Art, Creativity, and the Sacred

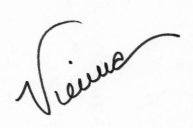

ART, CREATIVITY, AND THE SACRED

AN ANTHOLOGY IN RELIGION AND ART

Edited by
Diane Apostolos-Cappadona

CROSSROAD · NEW YORK

For Jane and John Dillenberger

1984

The Crossroad Publishing Company
370 Lexington Avenue, New York, N.Y. 10017

Printed in the United States of America

Library of Congress Cataloging in Publication Data

Main entry under title:

Art, creativity, and the sacred.

Bibliography: p. 319
1. Art and religion—Addresses, essays, lectures.
2. Christian art and symbolism—Addresses, essays,
lectures.   I. Apostolos-Cappadona, Diane.
N72.R4A77 1983   701'.04   83-15183
ISBN 0-8245-0609-X (pbk.)

Contents

Part V / Religion and Art: Interdisciplinary Vision 275

Part VI / Bibliographies 319

Introduction

In a treatise on education, Rabindranath Tagore wrote, "The object of education is to give man the unity of truth." Contemporary scholarship must recognize the need for such a unity, as well as the need for the diversity of specialization to which we are accustomed. The contributors to this anthology have all been trained in the primary discipline of their inquiry, and have extended themselves beyond its traditional boundaries in a quest for the unity of truth. A major theme of that quest is the understanding that the spiritual impinges on the artistic and that the artistic expresses the spiritual. As Martha Graham has testified, "Art is eternal; for it reveals the inner landscape, which is the soul of man."

This book has come into being as an attempt to understand the development and expression of that inner landscape. As a preliminary statement on the interdisciplinary field of religion and art, this anthology contains contributions by artists, art historians, historians of religion, philosophers, theologians, and specialists in religion and art. Therefore, the reader is presented with a breadth of knowledge that affords an interpretation, not just of art or religion, but of the fundamental nature of human experience. The writers of these essays approach their tasks with creativity, love, scholarly zeal, and a commitment to the quest for the unity of truth. Through the integrity of their interdisciplinary vision, each is a witness to the affirmation of Bernard of Clairvaux's suggestion that "he who understands truth without loving it, or loves without understanding, possesses neither the one nor the other."

The essays in this anthology have been selected with an eye to both methodological and thematic variety. There are many voices engaged in the dialogue of religion and art, as indicated by the bibliographic sources listed in Part VI. It has been my intention as editor of this anthology not to establish any "critical" line but to provide a forum for as many different voices as possible. The essays in this collection were chosen for their fundamental concern for works of art, as well as for the religious impulse that has both formed and been informed by the artistic process.

Part I presents the heart of the matter: the artists' own reflections on the spiritual possibilities of their artworks. It begins with a selection from Wassily Kandinsky's *Concerning the Spiritual in Art* as a guide for the ensuing essays by three contemporary artists. Kandinsky's understanding of the "spiritual" as being an inner necessity seeking expression has influenced the development of modern art. Those who create art as well as those of us who experience art are indebted to Kandinsky's creative reflections. The essays by Cecilia Davis Cunningham, Karen Laub-Novak, and Stephen DeStaebler offer contemporary artistic interpretations of "the spiritual in art."

Cunningham talks of the qualities of authenticity and genuineness in her craft, and of the expression of her deepest self in and through her artwork. Laub-Novak discusses the deceptive qualities of the creative experience: that twilight time when the artist walks a tightrope between the divine and the demoniac. DeStaebler suggests a series of relationships between the experience of art and the experience of religion as evidenced in his own life. The essays in Part I remind us that the artworks which are the focus and foundation of our inquiry come from human hands and out of human experiences. Art is not lifeless, static, or totally esoteric; it is alive, dynamic, and gutsy. No one knows this nor can express it better than artists themselves.

Part II contains essays by art historians who have considered the religious impulse in the artistic process. These scholars have examined and questioned not merely the traditional iconographic issues but the theological and spiritual possibilities that are crucial to the artistic process. Following a concern for interdisciplinary study, these art historians have presented interpretations of artworks that cause us to stand back and look with fresh eyes at the traditional and classic images we thought we knew and saw so well. Leo Steinberg's revision of his classic essay on Leonardo da Vinci's *Last Supper* challenges our preconceptions of Leonardo, Last Supper iconography, and Renaissance theology. Charles Scribner's essay on Caravaggio's *Last Supper* brings us to the controversies of Counter-Reformation theology as he raises the questions of artistic tradition and theological interpretation.

Barbara Novak's essay on the relationship between art, philosophy, and religion brings these issues into the American situation. Her examination of the symbolic quality of the landscape in American art is an attempt to consider the significance of the spiritual potential of nature as it was expressed by nineteenth-century American artists. Joshua Taylor's analysis of the religious impulse in American art surveys the transition from an iconographic to a symbolic understanding of religious art. He helps us to break through our preconceptions of American art and American religion. Jane Dillenberger's essay deals with the contemporary art scene as she examines George Segal's *Abraham and Isaac* in the context of the iconographic tradition of this motif. Her presentation of Segal's expression of the spiritual through sculpted forms is enlightened by his own understanding of the meaning of the Abraham and Isaac story.

The essays in Part III concentrate on the relationship between religion and art from the perspective of world religions. It begins with Ananda Coomaraswamy's essay on images in the Indian tradition and concludes with Mircea Eliade's essay on modern art. Richard B. Pilgrim offers an interpretation of the foundations of the relationship between religion and art in Japan, highlighting the total integration of the spiritual with the aesthetic and revealing the ritual dimension of art. Lois Ibsen al Faruqi examines the role of symbolism in religious art and applies her understanding to Islamic art to help us to pierce through our preconceptions about the nonfigural tradition of Islam. David and Linda Altshuler offer a survey of the role of art in Judaism, from ancient iconoclastic tendencies to the state of contemporary art.

Part IV presents philosophical and theological essays on art. Langdon Gilkey steps outside his usual role as a critical theologian to address the graduates of the School of the Art Institute of Chicago on the related roles of art and religion in our contemporary society. He finds several analogies between the experiential ground of art and religion as he challenges young artists to examine their motivation and commitment. John Dillenberger approaches a similar issue from a different perspective: the relationship between artists and the church that commissions them.

Thomas F. O'Meara suggests that contemporary theologians

have sought to recapture the aesthetic dimension in theology without recognizing its foundation in nineteenth-century Romantic idealism. In his essay, O'Meara examines the development of this dimension from the work of Friedrich Schelling to the contemporary theology of Hans Urs von Balthasar. Paul Tillich's essay "Art and Ultimate Reality" presents a methodological and theological approach to modern art. David Tracy takes his understanding of the religious classic into the world of art: the result is an interpretation of the interrelationship between religion and art as fundamental expressions of common human experience.

T. R. Martland uses the language and method of philosophy as he examines the fundamental issue of religion as art. He extends his inquiry beyond Western traditions to reveal the possibility of an universal religious aesthetic. Nicholas Wolterstorff also applies a philosopher's critical eye to a passage from André Malraux's *The Voices of Silence*. Wolterstorff's interpretation of high art as the religion of the elite is a challenge to theologians as well as artists.

Part V contains essays by scholars who specialize in the relationship between religion and art. John Dixon's revision of his essay on the art of Duccio and Giotto establishes a particular methodological approach to this study. His concern for the integrity of the artwork, the artist, and the philosophical/theological foundation informs his scholarly inquiry. Melinda Wortz's examination of Picasso's *Girl before a Mirror* brings the discussion of the relationship between religion and art into a nonecclesial and contemporary context. Roger Wedell considers the similarities in philosophy and spirituality between the writings of Nicholai Berdyaev and the chapel murals of Mark Rothko. Doug Adams voices concern for methodological development as he analyzes the contributions of Paul Tillich and Joshua Taylor to the study of religion and art.

This anthology concludes with two bibliographies. John Cook's survey of the materials available on Christianity and the arts progresses from Early Christian iconography to contemporary art. The Special Topic Bibliographies provide fine starting points for interdisciplinary study in the different areas of religion and art.

As with any creative encounter, the development of this volume is not an individual achievement. There have been many people upon whom I have depended for counsel and advice. Beyond the cooperation and understanding of each of the individual contributors, special mention of the continued support by my colleagues Doug Adams and David Altshuler is necessary. And I am indebted to Werner Mark Linz who guided this volume through its various incarnations from the "idea stage" to its present manifestation.

As this is the time and place to acknowledge debts, let me acknowledge a most important and personal one. Several years ago, I was fortunate enough to meet Jane Dillenberger. The time we spent together resulted in a renewal of my own commitment to the interdisciplinary study of religion and the arts. Since that time, this field of study has grown and my own endeavors have been professionally and personally rewarding. So, as editor, I have the singular pleasure of dedicating this volume to Jane Dillenberger in recognition of her scholarship and personal commitment to the religious impulse of the arts, and to John Dillenberger, whose achievement in theology and the arts stands for itself, and who is included in this dedication as theirs is truly a marriage of heart and mind.

Diane Apostolos-Cappadona

PART I

ARTISTS:
THE SPIRITUAL
DIMENSIONS

1

Concerning the Spiritual in Art

WASSILY KANDINSKY

Every work of art is the child of its time; often it is the mother of our emotions. It follows that each period of culture produces an art of its own, which cannot be repeated. Efforts to revive the art principles of the past at best produce works of art that resemble a stillborn child. For example, it is impossible for us to live and feel as did the ancient Greeks. For this reason those who follow Greek principles in sculpture reach only a similarity of form, while the work remains for all time without a soul. Such imitation resembles the antics of apes: externally a monkey resembles a human being; he will sit holding a book in front of his nose, turning over the pages with a thoughtful air, but his actions have no real significance.

But among the forms of art there is another kind of external similarity, which is founded on a fundamental necessity. When there is, as sometimes happens, a similarity of inner direction in an entire moral and spiritual milieu, a similarity of ideals, at first closely pursued but later lost to sight, a similarity of "inner mood" between one period and another, the logical consequence will be a revival of the external forms which served to express those insights in the earlier age. This may account partially for our sympathy and affinity with and our comprehension of the work of primitives. Like ourselves, these pure artists sought to express only inner[1] and essential feelings in their works; in this process they ignored as a matter of course the fortuitous.

This great point of inner contact is, in spite of its considerable importance, only one point. Only just now awakening after years

Reprinted from *Concerning the Spiritual in Art and Painting in Particular* by Wassily Kandinsky (New York: Wittenborn, Shultz, 1947), pp. 23–27.

of materialism, our soul is infected with the despair born of unbelief, of lack of purpose and aim. The nightmare of materialism, which turned life into an evil, senseless game, is not yet passed; it still darkens the awakening soul. Only a feeble light glimmers, a tiny point in an immense circle of darkness. This light is but a presentiment; and the mind, seeing it, trembles in doubt over whether the light is a dream and the surrounding darkness indeed reality. This doubt and the oppression of materialism separate us sharply from primitives. Our soul rings cracked when we sound it, like a precious vase, dug out of the earth, which has a flaw. For this reason, the primitive phase through which we are now passing, in its present derivative form, must be short-lived.

The two kinds of resemblance between the forms of art of today and of the past can be easily recognized as diametrically opposed. The first, since it is external, has no future. The second, being internal, contains the seed of the future. After a period of materialist temptation, to which the soul almost succumbed, and which it was able to shake off, the soul is emerging, refined by struggle and suffering. Cruder emotions, like fear, joy and grief, which belonged to this time of trial, will no longer attract the artist. He will attempt to arouse more refined emotions, as yet unnamed. Just as he will live a complicated and subtle life, so his work will give to those observers capable of feeling them emotions subtle beyond words.

The observer of today is seldom capable of feeling such vibrations. He seeks instead an imitation of nature with a practical function (for example, a portrait, in the ordinary sense) or an intuition of nature involving a certain interpretation (e.g., "impressionist" painting) or an inner feeling expressed by nature's forms (as we say, a picture of "mood"[2]). When they are true works of art, such forms fulfil their purposes and nourish the spirit. Though this remark applies to the first case, it applies more strongly to the third, in which the spectator hears an answering chord in himself. Such emotional chords cannot be superficial or without value; the feeling of such a picture can indeed deepen and purify the feeling of the spectator. The spirit at least is preserved from coarseness: such pictures tune it up, as a tuning fork does the strings of a musical instrument. But the subtilization and extension of this chord in time and space remained limited, and the potential power of art is not exhausted by it.

Imagine a building, large or small, divided into rooms; each room is covered with canvases of various sizes, perhaps thousands of them. They represent bits of nature in color—animals in sunlight or shadow, or drinking, standing in water, or lying on grass; close by, a "Crucifixion," by a painter who does not believe in Christ; then flowers, and human figures, sitting, standing, or walking, and often naked; there are many naked women foreshortened from behind; apples and silver dishes; a portrait of Mister So-and-So; sunsets; a lady in pink; a flying duck; a portrait of Lady X; flying geese; a lady in white; some cattle in shadow, flecked by brilliant sunlight; a portrait of Ambassador Y; a lady in green. All this is carefully reproduced in a book with the name of the artist and the name of the picture. Book in hand, people go from wall to wall, turning pages, reading names. Then they depart, neither richer nor poorer, again absorbed by their affairs, which have nothing to do with art. Why did they come? In every painting a whole life is mysteriously enclosed, a whole life of tortures, doubts, of hours of enthusiasm and inspiration.

What is the direction of that life? What is the cry of the artist's soul, if the soul was involved in the creation? "To send light into the darkness of men's hearts—such is the obligation of the artist," said Schumann. "A painter is a man who can draw and paint everything," said Tolstoi.

Of these two definitions we must choose the second, if we think of the exhibition just described. With more or less skill, virtuosity and vigor, objects are created on a canvas, "painted" either roughly or smoothly. To bring the whole into harmony on the canvas is what leads to a work of art. With cold eye and indifferent mind the public regards the work. Connoisseurs admire "technique," as one might admire a tight-rope walker, or enjoy the "painting quality," as one might enjoy a cake. But hungry souls go hungry away.

The public ambles through the rooms, saying "nice" or "interesting." Those who could speak have said nothing; those who could hear have heard nothing. This condition is called "art for art's sake." This annihilation of internal vibrations that constitute the life of the colors, this dwindling away of artistic force, is called "art for art's sake."

The artist seeks material rewards for his facility, inventiveness and sensitivity. His purpose becomes the satisfaction of ambition and greediness. In place of an intensive cooperation among artists, there is a battle for goods. There is excessive competition, over-production. Hatred, partisanship, cliques, jealousy, intrigues are the natural consequences of an aimless, materialist art.[3]

The public turns away from artists who have higher ideals, who find purpose in an art without purpose.

"Comprehension" is educating the spectator to the point of view of the artist. It has been said that art is the child of its time. But such an art can only repeat artistically what is already clearly realized by the contemporary. Since it is not germinative, but only a child of the age, and unable to become a mother of the future, it is a castrated art. It is transitory; it dies morally the moment the atmosphere that nourished it alters.

There is another art capable of further developments, which also springs from contemporary feeling. Not only is it simultaneously its echo and mirror but it possesses also an awakening prophetic power which can have far-reaching and profound effect.

The spiritual life to which art belongs, and of which it is one of the mightiest agents, is a complex but definite movement above and beyond, which can be translated into simplicity. This movement is that of cognition. Although it may take different forms, it holds basically to the same internal meaning and purpose.

The causes of the necessity to move forward and upward—through sweat, suffering, evil and torments—are obscure. When a stage has been reached at which obstacles have been cleared from the way, a hidden, malevolent hand scatters new obstacles. The path often seems blocked or destroyed. But someone always comes to the rescue—someone like ourselves in everything, but with a secretly implanted power of "vision."

He sees and points out. This high gift (often a heavy burden) at times he would gladly relinquish. But he cannot. Scorned and disliked, he drags the heavy weight of resisting humanity forward and upward.

Sometimes, after his body has vanished from the earth, men try by every means to recreate it in marble, iron, bronze, or stone, and on an enormous scale. As though there were any intrinsic value in the bodily existence of such divine martyrs and servants of humanity, who despised the flesh but wanted only to serve the spirit. But raising marble is evidence that a number of men have reached the point where the one they would now honor formerly stood alone.

NOTES

1. A work of art consists of two elements, the inner and the outer.
The inner is the emotion in the soul of the artist; this emotion has the capacity to evoke a similar emotion in the observer.
Being connected with the body, the soul is affected through the medium of the senses—the felt. Emotions are aroused and stirred by what is sensed. Thus the sensed is the bridge, i.e., the physical relation, between the immaterial (which is the artist's emotion) and the material, which results in the production of a work of art. And again, what is sensed is the bridge from the material (the artist and his work) to the immaterial (the emotion in the soul of the observer).
The sequence is: emotion (in the artist) → the sensed → the art-work → the sensed → emotion (in the observer).
The two emotions will be like and equivalent to the extent that the work of art is successful. In this respect painting is in no way different from a song: each is a communication. The successful singer arouses in listeners his emotions; the successful painter should do no less.
The inner element, i.e., emotion, must exist; otherwise the work of art is a sham. The inner element determines the form of the work of art.
In order that the inner element, which at first exists only as an emotion, may develop into a work of art, the second element, i.e., the outer, is used as an embodiment. Emotion is always seeking means of expression, a material form, a form that is able to stir the senses. The determining and vital element is the inner one, which controls the outer form, just as an idea in the mind determines the words we use, and not *vice versa*. The determination of the form of a work of art is therefore determined by the irresistible inner force: this is the only unchanging law in art. A beautiful work is the consequence of an harmonious cooperation of the inner and the outer; i.e., a painting is an intellectual organism which, like every other material organism, consists of many parts. (*This explanation by Kandinsky of the relation between internal and external, or inner and outer, is a slightly revised version of a translation by Arthur Jerome Eddy of part of an article by Kandinsky which appreaed in* Der Sturm, *Berlin, 1913; cf.* Cubists and Post-Impressionists, *A. C. McClurg, Chicago, 1914, pp. 119–20.*)
2. Alas, this word, which in the past was used to describe the poetical aspirations of an artist's soul, has been misued and finally ridiculed. Was there ever a great word that the crowd did not try immediately to desecrate?
3. A few exceptions do not affect the truth of this sad and ominous picture; even the exceptions are chiefly believers in the doctrine of art for art's sake. They serve, therefore, a higher ideal, but one which is ultimately a waste of their strength. External beauty is one element in a spiritual milieu. But beyond this positive fact (that what is beautiful is good) lies the weakness of a talent not used to the full (*talent* in the bibilical sense.)

2

Craft: Making and Being

CECILIA DAVIS CUNNINGHAM

I am a potter, a maker of things. For my work to be good now and better in the future requires doing. Every craftsperson seeks what Michelangelo called *sprezzatura:* the easy union of eye, hand, and brain that produces a worthy human work. It is only when a pot comes from my wheel that I am permitted to reflect on its form, its beauty, and its meaning. One does and then one reflects.

Potters by and large are practical people. Their conversations tend to focus on clay bodies, glaze recipes, recalcitrant kiln problems, new techniques, and—yes, let us be frank—sales. Nonetheless, potters today choose not only a job, but a way of life. Consciously or unconsciously they stand in a tradition that goes back thousands of years (a ceramic shard is the archaeologist's best friend) but that can be replaced in industrialized societies by machines. To be a potter today is to say that plastic cups, machine-stamped utensils, and mass-produced vessels are not enough. To be a potter, or any other craftsperson, is to opt for certain basic values that have informed our common humanity and seem worth nurturing.

The crafts are fundamental enterprises. Every craftsperson deals with the basic materials of the earth, works with tools that are part of a long common heritage, sets out criteria to establish the craft, accepts a discipline of work, and, into this fundamental framework, inserts the self as worker. It is the human self that enlarges the humanity of crafts. Every potter must obey the chemistry of clay, glazes, and fire, but the style, the technique, and the imagery used in transforming clay into vessels is limited only by the horizon of the worker.

The great English potter Bernard Leach (1887–1979) stressed in his teaching and writing that to be a potter is to be in a process that balances technology and humanity. Leach saw this process not merely as an acquisition of expertise but as a way of instilling *hope* into the human enterprise so that "out of our total inheritance, we are moving toward balance." He added, "Integration as I conceive it is the state in which a man attains a natural interrelatedness of his inner and outer capacities."[1]

Leach, true to the religious tradition he learned in the early years of this century in Japan, strongly emphasized the mindfulness of the potter and the responsibility that the potter must take for the integrity and wholeness of her work:

> The virtues of a pot are derived from the familiar virtues of life
> . . . the quality which appears to me fundamental in all pots is
> life in one or more of its modes: inner harmony, nobility, purity, strength, breadth, and generosity, or even exquisiteness and
> charm. But it's one thing to make a list of virtues of man and
> pot and another to interpret them in the counterpoint of convex
> and concave, hard or soft, growth or rest, for this is the breathing of the Universal in the particular.[2]

This process is not to be found in the single act of throwing a pot on the wheel. It devolves from the larger process of the potter's life, from the very rhythm of making. It may well be that one of the reasons why so many people are attracted to the various crafts today is that the craftsperson has a style of life that is marked by steady rhythms and engaged with elemental forces. There is a time for the labor of digging and mixing earths, a time for the heat of fire, and a time for contemplating what is done. The moment of turning a pot still warm in the hand to judge the result of labor is both the apex of a creative cycle and a gentle reminder that the next cycle is soon to begin. As Mary C. Richards shows in her classic meditation on craft, *Centering*,[3] the potter herself is at the very center of the cycle, mastering and being mastered by material.

Every great potter who has commented on his or her craft in our time has emphasized the closeness of the potter to the most elemental realities of nature. Those realities are palpable and timeless. Contemporary American potters, with all the world's technology available from catalogues, still feel a kinship (and a debt) to their "primitive" contemporaries. There is very little that separates my work in a neon-lighted lab with electric kilns and advanced glazes from the village potters of Nigeria. I learn from their work just as I learn from the potters who worked a millennium ago and whose works I now gaze at in museums.

The very basic nature of the potter's craft, however, should not blind us to the fact that the potter, like every artisan, works in an intensely historical milieu. Walk around any crafts fair or pottery gallery and look at the pots: they are very much like those done in the remote past, but their distinctiveness comes from history and historical forces. Although the average potter might not be aware of it, her work would be inconceivable without the insights of Zen provided by Bernard Leach and Shoji Hamada or the philosophy of crafts articulated by William Morris and the crafts movement in nineteenth-century England. A survey of books on ceramics will show that to the elemental craft of pottery has come the tugs and pulls of quite diverse cultural forces as potters have enlarged their aesthetic vocabulary by the study of African pottery (Michael Cardew and Charles Counts), abstract expressionism (Peter Voulkos), Amerindian culture (Maria Martinez), or the aesthetics of the Bauhaus (Marguerite Wildenhain).

That is as it should be, since at the most basic level we humans act both timelessly and historically. The potter is no different. She works at her craft in a particular time and place. Yet where her time intersects with history, there is of necessity something that the potter wishes to "say," something that speaks both to her time and to her tradition. That "something," I would assert, must be personal, beautiful, and lasting.

My person is in the pot by reason of my shaping hands and my intentionality. Every pot is the result of a decision to modify nature according to what I think, feel, and know. I must take responsibility for my work. The word may be a bit grandiose, but there is an *ethic* involved in artistic creation, since what I do communicates myself for better or worse to others.

It is every artisan's hope that what is produced will be considered beautiful both in its function and in its being. For the potter who creates the most utilitarian of objects—cups, vases, bowls, teapots—there is a constant challenge (and opportunity) to put beauty into work. This is our modest way of reaffirming the beauty of the larger creation. "Beauty will save the world," says Father Zosima in *The Brothers Karamazov*, and in that rather large task of world salvation the artist plays a modest but real role: to create epiphanies of beauty in the mundane surroundings of everyday life.

It is in the rhythm of my life, the successes and failures of my work, and the constant search for aesthetic perfection that I define myself as a potter and a craftsperson. Is that, in essence, a way of being religious in the world prior to, or in tandem with, my formal religious commitments? This is a very hard question to answer, but I do find myself in agreement with the observation of the eminent crafts critic Rose Slivka, who once wrote that serious craftspeople "quest for a deeper feeling of presence."[4] To that I can only add that the life of art is not only a quest but a communication about the process of the quest for that deeper feeling of presence.

NOTES

1. From the exhibition catalogue "Bernard Leach: Fifty Years a Potter" (Arts Council of Great Britain, 1961), p. 87. The same material may be found in Garth Clark, ed., *Ceramic Art Comment and Review, 1882–1977* (New York, 1978).
2. Ibid., p. 88.
3. Mary Caroline Richards, *Centering in Pottery, Poetry, and the Person* (Middletown, CT, 1964).
4. Rose Slivka, "The New Ceramic Presence." *Craft Horizons* 4 (1961), p. 36. See also Rose Slivka, "The Persistent Object," *The Crafts of the Modern World*, ed. Rose Slivka (New York, 1968).

3

The Art of Deception

KAREN LAUB-NOVAK

> Every intellectual work begins by a moment of ecstasy:
> only in the second place does the talent of arrangement,
> the technique of transitions, connections of idea, con-
> struction, come into play.
> Sertillanges, *The Intellectual Life*

There are similar stages of insight, preparation, discipline, dark night of the soul, and unity in both the spiritual quest and artistic activity. The artist is rooted in imagination, while the mystic seeks to transcend imagination. For the artist this rootedness affords special temptations. First, the imagination is especially embattled between the divine and the demonic. This warfare can be either fruitful or destructive to the artist and her creative work. But, second, there are many myths about creativity that the artist must sort through. One myth, that creativity is always spontaneous, inspired, prophetic, divine, and rebellious against tradition, applies to both the artist and the saint.

This essay will attempt, from an artist's point of view, to sift through several types of self-deception in the imagination and in the creative process.

I

Wassily Kandinsky (1866–1944) was widely regarded as a free spirit who worked in a fever of spontaniety. His wife fed this myth—as he often had—in her introduction to his book *Concerning the Spiritual in Art*. Were they self-deceived?

In 1913, the Armory Show introduced European avant-garde art to bewildered audiences in New York, Chicago, and Boston.

The show was angrily denounced by critics and artists alike, but in the end a generation of painters and their followers drew inspiration from these works.

Some critics consider Kandinsky to be the orginator of abstract art and point to his *Improvisations* as the first abstract paintings. The Armory Show included his *Improvisation 27*, filled with vibrant colors, almost watercolorlike washes, a few sketchy lines, no discernible images. He spoke of this work as "spontaneous," reflecting moods, tension, sounds, the spiritual in art. However, recent studies reveal that in Kandinsky's fury of brush strokes and color are encoded horses, riders, snakes, boats, cannons, cities, warrors, and lovers: clear ideas, although veiled images.[1]

From 1886 to 1896, Kandinsky had been a lawyer and an economist. At the age of thirty-one he decided to concentrate on painting, and at forty-three he became interested in theosophy. Theosophy's blending of Eastern and Western mysticism led him to a style that was considered purely abstract. Yet in 1953 Gabriele Munter, Kandinsky's companion from 1902 to 1916, gave the Stadtische Galerie im Lenbachhaus in Munich over one hundred of Kandinsky's paintings and drawings from that period, many of which had been preliminary drawings for the *Improvisations*. These sketches reveal a variety of images later disguised in the paintings. Furthermore, these preliminary sketches and watercolors were often simply enlarged and transposed to the final paintings. Recent studies show that much of Kandinsky's imagery was biblical; his favorite passages come from Genesis and Revelation. Furthermore, technical studies using infrared, ultraviolet, and macrophotography now reveal layers of pencil sketching underneath the paint.[2] Kandinsky's work is not, as we previously thought, purely abstract and spontaneous.

Classical Christian mysticism encourages beginners to use the visual, literal imagination in the early stages of prayer, but later to reject these levels of the imagination as impediments to spiritual growth. Kandinsky, of course, did not abandon imagination but he did reject the literal imagination. By encoding his imagery, he forces the viewer to enter into the process of the work, to pay attention to the medium of the work, and to look below the surface. This seems to be the rationale behind Kandinsky's expression "the paint is sound." It is also an excellent reason to call these paintings "Improvisations" rather than "Genesis" or "Revelation." The former pleased the avant-garde as the latter could not have.

Arthur Koestler said that the artist is on a tightrope between the practical world and the world of imagination: in that tension comes the creative impulse. Kandinsky, too, had a foot in each world. A curious contradiction are Kandinsky's demons of the Apocalypse, who march forth in joyful cadence. Kandinsky's color is vibrant: alizarin crimson, turquoise, ultramarine blue, gold, yellow. The paintings are full of life and excitement, a lyrical dance. However, the dominant mood of the Apocalypse is that of impending doom, death, violence, destruction. Despair comes in the fifth destruction, as the locusts sting but do not kill, and man seeks death but cannot find it. People cower, stars fall, cities crumble, the woman flees to the desert on eagle wings, the harlot's body is a cage of wild things, and the beast lies in wait to devour the child. The inner pulse of the passages is not that of a lyrical dance; it pounds with beating wings, and fiery armies march from the four corners of the world. These are the images Kandinsky chooses to veil. With his lyrical brush strokes, he evokes the New Jerusalem while covering the horsemen, floods, sea battles, and falling cities with layers of paint. His colors are visual analogies of joyful songs lightly covering wails of despair and darkness.

A small black spot in *Improvisation 31*, intended, according to Kandinsky, to represent the dark side of spiritual life, is not adequate to the darkness of the apocalyptic motif. Somehow Kandinsky's personal version of mysticism eliminated the dark side of the soul, perhaps weakened his interpretive skills, and led to a spirituality of too few notes.

Do these revelations diminish Kandinsky's reputation? Does it disappoint the viewer that the spontaneities of his imagination were harnessed by analytical intelligence? Because his work is not purely abstract, is it any less inventive and exciting? Kandinsky sought to challenge the viewer's imagination. His work still succeeds, but not perhaps according to his original intent. Abstract art no longer shocks the eye. The new shock lies in our detection of his imagery. Kandinsky's work forces us to exercise imagination and to bring a critical eye, both technical and interpretative, to what he has done on canvas. It forces us to believe not what he said but what he did.

II

Speaking for myself, the questions which interest me most when reading a poem are two. The first is technical: Here is a verbal contraption. How does it work? The second is, in the broadest sense, moral: What kind of a guy inhabits this poem? What is his notion of the good life or the good place? His notion of the Evil One? What does he conceal from the reader? What does he conceal even from himself?

W. H. Auden

Koestler's artist walks a tightrope and lives in tension, conflict, and risk. Mircea Eliade, writing of early religious beliefs, chose a similar metaphor to describe the spiritual quest: in the last part of the journey of the soul the soul must go over a bridge. This bridge is "as thin as a thread and as sharp as a sword." The goal ahead is divine presence. Below this bridge are the demons of the underworld.

This image can be used in another way: the artist often feels suspended between what she wants to reveal and what she wants to conceal in her paintings. Furthermore, the subjective struggles and technical problems of the work, which seem to be above and below this inner bridge, constantly change as the artist crosses. In the beginning the thin line seems stretched between clichés on the one side and obscure subjectivity on the other. As the artist develops her balancing act the scenery changes. Now she seems suspended between the choices of realistic rendering and abstract symbolism. Later on, the challenge becomes more complex. The artist may become more concerned with the exercise of either classic technique or experimental novelty. Again, themes and ideas may seem to dominate on one side, sheer images on the other.

All too often these decisions, temptations, and tensions become clear only in retrospect. As the artist does a balancing act other factors enter. Little furies buzz, poking and enticing. Their names are ambition, laziness, lack of direction, false imitation, dark humor, slick cleverness, pride, simplicity, writer's and artist's block, compulsive action, withdrawn passivity, overconfidence, loss of spirit. These furies are at least a nuisance and often the cause of melancholy. Yeats called them his frustrations, always interfering with his poetry. More deceptions.

III

The man without imagination . . . is cut off from the deeper reality of life and from his own soul.

                                                    Mircea Eliade

Imagination is the power of the inventor, scientist, artist, poet, philosopher, and saint. With imaginal power, we can live in other places, place ourselves in situations we've never experienced. Moreover, imagination contains several faculties.

Coleridge describes imagination as having two parts. The primary but finite imagination participates in the "eternal act of creation in the infinite I Am." The secondary imagination "dissolves, diffuses, dissipates, in order to re-create." It struggles to "idealize and to unify." By contrast, fantasy is "no more than a mode of memory emancipated from the order of time and space."

For most writers and philosophers, fantasy seems to be a poor cousin of imagination. Fantasy seems more accidental, without that ability to unify and order which we attribute to the imagination. It refers more to dreams, delusions, and playful perceptions. Jung wrote of fantasy as the "play of the imagination," and he considered it essential for creative work.

Thomas Aquinas divided the imagination into the reproductive and the creative. The reproductive imagination enables us to recall an event, to live it again, to bring back to the "screen of our consciousness pictures of things once but no longer present to our senses." He would also say that memory and imagination walk hand in hand, and that an original experience makes an impression on the "wax" of our memory. If the wax is too soft the impression is lost. If the wax is too hard the impression does not take.

Creative imagination has powers beyond the reproductive. It can invent images of things never perceived by the senses. The creative imagination has the ability to recall perceptions and then to recombine them. The creative imagination gathers all types of impressions and sees the similarities even between dissimilar things. It is the creative imagination that plays with veiling and unveiling, creates illusions, shocks the eye. Creative imagination simplifies, eliminates details or adds them, gives emphasis or distorts. In Kandinsky's case, it encoded the horses of the Apocalypse and shrouded the biblical images, so that the painting seems totally unattached to any imagery, past or present.

Imagination is fundamental to spiritual and aesthetic growth. It is the center of intuition, invention, and rational order. It is through the imagination that we appreciate beauty and experience awe. Why, then, does the mystic seek to transcend imagination? Why does the mystic see imagination as only one, and a very early, step on the mystical ladder—a ladder that artist and mystic climb again and again? Each new stage of understanding brings a repetition of the process of insight, critical reflection, and action. So, too, the artist will repeat with each new development in her work similar stages of understanding and action. What is present in these rooms of imagination that the mystic warns against? The artist is inspired by the idea that the imagination is ecstatic, awesome, divine, almost holy and prophetic, yet the mystic warns of its dangers.

In *Creative Intuition in Art and Poetry*, Jacques Maritain writes, "Art resides in the soul and is a certain perfection of the soul. It is . . . an inner quality . . . that raises the human subject . . . to a higher degree of vital formation and energy." In modern art he sees three steps. The first step transforms nature in order to disclose a reality closer to our dreams, anger, anguish, melancholy. The second step liberates us from conventional natural language. The third step is a rejection of reason and logic, an obscuring of plain meanings. Maritain sees in these three steps both advantages and a "diligent effort towards self-deception, narcissism, and surrealism." Lionel Abel published an autobiographical account of his friendship with the surrealists Breton, Matta, and Gorky. He noted the problems that arose from their philosophical espousal of sadism and the eventual havoc wreaked upon their personal lives.[3] In creation and destruction we call upon the same energies, the same inner demons. E. M. Cioran says, "to destroy is to act, to create backwards."

Without habits of hand and discipline of mind and memory, the imagination easily becomes self-pitying, sarcastic, helpless, passive; prefers fantasy; likes to wrap itself in its illusions. At other times, it is content to fill up work after work with images and ideas created by others. The imagination can be sloppy, careless, imprecise. It willfully rearranges thoughts and images. Imagination likes to fling its clothes to the floor assuming that reason and discipline will come along later and pick up the pieces. Imagination is a willful child, and at times a dangerous trickster.

We often hear praise for the delightful side of imagination. We think of the imagination as angelic, holistic, and divine. We avoid the other side, the side that is obscure, and vulnerable to self-deception.

IV

Everything that deceives may be said to enchant.
Plato

The awful thing is that beauty is mysterious as well as terrible. God and the devil are fighting there, and the battlefield is the heart of man.
Dostoevski

There is a struggle within the imagination. The temptations of illusion affect the artist and the work. The artist has two struggles with deception, one in herself and another with the surfaces of the work. Whatever the intentions of the artist, the construction of the work tells the final story, for the work is judged on its merits and not on the complicated personality of the artist.

The artist may see her own work as creating enigmas, not as revealing them. The artist may want not to be literal and univocal, but to create several levels of meaning, both to reveal and to hide. By hiding the literal meaning, the artist wants to reveal another level of our unconscious and conscious enigmas.

This whole business of veiling may fail. A trompe l'oeil may reveal deeper truths. On the other hand, despite all the pretensions—or even profound intentions—of the artist, the painting may still be a cliché. Depth of feeling is no guarantee of a fine product. A good technician may lack passion. A passionate person may lack technique. Both may lack originality, judgment, or proportion. There are infinite ways to fail.

The artist is enchanted by illusion, magic, visual deception, satire, wit, and humor. Viewers are often entranced by the deceptions the artist creates, enticed, for example, into many paintings by the device of perspective. Imaginary lines recede to a vanishing point with buildings, people, and trees following those lines and creating a three-dimensional effect.

In Geneva there is a very small painting with a very large frame, *The Tower of Babel*, by a sixteenth-century Flemish master. The canvas measures approximately twelve by fourteen inches. This small painting of a fantastic tower draws the viewer's eye into a small space and creates an illusion of vast space. One feels as if one is standing within the painting, becoming a part of this landscape with its towering citadel and struggling people. Even photographs of this painting re-create this strange experience of immense space, since those who see it assume that it represents a large painting rather than a small one. Part of the illusion is the skill of the draftsman and his control of perspective. Another part of the illusion is the fine detail of rocks, stones, ladders, and bodies. Yet another part is an uncanny use of color to suggest and emphasize the illusion of space.

Color both reveals and conceals the literal image. Certain colors seem to express moods: red for anger, violence, action; green for hope, nature, comfort, quiet; blue for melancholy, withdrawal, cold; black for despair and death. Cioran says that "the amount of chiaroscuro an idea harbors is the only index of its profundity, as the despairing accent of its playfulness is the index of its fascination." The artist employs chiaroscuro to conceal and reveal, to reveal and conceal.

Rembrandt, for example, cast his figures in soft shadows, at some points obscuring and at some points highlighting the painting. The proofs of his etching of a crucifixion show how he began with a clear rendering of the three crucified figures, the guards, and the attendants. Then, with cross-hatching, soft ground, and deep etching, he gradually made some figures merge into the dark background, while the crucified figures are focused in light. Each step from clarity to obscurity made the later print more powerful than the earlier.

Technique can be used in many ways, by accident or by intention, with insight and skill or without. The artist who is a master technician is blessed, but also has to be wary of being captured and deceived by her skill. There is more to being an artist than being a master of the crafts of illusion.

When an artist creates illusions in her work, she may loose the boundaries of her own experience of time, space, color, passion, mind. The illusions of the work may create illusions in the mind. Avoiding clear meanings, using veils, the artist may end up avoiding self-knowledge, consciously or unconsciously. She may become entangled in her own elaborate concoctions.

The inner rooms of illusion are a delight to the artist, but a bane of the mystic. What the artist seeks to experience the mystic seeks to transcend. For it is in these rooms that a person is at once most creative and also most destructive. In one sense, the person is freed from rational restraints but in another is vulnerable to self-deception and the worship of false idols.

V

The overarching metaphor for both the life of the spirit and the life of art is "the quest." We speak of the journey of the soul, the way, the pilgrimage. The power of this image is that it aptly describes the life of the spirit as a process, not static, but changing, developing. The spirit is energetic, not stagnant. It explores, questions, and moves, directly or indirectly, toward a goal. In *The Trial*, Kafka used the image of long corridors, with doors and rooms going nowhere, attended by persons who could tell the accused nothing of his charges. Keats said, "I compare human life to a large mansion of many apartments, two of which I can only describe, the doors of the rest being as yet shut upon me." The quest is not always happy.

The quest can also be taken as a metaphor for self-deception. Three wise men have a vision. They set out upon a journey. A star is to be their guide. Traveling through strange lands, they seek the guidance of jealous King Herod. Unthinking, focused on their goal, they ask foolish questions that have political and moral consequences. An enraged and threatened king orders the "slaughter of innocents" and kills all male children under the age of two. The quest has consequences unforeseen.

The quest may also be intoxicating. One may love the process more than the goal. One may center more on the questioning self than on transcending the self. It is easy for an artist to become enamored with the act of painting, the pursuit of fleeting images, the feelings and emotions that surround the moments of inspiration—and fail to complete the work. The quest becomes the goal.

A second dangerous metaphor that bewitches the artist is that of being prophetic. We have endowed the artist with the gift of prophecy, saying she sees the future with a clear eye. Every street corner has its resident prophet, Cioran writes. And Paul Valery in his introduction to *The Method of Leonardo da Vinci* says, "The folly of mistaking a paradox for a proof, a torrent of verbiage for a spring of capital truths, and oneself for an oracle, is born in us." The central problem is to complete the work. Such prophetic roles take care of themselves, if they are genuine. They seldom are.

VI

Lying, the wellspring of all tears! Such is the imposture of genius and the secret of art. Trifles swollen to the heavens: the improbable, generator of a universe! In every genius coexists a braggart and a god.
E. M. Cioran

Psychologists and philosophers often try to describe the attributes of an artist. Studying a range of individuals in various fields they usually come up with a list of traits that these individuals seem to share. In his book *Creativity*, Silvano Arieti lists "aloneness, inactivity, daydreaming, free thinking, state of readiness to catch similarities, gullibility, remembrances and inner replay of past traumatic experiences, conflict, alertness, and discipline." All of these creative attributes have a negative side. Solitude can become isolation. Free thinking can lead to anarchy. Inactivity can tend to a withdrawn and passive state. Remembrances can lead to psychic disorder. Conflict to violence. Discipline to tyranny. Each attribute opens a side door to self-deception.

Self-deception is more than being perplexed, different from inner conflict, tension or turmoil. It is not the same as being indecisive. It is an inability (or unwillingness) to see through our own fakeries. It is a form of lying to the self. Yet not all lying is self-deception. An intentional lie is quite clear to the individual who tells it. Even such a lie may conceal other self-deceptions. All the attributes of the creative person are vulnerable to self-deception. Two common ones are worth note: daydreaming and creative innocence.

Daydreaming is fundamental to creative work. But it is filled with dangers. Free floating fantasy is more pleasant than pulling oneself off the couch to make the painting or write the novel. Fantasy is more pleasant and immediate than taking up the pen, struggling with the words, and ordering the ideas. Inactive daydreaming is more pleasant than receiving the rejection slip from the publisher. Marcel Proust took to his bed with his asthma, neurosis, and memories of his doting mother. But he did manage to take his pen and paper to bed with him.

C. S. Lewis spent hours daydreaming as a child. But he warned later that had he not combined his daydreaming with invention and writing, the daydreaming alone would have led to a passive delight in fantasy. He also saw that without daydreams his adult work would have lacked a sense of awe.

Creative innocence is another trait attributed to both the artist and the saint. We need to be born again as a child to enter into the kingdom of God. The danger of this metaphor is to equate purity with naiveté. Many take this path, hoping for spiritual union or artistic inspiration. "Unfortunately, this rare purity of the mind is rare: when it does exist it is often allied with empty headedness," said Sertillanges.

Maritain notes, in *Creative Intuition in Art and Poetry*, that the purity of the artist is not moral purity. It is a special purity of vision open to sophistication. At the age of nine, Dante sees Beatrice and falls in love with her. This ideal, which envelopes Dante for the rest of his life, could have become maudlin. Neither naive nor blind, Dante was able to penetrate differences and make distinctions in human qualities, actions, and virtues. And with this ability he created *The Divine Comedy* to honor his ideal.

Willa Cather has written, "Artistic growth is, more than it is anything else, a refining of the sense of truthfulness. The stupid believe that to be truthful is easy: only the artist, the great artist, knows how difficult it is."

Those artists who have created the best work have been able to overcome for a short time many of their self-deceptions. They have developed the ability to make distinctions. Some are able to make these distinctions not only between their good work and their bad work (independently from what others say), not only between illusions leading to truth and illusions leading to deception, but also between their own honest voices and their many poses, their own self and its many disguises.

The journeys of the artist and the saint have similarities and differences. Artists and saints speak with quite individual voices about their struggles with their angels and their demons. For both, imagination is a source of inspiration and deception. Those who find the spiritual quest difficult and think that the artistic quest will be easier are mistaken.

Those who work with money, things, mundane affairs may be, however crafty, simple and direct. Those who work with the imagination, however noble in self-image, may be corrupted and dishonest, the most self-deceived. Their material is themselves, vague, obscure, and full of illusions. By itself, not reliable stuff.

To paraphrase Maritain: It is hard to be an artist. It is even harder to be a developed moral person (a saint). To be both is not twice as hard, but twice squared.

NOTES

1. Rose-Carol Washton Long and E. A. Carmean in an unpublished manuscript referred to in the brochure *Kandinsky: The Improvisations*, published for the Kandinsky exhibit at the National Gallery of Art in Washington, D.C., April 26 to August 2, 1981. See also Washton Long's *Kandinsky: The Development of an Abstract Style* (New York: Oxford, 1980), an expanded and revised version of her influential 1968 thesis. This work presents an extensive discussion of Kandinsky's abstraction and use of religious motifs in the Improvisations and other works.

2. E. A. Carmean and Ann Hoenigswald in unpublished research done in connection with the Kandinsky exhibit at the National Gallery mentioned in the previous note.

3. Lionel Abel, "The Surrealists in New York," *Commentary* 72, no. 4 (October 1981), pp. 44–54.

4

Reflections on Art and the Spirit:
A Conversation

STEPHEN DE STAEBLER AND
DIANE APOSTOLOS-CAPPADONA

Behind every artwork, there is a breathing, feeling human being called "the artist" who creates out of a drive and an energy that remain untapped in most of us. Too many of us, unfortunately, forget that the art we study comes from human hands and out of human experiences. The artist can be as much a focus of our interest as is the finished artwork. The "magic" of the initial creative process occurs within that individual, and we are the recipients of that magic, which somehow becomes our magic.

At the core of all artistic efforts is the concern to express and experience what it means to be human. To be human means more than to be able to think; it encompasses the integration of all the senses and faculties we associate with the human person. The fullness of the experience of the senses with the thoughts of the mind intepreted in and through the body is a holistic encounter that can be brought into being through the arts. As Thomas Merton reminds us, "Art enables us to find ourselves and lose ourselves at the same time." [1]

Stephen DeStaebler: I had difficulty with the formalism of religion and was very slow in understanding that there is a reality independent of formal religious thinking. My understanding developed as I progressed in my art. Art training involves many nonsensical rules that are turned into dogmas. Once you evolve into your own artist you realize that it is highly arbitrary what you choose to discard and what meanings you attach to all the variables. Then you realize that each person turns his own art into a bedrock experience. Well, if that is true in art, then why isn't it true in religion?

I felt lost, having no sense of belonging to the mainstream of either formal religion or art. I now take solace in the fact that human beings are so amazingly different. I like Jung's idea of the psyche having four major capacities: intellect, emotion, sensation, and intuition. He established a four-pointed circle. Each person is composed of varying strengths and weaknesses. It makes sense to realize that if you are oriented around one aspect of the mind's capacity you tend to build everything outward from that strength. And that makes you vulnerable to intolerance of other orientations.

Jung suggested that the lack of development of your weak capacity will result in its being an enemy within your own camp. You are apt to resent others who have developed the capacity that you have neglected in yourself, and, therefore, you have the foundation for internal conflicts, which create the seeds of external conflicts. It is clear to me now that strong allegiances, enmities, and struggles between groups are objectifications of inner battles that result from the failure to reconcile opposites.

Some people have the grace to seek out the opposite. Instead of marrying a person like yourself so that everything is easy or accommodating, for example, you marry your opposite. I have done that to a certain degree. Except for when I am really in conflict and can not bridge the gulf, I am grateful for the different point of view that helps to complete the incomplete circle. Maybe that is what art is all about—to bridge the gulf and to complete the circle.

You have to treat your self like a hunk of clay: you can shape it and do so much with it, but much of it is very recalcitrant and out of reach, and refuses to be shaped. So what do you do? How do you go through life? Well, I think you try to accommodate the inner, as much as you can reach it, with the outer, as much as you can perceive it; you try to create an equilibrium that is always in a state of process. You are not a fixed personality, and you keep adjusting to the greater awareness that you hope you gain along the way.

This is why artists do not work for masterpieces once they become themselves. When you are a young artist you think in terms of masterpieces, and tensions develop. I have seen some gifted artists literally paint themselves into a state of paralysis because they were afraid to take another step. In distinction to that, I think the function of art for the artist is to keep reaching closer to whatever it is that creates that equilibrium between the inner and the outer.

And so you go through a series of statements, one after the other, which can be highly repetitive and boring to another person if it is of no consequence to his perception of himself in the world, but highly engrossing if it is. The obsessive quality of art is an attempt to reconcile opposites and keep an equilibrium, and, as in religion, this is art's validity. If you strip away the dogmas and doctrines, religion becomes a very precarious relationship between a frail and finite reality and a sense of all-present infinite reality; and it is such a strange disequilibrium that this struggle to create an equilibrium creates religion.

If you acknowledge the fact that there is no absolute for human beings, then organized religion loses its punch and seems more like a straitjacket than a creative vehicle. When I was studying religion in college, I had no understanding of this fact. I thought, "I'm out of it," because what they are saying does not seem to touch me. Their vehicle was words, and words are not my avenue toward religious experience. The more I thought about it the more frustrating it became.

I discovered that in doing art certain obstacles evaporated. When I was a graduate student, I could not understand what other students were doing by painting abstractly and nonobjectively. It was just incomprehensible. Then, effortlessly, after a period of a year, I was doing it and not even wondering how. You just start like a baby learning how to talk, you make a lot of unintelligible noises and eventually they take shape as words and people understand you.

I realized that form has its own reality that does not depend on anything else. Whenever I encounter someone who does not have that awareness I empathize, because that is where I was once.

I feel basically the same way about formal religious experience, because I never really got over the hurdles to an essential experience. I suppose that is why going to liturgical services never became important to me. If anything, it seemed a little hokey to mouth condensations of truth, like the Nicene Creed. Even after having studied the history behind the strange terminology, it still did not come through clearly.

Christianity's strong sense of the family makes sense to me: It has built the crucial parent-child relationship into itself. That externalization of the internal family experience makes Christianity compelling. You have symbols or images to explain your own struggles of being a child within a family. Christianity uses a male-oriented family structure, and I imagine that for women the patriarchalism rankles. If you can get past the sex of Christ himself, you will not have all that much difficulty. The worship of the Virgin is a compensatory way of bringing the female principle into the family.

Diane Apostolos-Cappadona: The Holy Spirit has feminine qualities, such as the hovering "always with you" quality of a mother.

SDS: The church has become the mother faith and its architecture reflects that symbolism. I am fascinated how certain churches have become thinly veiled female vessels. The European church plan of a long nave, transept, apse, narthex and domes, like Saint Mark's in Venice, are so obviously the splayed female form. The space is the female space, and I think this womb-imaging is crucial.

DAC: Galla Placidia is like entering (or reentering) the womb; you feel the protective warmth all around you even in the darkness. When you are in the Rothko Chapel, it is dark and cool: characteristics of Jung's anima. This is an incredible experience. Then you walk outside into the blazing Houston sun as Barnett Newman's *Broken Obelisk* emerges from the reflecting pool. This male-female dichotomy was unconscious and not the architect's intention.

SDS: The language is a dead giveaway, because the church has been referred to as the mother church for a long time. With this awareness in mind, I remember a Spanish colonial church in Mexico. It was unbelievably graphic. It was a straightforward abstraction of the female figure with knees up, the pubic hair articulated by the statuary over the entrance, and the dome the breast. The image is so big that people over the ages probably have never seen it. I am convinced that this almost simplistic imagery is at the heart of art. It is nothing for which we should apologize. It is right that it should be that way, but it is also right that it be unconscious. Once we start poking around trying to make these images conscious, we do a disservice to the experience of what art or religion is.

DAC: That is the other part of the symbol: where a symbol "presences," as opposed to re-presents. It has all these levels of communication: conscious, unconscious, and its own.

SDS: I do not disparage consciousness, since within a given context it can be the basis of creativity; neither do I intend to suggest that the highest good in life is a nonconciousness attunement. What I like about Saint Francis's whole awareness is expressed by his saying, "You know as much as you do."[2] Knowledge that does not reach out into behavior and action is a stagnant layer of consciousness. When what you do is an embodiment of all that you know, you have a truly vital presence, and that Saint Francis really did express.

In my study of religion, I became aware of the two distinctive paths that religion has followed. One is a very male-oriented quest and the other is a very female-oriented quest. The highest good has been shaped two different ways. The male approach is to see God, and the female approach is to be absorbed in God. And this has everything to do with the question of individuation of each human being who comes from a mother and a father.

I had a teacher who referred to the quest of seeing the face of God as positive mysticism, and the quest of being absorbed in God as negative mysticism. The Eastern orientation is essentially female: Hinduism and Buddhism are involved with the nothingness of absorption, the drop of water into the ocean. In Christianity, with both Hebraic and Greek thought behind it, individuality is not obliterated but is consciously in relationship with God. That kind of relationship with ultimate reality leads to a different understanding of life and requires a different type of personality from the one that is seeking absorption.

You sensed that in my work there is a tension between separateness and fusion.[3] Either one alone is a highly edgy state, and the only way that I can accommodate my own psyche is to keep them in an equilibrium—sometimes more separateness, sometimes more fusion. The impulse, when I discovered two different colored clays, to stick the white, porcelain, bonelike forms into the stoneware, ocher, brownish clay is a very primitive expression of that separateness and fusion working simultaneously.

The role of color is significant because colors have instantaneous separateness. They only need to be a shade apart and they are separate colors. However, if you select two obviously separate colors, like opposites on the color wheel, they are as potently different as intellect is from emotion. And colors have certain emotional and symbolic connotations. I want to make a painting where blue and pink meet in lavender in that moment of fusion. How does the fused lavender get free of the pink and the blue? In terms of color, as soon as it becomes lavender, it is free. It is merely partaking of the two parent colors. There is an investment of your own life experience in something as innocent as color.

Then you add the form, and that is what I have been involved with for years: how you deal with the male-female polarity and the form of the body. All of my figures are either androgynous or nonsexual. Often, you do not know whether it is a male or a female figure. Or, if you see that it is a male figure, you see that it is also female. People who are insecure about their own sexual orientation, or who like things clear-cut, do not like this kind of ambiguity.

DAC: You are striving for that harmonious oneness: trying to get there but not staying since you have realized that people are always in process.

SDS: It is one of the great quests of being human, even though we are so involved with the polarity of man and woman. I do not know what to make of the Trinity. I keep thinking about it, as I

see the Holy Spirit as the vehicle for the fusion of opposites. It is
the force that allows us to transcend our separateness. Without
the Holy Spirit, we are caught in an almost frozen separation. It
is like the water that allows the fish to swim. It allows fusion or
unity to occur through the force of love; it bridges the gulf between parties who do love each other. The Bible is full of the
problem of separation, like the prodigal son: the conflict betwen
people who essentially love each other, but hate is there, also.

These religious concerns are not what make me a figurative artist, but they do help me to rationalize the validity of dealing
with figurative forms. I had to struggle with figurative art, as I
came out of a stronghold of non-objective Abstract Expressionism.
Willem deKooning had made that incredible fusion of abstract-
expressionist painting with the figure about ten years before I began my studies. He is perhaps the only abstract expressionist who
managed to achieve total spontaneity with a specific figure image. The only other artist I can think of who could do this, although in a different way, is Giacometti.

When you try to control an image in the midst of spontaneity
you usually fake it. You kind of sneak the image in and pretend
that it happened as spontaneously as the nonfigurative gestures.
Once your eyes are tuned, you can see the fakery instantly. That
is what has made me so hard on my own art. I developed a spontaneity with nonfigurative imagery, the landscapelike form, and
developed an attunement. Like a person develops a sense of pitch—
a realization that when something happens of its own accord, it
has a presence that is uniquely different from one that is manipulated. When I tried to achieve a figurative image with that presence, I only failed. That took me all of the 1960s to work through.

Early in my art, I realized that there is a state of honesty in a
form when it just happens. When I was a student I was laying a
big slab of clay onto my sculpture, and it didn't do what I wanted
it to do. Before I could act impulsively to correct the error, I
looked and saw the incredible vitality that was there. What was
given was infinitely greater than what I had wanted. That is when
I discovered the landscape in clay, the subtlety and softness of
flesh. My eyes were peeled open. Having had that experience, it
hurts my eyes to see a phony approximation of that kind of vitality. It hurts when I see my own, it hurts when I see others.

In *Zen in the Art of Archery*, by Eugen Herrigel, there is an exposition of the Western mind meeting the Eastern mind. Herrigel writes with such painstaking detail that you experience vicariously what happened to him. I remember the passage where he is in the archery class with people of smaller stature who pull the bow back effortlessly. He can only get the string back to about his nose and then his arm would begin to shake; by the time he got it back to his ear, the arrow was out of control. This went on for months. Finally the master said, "You might try a special way of breathing." He showed Herrigel how to breathe rhythmically with the drawing of the bow and the releasing of the arrow. Herrigel was able to pull the bow back all the way and release it without shaking. His first reaction was great relief. His second reaction was anger that the master had not shown him this earlier. Herrigel said, "Why didn't you tell me how to breathe at the beginning?" The master, in a very serene, detached way said, "If I had, you never would have known how important breathing is."

That helped me tremendously as I have tried to discover form honestly. Shortcuts to making form are like tricks. About two years into the experience, Herrigel took a seaside vacation with his wife and the master told him not to take his bow and arrow. He took them anyway. At the beach, he developed a completely Western method of aiming the arrow, until he could hit the bulls-eye. After vacation, the master asked Herrigel to shoot. He no sooner released the arrow than the master turned around and sat down with his back to Herrigel. Herrigel had been in Japan long enough to know what that meant: that was it.

It took weeks for an intermediary to rebuild the bridge. Reluctantly, the master took Herrigel back. What Herrigel was doing was defying the whole experience that the Zen tradition had discovered. By indulging in the gimmickry that is at the heart of Western culture, he was farther away from the experience than on the first day of class. If you are going to allow the experience to breathe and live, you are a co-worker who sets things in motion. The vitality is preserved. There are various words for it and the master talked about the arrow shooting him. You no longer are in the driver's seat state of mind.

Humanism is essentially working from the driver's seat: how you can shape things by a single-minded, left-brain control. Zen is always off center, askew, so that the human being is not at the center anymore. It is a dynamic participation of events occurring and you being there.[4] That is what Abstract Expressionism really was capturing. People did not realize how Eastern it was, since it was happening primarily in New York City. But it was a Zen awareness; small wonder that it could not perpetuate itself past the first generation.

In the second generation, artists like Rauschenberg and Johns, and in the second-and-a-half generation, Warhol and Lichtenstein and the Pop artists, realized that they could not do it in the way the masters could. They were too honest to become just second-rate Abstract Expressionists. They realized that if they were going to be themselves with any kind of individuality they could not just practice what the masters had unfolded, they had to defy it. So Rauschenberg began mocking the masters. There is his classic piece entitled *Erased deKooning*. The story is that when Rauschenberg asked deKooning for a drawing, deKooning was caught up in the historical spirit of the idea and gave him one of his best drawings.

In my own way and time, I have discovered that the unasked-for accident can also be the salvation of what you are doing. This is true in life, too, if you can get enough distance from the hot-headed front lines. Things go wrong in your life, and in some strange way they are really going right. I think that is what religion does. It addresses suffering. It is only through suffering that you become human. It hurts like hell, and nobody asks for it, unless he is masochistic or saintly. But once you have endured it, you invariably are richer and more alive than before you had to suffer. As you are aware, one of the themes in my work is the destruction of the body, and, to one degree or another, the healing of it again.

DAC: That is why I feel that even though your work has a fragmentation and a violence that caused the fragmentation, I do not find it hateful or vicious. I have always felt that your predominant theme is the healing and reuniting of the fragments. Whether these prove to be the fragments of the individual bodies or the fragments of one's life is left in the end to the experiences we each have, you in the making of the artwork and I in the perception of it. I can not imagine the possibility that either of us (or anyone else for that matter) does not add to the experience and interpretation of the artwork something of our own individuality and life experience.

SDS: Art lets us transform reality. So much of play, like when you are a child, is transforming reality: wanting to be big, driving a real truck, and not little, pushing a toy truck. Much of art is that kind of play in a serious sense, like magic, trying to restructure reality so that we can live with the suffering.

NOTES

1. *A Thomas Merton Reader*, ed. Thomas P. McDonnell (New York: Image Books, 1974), p. 387.

2. Stephen DeStaebler, "St. Francis of Assisi and His Imitation of Christ," Senior thesis, Princeton University, 1954.

3. See Diane Apostolos-Cappadona, "Art and the Spirit: The Sculptures of Stephen DeStaebler," American Academy of Religion Annual Meeting, 1981.

4. See Sharon Edwards, "A Conversation with Stephen DeStaebler," *Ceramics Monthly*, 29, no. 1 (April 1981), pp. 60–62.

PART II

ART HISTORIANS: THE RELIGIOUS IN ART

5

The Seven Functions of the Hands of Christ: Aspects of Leonardo's *Last Supper*

LEO STEINBERG

Introduction

Two questions arise at the mention of Leonardo's *Last Supper:* Is there anything left to see? and, Is there anything left to say? The answer to both questions is Yes.

Leonardo's mural is still where he painted it (Fig. 1). Despite its physical deterioration, despite the functional change of its setting from monastic refectory to public museum, and from a fifteenth-century structure shattered in World War II to a schematic modern replacement, the painting continues to build a unique situation. It transfigures the space it confronts, and there is no major feature within the mural that was not co-determined by considerations of site. That these considerations were formal is apparent from the effects achieved—the responsive articulation of the painted field and the fit of its perspectival construction.[1] But these same effects, as they couple the fictive world with the real, serve in abundant simultaneity to define the symbolic import of the occasion. The depicted action, unfolding from the pictorial center and overflowing, promotes the refectory itself to a condition of partnership; the space addressed becomes the recipient of an influence that proceeds, visibly, from an embodiment of the

Adapted from the Introduction and from chaps. I and V of a six-chapter essay, "Leonardo's *Last Supper*," published in *The Art Quarterly* 36 (1973), pp. 297–410. The material was originally delivered in a series of lectures at the Metropolitan Museum of Art, New York, in November 1967.

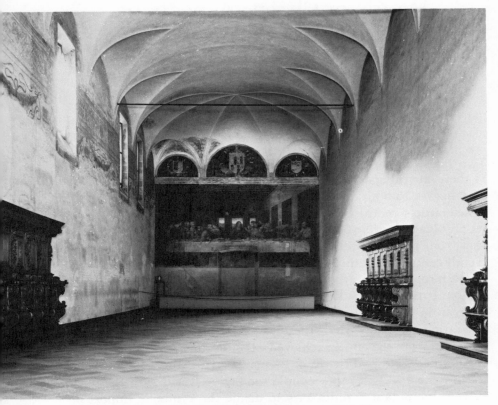

Fig. 1. Leonardo da Vinci. *The Last Supper*, c. 1495-97.
Refectory, S. Maria delle Grazie, Milan.

innermost Christian mystery, the union in Christ of two natures. To a holistic intuition, the painting *in situ* offers a parallel incarnation, wherein meekness and power, submissiveness and the potency of the prime mover, are beheld as coincident.

None of these visual effects, none of these meanings, survive the transfer of the image in reproduction. Leonardo's great mural painting participates in a close-knit collocation, and—though it has been more than any painting in history copied, adapted, abused and lampooned—it remains essentially unreproduceable. Quarantined in a frame, insulated on a book page, the image is demythologized, cut back to the dimension of narrative. What the artist conceived demands to be seen, and to be thought of, *in situ.* And the uniqueness of the *in situ* experience forms one theme of the present essay.

The answer to the second of the two opening questions is equally positive. What remains to be told about Leonardo's *Last Supper* is not some residual matter previously overlooked; the novelty of the subject is the whole of the work responding to another interrogation. In the present study the picture emerges as both less secular and less simple; contrary to received notions, it is nowhere "unambiguous and clear," but consistently polysemantic.

The common view of Leonardo's *Last Supper* as a feat of dramatic verisimilitude and a revelation of human nature perpetuates two dominant attitudes of the nineteenth century—its secularism and its relish for scientific statement. The latter called for precise representation and required not only that a statement be consistent with what it means, but that it be inconsistent with alternative meanings. Hence the aversion to ambiguity, and the assurance that Leonardo's outstanding artistic creation must be as forthright in meaning as his anatomical drawing or his didactic prose.[2]

Nineteenth-century secularism led to the same result. In the art of the Renaissance, the obscurantism attributed to religious preoccupations seemed happily superseded. Art at its ideal best was believed to reveal humane truths which the cult of religion could only dim or distort. And it was again Leonardo in whom the highest artistic goals, originally envisaged in ancient Greece, seemed reaffirmed. In this projection of nineteenth-century values upon the Renaissance, the masterworks of religious Renaissance painting, depleted of content and connotation, were pinned to the utmost simplicity of intention. So Mantegna's *Dead Christ* was declared to be only an exercise in anatomic perspective; Michelangelo's *Doni Tondo*, no more than a family group sporting outdoors; and Leonardo's *Last Supper* nothing but a behavioral study of twelve individuals responding to psychic shock. In the words of a still popular textbook, Leonardo chose to "bypass the traditional meaning of the Last Supper in Christian art. He is not in the least concerned with the institution of the Eucharist, nor with the mystery of sacrificial death . . . but with a single aspect of the narrative—the speculation regarding the identity of the betrayer. . . ."[3]

It is the wonder of great art to be so richly dowered that it satisfies even under restricting assumptions. The proponents of positivism who took Leonardo's picture for pure psychodrama felt fully rewarded. So do we who see the work steeped in exquisite ambiguity. But in differing from interpreters such as Goethe, Burckhardt, and Wölfflin, we need not claim greater wisdom; we claim only to be writing out of the latter twentieth century, as they did not. Our task is to announce how the work looks to an age that no longer insists on seeing the Renaissance as a movement of triumphant secularism; to declare how it appears in a climate no longer averse to reading pictorial symbols as multiplex signs. The word "ambiguity," a Latin rendering of the Greek *amphibolia*, referred originally to a predicament; it meant being attacked from two sides at once. The modern consciousness has inverted the primitive model to suggest effective action in more directions than one. Ambiguity becomes enhanced capability, a species of power revealed in its maximum density in the artist's conception of the protagonist at the Last Supper (Fig. 2).

I. Christ lowers his arms in resignation. Done with the ministry, he is about to submit to the Passion (Fig. 3). Ever since the late eighteenth century, the pathetic humanity of the gesture has won admiration.[4] The foremost Leonardo enthusiast of the Neo-Classical age—the painter Giuseppe Bossi, who spent ten years studying and copying the work (Fig. 4)—rejoiced to see the divinity of the Christ figure "abstracted," its human pathos intensified.[5] Walter Pater (1869) was pleased to perceive ". . . not the pale Host of the altar, but one taking leave of his friends." And a

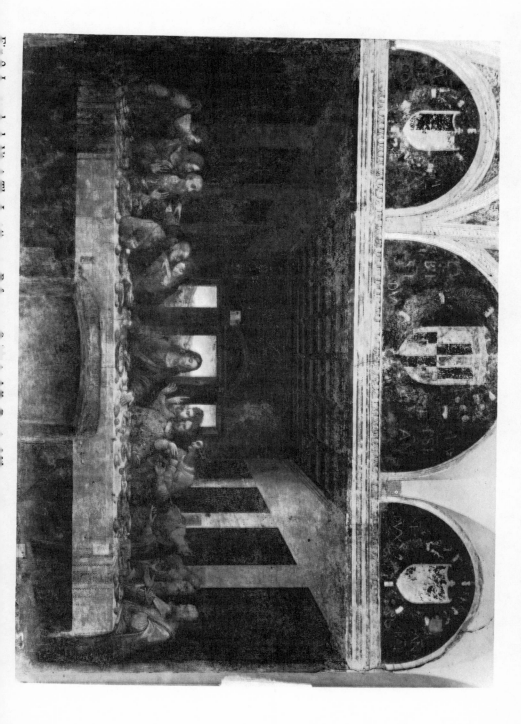

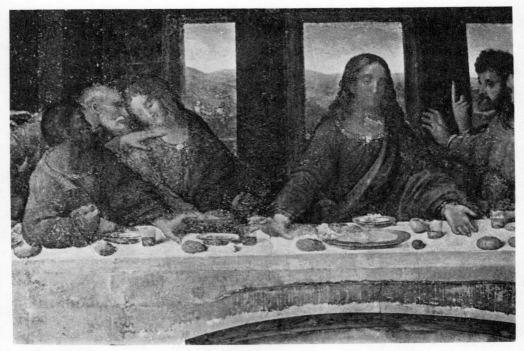

Fig. 3. Leonardo da Vinci. *The Last Supper*, detail.

hundred years later, Herbert von Einem: "Gone is the formal gesture of blessing. . . . The sorrowful inclination of the head converts the sublimity of the divine into gentle humanity."[6]

We almost see how it is done—how the cadence of resignation
is conveyed by the droop of the shoulders (Fig. 3). The morphol-
ogy of acquiescence was never fixed more precisely, never more
accurately defined as the obverse of resistance. Squared shoulders
assert themselves; they withstand. Those of the Christ signal surrender. Insistently Leonardo's choreography drives the effect
home: from left to center, in one figure after another, a repeated
stress falls on sturdy shoulders—three hands in succession set-
tling like epaulets. Then, silhouetted by the rear window, a sharp
incline at the St. John; and, finally, brought down by the lowered
hand, the responding slope of Christ's body: figure and hieroglyph
of submission.[7]

II. Strangely enough, it is exactly these shrinking shoulders that
also serve to triangulate the body's shape. Aligned with the fall-

ing hair, they trace a nearly regular, three-sided figure, so that the incarnation of triune godhead reigns at the table under the aspect of an equilateral triangle. The very contour that reduces Christ's manhood to meekness evokes his divinity in emblematic abstraction. We are given a double value: in one reading, a full-bodied presence, a person in a fugitive moment swayed by emotion; in another, a stable triangular shape—centered, discrete and immovable. A single posture is made to meet contradictory ends, projecting a figure as paradoxical as the dual nature of Christ.[8]

III. Yet this is but the beginning. That same gesture, which configures in simple shape both affect and emblem, also promotes the dramatic plot by designating the traitor. Words of ill omen—"he that dips with me in the dish, the same shall betray me"—these just-spoken words are accompanied by a right-handed motion which the given context renders accusatory. Christ's pronated hand stops the recoiling left hand of Judas—the two hands, in the symmetry of their mutual approach, suddenly similar, almost identical (Figs. 3, 4). They are antagonists, sundered only by the foreboding dish.[9]

Are we now seeing more than the artist intended? Could not this fleeting coordination of hands approaching a plate be a mirage—or, as Otto Hoerth in his long-definitive monograph on the *Last Supper* put it (1907), "an accidental optical constellation"? Hoerth argued (and some younger writers agree) that the bracketed dish can have no special role to play in the picture; that it is merely John's personal plate, ergo, not a communal dish to be dipped into by fellow diners. We are, in effect, cautioned against imputing a breach of good table manners to the sacred assembly. On the other hand, all our knowledge of Leonardo, and everything in the design of this mural, warns us against attributing any of its dispositions to chance. Could it be that the seeming fortuity of that "optical constellation" was planned?

In quandaries of this sort it is advisable to start looking afresh and to tabulate the pertinent data. Yes indeed, the plate is St. John's. You may verify this by matching tableware and Apostles down the length of the board. But who keeps such tallies? As we watch the commotion that shakes the Peter-John-Judas group in responding to Christ, we perceive their gestural reflexes without counting dishes. And if we allow that just this negligence about keeping count is what the artist expects of us, then it follows that Leonardo is again doing more than one thing at a time. In a literal sense, the disputed plate belongs to St. John; visually, its insertion between Christ and Judas announces the imminent clash of protagonist and betrayer. Observe how St. John's own passive gesture sets off the encounter, hyphening the affronted hands of his neighbors. John's peaceably folded hands advance no possessive claims; they withdraw to his edge of the table, furthest removed from the plate which sits far forward across the board, as if disowned. By way of this optical manumission, John succeeds in leaving his plate more closely engaged by Christ's spreading fingers than by his own. The retreat of John's interlocked fingers frees his "personal" plate for symbolic performance.

We conclude that the apparently simple, "straightforward" gesture of Christ achieves no less than three things: it expresses submission; it triangulates a symbolic form; and it accuses the traitor. And this bring us to Function IV.

IV. In relation to Judas' hand, Christ's gesture is ambiguous enough; it holds down what it condemns—this being the third of its tasks. But there is yet another. We observe that the fingers of Christ's right hand are splayed for the widest span, like a pianist's striking an octave; and we note that a wineglass (omitted in Fig. 5) as well as the treason dish enters their grasp. The maneuver is complex, or rather, it is made so by the context: in a sidelong reading, parallel to the board, the gesture directs itself to the dish and the hand of Judas; in a hitherward reading—paired and concerted with the advancing left hand—the gesture addresses the glass. Seeing Christ's two hands together, we witness one reaching toward the wine—symbol of the Passion which Judas is about to initiate—while the other tips toward a loaf of bread. Such clear exposition of the Eucharistic species, however disguised as still-life, cannot be fortuitous. Nor is it by accident that the reach for the wine occurs on the shadowed, descending side of the mural, the side of John, Peter and Judas—the three disciples who participate in the Passion; whereas the showing forth of the bread falls on the rising, illumined side, and under that

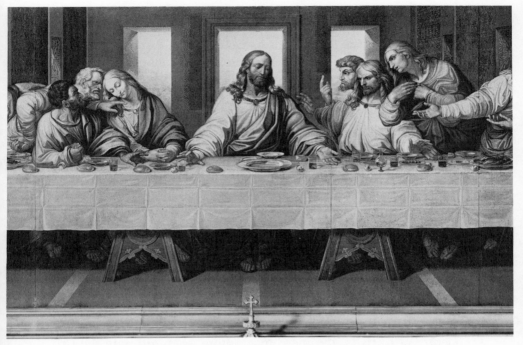

Fig. 4. Giacomo Raffaelli after Giuseppe Bossi's "reconstruction" of *The Last Supper*, mosaic, 1819. Vienna, Minoritenkirche.

earnest finger by which, three days hence, doubting Thomas will verify the Resurrection.

The hands of Christ "show forth" the elements of the Eucharist (Figs. 3, 4). More precisely, they address those homely species of bread and wine which will be consecrated for Christian communion by the event of this night. But "showing forth" and "addressing" are words inadequate to the work in hand—the figure of Leonardo's Christ is more richly tasked. By the subtlest of collocations, Leonardo empowered Christ's gesture not only to point but to transmit and bestow. The pictorial conception was to effect a near-magical process—a perpetual outflow, or effusion of grace, from the heart of the painting upon those who breathed in its presence.

To accomplish this end, Leonardo enlisted the floor pattern beneath the Christ figure, the center part that directly supports the feet, as well as the flanking units that lie at a distance under his hands. Unfortunately, the lower center of Leonardo's work perished in 1652 to accommodate a large portal in place of the low fifteenth-century door under the mural (Fig. 1). To reconstruct Leonardo's pavement design we therefore consult the earliest copies and replicas. And the most authoritative of these copies inform us that Leonardo's pavement had been articulated as an exact counterpart to the ceiling (Figs. 4, 5).[10] In other words, the pavement was originally divided into six lanes by means of five inlaid bands, light on dark ground; of which the median, the central floor band, defined the pictorial axis as the site of Christ's tangent feet.

These feet, pressed close against one another, are a troubling sign. Neither in normal life situations nor in the conventions of art do the lower limbs of seated male figures so cleave together. As Leonardo disposed them, these centered feet, seeking the central band of the pavement, prompt an irresistible association; they evoke the feet nailed to the stem of the Cross. Anticipating the posture of Christ's imminent martyrdom, they intimate the Crucifixion and declare the readiness of the victim. For we cannot unthink the Passion when Christ's feet appear joined on an upright stave.[11]

Nor is this an adventitious allusion, since the image of the Last Supper on a refectory wall was traditionally associated with a representation of the Crucifixion.[12] In Leonardo's mural, which faced a *Crucifixion* fresco already emplaced at the opposite end of the hall, the reference to the Cross must be understood as proleptic—an allusion retained in shadow as to a moment unborn. But this prolepsis is central to the whole argument, as central to the mural's design and conceptual program as it is to the theology of the Mass.[13] The Eucharist, a meal in its outward form, renders present Christ's death on the Cross. Of that death, Christ's feet, the dutiful tokens of his mortal nature, are the appropriate heralds.[14] Hence their location and posture in the *Last Supper:* they transfigured the lowliest element in the design, the axial floor band, into a sign.

So much for the centerline as it rises toward the feet. Let us

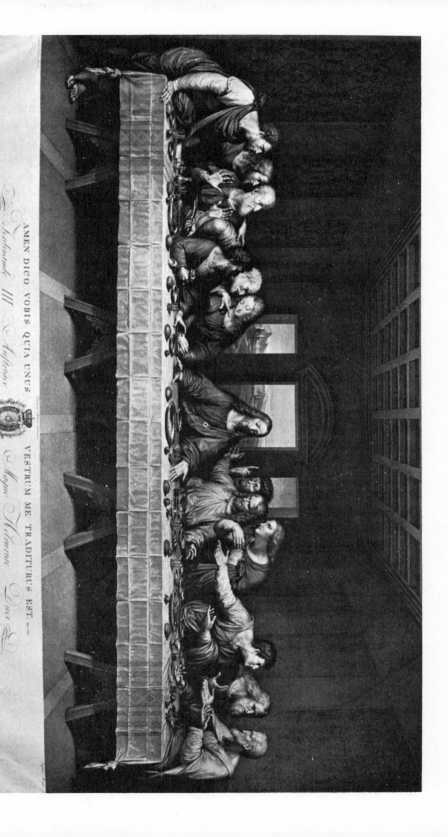

Fig. 5. Raphael Morghen after Leonardo, *The Last Supper*, engraving, 1800.

turn next to the nearest pair of floor bands and consider their original relationship to Christ's hands. We have seen these hands propound the elements of the Eucharist—but almost casually, as if shy of their meaning; the bread indicated is no different from the other loaves on the table, while the half-empty cup, strictly speaking, belongs to St. John. But Leonardo's meanings are not simply embodied in objects. The very location of these elements in the composition supports their symbolic role. Thus the cup and the roll of bread are of a character entirely ordinary when read lengthwise along the table; they are transubstantiated in their relation to Christ and to the vectors released by his gesture. Christ's outspread arms initiate a forward directional flow that continues, under the drop of the tablecloth, in two orthogonal floorlines in front of the table.[15] As these lines converge, moving inward and upward, Christ becomes the capstone of a great central pyramid. But as Christ launches the action, the floorlines diverge and stream toward us. And midway between the descending slopes of Christ's arms and the floorlines that align with these arms and prolong their course lie bread and wine. Wineglass and breadroll together bring the thrust of Christ's hands hitherward to the fore edge of the table—below which the bands of the pavement proceed again, down to the threshold of the depicted field. Are we hallucinating? Is this freighted symmetry consisting of arms, Eucharistic species and floor bands another chance optical configuration? Shall it be written off as a formal arrangement that happens accidentally to suggest a possible Christian meaning; or is it a willed visual metaphor? The situation calls upon every interpreter to declare himself—whether to admit a coded signal, or shrug it off as a fluke.

The elements at Christ's fingertips, placed in extension of his own body, are points of transmission between the divine presence and our own. And just as the symbol of imminent Crucifixion is drawn inward upon Christ's body—drawn up from the pictorial threshold as though incurred from the actual world—so the symbolic wineglass and loaf relay beams of energy that pass from the picture outward, as things bestowed. The strategic positioning of that bread and wine comes too close to defining the nature of the sacrament to be dismissed as the product of chance. Rather, their placement suggests that Leonardo's pictorial syntax includes location as a factor of meaning, and that neither the pavement nor the bread and wine at the reach of Christ's hands were meant to be overlooked. The sum of Christ's traffic with man—Crucifixion received, sacrament given—inheres in the pattern.

V. The discernible meanings multiply before one's eyes. But so, we must add, does the resistance of those who dislike ambiguity—a resistance expressed not only in simplistic literary descriptions, but already apparent in the numerous replicas of Leonardo's *Last Supper* produced in the sixteenth century. Nearly all of these change the floor pattern to dispel whatever burden of meaning might lurk in the conjunction of feet with a figured floor. For the sake of simplification many copyists and adapters pry the closed feet apart. Some omit the wineglass (Fig. 5); others let the dish go. Not one preserves the pluralities of the original. Even Raphael, in the very act of paying homage to the *Cenacolo*, feels the need to pare down. His drawing for Marcantonio's famous engraving shows a protagonist moved by a simple impulse to a single gesture: the laying down of both palms on the table. Implicitly the surcharged complexity of the original is rebuked. For Leonardo's Christ—gesturing with both palms displayed, but one open, the other turned down—assumes yet another symbolic role— the fifth in the present inventory. His hands, alternately prone and supine, project a familiar vision, the dual form under which Christ's hands appear in numberless images of the Last Judgment, one summoning, one putting away. Seeing this act of ultimate segregation anticipated in the ordained body of Christ—and the pronated hand directed at the first of the damned—we cannot dismiss the intuition that the Christ of the Parousia and of the concomitant Judgment is being prefigured. We are indeed witnessing the institution of that central sacrament wherein Christ makes present the fullness of his redemptive work from Incarnation to Second Coming.[16]

Some may object that the wrong hand is open, since the auspicious hand should be the right. And it has been suggested that Leonardo reversed the actions of right and left because he himself was left-handed.[17] But this is improbable since the picture is not a private notation. More to the point, it is not a self-contained image, but part of an architectural complex, an end wall in a monastic refectory, adjoined to a cloister and church. In considering right and left, this contexture may not be ignored. When Leonardo embarked on the painting, Montorfano's fresco of the *Crucifixion*, completed in 1495, already occupied the wall opposite. And there, on the south wall, the right side of Christ turns, as required, toward the Madonna and the Good Thief. The direction of blessedness was thus prefixed for the entire refectory. In conformity with Christ's own inclination, the longitudinal hall was, as it were, oriented laterally to its pulpit, eastward, and to what lay beyond its east wall—the graveyard and church (Figs. 6, 7).

Could these conditions be slighted? Another painter, commissioned to place a Last Supper on the north wall of the refectory, might have tried to think them away. The subject, after all, was not like a Crucifixion or a Last Judgment—subjects that automatically rank right versus left. Since a Last Supper disposes six Apostles of equal dignity on either side of their Lord, it would have been possible to repeat the standard symmetrical scheme without finding significance in bilateral differentiation. But Leonardo, bound though he was to a general compositional symmetry, committed himself no less to meaningful oppositions of right and left. And the inequalities he assigned to the two halves of the mural dramatize a contrast that runs deep in the duality of the subject. The Lord's Supper was to be understood in its two senses: historically, as the announcement of the Passion, and mystically, as the promise of eternal life conveyed in the sacrament of the Mass. So the darkened side of the mural became that of Judas, Peter and John—the three disciples associated with the Crucifixion; while the right side was made to begin at St. Thomas' finger—witness to the Resurrection (Fig. 3). The opposition is further sustained by the changing densities of the groups (Fig. 2). A cluster of five heads on the left packs a surface measurable from between the foremost tapestries to the wall corner; the corresponding span on the right is loosely manned by no more than three. The want of elbow-room at left contrasts at right with free-flowing motion; and on the constricted dark side, ten hands out of twelve (excepting only those of St. Andrew) bear down, weighing on table or shoulders; whereas on the right, ten out of twelve hands are aloft. Even the perspectival construction was persuaded to yield more than the normal convergence upon a centric vanishing point. By a pervasive eastward drift, rightward throughout the design, Leonardo contrived to make the orthogonals on the left seem to dip, then mount on the other side. And the effect of falling and rising agreed not only with the depicted opposition of shadow and brightness, but was keyed in symbolic asymmetry to the real illumination of the refectory.[18]

No earlier painting displayed within its own feigned interior a comparable susceptibility to an external light source (Fig. 8). Evening light, entering from the left, bleaches—or appears to bleach— the depicted east wall of the painted chamber. As the westering sun streams through the high windows in the west wall of the refectory, reality and illusion together are suffused in its radiance. When the mural was new, this vision of actual light irradiating a faerie space must have been the most magical feature of Leonardo's illusionism. The assembled friars, seated at supper, were embraced in one glow with the sacred assembly. And even today, after nearly five centuries of irreversible ruin, the sense of disparate worlds in communion sometimes returns at the hour of dusk. In their common reception of the evening light, no less than in their jointed perspectives, the two interfaced spaces were to be experienced in continuity. The painted world of the *Last Supper* was to be felt as a real presence, sensitive to the points of the compass and the determinants of the site.

It follows that the Christ of the mural had to favor his left—our right as we face him; he would not incline to the side of darkness. Once the work was lodged in its topographical context, the orientation of the life-giving hand was determined. The painter could not avert his Christ from the east.

VI. We are beginning to see the figure—not as it appears in reproduction on a book page, but as it would have loomed before a man entering the refectory by way of its original entrance in the east wall (Fig. 6). One discovers that the propitious left hand in the mural is extended illusionistically toward the visitant. The depicted Christ points directly to the door (now walled up) that formerly gave on the Grand Cloister, the Chiostro dei Morti, or burial ground. To a person passing through this door, the offer of Christ's extended hand must have come like a token of reassurance. Whatever message the visitor was prepared to impute to the

gesture, he would have seen the open hand put forth in his direction. And not toward him alone, for the hand reached out toward
those who, dying in Christian hope, await Christ's call in the
grave—those asleep in the Chiostro dei Morti and, directly beyond, those dead of the house of Sforza who were to be buried
under the dome of the church (Fig. 7).[19]

It is improbable that the connection between the depicted Christ
figure, the burial ground, and the church of S. Maria delle Grazie
was lost upon Leonardo's ducal patron, Lodovico il Moro. The
Last Supper commission was part of a grandiose scheme to turn
the monastery-church complex into a Sforza family mausoleum—
and there had been enough recent deaths to lend urgency to the
project. The former Duke Gian Galeazzo had died (October 22,
1494) shortly before the commission was given. While Leonardo's

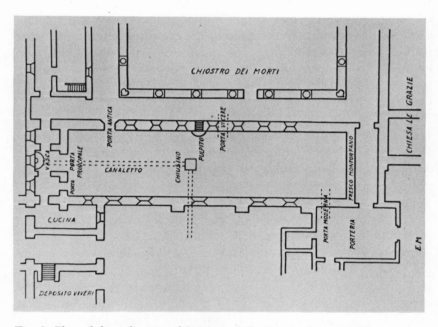

Fig. 6. Plan of the refectory of S. Maria delle Grazie (from Möller,
fig. 48), showing the 17th-century *porta principale* in the wall of
the *Last Supper* mural, the *porta antica* in the east wall, and the
adjoining Chiostro dei Morti.

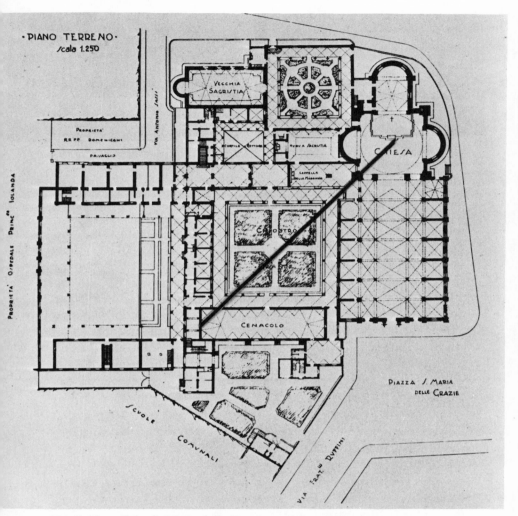

Fig. 7. Plan of the S. Maria delle Grazie complex, east at top (from Mezzanotte, *Milano nell'arte . . .*, p. 652), with directional line superimposed.

mural was taking form, Duke Lodovico's daughter died (November 22, 1496); then, six weeks later, Beatrice d'Este, his wife. The grief-stricken Sforza usurper continually frequented the Grazie altar and dined every Tuesday and Saturday at the prior's table in the refectory, facing the Christ.[20] And the emotional effect of his weekly itinerary is not hard to conceive: leaving behind the high altar and burial ground to enter the refectory by the *porta antica* in its east wall, he must have sensed the felicity of the divine hand motioning toward the graves as it indicated the "bread which is the medicine of immortality."[21]

Needless to say, the duke's feelings on these occasions are not recorded. But a glance at the plan of the Grazie complex confirms that the felicitous correlation between depicted gesture and actual topography must have been a deliberated effect. Consider the north wall of the refectory, the wall that contains the *Last Supper*. If we trace a line from its midpoint southeast at 45 degrees— the angle at which the foreshortened left arm of the Christ projects illusionistically across the depicted table—we find that this line, clearing the *porta antica* and traversing the Chiostro dei Morti, homes to the exact midpoint of Bramante's *tribuna*, the church's domed crossing. Or, reversing the sequence: the center-point of the new dome was located to lie on one rectilinear diagonal with the refectory entrance and the midpoint of the *Last Supper* wall—the point whence Leonardo's Christ initiates that commanding axis by the gesture of the left hand. In other words, the direction of Christ's life-giving motion defines the radius of the dome. And since, as Carlo Pedretti has shown, Leonardo collaborated with Bramante in replanning the church; since he was simultaneously engaged in both projects, we need not suppose that this precise correlation between dome and refectory mural escaped his attention, or that it fell into place by chance.[22] The siting of Bramante's great domed *tribuna*—its exact distance from the preexistent old Gothic nave—must have been calculated to correspond with the central event in the projected wall painting, the gesture of its protagonist.

But is it conceivable that Leonardo intended so many meanings while designing his Christ? So formulated, the question is sterile, because Leonardo's unrecorded intentions are not available. The question rebounds on the modern viewer who has to choose between probabilities. If he overloads the mystery of Christ's gesture with meanings, he may be reading in more than was meant. Conversely, if he resists possible levels of meaning, he may be projecting upon Leonardo a personal preference for simplicity. The risk of projecting attends both alternatives, and, judged by the historical record, the *Last Supper* has been more grossly wronged by simplism and mental sloth than by exorbitant subtlety.

For this writer there is one determining consideration: that it is methodologically unsound to imagine Leonardo blind or insensitive to the implications of his inventions. He was creating the most excogitated picture in the history of art, and we do less violence to probability if we grant him awareness that the action he assigned to his Christ yields at least six intelligible connotations: (1) Christ spreads his hands to express willing surrender; (2) the gesture accuses the traitor; (3) it contours Christ's shape so as to allude to the Trinity; (4) both hands together, pointing to bread and wine, evoke the sacrament of communion; (5) the open hand, defining the radius of the church dome, extends the promise of life to the sleeping dead; (6) the palms, alternately prone and uplifting, prefigure the Judge of the Second Coming.[23]

It is as though that single pose held the whole meaning of the Eucharistic sacrifice, the locked feet and dispensing hands reminding the faithful that the Last Supper anticipates the sacrifice of the Cross, while enshrining it in a perpetual rite till he come again. In the working of the Christ figure, Leonardo visualized the continuum of salvation.

VII. And there is yet a seventh function that depends once again on the apparent forward thrust of Christ's arms, their emphatic reach half-way across the table. Standing in the refectory (photographs tend to flatten and reduce the effect), one becomes intensely aware that the arms of Christ do more than triangulate his upper body; they give the figure a projective "ground plan." The body in depth describes an open trapezoid formed by arms diverging from the plane of the chest. The arms fan out, obliquely foreshortened and with far-reaching consequence (Fig. 8).

When Goethe—in the most influential text ever written about our topic—declared that Leonardo's *Last Supper* represents the impact of a spoken word on an assembly, he was thinking as a dramatist, not as a painter. In his description, the picture becomes the illustration of an auditory event, the visible sequel to a vocal stimulus which itself lies outside the scope of visualization. Thus, in the Goethean conception, the picture, lacking the

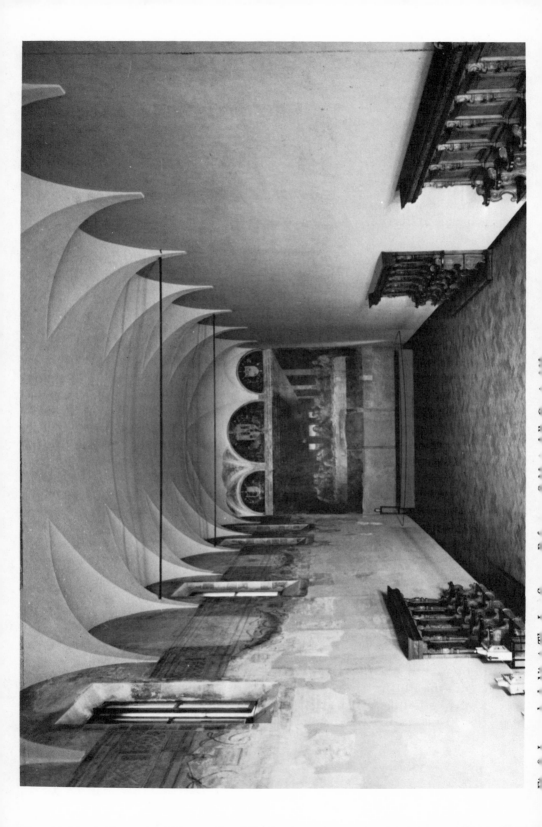

voice of Christ, remains incomplete; it does not evince the speech that supposedly caused what we are seeing. This literary approach to Leonardo's pictorial thinking misses the plenitude, the sufficiency of the image. It misses the thrust of a picture whose vitality is not fed by an absent stimulus—a spoken word that has died on the air—but by an ongoing process, like the beat of a heart or the emission of light. Of course Leonardo expects us to recognize Christ as the speaker, the *proponitore*. But what is optically manifest, what we are made to see as the impetus to all motion, is not a word but a gesture. That gesture is causal. Visually, choreographically, the motive force in the picture is the flare of those arms, and it is to their action that the whole picture responds. As Christ's hands clear a site for themselves, his nearest neighbors roll back, make way, and fall into responsive diagonals. The redisposition of the two flanking triads with respect to the table's edge is instantaneous: on our left, parallel to the right arm of Christ, one slanted course runs elbows-out from John to Judas; on our right, Thomas and Philip line up obliquely with the recoiling St. James. Both groups together confirm the divergence of that central arms' spread; they take up its momentum, and they transmit it, further amplified, to the tapestried walls, so that the walls, too, seem to expand, fanning out in remote obedience to the initial impulse of Christ's spreading arms. One cannot unsee the optical correspondence between the induced obliquity of these walls and the mediating diagonals of the inner groups of disciples. Seen synoptically with the Christ, the depicted room in its splayed-out perspective adapts itself to the "ground plan" of Christ's action. For as the rear wall of the depicted chamber parallels the expanse of Christ's shoulders, so by virtue of the perspectival projection, the foreshortened side walls (like the stripes in the floor) obey the course set and shaped by his arms. The very perspective becomes, as it were, a consequence of the event. From the closest disciples to the hithermost reach of the chamber, the response is to one source of energy, dramatic action and geometric projection reacting together as in a fluid medium. The walls amplify the motion initiated in Christ. We are witness to a spectacular symboisis of the vital and the inanimate—and receive the shock of this visual equation: what motor action is to the body, perspective is to the walls; it is their adaptive response, their form of commotion, their way of being ensouled. Perspective and body movement alike are revealed as modes of reactivity to an impulse absorbed from the prime mover.[24]

We touch here on the most sensitive of Leonardo's paradoxes. Obviously, these tapestried walls, being the facing sides of a projected rectangular hall, must run parallel to each other; hence they cannot assimilate the divergence of Christ's arms in a structural sense. We resist being tricked into an erroneous reading of perspectival directions. As we observe the walls and the diagonally disposed groups of Apostles together, we may relish their mutual rhyming as a compositional artifice, but when it comes to understanding what we are seeing, our minds pry them apart as being different things. It is hard for the intelligence to concede that the flanks of a rectangular box can be so double-dealing as to approximate two spreading radii. Yet the paradox is no greater than that contained in the postulate that parallels meet at infinity. And it seems that Leonardo's design, for all its appeal to the intellect which decodes a one-point perspective, appeals no less to that optical intuition which exactly sees what appears. In the *Last Supper*, the course of the tapestried walls is doubly charged. One charge is rational—to define the locale of the narrative as a rectangular chamber; the other is visionary—to exhibit space in mysterious congruity with the divine influence from the center.

We are asked to share the master's profound acquiescence in the ambivalence of perspective, an acquiescence that actually wills ambiguity. The seeming convergence of the side walls as well as their known non-convergence—the thing seen and the thing understood—both in parity assume the same significant status. They may contradict one another, but they co-exist like sight and thought in the mind.

Leonardo's depicted space, then, is not an inert shell but a reactive presence. Informed and moved by the action onstage and concerted with the gesticulation of Christ, the wall planes diverge as if launched on their hithering course by divine ordinance. The result is an image of uncanny vitality. Through the valve-like gap formed by the inner groups of disciples, the picture pours itself out toward us. And as this effluent energy, discharged from the center, expands into the three-dimensional space we ourselves occupy, the perspective even of the refectory walls seems to reverse itself. Their spatial motion, their normal convergence upon a remote vanishing point, is perceived instead as an outcome—the ultimate propagation of a movement engendered in Christ. Leonardo makes actual space seem contingent on the divine presence. As Christ's arms anticipate and embrace even the real perspective, our physical ambience is subsumed in his influence. All visible space is defined in his aura, and perspective itself becomes sanctified. Christ, the submissive Christ of the Passion, literally imparts himself to the world. He moves his hands—no more than that; and at his motion, the very order of space, the laws governing visibility, are revealed as a divine emanation.

NOTES

1. The subject of Leonardo's perspectival construction, in its collocation with the actual refectory, is discussed at length in Steinberg, "Leonardo's *Last Supper*," chaps. IV and VI; and, more definitively, in Francis Naumann, "The 'costruzione legittima' in the Reconstruction of Leonardo da Vinci's 'Last Supper,' " *Arte Lombarda* 52 (1979), pp. 63–89. See also Warman Welliver, "Symbolic Meaning in Leonardo's and Raphael's Painted Architecture," *The Art Quarterly* 2 (1979), pp. 37–66.

2. It is a tribute to Leonardo's success that every ambiguity in his picture earns praise for being straightforward and clear—even though disagreements over what it is that is clearly presented never subside. Confirming instances are cited in Steinberg, p. 382, n. 12.

3. Frederick Hartt, *Italian Renaissance Art*, New York, 1969, p. 399.

4. Thus Domenico Pino (*Storia genuina del cenacolo* . . . , Milan, 1796): "Il volto è dolcemente maestoso, gli occhi abbassati in maniera di chi dice cosa, cui dispiace il dirla." And Stendhal twenty years later: "Voyant les hommes si méchants, il [Christ] se dégoûte de vivre. . . . 'Je me suis trompé, se dit-il, j'ai jugé des hommes d'après mon coeur.' Son attendrissement est tel, qu'en disant aux disciples ces tristes paroles: 'L'un de vous va me trahir,' il n'ose regarder aucun d'eux" (Stendhal, *Histoire de la Peinture en Italie*, ed. Paul Arbelet, Paris, 1924, I, p. 196).

5. Bossi's pertinent paragraph reads (in the author's translation): "Unlike his predecessors, the divine Leonardo was not content with the approval of religious souls . . . rather, he wished to engage the spirits of all men capable of feeling, men of all times and of every creed; to engage all those hearts to whom friendship and the horror of treason are not unknown. Guided by philosophy, he pondered how greatly those feelings would be enhanced when directed toward the Man-God as the principal personage; but he so ordered his work that, even while abstracting the divinity of the protagonist, his subject retained such general import, that art here sacrificed nothing to private opinions or religious ceremonies, which are neither as eternal nor as universal as human feelings" (Giuseppe Bossi, *Del Cenacolo di Leonardo da Vinci*, Milan, 1810, p. 78).

6. Walter Pater, "Leonardo da Vinci" (1869), in *The Renaissance*, Modern Library edition, New York, n.d., p. 99; Herbert von Einem, "Das Abendmahl des Leonardo da Vinci," *Arbeitsgemeinschaft für Forschung des Landes Nordrhein-Westfalen* 99 (1961), p. 58.

7. St. John's abridged shoulder was first remarked by Guillon, who attributed its disfigurement to the incompetence of some eighteenth-century restorer (Aimé Guillon de Montléon, *Le cénacle de Léonard de Vinci*, Paris, 1811). Hoerth followed at a century's distance: "Not without justice did Guillon de Montléon blame the overpainters for the unnatural shrinkage of St. John's left shoulder, whose collarbone seems to be missing" (Otto Hoerth, *Das Abendmahl des Leonardo da Vinci*, Leipzig, 1907, p. 22, n. 10). As for the narrow shoulders of Christ—broadened somewhat in most early copies—they grow immense in Bossi's "reconstruction" (Fig. 4, and Steinberg, fig. 28, for Bossi's destroyed original). Bossi justifies his spectacular alteration on the grounds that Christ's principal virtue was "la potenza," to which the virtues of gentleness, resignation and love were "secondary" (*Del Cenacolo*, pp. 181ff.). He concluded that the shrinking shoulders in the original mural must be the result of inept restoration. There is no question, however, that the sloping contours of both the Christ and the St. John figure survive as Leonardo designed them. He was willing to forgo local anatomical accuracy for the sake of larger connections.

8. For similar renderings of embodied divinity in the symbolic form of a triangle (not, however, in a narrative context!), see the *Padre Eterno* in the gables of Florentine fifteenth-century wall tombs and tabernacles (e.g., by Luca della Robbia), or the enskied God the Father in Dürer's engraving, *Virgin and Child with St. Anne*, c. 1500 (Bartsch 29). Since such triangulation is commoner in visions of the Father than of the incarnate Son, it may, in Leonardo's picture, allude to Christ's words at the Last Supper—"he that hath seen me hath seen the Father" (John 14:9).

9. Bossi (*Del Cenacolo*, p. 185) was the first to suspect that Christ's right hand (more precisely its lowered index) expressed St. Matthew's "Qui intingit mecum manum in paropside."

10. The most authoritative copy of Leonardo's mural was a fresco produced during the master's lifetime for the monastery at Castellazzo near Milan. During the nineteenth century it was detached and severely damaged; and it perished in World War II. But the floor pattern displayed in the Castellazzo fresco is recorded (a) in Bossi's description ("Il pavimento è di un rosso vivace interrotto d'alto in basso da cinque strisce verdi," *Del Cenacolo*, p. 135); (b) in Bossi's copy of the *Last Supper* (Fig. 4); and (c) in the famous Raphael Morghen engraving (and its countless derivatives). Both Bossi and Morghen knew the Castellazzo fresco in its original setting. Thus, as regards the design of the pavement, their copies are our best evidence of Leonardo's intention.

11. The majority of *Crucifixion* images since the Renaissance show the feet of Christ overlapping, not side by side. But though this has become the familiar form, it was formerly a contested and deplored innovation. By the thirteenth century, the correct posture of the feet on the Cross, and the right number of nails employed, could arouse heated controversy; as when Bishop Luke of Tuy in Spain composed a diatribe against the Albigensian heretics (c. 1230), accusing them of deceiving the people even by the use of unorthodox paintings: "They paint mostly deformed images of the saints, to the end that the aspect may transform the devotion of the plain Christian people into disgust. As a mockery and as an insult of the Cross they represent the crucified Christ with one foot above the other and pierced by one nail. . . ." The bishop proceeds to put a defense of such license into a heretic's mouth: "We wish to change the practice of the Church, so that we may be able to excite the devotion of the people by the greater intensity of the passion of Christ and to prevent tedium by replacing the customs of long standing by something new. . . . It suffices for the salvation to believe that Christ has been crucified and to believe it immaterial whether . . . he was pierced by four or three nails. . . . That and suchlike they say so that it seems almost rational" (quoted in Rudolf Berliner, "The Freedom of Medieval Art," *Gazette des Beaux-Arts* 28 [1945], p. 278, n. 54).

Nevertheless, the overlapped feet of the Crucified—not ranked but filed and pierceable by one nail—became increasingly common after 1300; so that Boccaccio, in the "Author's Conclusion" to the *Decameron* could cite the interchangeability of the two variants as proof of permissible artistic license. (Both variants occur in the work of Dürer, Burgkmair, and Michelangelo.) By the late sixteenth century, in the general turn toward orthodoxy following the Council of Trent, the Church sought once again to reestablish the "four nails" as the canonic form. Francisco Pacheco, supervisor of religious iconography for the Inquisition in Spain, wrote an entire chapter, "En favor de la pintura de los cuatro clavos . . . ," citing authorities from Gregory of Tours to Pope Innocent III and St. Bridget (*Arte de la Pintura* [1638], III, 15, ed. F. J. Sanchez Cantón, Madrid, 1956, pp. 362–78). Thus, insofar as the feet of Leonardo's Christ in the *Last Supper* allude to the Crucifixion, they revert to the venerable canonic tradition.

12. Recent precedents in refectory decoration, Ghirlandaio's especially, depicted the *Last Supper* alone. But once again, Leonardo would have had more respect for the venerable tradition—that of Taddeo Gaddi, Orcagna, Castagno—than for Ghirlandaio's impoverished modernism. At S. Croce, where the Florentine practice of placing a *Last Supper* on a refectory wall commenced, Taddeo Gaddi's fresco of the 1340s took the form of a kind of predella to a wall-sized representation of St. Bonaventure's *Lignum vitae*. In the refectory of S. Spirito, the *Last Supper* (of which only a vestige survives) appeared similarly under a representation of the *Crucifixion* (formerly ascribed to Orcagna). In Castagno's *Cenacolo* in S. Apollonia, the *Last Supper*, represented as though "enshrined," is surmounted by a fresco of a *Crucifixion* flanked by scenes of *Entombment* and *Resurrection*. On the other hand, painters following upon Ghirlandaio's Ognissanti *Cenacolo* of 1480 often made up for the apparent depletion of symbolic content by inserting scenes from the Passion in small background vistas (e.g., Perugino in the Foligno monastery in Florence; Cosimo Rosselli in the Sistine Chapel; and several copyists in replicas of Leonardo's *Last Supper*).

13. In the Mass, "the sacrifice of the Cross is made present sacramentally" (Joseph A. Jungmann, *The Mass of the Roman Rite: Its Origins and Development*, New York, 1951, II, p. 144 and n. 33, referring to St. Thomas Aquinas). Adolf Katzenellenbogen has discussed the iconographic effects of the doctrine that the substance of the Eucharist is not the spiritual flesh of the risen Christ, but that of his crucified mortal body. After the twelfth century, when the latter doctrine prevailed, scenes of the *Last Supper* were commonly associated with the *Crucifixion* (*The Sculptural Programs of Chartres Cathedral*, Baltimore, 1959, pp. 13f.). The same doctrinal shift dictated the placing of a cross on the altar; see Joseph Braun, *Das christliche Altargerät*, Munich, 1932, p. 467.

14. The symbolic polarization of Christ's upper and lower body is Early Christian. "The head means the godhead of Christ; the feet, his manhood," writes Cyril of Jerusalem (*Catechesis*, XII, 1, *P.G.*, 33, col. 726). And Eusebius: "The nature of Christ is twofold: it is like the head of the body in that He is recognized as God, and comparable to the feet in that for our salvation He put on manhood as frail as our own" (*History of the Church*, I, 2; English ed., G. A. Williamson, New York, 1966, p. 33). The seventh-century Byzantine theologian, St. Maximus Confessor, maintained that "whoever says that the words of theology 'stand at the head' because of the deity of Christ, while the words of the dispensation 'stand at the feet' because of the incarnation, and whoever calls the head of Christ his divinity, and the feet his humanity, he does not stray from the truth" (*Liber Ambiguorum*, *P.G.*, 91, col. 1379). In the ninth century, a medallion bust portrait of Christ is explained as excluding the lower body to emphasize the divine part of his nature (see R. J. H. Jenkins and C. A. Mango in *Dumbarton Oaks Papers* 9–10 [1956], p. 132). The idea is restated by St. Bernard: "If it seemed right to St. Paul to describe Christ's head in terms of his divinity (I Cor. 11:3), it should not seem unreasonable to us to ascribe the feet to his humanity" (*On the Song of Songs*, Sermon 6, 6,

trans. K. Walsh, Spencer, Mass., 1971, p. 35). The *topos* is discussed by Ernst Kantorowicz, *The King's Two Bodies*, Princeton, 1957, pp. 70–75, with emphasis on St. Augustine's exegesis of Psalms 90 and 91, whose drift Kantorowicz summarizes as *pedes in terra, caput in coelo*. Kantorowicz adduces the familiar image of the Ascension, wherein Western artists, from Ottonian times to the Cinquecento, depicted a "disappearing Christ," whose "feet alone—the symbol of the Incarnation—remain as a visible token of the historical fact that the Incarnate has migrated on earth." As Renaissance artists took this symbolism for granted, we are surely permitted to recognize the trope *pedes in terra, caput in coelo* in the naturalistic *mise-en-scène* of Leonardo's mural. In a near contemporary image, Mazzolino's *Nativity* of 1510 in the Ferrara Pinacoteca, the idea is spelled out with quaint literalness: the Christ Child inhabits a body-sized bubble halo from which the loins and legs are excluded. The Christ of Michelangelo's *Last Judgment* still honors this ancient tradition.

15. For a discussion of the pavement, see Steinberg, chap. III, n. 18, and Appendix C. The thin, asymmetrically misplaced floorlines that now show up faintly in the original mural were ineptly inserted after the destruction of its lower center in 1652.

16. Cf. Pius Parsch, *The Liturgy of the Mass*, 3rd ed., London, 1957, pp. 19 and 238: "In the Consecration . . . He comes in Flesh and Blood, as in the days of his first coming; at the same time He is the transfigured King of glory, and comes in the glory that will be revealed in His second coming."

17. "Und so hat nun der Meister auch diesmal der linken Hand, der vertrauten und folgsamen Vollstreckerin seiner künstlerischen Absichten und Gedanken die hehre Aufgabe anvertraut, in klarer, anschaulicher, unzweideutiger Weise die Handlung einzuleiten" (Johann Boloz Antoniewicz, "Das Abendmahl Lionardos," *Anzeiger der Akademie der Wissenschaften in Krakau*, Philologische Klasse. Historisch-Philosophische Klasse, Cracow, 1904, p. 65; observe again the emphasis on the allegedly "unambiguous" character of the action).

18. Leonardo's inspired asymmetries are analyzed in the section called "Coincident Opposites" in Steinberg, pp. 337ff. I repeat the conclusion (p. 340): "The symmetry of Leonardo's *Cenacolo* surpasses that of, say, Ghirlandaio, in more than dynamic articulation; more is achieved than the substitution of four triads in flux and reflux for the monotony of monadic figures in series. Challenged by strong left-right contrasts as well as by sideward drift, Leonardo's abiding symmetry emerges as a heroic conciliation. It becomes, as it were, iconographic. What his bilateral equilibrium holds in balance is not six against half a dozen, but contradictory principles—shade versus brightness, descent and ascent, constraint and expansion, prospect of pain against promise of life—while an irresistible impetus propels the entire system toward the positive pole."

19. The Sforza tomb was dismembered before its definitive installation. Its intended location under the dome of the church—comparable to that of Cosimo de'Medici's tomb in S. Lorenzo, Florence—remains, for the present, conjectural. Carlo Pedretti, responding to the argument presented in my original essay, takes up the problem in his article, "The Sforza Sepulchre," *Gazette des Beaux-Arts* 89 (1977), p. 125: "Any information about the funerary monument as a whole in its original setting would be an invaluable contribution to our knowledge of the overall program of rebuilding S. Maria delle Grazie, since it was certainly meant as the visual and symbolic focus of the new church." Though Pedretti seems to remain undecided, his article closes by citing the last-known mention of the Sforza sepulchre (by Abraham Ortelius in 1579) "as a monument planned to be placed under the cupola of S. Maria delle Grazie." For the important Florentine precedent cited above, see Janis Clearfield, "The Tomb of Cosimo de'Medici in San Lorenzo," *The Rutgers Art Review* 2 (1981), pp. 13ff.

20. See Emil Möller, *Das Abendmahl des Lionardo da Vinci*, Baden-Baden, 1952, p. 9.

21. The phrase comes from St. Ignatius, Bishop of Antioch (c. 112 A.D.); quoted in *Documents of the Christian Church*, ed. H. Bettenson, Oxford, 1947, p. 104.

22. Carlo Pedretti, "The Original Project for Santa Maria delle Grazie," *Journal of the Society of Architectural Historians* 32 (1973), pp. 30ff. Pedretti's earlier article ("Leonardo Architetto a Imola," *Architectura*, 1972, fig. 8) reproduces in revealing comparison the actual plan of the complex and a Leonardo sketch for the Bramante design of S. Maria delle Grazie. Note that the length of the narrow "corridor" joining the new construction to the old nave is an unfixed variable in the drawing. The final design lengthened the corridor to locate the dome's center on a single diagonal axis with the refectory, the *porta antica*, and the midpoint of the mural.

23. Two further functions of Christ's hands (bringing the total to nine) are discussed in Steinberg, pp. 330 and 340, respectively: the mystic "rebus" rising over Christ's open palm, and the influence of the downturned and upturned hands on the corresponding optical movement of the piers behind the Christ figure.

24. The sensible influence of Leonardo's Christ on the spatial perspective answers Goethe's rhetorical question whether even the most inspired brush can unite in a single countenance human pathos and divine power. Granted that no human visage—whether depicted or real—can convey the "sublimity, strength and puissance of the divine." But Leonardo's portrayal of the God-man is not confined to type-casting, since he displays, along with the gesture and physiognomy of the man, the impact of his divine nature upon the world.

6

In Alia Effigie: Caravaggio's London *Supper at Emmaus*

CHARLES SCRIBNER III

According to the biographer and critic Gian Pietro Bellori, Caravaggio is an artist who "often degenerates into low and vulgar forms." As examples justifying his familiar complaint, Bellori cites the two versions of the *Supper at Emmaus* (London, National Gallery, and Milan, Brera).[1] Both works, dating approximately six years apart, "imitate natural color very well while failing in decorum," Bellori writes. But his particular scorn is directed at the earlier, London version (Fig. 1), painted around 1599–1600:[2] "Besides the rustic character of the two apostles and of the Lord who is shown young and without a beard, Caravaggio shows the innkeeper serving with a cap on his head, and on the table there is a plate of grapes, figs and pomegranates out of season."[3]

To a large degree, these remarks merely reflect a certain academic bias of the late seventeenth-century critic, and as such they pose no problem to the present-day art historian. A brief survey of the *Supper at Emmaus* in Renaissance and early Baroque art soon reveals that several of Caravaggio's supposed errors are simply part of an artistic tradition. The "rustic apostles" were anticipated in versions of this popular subject by Romanino,[4] Mor-

Reprinted from *The Art Bulletin* 59, no. 3 (1977): 375–82.

This paper originated in a colloquium on Caravaggio given by Irving Lavin at Princeton University in the spring of 1974. It was presented at the Annual Meeting of the College Art Association (17th Century Session) in Los Angeles in February 1977. I am most grateful to Professor Lavin for his generous encouragement and guidance. I also wish to thank the following for their helpful suggestions: Jacques Barzun, Julius S. Held, Howard Hibbard, John Rupert Martin, and Charles Scribner, Jr.

etto,[5] Titian[6] and Veronese[7]—just to mention four well-known precedents with which Caravaggio was probably familiar.[8]

Furthermore, each of these examples includes an "innkeeper who serves with a cap on his head." If Bellori considered it indecorous or disrespectful to show the servant's head covered when waiting on the Lord, he missed the simple point that Caravaggio—like his predecessors—took care to stress: the innkeeper has not removed his cap because he remains totally unaware of Christ's identity, even at the moment when he reveals himself to his two disciples in the blessing or breaking of the bread. The covered head deliberately underscores the servant's exclusion from the miracle of divine revelation.

Likewise, Bellori's observation that the basket of fruit is "out of season" (since the supper took place on Easter Sunday evening— or in springtime), a criticism that Friedlaender considered a "pedantic remark,"[9] may represent an equally naïve misreading of the painting. It has recently been suggested that the fruit here has emblematic meaning, just as in Caravaggio's early genre paintings such as the *Boy Bitten by a Lizard*.[10] In any event, Caravaggio could have cited for this apparent lapse a rather weighty precedent: the tapestry by the School of Raphael, hanging in the Vatican.[11] In that representation of the *Supper at Emmaus* the meal is set under an arbor of hanging grapes, equally "out of season" but clearly included as a reference to Christ's Eucharistic (supernatural) presence in the sacramental wine as well as in the bread.

There is, however, one criticism by Bellori that seems far more substantial than any of the above and requires serious attention: the observation that Christ is shown as a beardless youth. Not only has this unusual portrayal disturbed or at least puzzled critics and scholars down to the present day, but it evidently troubled Caravaggio's contemporaries as well. One early copyist (J. B. Maino?) "corrected" Caravaggio by substituting an older, bearded Christ for the original figure.[12] He was followed by Pierre Fatoure (d. 1629), whose engraving likewise includes the conventional beard.[13] Finally, even Caravaggio himself, when he turned again to the subject several years later, reverted to the traditional representation of Christ for the Patrizi version of the *Supper at Emmaus*.[14]

In more recent times, it is fair to say that Christ's boyish looks

and emphatic gesture have discouraged scholars from considering this work an example of serious religious painting.[15] In the
light of the most recent scholarship, however, especially Irving
Lavin's illuminating article on Caravaggio's two Saint Matthews,[16] it is no longer possible to attribute such a troublesome
element to artistic license, or worse, to a lack of seriousness on
Caravaggio's part. Nor is it sufficient to analyze the formal qualities of the painting without seeking its meaning. That the beardless Christ indeed had deliberate significance is suggested by a
double anomaly: not only does this visage differ from previous
depictions of the *Supper at Emmaus*[17] but it also conflicts with
Caravaggio's own canonical portrayal of Christ in contempora-
neous works.[18] One need only compare this painting, on the one
hand, with such antecedents as Titian's and Tintoretto's *Supper
at Emmaus*,[19] or, on the other, with Caravaggio's image of Christ
in the *Calling of Saint Matthew* (1599, S. Luigi dei Francesi, Rome)
and the *Incredulity of Saint Thomas* (1599–1600, Potsdam) to recognize how great a departure was taken in the London *Emmaus*.[20]

It is the purpose of this paper to show that Caravaggio's apparent aberration represents a bold visual formula deliberately chosen in order to convey the essential meaning of the painting. In
this respect, Caravaggio's unusual portrayal of Christ at Emmaus
actually anticipates, both formally and conceptually, the first Saint
Matthew altarpiece for the Contarelli Chapel, commissioned in
1602. In each case, Caravaggio relied on physiognomic anomaly
and gesture to express a theological point that was central to
Catholic belief.[21]

The story of the journey to Emmaus is told by the Evangelist
Luke (24:13–35), but there is also a brief mention of this appearance of the resurrected Christ in Saint Mark's Gospel (16:12), a
reference that, although hitherto ignored, provides the key to Caravaggio's interpretation. Traditionally, Saint Luke's narrative
offered three main subjects for illustration: the "Walk to Emmaus," during which the unrecognized Christ converses with his
two disciples; the "Supper at Emmaus," at which he suddenly
reveals his identity; and finally the "Vanishing Christ," immediately following the recognition.[22]

Caravaggio's London painting focuses on the moment most often

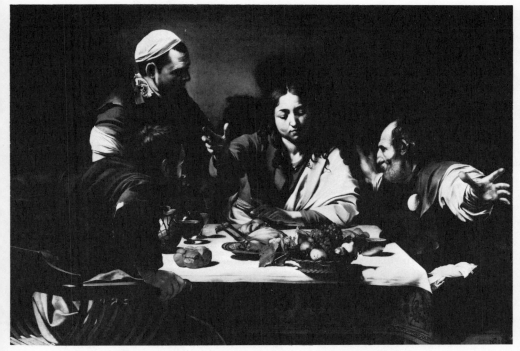

Fig. 1. Caravaggio, *Supper at Emmaus*. London, National Gallery.

Fig. 2. Attributed to Marco d'Oggiono, *Salvator Mundi*. Rome, Borghese Gallery.

Fig. 3. Michelangelo, *Last Judgment* (detail). Rome, Vatican, Sistine Chapel.

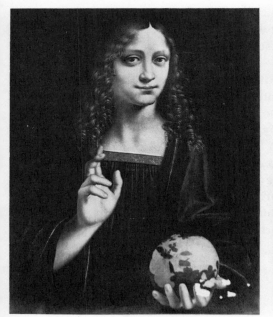

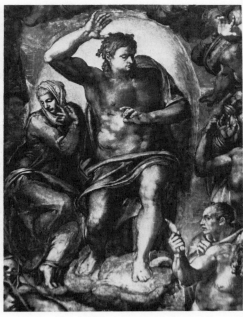

depicted by Renaissance and Baroque artists: Christ's sudden revelation and the disciples' startled recognition. The artist here followed, as Friedlaender has pointed out, a Venetian tradition of showing Christ blessing rather than breaking the bread.[23] Caravaggio raises the familiar subject to a new level of drama by throwing unprecedented emphasis on extended gesture as both the cause and effect of the miracle. As Christ thrusts his right hand forward to bless the loaf of bread, the disciples react as if thunderstruck. One grasps the arm of his chair[24] and leans forward while the other throws out both arms, his left hand breaking into the viewer's own space.

Given this dramatic emphasis on the moment of recognition, it is surely paradoxical that the artist has described the protagonist, Christ himself, in such an unfamiliar, unorthodox, and indeed almost unrecognizable fashion. One might well wonder whether this face, taken out of context, would be identifiable as Christ's at all. In other words, at the very point when he reveals himself to his disciples Caravaggio's savior presents to the viewer a problem of recognition.

It was, however, precisely by creating this uncertainty that Caravaggio succeeded in making the miracle at once more rational and more miraculous; that is, more profoundly sacramental than ever before in the history of art. By revealing an unexpected Christ—*one who does not look like himself*—Caravaggio was the first painter to justify the disciples' lack of recognition along their journey to Emmaus.[25] Yet in seeking to explain visually the central problem of recognition by substituting an unfamiliar image for the canonical face of Christ—as "recorded" on Veronica's veil and adopted by tradition in both Eastern and Western art[26]—Caravaggio did not simply abandon the biblical account of Saint Luke's Gospel in favor of a personal interpretation. He presented a more biblical interpretation by doing what no artist, so far as I know, had attempted before: to base his representation on more than just Luke's account and to create a synthesis, as it were, of two Gospel texts. Saint Luke never fully explains why the disciples had failed to recognize Christ. His narrative mentions only that "their eyes were kept from recognizing him." But Saint Mark's brief reference to the appearance (16:12), on the other hand, is explicit on this very point. He states that Christ appeared to the disciples *"in another likeness [in alia effigie]."*

Evidently this single phrase suggested to Caravaggio a solution to the problem of recognition. It also offered a clear biblical sanction for showing Christ in a different guise, *in alia effigie*, as the Evangelist describes him. It is possible that Caravaggio was aware of the various apocryphal stories wherein Christ appears to his disciples and saints under different guises, an Early Christian tradition that was recorded in the writings of Origen.[27] But one need not attribute to Caravaggio a knowledge of Early Christian literature to explain his new formulation of the Emmaus miracle.[28] He had only to turn to the Bible.

So far, we have considered only the first half of a paradox: how Caravaggio dealt with the problem of recognition by following Mark's account and adopting a new face for Christ. Yet Caravaggio's intent was not merely to make the miracle rational; it was ultimately to make it *sacramental*. Traditionally the appearance at supper was interpreted by theologians as a confirmation not only of Christ's physical Resurrection but also of his bodily presence in the Eucharist, a doctrine of central importance to the Counter-Reformatory Church. The doctrinal controversy between Catholics and Protestants over the nature of Christ's identification with the sacrament had by Caravaggio's time led to an intensified Catholic emphasis upon the centrality of the Eucharist and the belief in Transubstantiation. The Church reaffirmed this tenet of faith by every available means, including artistic representations of Eucharistic subjects such as the *Supper at Emmaus*.[29] In the Jesuit book of engravings, Geronimo Nadal's *Evangelicae Historiae Imagines* (1593), the *Supper at Emmaus* was illustrated as a prefiguration of the Mass, in which Christ himself distributes the broken bread to his two disciples.[30] Caravaggio intended his monumental version to be no less sacramental. He merely sought a more persuasive way to convey the same idea.

For Caravaggio, the disciples' recognition of Christ is achieved solely through the Eucharist.[31] To underscore this point he has deliberately removed all other clues to Christ's identity. We look in vain for the nail prints or the side wound. His hands have been placed in such a way that it is impossible to determine whether the wounds are there or not, and the new garments cover his side completely. Most striking of all, Christ's face is not that of the Crucified, even at the moment of recognition. That recognition, therefore, is the result of his gesture alone, the extended hand blessing the bread, an allusion to the priest's act of blessing at the consecration of bread into the Body of Christ during the Mass. (Appropriately, beside the loaf of bread are the vessels of water and wine.) Thus Christ's sacramental gesture becomes the *sine qua non* of his self-revelation to the disciples, for we are to understand that only in the Eucharist does Christ reveal himself both physically and spiritually to the faithful.

At this point it should be observed that for all its formal and iconographic originality, Caravaggio's interpretation was theologically orthodox and traditional. Such a sacramental explanation of the miracle had been clearly spelled out in the standard Catholic gloss on the Scriptures, the medieval *Glossa Ordinaria* (Luke 24:32):

> The mystical interpretation: therefore Christ was shown to the disciples in another likeness [*alia effigies*] so that they would recognize him only in the breaking of bread, in order that all should understand that they do not recognize Christ unless they become partakers of His body; that is, of the Church, whose unity the Apostle [Paul] commends in the sacrament of bread, saying; "Although we are many, yet are we one bread, one body" [I Cor. 10]. When, therefore, He extends the blessed bread, their eyes are opened so that they may recognize Him, and the impediment that Satan placed in their eyes, to prevent them from recognizing Jesus, is removed. The Lord, moreover, allows this impediment to remain until they come to the sacrament of bread. But in the shared unity of the Body the impediment of the enemy is taken away so that Christ can be recognized.[32]

To be sure, the point was already implicit in Saint Luke's Gospel (24:35): "Then they recounted what had happened on the road and how they had come to know him in the breaking of the bread." It was left to Caravaggio simply to translate the biblical texts into a persuasive visual form. Significantly, in his otherwise literal translation he substituted a gesture of blessing for the breaking of bread (*fractio panis*) as the cause of revelation. But the choice of gesture was as deliberate and meaningful as the particular visage; indeed the two, as we shall see, are closely related.

The distinguishing aspects of Christ's *alia effigies*—youthful, long-haired, and beardless—represent no arbitrary invention of the artist's imagination but rather a specific alternative to his conventional portrayal. Although seemingly unorthodox, it was no less "authentic," for it derived from an ancient prototype: the earliest representation of Christ in art, the so-called Apollonian type preserved in Early Christian catacomb painting, mosaics, and relief sculpture, especially sarcophagi, many of which were surely known to Caravaggio. The preceding decade of the 1590's had witnessed extensive excavations of these Early Christian monuments in Rome. One outstanding example of a contemporary discovery is the Junius Bassus sarcophagus, unearthed in 1595.[33] In the center, a youthful beardless Christ sits enthroned between two Apostles, and his appearance suggests a possible source for Caravaggio's figure.

It is, to be sure, fruitless to attempt to identify any one monument as Caravaggio's Early Christian model—so many were available to him in Rome. The true source was the distinctive *type*, and its Early Christian status provided historical justification, so to speak, for its adoption as Christ's *alia effigies*. At this time the post-Tridentine Church was engaged in a general revival of Early Christian sources to buttress its historical and sacramental claims. Caravaggio's selection of the Early Christian type for Christ's *alia effigies* may then be viewed as consistent with the spiritual aims of this archaeological revival.[34]

The adoption of the Apollonian type by Caravaggio should not, however, be seen as an isolated, personal revival of an abandoned and forgotten image. Although the latter had long since been displaced by the bearded Zeus type, nevertheless it occasionally recurred throughout the Middle Ages[35] and during the Italian Renaissance.[36] Two important examples of its revival not only were accessible to Caravaggio but may have served as actual sources for his image of the beardless Christ. One was a small devotional panel, then believed to have been painted by Leonardo; the other, a monumental fresco by Michelangelo.

Among the several variants of the lost *Salvator Mundi* by Leonardo is the panel (Fig. 2) now attributed to Marco d'Oggiono and preserved in the Borghese Gallery. At one time it hung in the bedroom of Pope Paul V as his most cherished painting before he relinquished it in 1611 to his acquisitive nephew, Scipione Borghese, who desired a Leonardo for his vast collection.[37] This representation of a strikingly youthful and beardless Christ provides an iconographically suitable—and highly regarded—precedent for Caravaggio's Christ in alia effigie. The formal analogies between the two are self-evident.[38] What is not so apparent at first is the iconological bond between them. Like his counterpart at Emmaus, the young Salvator Mundi is described in the act of blessing, here literally a gesture of salvation with clearly sacramental overtones.[39] This iconic image of an eternally youthful Savior offered to Caravaggio a highly esteemed prototype for the Savior at Emmaus who reveals himself also in a gesture of blessing.

According to Catholic doctrine, salvation is inseparable from the Resurrection and the Second Coming of Christ, and so it is singularly appropriate that another likely source for Caravaggio's Christ was the most prominent scene of Resurrection and Judgment in Rome: Michelangelo's Sistine Chapel fresco, wherein Christ appears at the end of time as a youthful, beardless deity (Fig. 3). His extraordinary appearance has been the subject of much discussion by art historians.[40] More important is the fact that it was severely criticized by Michelangelo's contemporaries, such as Giglio da Fabriano, to whom it represented a grave breach of decorum.[41]

Caravaggio, then, was not the first artist to be censured for painting Christ without a beard. His image, moreover, shares with Michelangelo's not only the distinctive facial type, but also a crucial gesture.[42] In Michelangelo's fresco, Christ's right arm is raised while the left and less active one reaches across his side as if to point to his side wound. Caravaggio has lowered the dramatically extended right arm, thereby transfoming a gesture of judgment into one of blessing. But the left arm remains relatively unaltered and thus recalls what is no longer visible: the side wound.

The formal allusion to Michelangelo's Christ of the Last Judgment suggests a deeper connection between the two subjects, namely the idea that Christ's appearance to his disciples at Emmaus anticipates, proleptically, his final appearance to all mankind.[43] Michelangelo's Last Judgment and Caravaggio's Emmaus share a common theme: both represent epiphanies of the Resurrected Christ. The fact that Caravaggio substituted a liturgical act of blessing for the breaking of bread may therefore be seen as a means of relating his image in gesture as well as visage to Leonardo's *Salvator Mundi* and Michelangelo's *Judge*.

If Christ's gesture conveys at once the liturgical act of consecration and an allusion to Salvation and the Second Coming, how then should one interpret the equally emphatic response of the disciple on the right? Of course, the outthrust arms are surely meant to express his immediate shock of recognition. Yet, like Christ's, the disciple's gesture may have a secondary meaning. The fact that his arms are fully extended, cross-like, inevitably suggests a reference to the Crucifixion. On a dramatic level, the allusion is a natural one. Were he to speak, he might well exclaim: "But, Lord, you were crucified!" Sacramentally, it complements Christ's liturgical gesture by recalling the sacrifice on Calvary which, according to Catholic doctrine, is renewed at every celebration of the Mass.[44]

Taken together, Caravaggio's three most likely sources for Christ *in alia effigie*—the Early Christian type, the Leonardesque *Salvator Mundi*, and Michelangelo's *Judge*—can all be reduced to a common referent: the image of the eternal, divine Savior; that is, they all represent not the earthly, historical Jesus but the heavenly, glorified Christ of the Second Coming.

The dramatic confrontation of youth and age, of Christ and his two disciples (as well as the server), is exploited by Caravaggio as a metaphor for the Christian promise of New Life, both in the final Resurrection of all flesh and in the sacramental form of the Eucharist, the heavenly food that is likewise juxtaposed with its earthly opposite: the roast fowl and the perishable, overripe fruit set precariously at the table's edge, about to tumble to the viewer's feet.[45]

Thus Caravaggio reinterprets a familiar subject as a vivid confirmation of the Resurrection and the efficacy of the Eucharist. Basing his deceptively "unorthodox" representation of Christ *in alia effigie* on a verse in Saint Mark's Gospel, he fuses in one image the earliest visual expression of Christ's divinity, the *Salvator Mundi*, and the Christ of the Second Coming, whose triumphant revelation is here accompanied by a stark reminder of the Crucifixion—two gestures that intrude into the viewer's own space. In the London *Supper at Emmaus,* one of his very rare miracle scenes, Caravaggio confronts us with nothing less than an affirmation of salvation.

NOTES

N.B.: A bibliography of frequently cited sources follows the notes.

1. W. Friedlaender, *Caravaggio Studies,* Princeton, 1955, 164f. (Cat. Nos. 18A, 18B).

2. The date of this work has been subject to disagreement. R. Hinks (*Michelangelo Merisi da Caravaggio: His Life—His Legend—His Works,* London, 1953, 103, Cat. No. 21) dated it 1598; D. Mahon ("Addenda to Caravaggio," *Burlington Magazine,* xciv, 1952, 19) 1599–1600; W. Friedlaender (*Caravaggio,* 167) 1598–1599; H. Röttgen ("Die Stellung der Contarelli-Kapelle in Caravaggios Werk," *Zeitschrift für Kunstgeschichte,* xxviii, 1965, 59, fig. 5., and 62–64) 1601–02. I prefer 1599–1600, considering it contemporary with the side paintings of the Contarelli Chapel and preceding the first Saint Matthew Altarpiece.

3. G. P. Bellori, *Le vite de'pittori, scultori et architetti moderni,* Rome, 1672, 213. For English translation, see W. Friedlaender, *Caravaggio,* 164.

4. Brescia, Pinacoteca Tosio e Martinengo: see *Mostra di Girolamo Romanino,* Brescia, 1965, fig. 103 (Cat. No. 46).

5. Brescia, Pinacoteca Tosio e Martinengo: see G. Gombosi, *Moretto da Brescia,* Basel, 1943, fig. 57 (Cat. No. 80).

6. Paris, Louvre (see H. E. Wethey, *The Paintings of Titian,* I [*The Religious Paintings*], London, 1969, No. 143, pls. 88, 89); and Brocklesby Park, Lincolnshire, Coll. Earl of Yarborough (*ibid.,* No. 142, pl. 87).

7. Dresden, Gemäldegalerie; and Paris, Louvre.

8. For a brief discussion of Caravaggio's relation to such precedents, see W. Friedlaender, *Caravaggio,* 164.

9. *Ibid.,* 166.

10. See D. T. Kinkead, "Poesia e simboli nel Caravaggio: Temi religiosi," *Palatino,* X, 1966, 114–15. For other instances of Caravaggio's possible use of emblematic still-life see L. J. Slatkes, "Caravaggio's *Boy Bitten by a Lizard,*" *Print Review No. 5, Tribute to Wolfgang Stechow,* New York, 1976, 152–53. See also D. Posner, "Caravaggio's Homo-Erotic Early Works," *Art Quarterly,* xxxiv, 1971, 301–324. Even the shadow cast by the basket of fruit may have emblematic significance, for, as Professor Walter Liedtke has called to my attention, it describes the partial outline of a fish, the Early Christian symbol for Christ. The probability of a symbolic meaning here is strengthened by Liedtke's further observation that the innkeeper's shadow creates a naturalistic halo around Christ's head. This dark, "negative" halo in the form of a foreshortened disc is effectively juxtaposed with Christ's fully illumined face—a clear indication of the metaphysical qualities of Caravaggio's chiaroscuro.

11. Illustrated in L. Rudrauf, *Le Repas d'Emmaus,* Paris, 1955, fig. 172. Here, too, a roast chicken is placed on the table, representing the ordinary meal that is juxtaposed with the sacramental food.

12. See A. Moir, *Caravaggio and His Copyists,* New York, 1976, 126–27, fig. 54. One of Caravaggio's followers, however, did retain the beardless face in his version of the subject: the *Supper at Emmaus,* attributed to Aniello Falcone (J. Paul Getty Museum, Malibu). See R. Spear, *Caravaggio and His Followers,* Cleveland, 1971, 90–91.

13. According to Moir (*Copyists*, 126), Fatoure based his print on a contemporary copy that included the beard.

14. For reasons about which we can only conjecture. It is possible that his patron requested a more conventional representation than the earlier version, in which case Caravaggio's two *Emmaus* paintings parallel the two *Saint Matthews*.

15. See B. Berenson, *Caravaggio: His Incongruity and His Fame*, London, 1953, 64; R. Hinks, *Caravaggio*, 58; and W. Friedlaender, *Caravaggio*, 166.

16. I. Lavin, "Divine Inspiration in Caravaggio's Two *St. Matthews*," *Art Bulletin*, LVI, 1974. 59f.

17. For a useful survey of this subject in art, see L. Rudrauf, *Repas, passim*. Although the beardless Christ is unprecedented in earlier paintings of the subject (most of which date from the 15th and 16th centuries) he does, to be sure, appear occasionally in early medieval manuscript illuminations and ivories illustrating the Supper at Emmaus: see note 35, below. The likelihood that Caravaggio knew of such rare precedents seems remote.

18. One possible exception "that proves the rule" is to be found in the Hampton Court copy of a lost Caravaggio. The subject of this painting has been disputed: see M. Kitson, *The Complete Paintings of Caravaggio*, London, 1969, 97, Cat. No. 48. But Friedlaender's identification of it as the *Walk to Emmaus* is the most convincing (Friedlaender, *Caravaggio*, 168, Cat. No. 19). Friedlaender does not raise the question of Christ's unusual appearance in this painting, but the fact that he is shown as a beardless youth is strong evidence in favor of this identification and suggests a connection with the London *Emmaus*. In fact, one should not rule out the possibility that the original canvas was intended not only to be iconographically consonant with the latter but actually to serve as a pendant. Of course, this must remain pure speculation since the original is lost and its precise dimensions are therefore unknown, but the fact that Christ is similarly described in two episodes of the same narrative makes the hypothesis an attractive one.

19. Paris, Louvre and Budapest, Museum of Fine Arts respectively.

20. R. Hinks (*Caravaggio*, 58) believed the Potsdam version to be a copy of a lost original and even suggested that the latter may have been a pendant to the London *Emmaus*, in which case the sharp contrast between Christ's two visages would have been inescapable. In any event, the two paintings are contemporary and both illustrate post-Resurrection appearances of Christ to his disciples, so that the radically different portrayals of the protagonist require some explanation.

21. For an analysis of gesture and physiognomy in Caravaggio's two *Saint Matthews*, see Lavin, "Inspiration," *passim*.

22. For iconographical surveys of this subject in art, see L. Réau, *Iconographie de l'art chrétien*, II, 2, Paris, 1957, 561–567; E. Kirschbaum, *Lexikon der christlichen Ikonographie*, Rome-Freiburg-Basel-Vienna, 1968, I, cols. 622–626 (s.v. "Emmaus"); and W. Stechow in *Reallexikon zur deutschen Kunstgeschichte*, Stuttgart, 1967, V, cols. 228–242 (s.v. "Emmaus").

23. W. Friedlaender, *Caravaggio*, 164.

24. It is worth noting, in passing, that the same "Savonarola chair" appears in both the *Calling of Saint Matthew* and the first Saint Matthew Altarpiece—an additional (albeit minor) link between the London canvas and the Contarelli Chapel. For a comparison of Christ at Emmaus and the Angel in the first *Saint Matthew*, see H. Röttgen, "Stellung," 63 ("beide mit entschieden androgynem Einschlag").

25. I owe this observation to Irving Lavin.

26. For a discussion of Christ's visage in art, see L. Réau, *Iconographie*, II, 2, 36f. See also H. Aurenhammer, *Lexikon der christlichen Ikonographie*, Vienna, 1967, 457–58.

27. E. Hennecke, *New Testament Apocrypha*, ed. W. Schneemelcher, I, Philadelphia, 1963, 434.

28. Caravaggio's representation of an "illiterate Socrates," however, may depend upon an Early Christian author: see I. Lavin, "Inspiration," 74–75.

29. For Catholic art in defense of the sacraments, see E. Mâle, *L'Art religieux après le Concile de Trente*, Paris, 1932, 72f.

30. Hieronymus Natalis (Geronimo Nadal), *Evangelicae Historiae Imagines*, Antwerp, 1593, pl. 141, engraved by Anton Wierx. Significantly this plate includes a verse reference not only to Saint Luke's Gospel but also to Saint Mark's. It is therefore possible that Caravaggio was alerted to the existence of a second biblical source by such an engraving.

31. I am grateful to Irving Lavin for this suggestion.

32. The passage is found in the *Patrologiae Cursus Completus, Series Latina*, CXIV, ed. J. P. Migne, Petit-Montrouge, 1852, cols. 352–353:

> [Verse 32] *Et dixerunt*, etc. Mystice: Ideo in Christo illis ostensa est alia effigies, ne eum nisi in fractione panis cognoscerent, ut omnes intelligant se Christum non agnoscere, nisi fiant participes corporis ejus, id est Ecclesiae, cujus unitatem commendat Apostolus in sacramento panis, dicens: 'Unus panis, unum corpus multi sumus (I Cor. X).' Cum ergo panem benedictum porrigit, aperiuntur oculi ut eum cognoscant, et removetur impedimentum quod a Satana in oculis erat, ne agnosceretur Jesus. Et hoc impedimentum permittit inesse Dominus donec ad sacramentum panis veniatur. Sed participata unitate corporis, aufertur impedimentum inimici, ut possit Christus agnosci.

I am grateful to Roderick B. Porter for locating this gloss for me.

33. For further analysis of the earliest representations of Christ in art, see H. Aurenhammer, *Lexikon*, s.v. "Christus"; A. Grabar, *Christian Iconography*, Princeton, 1968, 119f.; F. Gerke, *Christus in der spätantiken Plastik*, Berlin, 1940; L. Heilmaier, "Der jugendliche Christus in der altchristlichen Volkskunst," *Die christliche Kunst*, xv, 1918/1919, 236f.; E. Hempel in *Reallexikon zur deutschen Kunstgeschichte*, III, cols. 732f., s.v. "Christustypus"; J. Kollwitz, "Das Christusbild der früchristlichen Kunst" in E. Kirschbaum, *Lexikon der christlichen Ikonographie*, I, 355f; F. Poulsen, *Das Christusbild in der ersten Christenzeit*, Dresden and Leipzig, n.d.; and L. Réau, *Iconographie*, II, 2, 36–37.

A good idea of the extensive discoveries of the 1590's can be had from F. W. Deichman, *Repertorium der christlich-antiken Sarkophage*, Wiesbaden, 1967, *passim*. For the Junius Bassus sarcophagus, see F. Gerke, *Der Sarkophag des Iunius Bassus*, Berlin, 1936.

34. Antonio Bosio (1575–1629), the first serious Christian archaeologist, explained the youthful, beardless type as signifying Christ's eternal nature and cited Early Christian writers in his *Roma sotterranea*, first published in 1632, but with information that had been widely circulated for years: see Libro IV, cap. XXVIII (*Dell' imagine di Christo in aspetto giovanile. . . .*), 623. Caravaggio's interpretation of the type, as we shall see, is consistent with Bosio's and may therefore reflect current archaeological ideas.

35. The following two examples actually represent the Emmaus story: (a) the 9th-century Carolingian ivory (Aachen, Cathedral), illustrated in E. Kirschbaum, *Lexikon der christlichen Ikonographie*, I, col. 623, fig. 1.; and (b) the Ottonian manuscript illumination in the Egbertkodex (ca. 980, Trier), illustrated in *Reallexikon zur deutschen Kunstgeschichte*, col. 228, fig. 1.

36. e.g. Botticelli's *Pietà* (Munich, Alte Pinakothek), Andrea del Castagno's *Christ and Saint Julian* (Florence, SS. Annunziata), and Palma Vecchio's *Resurrected Christ* (Florence, Coll. Contini-Bonacossi).

37. See P. della Pergola, *Galleria Borghese, i dipinti*, Rome, 1955, I, 82, No. 146. For a discussion of the lost Leonardo original on which this and several other variants were based, see S. Ringbom, *Icon to Narrative*, Abo, 1965, 69f. and 171f. The original *Salvator Mundi* was commissioned by Isabella d'Este, who specifi-

cally asked Leonardo to paint "uno Christo giovanetto di anni circa duodeci che seria di quella età che l'haveva quando disputò nel tempio" (*ibid.*, 175). Ringbom believes that of all the known variants the Borghese D'Oggiono is probably the closest to Leonardo's original (*ibid.*, 177). For further study of the subject in Leonardo's art, see L. Heydenreich, "Leonardo's *Salvator Mundi*," *Raccolta vinciana*, xx, 1964, 83–109. It is, of course, possible that Caravaggio was aware of other "copies" of Leonardo's composition, three of which are illustrated in W. Suida, *Leonardo und sein Kreis*, Munich, 1929, figs. 147, 148, and 233. In any case, the D'Oggiono was by no means an exclusive source, and Caravaggio's knowledge of the Leonardo type may have depended on another version.

H. Wagner (*Michelangelo da Caravaggio*, Bern, 1958, 52–53) mentioned the D'Oggiono as a formal precedent but suggested no possible iconographic parallels.

38. W. Friedlaender (*Caravaggio*, 166) recognized in the delicate, even somewhat effeminate features of Caravaggio's Christ a "Leonardesque" quality, without citing a specific work. After the completion of this article, Howard Hibbard brought to my attention Maurizio Calvesi's extraordinary reinterpretations of Caravaggio's genre paintings ("Caravaggio o la ricerca della salvazione," *Storia dell' arte*, ix/x, 1971, 93f.) in which he, too, compares Caravaggio's adolescent Christ type to those of the Junius Bassus sarcophagus and D'Oggiono's *Salvator Mundi*. Calvesi sees Christ's androgynous features as an emblem of divine unity, the union of opposites, and he associates the Christ at Emmaus with Caravaggio's *Bacchus* (Florence, Uffizi), which is interpreted as an allegory of Christ the Redeemer. Although I cannot agree with Calvesi's farfetched (if imaginative) interpretations, I am pleased to discover that we both—independently—assumed that the Early Christian type and D'Oggiono's *Salvator Mundi* play an important part in the meaning of Caravaggio's youthful Christ.

39. See C. Gottlieb, "The Mystical Window in Paintings of the *Salvator Mundi*," *Gazette des beaux-arts*, lvi, 1960, 313–332.

40. For example, E. Steinmann (*Die sixtinische Kapelle*, Munich, 1905, ii, 529–533) noted that Michelangelo's Christ was not entirely without precedent, for Giovanni di Paolo's *Last Judgment* (Siena, Accademia di Belle Arti) had included "den richtenden Christus fast nackt und unbärtig" (*ibid.*, 530). C. de Tolnay (*Michelangelo*, Princeton, 1960, v, 47–49) saw the youthful, beardless, and idealized Christ as an allusion to Apollo. D. Kinkead ("Temi," 114) noted in passing its similarity to Caravaggio's Christ in the London canvas but took the observation no further.

41. For contemporary comments and criticisms, see G. Vasari, *La vita di Michelangelo nelle redazioni del 1550 e del 1568, curata e commentata da Paola Barocchi*, Milan-Naples, 1962, iii, 1317–19 (No. 569):
In a letter to E. Gonzaga (19 November 1541) Nino Sernini wrote: "Altri dicono che ha fatto Cristo senza barba e troppo giovane e che non ha in sé quella maestà che gli si conviene" (*ibid.*, 1317). Giglio da Fabriano considered it simply "un altro capriccio" on Michelangelo's part (*ibid.*, 1318–19). And within a decade of Caravaggio's London painting a similar complaint was expressed by Comanini in 1591 (*ibid.*, 1319). It is likely, therefore, that Caravaggio was well aware of such repeated criticisms of Michelangelo's portrayal of the beardless Judge.

42. It should be noted that during the execution of his *Calling of Saint Matthew* for the Contarelli Chapel Caravaggio had similarly given his Christ a gesture "lifted" from a famous Michelangelo fresco in the Sistine Chapel: in this case, Adam's extended hand which reaches toward God the Father's. In adapting the gesture for a representation of Christ calling Matthew to a new life as his Apostle, the artist surely intended to evoke its prototype. Christ was thus identified as the *Second Adam* (one of his traditional epithets) and, furthermore, was to be understood as engaged in a new act of Creation. Caravaggio did not re-use a gesture simply for its formal qualities but reinterpreted its original meaning when introducing it into a new context.

It has recently come to my attention that Homan Potterton (*Painting in Focus,*

No. 3, London, National Gallery, 1975) also—and independently—recognized that the pose of Caravaggio's *Christ at Emmaus* derives from the Christ of Michelangelo's *Last Judgment,* but he suggested no relationship between them beyond a formal similarity.

43. For an interpretation of Michelangelo's fresco as representing, above all, the dramatic *appearance* of Christ—specifically, the *Adventus Domini* described in Matthew 24:30–31—see C. de Tolnay, *Michelangelo,* v, 33. See also M. B. Hall, "Michelangelo's *Last Judgment:* Resurrection of the Body and Predestination," *Art Bulletin,* LVIII, 1976, 89.

44. Leo Steinberg ("Leonardo's *Last Supper,*" *Art Quarterly,* XXXVI, 1973, 387, n. 29) has suggested that Caravaggio adapted this gesture from that of Saint James in Leonardo's *Last Supper.* The suggestion is an attractive one, for each gesture expresses a reaction of surprise to a revelation by Christ: in one case, betrayal; in the other, Resurrection. Also each subject is centered on the Eucharist; and, as we have seen, Caravaggio's Christ was similarly related to a Leonardesque prototype. In view of Steinberg's suggestion, it would be tempting also to identify Caravaggio's disciple on the right as Saint James, as Röttgen has done ("Caravaggio," 64), evidently because he wears a cockle shell, the traditional attribute of the saint. Friedlaender identifies him as Simon Peter, however (*Caravaggio,* 164). Indeed, there was an old tradition that Saint Peter was the unnamed companion of Cleopas at Emmaus (see W. Stechow, "Emmaus," cols. 228–229); I have found no mention of Saint James as the "other" disciple. Since the cockle shell was frequently introduced into representations of the Emmaus story as an attribute of pilgrims or a symbol of the Resurrection, it need not be here associated with Saint James, and the question of the disciple's identity should be left open. In favor of Friedlaender's identification is the fact that in the Hampton Court copy of Caravaggio's *Walk to Emmaus* (see note 18, above) the foremost disciple carries a fish, an attribute of Saint Peter. If, moreover, Caravaggio's disciple seated at the right in the London painting is Saint Peter, then his violent gesture may allude not only to Christ's Crucifixion but also to his own eventual martyrdom, which Caravaggio was to represent a year later (1601) for the Cerasi Chapel of S. Maria del Popolo.

45. Cf. M. Calvesi ("Caravaggio," cited in note 38, 97–98), who interprets the roast fowl juxtaposed with the basket of fruit as allusions to Christ's death and Resurrection, respectively. Whether the fowl carries symbolic meaning is, of course, a matter of speculation. But I prefer the simpler and more general contrast between the sacramental and the earthly food.

BIBLIOGRAPHY OF FREQUENTLY CITED SOURCES

Aurenhammer, H., *Lexikon der christlichen Ikonographie,* Vienna, 1967

Friedlaender, W., *Caravaggio Studies,* Princeton, 1955

Hinks, R., *Michelangelo Merisi da Caravaggio: His Life—His Legend—His Works,* London, 1952

Kinkead, D., "Poesia e simboli nel Caravaggio: Temi religiosi," *Palatino,* x, 1966, 112f.

Kirschbaum, R., *Lexikon der christlichen Ikonographie,* I, Rome-Freiburg-Basel-Vienna, 1968

Lavin, I., "Divine Inspiration in Caravaggio's Two *St. Matthews,*" *Art Bulletin,* LVI, 1974, 59f.

Mâle, E., *L'Art religieux après le Concile de Trente,* Paris, 1932

Réau, L., *Iconographie de l'art chrétien,* II, Paris, 1957

Röttgen, H., "Die Stellung der Contarelli-Kapelle in Caravaggios Werk," *Zeit-*

schrift für Kunstgeschichte, XXVIII, 1965, 47f. (repr. and trans. in H. Röttgen, *Il Caravaggio ricerche e interpretazioni*, Rome, 1974, 47f.)

Rudrauf, L., *Le Repas d'Emmaus*, Paris, 1955

Stechow, W., "Emmaus," *Reallexikon zur deutschen Kunstgeschichte*, V, Stuttgart, 1967, cols. 228–242

Tolnay, C. de, *Michelangelo*, V, Princeton, 1960

7

The Nationalist Garden
and the Holy Book

BARBARA NOVAK

In the beginning all the world was America.
John Locke [1]

In the early nineteenth century in America, nature couldn't do
without God, and God apparently couldn't do without nature. By
the time Emerson wrote *Nature* in 1836, the terms "God" and
"nature" were often the same thing, and could be used inter-
changeably. The transcendentalists accepted God's immanence.
More orthodox religions, which had always insisted on a separation of God and nature, also capitulated to their union. A "Christianized naturalism," to use Perry Miller's phrase, transcended
theological boundaries, so that one could find "sermons in stones,
and good in every thing." "Nature," wrote Miller, "somehow, by
a legerdemain that even so highly literate Christians as the edi-
tors of *The New York Review* could not quite admit to themselves,
had effectually taken the place of the Bible. . . ." [2]

That legerdemain was facilitated by the pervasive nature worship not only of Emerson, but of Wordsworth, Rousseau, and
Schelling. With this added international force it is not surprising
that most religious orthodoxies in America obligingly expanded
to accommodate a kind of Christianized pantheism. Ideas of God's
nature and of God *in* nature became hopelessly entangled, and

only the most scrupulous theologians even tried to separate them. If nature was God's Holy Book, it *was* God.

The implications of this for morality, religion, and nationalism make the concept of nature before the Civil War indispensable to an understanding of American culture. Like every age, the early nineteenth century entertained contradictions it did not attempt, or perhaps dare, to resolve. By asking the apparently simple question "How did Americans see and interpret nature?" we are quickly brought into the heart of these contradictions.

In recent years a number of brilliant historians have tried to isolate and define the ideas the nineteenth century projected on nature, ideas that strove to reconcile America, nature, and God. In *Errand into the Wilderness*, Perry Miller suggests that "Nature—not to be too tedious—in America means the wilderness."[3] In *Virgin Land*, Henry Nash Smith speaks of the American agrarian dream as the Garden of the World.[4] In *The American Adam*, R. W. B. Lewis suggests the idea of Adamic innocence before the Fall.[5] To these three (nature as Primordial Wilderness, as the Garden of the World, as the original Paradise) we can add a fourth— America awaiting the regained Paradise attending the millennium. These myths of nature in America change according to the religious or philosophical lenses through which they are examined. Accepting this lability, Leo Marx found it convenient to discriminate between two concepts of the Garden, the primitive and the pastoral[6]—a distinction that fortuitously resolves an important antinomy between ideas of wilderness (God's original creation, untamed, untouched, savage) and the agrarian Garden of man's cultivation. The mutability of these myths assisted the powerful hold nature had on the nineteenth-century imagination. As with any shared overriding concept whose terms are not strictly defined, each man could interpret it according to his needs. Nature's text, like the Bible, could be interpreted with Protestant independence.

The new significance of nature and the development of landscape painting coincided paradoxically with the relentless destruction of the wilderness in the early nineteenth century. The ravages of man on nature were a repeated concern in artists' writings, and the symbol of this attack was usually "the axe," cutting into nature's pristine—and thus godly—state. In his "Essay on

American Scenery" (1835), an essay that articulates the spirit that was to dominate much American landscape painting for thirty years, Thomas Cole found America's wildness its most distinctive feature,

> because in civilized Europe the primitive features of scenery have long since been destroyed or modified. . . . And to this cultivated state our western world is fast approaching; but nature is still predominant, and there are those who regret that with the improvements of cultivation the sublimity of the wilderness should pass away; for those scenes of solitude from which the hand of nature has never been lifted, affect the mind with a more deep toned emotion than aught which the hand of man has touched. Amid them the consequent associations are of God the creator—they are his undefiled works, and the mind is cast into the contemplation of eternal things.[7]

In his funeral oration for Cole, William Cullen Bryant extolled the early landscapes and noted "delight . . . at the opportunity of contemplating pictures which carried the eye over scenes of wild grandeur peculiar to our country, over our ariel mountaintops with their mighty growth of forest never touched by the axe, along the banks of streams never deformed by culture. . . ."[8] This consciousness of destruction is never far from contemporary criticism. Reviewing two landscapes by Cole's Hudson River colleague, J. F. Cropsey, in 1847, *The Literary World* pointed out the artist's role in preserving the last evidences of the golden age of wilderness: "The axe of civilization is busy with our old forests, and artisan ingenuity is fast sweeping away the relics of our national infancy. . . . What were once the wild and picturesque haunts of the Red Man, and where the wild deer roamed in freedom, are becoming the abodes of commerce and the seats of manufactures. . . . Yankee enterprise has little sympathy with the picturesque, and it behooves our artists to rescue from its grasp the little that is left, before it is too late."[9] Such intense reverence for nature came only with the realization that nature could be lost. Given the indissoluble union of God and nature at this moment, the fate of both God and nature is obvious. A future mourning the loss of faith and consumed with ecological nostalgia was not far away. But though the nineteenth century acknowledged its fears to some extent, it worked hard to reconcile the various myths, to retain God and nature in any combination that seemed workable. Thus, if Wilderness became cultivated ("deformed by culture," in Bryant's phrase), it could still be a Garden. If the Garden was not Paradise, it could offer the possibility of a Paradise to be regained. To this idea of Paradise, original or regained, much energy was devoted.

Though the idea of primal innocence received its main exposition from Whitman rather late in the pre-Civil War period we are discussing, the reconciliation to its loss was premised on the idea of Adam's "fortunate Fall." The elder Henry James felt that Adam's original estate had all the happy blindness of the state of nature, undisturbed by the rigors of self-consciousness. Adam's state was

> purely genetic and premoral . . . a state of blissful infantile delight unperturbed as yet by those fierce storms of the intellect which are soon to envelope and sweep it away, but also unvisited by a single glimpse of that Divine and halcyon calm of the heart in which these hideous storms will finally rock themselves to sleep. Nothing can indeed be more remote (except in pure imagery) from distinctively *human* attributes, or from the spontaneous life of man, than this sleek and comely Adamic condition, provided it should turn out an abiding one: because man in that case would prove a mere dimpled nursling of the skies, without ever rising into the slightest Divine communion or fellowship, without ever realizing a truly Divine manhood and dignity.[10]

So after detailing the drawbacks of Paradise on the basis that perfect happiness is hardly worth having unless one knows one has it, the stage was set for the fortunate Fall, putting an optimistic complexion on Original Sin. The notion of the fortunate Fall, R. W. B. Lewis points out, can be traced back almost to the fourth century in Christian theology, and allows for "the necessary transforming shocks and sufferings, the experiments and errors, in short, the experience—through which maturity and identity may be arrived at."[11]

For those who did not subscribe to the concept of Adamic innocence, or to the fortunate aspect of the Fall, the recovery of Paradise, the coming of the millennium prophesied in the Book of Revelation, might also be discerned in American nature, which now took on the aspect of the New Jerusalem. The series of awakenings, of evangelical revivals, that spread through many American towns from upstate New York to the newer territories in the West, were a powerful force in the national psyche. Apocalyptic shudders of remorse carried with them an ardent belief that the believers were chosen, that America itself was the chosen land, and that the millennium was at hand.

Each view of nature, then, carried with it not only an esthetic view, but a powerful self-image, a moral and social energy that could be translated into action. Many of these projections on nature augmented the American's sense of his own unique nature, his unique opportunity, and could indeed foster a sense of destiny which, when it served to rationalize questionable acts with elevated thoughts, could have a darker side. And the apparently innocent nationalism, so mingled with moral and religious ideas, could survive into another century as an imperial iconography.

> . . . The noblest ministry of nature is to stand as the apparition of God. It is the organ through which the universal spirit speaks to the individual, and strives to lead back the individual to it.
>
> Emerson, *Nature*

> We can never see Christianity from the catechism—from the pastures, from a boat in the pond, from amidst the songs of wood-birds, we possibly may.
>
> Emerson, "Circles"[12]

Since the landscape was a holy text which revealed truth and also offered it for interpretation, artists who painted the landscape had a choice of what to transcribe and interpret. They could paint what Lewis calls "Yankee Genesis," or they could paint Revelation, with or without evangelical overtones. Creation and revelation were in fact key words in nineteenth-century philosophy, theology, and esthetics—though, again, their meanings varied enormously according to context.

"We distinguish the announcements of the soul, its manifestations of its own nature, by the term *Revelation*," wrote Emerson. "These are always attended by the emotion of the sublime."[13] "Sublimity" is also an important word in nineteenth-century nature terminology. By the time Emerson was writing, the sublime had been largely transformed from an esthetic to a Christianized mark of the Deity resident in nature. Indeed the gradual fusion of esthetic and religious terms is an index of the appropriation of the landscape for religious and ultimately, as we shall see, nationalist purposes. Science, so prominent in the nineteenth-century consciousness, could hardly be left out either. Landscape, according to the mid-century critic James Jackson Jarves, was "the creation of the one God—his sensuous image and revelation, through the investigation of which by science or its representation by art men's hearts are lifted toward him."[14] Science and art are both cited here as routes to God; and this continued attempt to Christianize science was made urgent by the growing stress it was placing on the traditional interpretations of God's nature. It was hoped that art's interpretive capacities would reconcile the contradictions science was forcing on the nineteenth-century mind.

Revelation and creation, the sublime as a religious idea, science as a mode of knowledge to be urgently enlisted on God's side—with these the artist, approaching a nature in which his society had located powerful vested interests, was already in a difficult position. In painting landscape, the artist was tampering with some of his society's most touchy ideas, ideas involved in many of its pursuits. Any irresponsibility on his part might result in a kind of excommunication. The nineteenth century rings with exhortations to the artist on the high moral duties of his exceptional calling—entirely proper for landscape painters, those priests of the natural church. There is no question, in early-nineteenth-century America, of the intimate relation between art and society, a fact that has to be emphasized after a century of modernism.

Since artists were created by God and generously endowed by him with special gifts, the powers of revelation and creation extended to them too. How to exercise these divine rights was the subject of much discussion. Asher B. Durand cautioned the young artist "not to transcribe whole pages [of nature] indiscriminately 'verbatim ad literature'; but such texts as most clearly and simply declare her great truths, and then he cannot transcribe with too much care and faithfulness."[15] He suggested starting with a humble naturalism, for "the humblest scenes of your successful labors will become hallowed ground to which, in memory at least, you will make many a joyous pilgrimage, and, like Rousseau, in the fullness of your emotions, kiss the very earth that bore the print of your oft-repeated footsteps."[16] As is clear from this passage, Durand's famous "Letters on Landscape Painting" (1855) frequently adopt the tone of a religious manual instructing a novice. And as a spiritual instructor sometimes does, Durand tried to make the burden of humble labors less heavy by pointing to their goal. Landscape painting, he wrote, "will be great in proportion as it declares the glory of God, by representation of his works, and not of the works of man . . . every *truthful* study of near and simple objects will qualify you for the more difficult and complex; it is only thus you can learn to read the great book of Nature, to comprehend it, and eventually transcribe from its pages, and attach to the transcript your own commentaries." But he immediately cautions on the priorities involved and warns the acolyte not to overvalue hard-won technical facility: "There is the letter and the spirit in the true Scripture of Art, the former being tributary to the latter, but never overruling it. All the technicalities above named are but the language and the rhetoric which expresses and enforces the doctrine. . . ."[17]

Thomas Cole, though no less reverent, was more assertive in emphasizing the creative role of the artist than was Durand, who always remained the devout naturalist: "Art is in fact man's lowly imitation of the creative power of the Almighty."[18] Cole also said, "We are still in Eden; the wall that shuts us out of the garden is our ignorance and folly."[19] This reinforces a matter often indispensable to the whole machinery of nature worship—morality. Cole implies that, seen with the guiltless eye, nature would be perceived as perfection, as Eden. The flaws are not in nature, but in ourselves.

From this point of view Cole's own development is instructive. The first two paintings in the *Course of Empire* series, the savage and pastoral states, move from the Wilderness to the Garden, two powerful mythic conceits in America, as we have seen. Then, consummation of empire, lush, sensual, and hedonistic, is followed by destruction and desolation. The moral of Cole's parable was mused over in the contemporary reviews. "Will it always be so?" wrote one reviewer. "Philosophy and religion forbid." For when "the lust to destroy shall cease and the arts, the sciences, and the ambition to excell in all good shall characterize man, instead of the pride of the triumph, or the desire of conquests, then will the empire of love be permanent."[20] The expression of such pious sentiments penetrated to the furthest reaches of secular society, even when their incongruity was marked. Cole himself projected a sequel to this series, based on Christianity (*The Cross and the World*, left incomplete at his death), in which the empire of love would triumph. The two series may be seen as parables of the fate of pagan and of Christian man. Christianity could redeem history, the landscape, the world.

So the strongly moral reception of Cole's *Course of Empire* was a salient part of the age. If, like nature, art was a divine force, and the artist himself bound by his divine task, morality, served by art and nature, was enlisted to assist man toward his divinity, and didactically encouraged at all turns. Despite the suggestions of some critics that the love of nature had its amoral aspects, the opposite idea was energetically cultivated. ". . . In regard to landscape art," wrote the critic H. T. Tuckerman, "it is apparent that the impression must depend upon the habits of observation and the degree of moral sensibility of the spectator."[21] Emerson was, as usual, more optimistic: "Nor can it be doubted that this moral sentiment which thus scents the air, grows in the grain, and impregnates the waters of the world, is caught by man and sinks into his soul. The moral influence of nature upon every individual is that amount of truth which it illustrates to him."[22] To a writer in *The Crayon* in 1855, "the man to whom nature, in her inanimate forms, has been a delight all his early life, will love a landscape, and be better capable of feeling the merits of it than any city-bred artist. . . ."[23] The *Southern Literary Messenger* in 1844 treated the problem in an article called "The Influence of the Fine Arts on the Moral Sensibilities," by the Reverend J. N. Danforth, who observed: "[The painter] seeks to stir the deep sea of human sensibility. He desires to reach the most retired and secret foundations of feeling in man, and hence he must commune for days and nights with nature herself in her multiplied forms and in her beautiful developments. Some minds are more affected by *natural scenery* than by any other source of moral influence."[24]

So it was "the legitimate and holy task of the scenic limner," as Tuckerman put it, to interpret nature.[25] And Durand, whose writings on the whole lack the sententiousness that afflicted many of his contemporaries, concluded:

It is impossible to contemplate with right-minded, reverent feeling, [nature's] inexpressible beauty and grandeur, for ever assuming new forms of impressiveness under the varying phases of cloud and sunshine, time and season, without arriving at the conviction

—"That all which we behold
Is full of blessings"—

that the Great Designer of these glorious pictures has placed them before us as types of the Divine attributes, and we insensibly, as it were, in our daily contemplations,

—"To the beautiful order of his works
Learn to conform the order of our lives."[26]

All that the artists and public had to do was to read what William Sidney Mount called "the volume of nature—a lecture always ready and bound by the Almighty," and virtue presumably would triumph.[27] For the Holy Book was open to all. To read, interpret, and express its truths required dedication, cultivation, and sensibilities enlightened by Christian morals.

The close connection between nature and art as routes to spiritual understanding had been asserted earlier by the German writer Wilhelm Wackenroder in "Outpourings from the Heart of an Art-Loving Friar" (1797):

I know of *two miraculous languages* through which the Creator has enabled men to grasp and understand things in all their power, or at least so much of them—to put it more modestly— as mortals can grasp. They enter into us by ways other than words, they move us suddenly, miraculously seizing our entire self, penetrating into our every nerve and drop of blood. One of these miraculous languages is spoken only by God, the other is spoken by a few chosen men whom he has lovingly anointed. They are: *Nature and Art.*

Since my early youth, when I first learned about God from the ancient sacred books of our faith, *Nature* has seemed to me the fullest and clearest index to His being and character. The rustling in the trees of the forest and the rolling thunder have told me secrets about Him which I cannot put into words. A beautiful valley enclosed by bizarre rocks, a smooth-flowing river reflecting overhanging trees, a pleasant green meadow under a blue sky—all these stirred my innermost spirit more, gave me a more intense feeling of God's power and benevolence, purified and uplifted my soul more than any language of words could have done. Words, I think, are tools too earthly and crude to express the incorporeal as well as they do express material reality.[28]

Like such German contemporaries as Caspar David Friedrich, nineteenth-century American artists united nature and art in the single votive act of landscape painting. Thus they spoke the two "miraculous languages" at once. In that they were blessed with creative gifts, they reproduced in little the divine act of Creation. Their interpretation of their duties ranged from a humble naturalism to a baroque romanticism. Humble in their exaltation and exalted in their humility, they were perfect media between nature and their fellow man, between the God in them and their human estate. As curates of nature interpreting its Holy Book, as proxies for the divine, they were implicated in tasks that demanded as fine discriminations as modernist art, though the terms of their involvement were, if anything, more complex.

> God has promised us a renowned existence, if we will but deserve it. He speaks this promise in the sublimity of Nature. It resounds all along the crags of the Alleghanies. It is uttered in the thunder of Niagara. It is heard in the roar of two oceans, from the great Pacific to the rocky ramparts of the Bay of Fundy. His finger has written it in the broad expanse of our Inland Seas, and traced it out by the mighty Father of Waters! The august TEMPLE in which we dwell was built for lofty purposes. Oh! that we may consecrate it to LIBERTY and CONCORD, and be found fit worshippers within its holy wall!
>
> James Brooks
> *The Knickerbocker*, 1835[29]

With such a range of religious, moral, philosophic, and social ideas projected onto the American landscape, it is clear that the painters who took it upon themselves to deal with this "loaded" subject were involved not only with art, but with the iconography of nationalism. In painting the face of God in the landscape so that the less gifted might recognize and share in that benevolent spirituality, they were among the spiritual leaders of America's flock. Through this idea of *community* we can approach a firm understanding of the role of landscape not only in American art, but in

American life, especially before the Civil War. The idea of this community through nature runs clearly through all aspects of American social life in the first half of the nineteenth century, and its durability is still evidenced by its partial survival as the myth of rural America.

While I am not concerned here with the reasons why this myth was so necessary and durable, we should investigate further the idea of community. God in or revealed through nature is accessible to every man, and every man can thus "commune" (as the word was) with nature and partake in the divine. God in nature speaks to God in man. (This can be seen as a way of moving man back to the center of the universe, using as passport a discreet humility, which is confident, however, of its ultimate virtue and godliness.) And man can also commune with *man* through nature—a communing which requires for its representation not the solitary figure, but two figures in a landscape, the classic exemplar of which, in American landscape art, is Durand's portrait of Cole and Bryant, *Kindred Spirits*. This picture is evidence not only of singular contemplation after a transcendental model, but of a sharing through communion, of a potential community.

The sense of community fostered by the natural church was reinforced by an all-pervasive nationalism that identified America's destiny with the American landscape. In 1848, James Batchelder, in a book called *The United States as a Missionary Field*, wrote: "Its sublime mountain ranges—its capacious valleys—its majestic rivers—its inland seas—its productiveness of soil, immense mineral resources, and salubrity of climate, render it a most desirable habitation for man, and are all worthy of the sublime destiny which awaits it, as the foster mother of future billions, who will be the *governing* race of man." [30]

There was a widespread belief that America's natural riches were God's blessings on a chosen people. Perhaps it is safe to say that despite its international complexion, nineteenth-century nature worship was more strongly nationalistic in America than elsewhere. For nature was tied to the group destiny of Americans united within a still-new nation, "one nation, under God." This is perhaps a key explanation for the acceptance of immanence by the religious orthodoxy.

The community awareness of that one nation, united under God

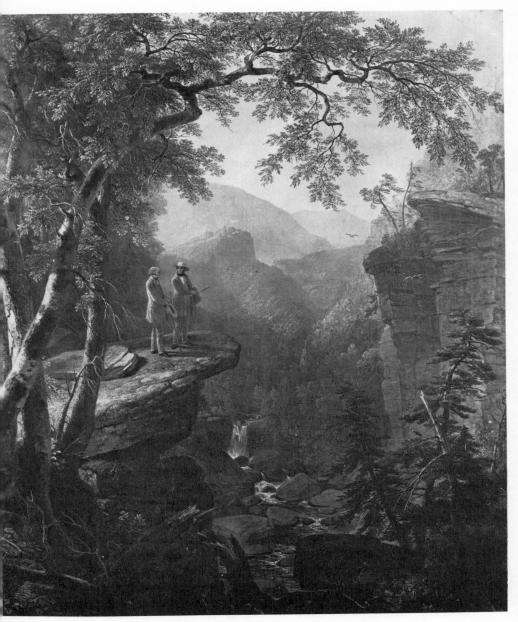

Asher Brown Durand, *Kindred Spirits*. 1849. Oil on canvas, 44 x 36″.
Photo: The New York Public Library.

and nature (or under God *as* nature), received further reinforcement early in the nineteenth century from the evangelical revivalism sweeping the country. Thus, a writer in the *Spectator* in 1829 observed that the Gospel could "renew the face of communities and nations. The same heavenly influence which, in revivals of religion, descends on families and villages . . . may in like manner, when it shall please him who hath the residue of the spirit, descend to refresh and beautify a whole land."[31] It was only God's grace, according to the Reverend David Riddle in 1851, "not enterprise, or physical improvements, or a glorious constitution and good laws, or free trade, or a tariff, or railroads and steamships, or philosophy, or science, or taste . . . that bringeth salvation, appearing to every man, and inwrought into the heart of every man, that can save us from the fate of former republics, and make us a blessing to all nations."[32]

That grace had been apparent to the earliest settlers in the midst of America's natural bounties. As Tocqueville had said: "There is no country in the world in which the Christian religion retains a greater hold over the souls of men, than in America. . . . Religion is the foremost of the institutions of the country."[33] If, within the decade of the Reverend Riddle's writing, the axe, growing technology, and a dawning sense of Darwinian savageries began to threaten the dream of an American Paradise, and of a nature which was both benevolent and godly, the belief in a chosen national destiny did a lot to keep such awareness at bay. No wonder that Christianity and nationalism, two forms of hope, two imprimaturs of destiny, continually emerged from the face of American nature.

The unity of nature bespoke the unity of God. The unity of man with nature assumed an optimistic attitude toward human perfectibility. Nature, God, and Man composed an infinitely mutable Trinity within this para-religion. This gave confidence to all aspects of nature study, from the detail with its microscopic perfection (the microscope further revealed divine truths) to the grandeur of huge spaces. And in the mutability which landscape presents, God's moods could be read through a key symbol of God's immanence—light, the mystic substance of the landscape artist. Thus the landscape painters, the leaders of the national flock, could remind the nation of divine benevolence and of a chosen destiny by keeping before their eyes the mountains, trees, forests, and lakes which revealed the Word in each shining image.

NOTES

1. Quoted in Leo Marx, *The Machine in the Garden* (New York: Oxford University Press, 1964), p. 210.

2. Perry Miller, "Nature and the National Ego," in *Errand into the Wilderness* (New York: Harper & Row, 1964), p. 211.

3. Ibid., p. 204.

4. Henry Nash Smith, *Virgin Land* (New York: Random House—Knopf, 1950); see Book 3.

5. R. W. B. Lewis, *The American Adam* (Chicago: University of Chicago Press, Phoenix Books, 1958).

6. See Marx, op. cit.

7. Thomas Cole, "Essay on American Scenery" (1835), in John McCoubrey, ed., *American Art, 1700–1960*, Sources and Documents in the History of Art Series (Englewood Cliffs, N.J.: Prentice-Hall, 1965), p. 102.

8. Quoted in Louis L. Noble, *The Course of Empire, Voyage of Life and Other Pictures of Thomas Cole, N.A.* (New York: Cornish, Lamport & Co., 1853), pp. 58–59.

9. Quoted in Miller, op. cit., pp. 205–6.

10. Quoted in Lewis, op. cit., p. 59.

11. Ibid., p. 61.

12. Ralph Waldo Emerson, *The Selected Writings of Ralph Waldo Emerson*, ed. Brooks Atkinson (New York: Random House, Modern Library, 1950), pp. 34, 285–86.

13. "The Over-Soul," ibid., p. 269.

14. James Jackson Jarves, *The Art-Idea* (Hurd and Houghton, 1864; reprint, ed. Benjamin Rowland, Jr., Cambridge: Harvard University Press, Belknap Press, 1960), p. 86.

15. Asher B. Durand, undated ms., Durand papers, New York Public Library.

16. Asher B. Durand, "Letters on Landscape Painting," Letter II, *Crayon* 1 (Jan. 17, 1855):34; also in McCoubrey, op. cit., p. 111.

17. Durand, "Letters," Letter III, *Crayon* 1 (Jan. 31, 1855):66.

18. Thomas Cole, "Thoughts and Occurrences," undated entry, c. 1842, New York State Library, Albany; photostat, New-York Historical Society; microfilm, Archives of American Art.

19. Cole, "Essay on American Scenery," p. 109.

20. *New York Mirror* 14, no. 17 (Oct. 22, 1856):135.

21. Henry T. Tuckerman, *Book of the Artists* (1867; New York: James F. Carr, 1966), p. 531.

22. Emerson, *Nature*, in *Selected Writings*, pp. 23–24.

23. *Crayon* 1 (1855):81.

24. *Southern Literary Messenger* 10 (1844):112.

25. Tuckerman, op. cit., p. 512.

26. Durand, Letter II, p. 34; in McCoubrey, op. cit., p. 112.

27. William Sidney Mount, quoted in John I. H. Baur, "Trends in American Painting," introduction to *M. & M. Karolik Collection of American Paintings, 1815–1865*, Museum of Fine Arts, Boston (Cambridge, Mass.: Harvard University Press, 1949), p. xxvi.

28. Quoted in Lorenz Eitner, *Neoclassicism and Romanticism, 1750–1850*, Sources

and Documents in the History of Art Series (Englewood Cliffs, N.J.: Prentice-Hall, 1970), 2:26.

29. Quoted in Miller, op. cit., p. 210.

30. Quoted in Perry Miller, *The Life of the Mind in America from the Revolution to the Civil War* (New York: Harcourt, Brace & World, 1965), p. 57.

31. Ibid., p. 11.

32. Ibid., p. 13.

33. Quoted in Russel Blaine Nye, *The Cultural Life of the New Nation, 1776–1830* (New York: Harper Torchbooks, 1960); p. 219 from *Democracy in America*, ed. Phillips Bradley (New York, 1948), 1:303–4.

8

The Religious Impulse in American Art

JOSHUA C. TAYLOR

Historians have generally assumed in studies of American art through its first century or so that the religious impulse played little part. On those few occasions when it has been felt necessary to rationalize this fact one has fallen back on the principle that the predominantly Protestant sects in the United States had little need for art in their religious practices; sometimes it has been suggested that religious institutions were actually in opposition to art.

But this is to consider religion and the religious impulse in a very narrow sense. In Europe as well as America from the late eighteenth century on, the artists who were most committed to religion tended not to identify themselves with the church and rarely looked upon biblical subject matter as the only key to religious expression. When the artists did take the church into their consideration, they were likely to see it in an allegorical sense, as a symbolic force—as in the various allegories of religion and the arts—or as a mysterious place in which personal meditations might be encouraged, rather than to see it as a guiding mother for the arts. Protestant American artists traveling in Europe never failed to visit the churches and wayside shrines of Italy and expressed a proper horror at the institution, and a deep fascination with the tradition of piety that it represented. Some few tried their hand at works based on the traditional repertory—Copley, Trumbull, Robert Weir among others—but they hardly con-

Reprinted from *Papers in American Art*, edited by John C. Milley (Maple Shade, N.J.: The Edinburgh Press, 1976), pp. 113–32.

sidered religious subject matter a center around which to build their serious work. Even those who worked with Benjamin West at the very time he was creating his large paintings based on Christian and sometimes liturgical themes, seem to have been little persuaded to find their subjects in the traditional Christian repertory. In early exhibitions in this country works of religious subject matter were shown, but with rare exception they were works by earlier European artists or copies. There was even a prejudice against some kinds of traditional subjects for American consumption. As one critic as late as the 1840s said, the Europeans could keep their licentious renderings of Adam and Eve and Lot and his daughters at home and not sully the minds of good moral Americans with them.

No one can doubt, however, the religious commitments of artists and their publics in America. Religion was the center of university life, of both rural and urban society, and certainly constituted one of the major subjects of literary concern. There was no aspect of life that was not likely to be described in religious terminology. But it was part of the change both in religion and in art that the way religious impulse was to be expressed was a matter of personal, not institutional, pursuit. This does not mean that the artist was free to seek some capricious and personal manner of expression, but rather that he might find formulations within the terms of his own art and not borrow religiosity simply from the pronouncements of the theologians. He was encouraged to do this by the nature of current art theory itself. In fact it is difficult at times to decide whether aesthetic language at the end of the eighteenth century is talking in terms of the pulpit or whether the minister discussing the nature of virtue and the world beyond is using the terms of the artist.

The dedicated revival of academic thought at the end of the eighteenth century, particularly in England, put the artist in contact with an ideal world that eschewed the sensuous distractions of the particular and the everyday, and encouraged him to believe that an order of beauty was the physical equivalent of a morally ordered life. Both artists and theologians talked about elevating the spirit, about gaining distance from mundane entanglements. One might consider that the systematic step by step use of classical models to create a perfection of form, and thus establish an aesthetic distance, was a ladder of virtue leading to moral exaltation. There was even a kind of moral purpose in simply being an artist; one was called to art much as one was called to the ministry. It became a kind of sacred obligation. And no where was the obligation more important than in the new republic in which art was calculated to perform an ennobling role.

Much eighteenth century thought about art rested on the principle that form had consequences. That is, that a given kind of form produced a predictable state of mind. There were, moreover, those theories that would hold that the mind could be taught through sight and through action. (This was in counter distinction to those who believed that the mind had within itself full knowledge of moral direction, which needed only to be brought out.) It was the obligation of the artist to create those forms which would lead the mind to orderly thinking, to allow it to understand the nature of the good. Consider for example what it meant to write a good hand. One practiced rhythmical and proportional exercises until the hand automatically created well-balanced forms with lucid continuity. It is not by chance that the mottos used for practice in penmanship were invariably of a moral and religious nature. To write in a disorderly ill-formed way was, the children were given to understand, a kind of moral lapse. Similarly the artist early was given to understand that if his art was to reach the proper level of moral truth it must be formally perfect and speak only the highest beauty. Style, which is often misunderstood as classical copying, was actually moral content.

Of course this systematic education of the spirit spoke of only one aspect of religion. It accorded well with the Protestant sermon that exalted labor and seemed to look upon success as a manifestation of spiritual virtue. The emphasis was on justice and morality not on spiritual transport. There is little in such an art that lends itself to expressing the admonitions of guilt, the constant terror of Hell, and the need for human redemption. When the need to strike this mortal fear was recognized, the artist had to put aside his regularity of form, his beauty of finish, and plunge the viewer into a world of jagged shapes and their resultant conflict. Although this was a well recognized mode of expression, it took second place in America to an art of formal exaltation.

Possibly the man who brought religious enthusiasm into art in

America was Thomas Cole. Enthusiasm was not a quality highly regarded in the eighteenth century in either religion or art. Regardless of how virtuous the goal, to be carried away as if possessed was not looked upon as a proper mode of human conduct. And yet there was that strain of religion, prominent in the eighteenth century and developing more and more in the nineteenth in America in the fiery exhortations of itinerant ministers and in the excitement of camp meetings, which depended on a kind of spiritual possession. Thomas Cole did not paint camp meetings nor did he attend them. In fact he eventually became a devout Episcopalian. But he became an artist possessed, believing every tree and cloud spoke to him of man's struggle and man's fate, reflecting in the changing conformations both the spiritual and the physical state of man. Although he could record the most extraordinary quantity of detailed fact about nature and its changes in his bulging notebooks, Cole could switch from the language of the naturalist to the language of the religious poet without seeming to have changed his mode. When Cole painted a tree he became the tree and seemed quite incapable of that aesthetic and moral distance that had served as a basis for an earlier style. His is not an art of moral reasoning but of histrionic identity in which man continuously acts out his struggle for salvation. He taught people to see the American wilderness as a religious drama, and his followers never forgot the lesson even though their own discourse was to be formulated on a totally different plane. Although Cole was devoted to the close examination of nature and in some of his paintings he was content to render only that which he saw, when one looks at the bulk of his art it is evident that he considered his vocation chiefly as that of teacher. His art is as persuasive as an evangelical hymn and philosophically not much more profound. His power comes not from any systematic expounding of doctrine but through creating a sympathetic bond between man and the world around him. Taught to see nature through the eyes of Cole the common man could find sermons in his every environment.

There is a distinction between the persuasive sentiment of Cole and a rather more complex contemplative view of nature expressed by Ralph Waldo Emerson. There is little of transcendental calm in Cole's eager use of every twig and leaf to express a human state of mind. It is not surprising that a later group of painters looked upon Cole as well-meaning but untruthful. The writing of Emerson and that of Ruskin both taught that nature was itself the voice of God and needed no help from man to perfect its spiritual communication. Art, said Emerson, is only the gymnastics of the eye, a preparation of the eye in order to see the beauties of nature. The ultimate experience is that of nature, and art is simply an advertisement for the ultimate truth. From quite a different background, John Ruskin said much the same thing. He spoke of the anonymous artist who gave over his individual personality to the truth of nature, copying nature both in its part and in its whole. What was created as a result of this prompting by artists such as Durand and Kensett or the later painters who adhered to that curious organization called the Society for the Advancement of Truth in Art, was a kind of art that implies that spiritual content is to be assumed not expressed. But how is one to recognize that a detailed painting of nature carries spiritual content and is not simply the rendering of material fact?

In a way what had been developing by mid-century was a kind of irreconcilable opposition. On one hand *style* was itself content. Morality was reached by the formal treatment of an object, a treatment that placed it well beyond the complexities and particularities of ordinary life. On the other hand *non-style* was the only true content because style was simply the manipulation of man and non-style allowed nature to speak with the direct voice of God. The argument of some against nature as content was that it was a mindless and therefore soulless representation. Others found in nature the mind of God. The clue for finding God in nature for the latter artists, came not from any formal prompting but from a well established philosophical or religious stand. Meaning in the work of art depended not on narrative or on formal beauty but on a religious belief. Art became not an illustration but a complement to religion or at least to a strong mystical, philosophical view of life.

It is not surprising that in the 1840s and 50s the teachings of Emanuel Swedenborg became of particular importance for artists and patrons alike. Swedenborg provided the unusual attraction of expressing a clinical concern for nature and yet, through the simple device of a spiritual metaphor, could remain in touch with the spiritual world. For Swedenborg the spiritual world was not something above or beyond but coexisted with the material world. It was simply a matter of dimension: the material world existed in terms of the dimensions of time and space; the spiritual world was to be measured in moral dimensions. It was the highest achievement of man to be able to read material dimension in terms of their true moral equivalents. Man's physical growth was the material manifestation of his moral growth, just as a tree was the visual manifestation of the vital forces that brought it into existence. Beauty occurred at that moment when the outer form expressed the purity of the inner growth. It was not a beauty beyond sense but rather a beauty within sense; paradoxically, it was a sensuous spirituality.

This untraditional combination of formal beauty and sensuous precision occurs in the work of Hiram Powers which is so often mislabeled Neo-Classical, whatever that term ever means. Powers was a man of extraordinary literalness and yet was devoted to a spiritual ideal. Possibly it was because of his Swedenborgian teaching that he saw no conflict in this combination. His figure of "Eve Tempted" is a winningly transient creation existing equally in the world of flesh and the world of perfect style. Every curve and line corresponds to those elegant forms that once spoke of high morality, and yet there is no denying the fleshly softness and even voluptuous carving of the work. Evidently Hiram Powers had some fear that the American eye was not yet attuned to the perception of the spiritual quality in sensuous form and might be mislead by the natural condition of Eve's materiality state, because he chose to send first to the United States for exhibition not the Eve but the "Greek Slave." In one sense this is a more chaste work, slimmer in figure and expressing an appropriate modesty, and yet it, too, combines the persuasive surfaces of flesh minutely observed with the general perfection of harmonious form. To the sensitive eye it provides a lesson in seeing the beauty of spiritual harmony in nature itself. In its way it was meant as a lesson in spiritual vision. When Powers modeled his head of Christ he was concerned, as later was his friend William Page, in combining the earthly with the spiritual. He did not hesitate to give Christ the character of a sensuous man since it was only through the sensuous that the spiritual could be revealed. That was the meaning of the incarnation. To be non-human was to be likewise non-divine.

The function of the artist then was not to transcend nature, but to reveal within nature itself a high spiritual order. An artist was one who could see spiritually. William Page, who reformulated his entire theory of art in the terms of Swedenborg, was persuaded that each work had to have the complex many-layered color of nature yet be bounded by the intellect of form. For him color and form worked together much the way that Swedenborg's Divine Love and Divine Wisdom served to produce both the spiritual and physical entity. The work of art carried its spiritual message, then, not simply through its subject matter but through its very fabric. The artist in turn was a maker, as God was a maker. Through his works he maintained for human kind that tenuous relationship between the world of matter and the mind of God. He made it possible, again in Swedenborgian terms, for man to realize heaven rather than to suffer in Hell. In the late 1850s William Page painted a very large painting of "Moses on Mount Horeb." It is based on that passage in Exodus in which the Israelites are to prevail so long as Moses can hold up his arms. He is being helped by Aaron and Hur. This model of a hero sustaining the faith might be taken as a general allegory of the time, as Page himself later said, after the Civil War. Curiously enough, however, the face of Moses bears a striking resemblance to that of the artist himself. Possibly Page was indicating that it was up to the artist to sustain the spirituality of the time, to struggle against the odds of materialism, in order that spirituality could prevail.

What emerges is the idea that artistic creativity itself has spiritual value, and for the observer to enter into that creativity to some degree is to achieve a kind of spiritual insight. William Rimmer's eloquent drawing of the *Fall of Day* is an extraordinary mixture of cosmic expression and personal anguish. It is impossible to see the drawing without thinking of the artist who created it, yet to call it a personal expression would be to miss its extraordinary power. The artist becomes, in a sense, the soul of the world dramatizing in his own act of creation a fresh spiritual insight. At this point, the way artists lived became almost as important as what artists painted. The artist's life was a special life, lived in a special environment in which all spiritual values were somehow heightened. Possibly it was this new recognition of the artist as seer that permitted him in the 1860s and 70s to create paintings that were neither direct transcriptions of nature in all of its detail nor formal organization in the architectonic sense of earlier art. In the later works of George Inness, another artist who found great satisfaction in Swedenborg, the spectator is invited to join the artist in the shadowy reaches of a richly colored landscape where the mind is provoked to think and remember, to seek for definition and never find it. Inness not only opens up to view the landscape in front of him but the whole range of speculation for the mind. Each painting provides a venture into sense in which the mind discovers new routes and fruitful ruminations. Art was a means to spiritual freedom.

Sometimes in this landscape of the mind one encounters unexpected figures. In Robert Loftin Newman, they occasionally act out well known religious scenes. But the setting is strange. It is not Bethlehem or a local township, but rather a land of art. The land is a special land inhabited by artists and poets in which each shadow, each formless shape takes on a special mysterious meaning. One can say as well that it is the land of belief, of human sympathy and spiritual values, where one might seek a kind of solace from a more material world. If it is not religious in the strict sense of that word, it at least provides the solace of religion to those who are won by its artistic persuasion.

More potent a persuader was Ryder who did not leave to chance the relationship between the observer and the painting. The strong forms, pushing and pulling, of Ryder's "Jonah" are irresistible, and one thrashes with Jonah amongst the powerful waves. It is a visual parable, in effect, since one learns a spiritual lesson in the potent narrative of its forms. The painting is not so much to be looked at as to be acted out, and yet for all its sensuousness the artistic "place" escapes the limits of the mundane world. It is as if the soul were provided with a special environment in which it can recognize its own nature.

This kind of spiritual persuasiveness became the special province of art. In 1868 Daniel Huntington, so long a prominent figure in American art, painted his "Philosophy and Christian Art." Philosophy is a Renaissance scientist pointing to the accurate configurations in his book, which is lit by a traditional ancient lamp of learning. Christian art, however, is an attractive young woman,

seated before a natural landscape, pointing to a painting of the
nativity. Art has to do with nature, charm, and human feelings.
Its identity with Christianity is not here to be taken lightly. In
opposing classical tendencies in art in an earlier generation, Cha-
teaubriand pointed out that it was only Christianity that provided the strong human feeling necessary for what he considered
to be great art. That is he equated Christianity with human compassion and emotional intensity. It would seem that Daniel Huntington was pointing out once more the identity between artistic
expression and religious awareness.

It is also worth remarking that the art to which Huntington's
allegorical figure points is a work from the past, the work from
the great Renaissance tradition of Italian painting. Together with
the new awareness of an identity between art and spirituality
came an awareness of art's history. In fact, in the 1870s art and
historical values became curiously intertwined. Possibly it was
because of a belief in the persisting qualities of art, its existence
over many centuries in which it served as a link between man
and man, a kind of persistent line of spiritual contact. An anti-
quarian environment at times became almost the same as an artistic environment, and many artist's studios were well supplied
with pious artifacts from the past. But there was something deeper
in this than simply modish historicism. Joining with the past the
artist lost his lonely isolation and became a member of a great
cultural community. Armed with tradition he could face the complexities and disappointments of an increasingly materialistic
time. The past was summoned in support of faith. Richardson's
Trinity Church in Boston built in the 1870s is a great monument
to this concept. It creates an environment of art which belongs to
the past and to the continuing present being both a sensuous
pleasure and a carefully presented record of archeological knowledge. The worshipper is not transported back to a remote and
spiritual time but adds that time's perceptions to his own. Here
art, not theology, teaches man about the persistence of spirit and
allows him to live for a moment in a heightened spiritual world.
Everywhere one looks he encounters art, decoration and other re-
minders of churches and galleries seen elsewhere. No less than in
the shadowy forests of Newman or Inness, the artistic environment serves to free the exploring spirit. In a way, art itself be-

comes the subject of art and the means to a religious experience. By recalling the art of Florence, Renaissance palaces, and biographies of great painters, the wealth of artistic learning could support a suggestive style that could transform the world. Who is Abbott Thayer's placid "Virgin"? Is she the Virgin of the Bible, a re-enactment of the Renaissance, or the girl next door? In a strange way she is all of these. She represents, in her way, the persistence of faith, of human goodness. She expresses the spirituality of aesthetic optimism. Significantly, when Elihu Vedder represented the conflict of the soul placed between doubt and faith, doubt was the thoughtful Greek philosopher; faith was the Raphaelesque angel. Art, not argument, was the vehicle of faith.

Looking back over the century, then, we might say that art has rarely served in America as an illustration of religious thought, but rather has often striven to create that environment of mind that makes religion possible. It passed from the moral logic of form to a free sensuous persuasion. Eventually art itself became both symbol and proof of a persistent human spirituality. The artists never doubted their religious purpose, and it behooves us to recognize the seriousness of their intent.

9

George Segal's *Abraham and Isaac:* Some Iconographic Reflections

JANE DILLENBERGER

George Segal's two sculptural interpretations of the sacrifice of Isaac stand conspicuously alone in the art of the twentieth century. They are biblical and figurative at a time when little significant art is either figurative or traditionally religious. And both sculptures have been controversial; an abstract rendering of this theme might cause criticism or bewilderment, but the hostility that these two distinguished sculptures have evoked is of another order.

Although Segal's two sculptures of the sacrifice of Isaac stand alone in twentieth-century art in their bold figuration of this biblical theme, they join a great company of works of art on the theme from past centuries. From these many earlier interpretations of the Abraham and Isaac story, a selection has been made for comparison and contrast with Segal's sculptures. A review of some of these major works from earlier art will give perspective and depth to the interpretation of the contemporary artist's work.

One of the earliest representations of the sacrifice of Isaac to have been created within the Christian context[1] is on the famous Early Christian sarcophagus of Junius Bassus, a prefect of Rome (Fig. 1). The sarcophagus was made sometime before A.D. 359, since the inscription reads that in that year, "Junius Bassus, who lived forty-two years and two months, during his tenure of the city went to God, as a neophyte."

This essay is based on a lecture given at Nassau Presbyterian Church, Princeton, New Jersey, 2 March 1981. George Segal attended and participated in the discussion period.

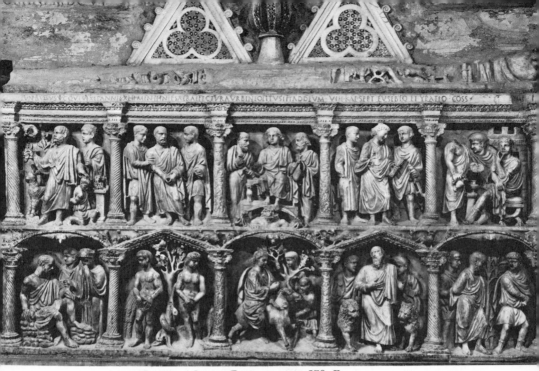

Fig. 1. *Sarcophagus of Junius Bassus*, c. A.D. 350. Rome,
Crypt of St. Peter's. Photo: Alinari/Art Resource, Inc..

Fig. 2. *Abraham Receives the Three Angels and the Sacrifice of Isaac.* Mosaic.
c. 546-48. Ravenna, San Vitale. Photo: Alinari/Art Resource, Inc.

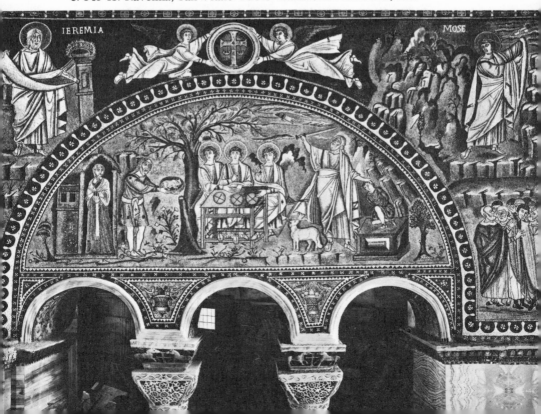

The sarcophagus is divided architecturally into a succession of niches, each containing a separate episode. The subjects are from the Old and the New Testament. The upper-left niche is devoted to Abraham and Isaac. Abraham stands facing us with his right hand grasping the knife, which is stayed by the angel of the Lord who called to him from heaven. His left hand is on the head of the kneeling Isaac, perhaps grasping his hair. The boy's hands appear to be bound behind his back. The ram is seen at the lower left, and one of Abraham's servants witnesses the event at our right.

Other Old Testament subjects are Adam and Eve, Daniel between two lions, and Job seated on the ash heap and visited by his wife and friends. The two latter subjects, as well as the Abraham and Isaac episode, were often represented in Early Christian art. They are all subjects on the theme of deliverance, showing God's merciful intervention in human history. An ancient liturgy of the church begins with the supplication:

> Receive, O Lord, thy servant into the place
>   of salvation which he may hope of thy mercy.
> Deliver, O Lord, his soul as thou didst deliver
>   Isaac from sacrifice and from the hand of
>   his father.[2]

Stylistically, the sarcophagus shows the persistence of the classical style and vocabulary of forms, even during the fourth century A.D.—almost nine hundred years after classical art reached its apogee in the fifth century B.C. in Greece. The Abraham is a statesman-philosopher type; the figures stand in attitudes familiar to us through their Greek prototypes. However, the arrangement of the figures in the narrow space, as in a tableau, suggest the ancient liturgy: the solemn gestures of Abraham and the compliant kneeling of the obedient Isaac have a liturgical character. This is an unemotional enactment, a symbolic replay of the mighty story: we recognize the event, but the meaning of the event seems circumscribed. All of the intolerable ambiguities and incipient tragedies are evaded.

The first flowering of Byzantine art occurred in Ravenna in the middle of the sixth century, and it is within the glorious and historically important church of San Vitale (dedicated in 548) that the next example of the theme of the sacrifice of Isaac is found (Fig. 2). Inasmuch as the mosaics of the entire apse form a symphonic unity, the theme of the whole must be considered. "In different symbols and imagery they all convey one idea: the redemption of mankind by Christ and the Sacramental reenactment of this event in the eucharistic sacrifice."[3] Thus, the Lamb of God slain before the foundations of the earth is depicted at the center of the vault; medallions about the arches depict the twelve apostles and all the saints mentioned in the "Book of Life," listing those the church remembers at every mass; on either side of the sanctuary are sacrificial scenes from the Old Testament: on the right are Abel and Melchizedek, and between them on an altar are a chalice and loaves of bread like those used for the mass.

At the left of the sanctuary is the Abraham and Isaac story, shown as two episodes in one continuous landscape setting (Fig. 4): on the left is Sarah standing before her tent looking doubtfully toward the three strangers, for whom she has prepared cakes. Abraham bears the "calf, tender and good"[4] prepared by his servants. Standing under one of the oaks of Mamre, he proffers it to the three men. At the right Abraham is seen again, no longer dressed in the simple, short garment, but in the ample, flowing garments worn by Moses and the prophets and the apostles in the surrounding mosaics. As Abraham lifts his great sword, obedient to the word of the Lord (here symbolized by a hand issuing from the clouds above), he is dressed as a priest; his other hand rests on the head of the obedient Isaac who kneels on the sacrificial altar built by Abraham. Like the carving on the Junius Bassus sarcophagus, the event seems enacted liturgically, the human relationships and feelings minimized. In fact, in the narrative in Genesis, the laconic account says nothing of Abraham's or Isaac's feelings. It is the Lord who says, "your son, your only son, whom you love."[5] Father and son are described as simply acting, not feeling, in the biblical narrative.

It is the priestly role of Abraham that the choreographer of the San Vitale mosaics emphasizes. Abraham's sacrifice is paralleled by Abel's offering, and by Melchizedek, the priest-king who blessed Abraham and brought him bread and wine. These three Old Testament priestly figures and their sacrifices and ceremonials are types of the sacrifice of Jesus Christ, which is reenacted in the mass. The significance of Abraham's willing sacrifice of his son, is the type of God the Father, who gave his son that through him all men may be saved. The altar built by Abraham becomes the altar at which the eucharist is celebrated.

This kind of typological interpretation, in which the events of the Old Testament are seen as prefiguring those of the New Testament, began in the early centuries and was expressed in the writings of Origen, Ambrose, Clement, and Augustine, was further elaborated, and, in the tenth century, was issued as the *Glossa Ordinaria*. This book was an important source for the medieval world. The *Glossa Ordinaria* teaches that Isaac is a figure of God the Son, as Abraham is a figure of God the Father. God, who gave his son for mankind, willed that the people of the Old Covenant should catch a faint foreshadowing of the sacrifice yet to be.

It is this kind of typological interpretation that is present in the Abraham and Isaac figures represented at the Chartres cathedral (Fig. 3), where they are part of the noble group of patriarchs and prophets who line the entrance to the north porch of the cathedral. Again the sacrifice is part of a thematic grouping referring to the priestly role. Each of the patriarchs and prophets bears a symbol, which, as Emile Mâle says,

> . . . announces Jesus Christ, which is Jesus Christ. Melchizedek has the chalice, Abraham rests his hand upon the head of Isaac, Moses holds the brazen serpent, Samuel the sacrificial lamb, David the crown of thorns . . . and Saint Peter, at the end, also has the chalice. Thus the mysterious chalice which appears at the beginning of history in the hands of Melchizedek reappears in the hands of Saint Peter. The circle is closed. Each of the figures is a Christ-bearer, a christophorous, transmitting from generation to generation the mysterious sign.[6]

At Chartres, Abraham is seen at the moment when the angel of the Lord called to him from heaven and said, "Abraham, Abraham, . . . do not lay your hand on the lad or do anything to him; for now I know that you fear God, seeing that you have not withheld your son, your only son, from me."[7] The angel is seen in the canopy above the neighboring statue of Melchizedek. The urgent gesture of the angel's arm and the downward thrust of his head, as he beckons to Abraham, communicate something of the drama

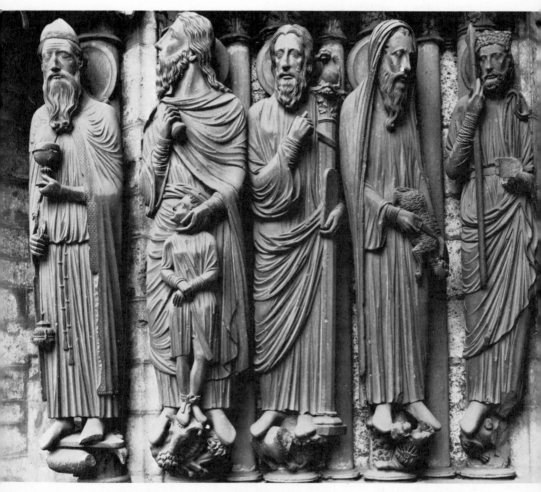

Fig. 3. *Abraham and Isaac,* from the North Porch, Cathedral of Nôtre Dame, Chartres, France. c. 1230-50.

of the biblical text. The upward glance of Abraham and his expression of deep sorrow are movingly delineated. Abraham's gesture with the hand that holds the knife convincingly suggests an interrupted movement. The other hand tenderly clasps the head of Isaac, whose small body is pressed against the old patriarch's body.

The biblical passage tells how Abraham bound Isaac, and it is of interest that the Chartres sculptor shows the boy's ankles as bound by a carefully knotted double cord. But Isaac's hands are not bound. They are placed one across the other, as if in obedient preparation for binding. Whereas the old Abraham's face is full of sorrow, the young Isaac's expression is serene, and even has a suggestion of a smile. The two figures stand upon the ram "which was caught in the thicket by his horns,"[8] and which was provided for the burnt offering.

These three examples of the sacrifice of Isaac from the Early Christian, Byzantine, and Gothic eras share a characteristic not to be found in the later examples of this motif. Each is part of a larger, overarching theme. In each case, not only is the biblical story evoked, but a theological interpretation of that story that is presented. For the fourth-century Christian, the sacrifice of Isaac was an example along with others from the Old and the New Testament on the theme of deliverance, showing God's intervention into history to save his own. For the sixth-century believer who worshiped in San Vitale, the sacrifice of Isaac was a paradigm of the eucharist. For the thirteenth-century worshiper at Chartres, Abraham was one of the patriarchs and prophets whose acts mysteriously foretold the sacrifice of Christ. However, the early Renaissance sculptures of the sacrifice of Isaac, and the later interpretations of the theme selected for this study were created as individual works of art, and not related to a larger iconographic and theological scheme.

The sacrifice of Isaac was the subject chosen for a historic sculptural competition that took place in 1401 in the city of Florence. Seven sculptors selected from a much larger group competed for the commission for the new doors for the great octagonal baptistry in front of the cathedral. The size of the sculpture, the amount of bronze, and the quatrefoil frame were specified by the rules of the competition. Two of the sculptures, those by Ghiberti and Brunelleschi (Figs. 4 and 5), are to be seen today in the Bargello Gallery in Florence. For some decades, these two reliefs have provided a neat examination question for budding art historians who were asked which of these two sculptures won the competition and why.

In the two reliefs, the components are the same: the two men servants, the saddled ass, Abraham with the knife, Isaac bound, the angel of the Lord, the rams, the mountain. By including the servants and the ass, the storytelling aspects are emphasized, rather than the liturgical aspects emphasized in the Early Christian, Byzantine, and Gothic examples.

These two Renaissance artists have observed, delighted in, and realistically represented persons, places, animals, things. In Brunelleschi's relief (Fig. 5), the angel grasps Abraham's arm firmly and Abraham thrusts the knife with vigor; Abraham's hand, which cups the boy's throat, and his thumb, which pushes back the chin, are delineated, not only accurately, but with a sense of terrible urgency. Abraham rushes at his dread task, his brows contracted, his hair flowing back in the haste of his movement. Isaac seems to feel the flames already issuing from the altar, for his feet lift off the altar as his knee alone supports him. The bone and muscle beneath the flesh of Isaac's young body are delineated with care, juxtaposing this innocent, vulnerable flesh to the all-encasing garments of the elderly father.

Nearby, the ram, unconscious of his role in the drama, quite realistically scratches one ear with a back leg. The ram, like the ass, is delineated, with an affectionate realism that stresses the texture of the fur, the anatomical structure, and the spontaneous movement. The same can be said of the details in Ghiberti's relief (Fig. 4) of the scene, but Ghiberti's Abraham is more ceremonial in his stance, his gesture, and his solemn but not frantic expression; Isaac seems aware already of the angel's message of deliverance. Ghiberti has placed Isaac's lithe young torso frontally, and given it a graceful contraposto as he looks upward, tilting his shoulders in one direction and his hips in the other. The structure of the body is delineated, stressing both its mobility and details such as the genitals, which are here shown quite explicitly as circumcised, this latter detail based upon Scripture.[9] Isaac's body, which was cast separately, reflects the influence of classical sculpture, in its frontal posture and in the artist's delight in the supple, sensuous, ideal young torso.

It was Ghiberti's relief that won the competition, though to twentieth-century eyes, Brunelleschi's composition, with its vigorous angles and movement and the terrible intensity of the frantic father's assault upon the terrified son, may be more appealing. However, Ghiberti's design is more integrated, the dramatic action more balanced—these are qualities that the creators of the Renaissance, with their emulation of classical art, prized.

At the time Ghiberti's relief was created, it was the more "modern" of the two. Florence was experiencing the impulses and creative ferment that developed into the Renaissance. The Renaissance led to a rebirth of classical motifs and classical style, and it was Ghiberti's composition of harmonious and balanced forms and content that best accorded with classical ideals.

It is a long jump from the Byzantine mosaic and the Renaissance reliefs to Caravaggio's dramatic painting *Sacrifice of Isaac* (Fig. 6). Almost two hundred years separate the Ghiberti and Brunelleschi reliefs from Caravaggio's oil painting, and during those years all of the masterpieces we associate with the Renaissance were created: Leonardo's *Last Supper*, the murals of the Sistine Chapel and all of Michelangelo's sculptures, Raphael's *Stanza*, and Titian's religious and mythological works. Caravaggio was heir to their discoveries and was a revolutionary genius, a key figure in the development of baroque painting, and also of realism.

Most of Caravaggio's religious paintings were commissioned by clerics or religious orders, as was the *Sacrifice of Isaac*, which Caravaggio painted, probably in 1599, for Cardinal Maffeo Barberini, who later became Pope Urban VIII. The drama and emotional intensity of this picture are typical of Caravaggio's style. Throughout his career, he contended with violent objections from both ecclesiastics and from artistic circles, yet he continued to receive commissions from clerics and churches.

In the painting a grim and desperate Abraham forces the head of the terrified, howling Isaac to the altar; his right hand, with the knife perilously close to Isaac's neck, is stayed by the hand of another adolescent, whom we take to be the angel of the Lord and who points to the ram. The terrible event is further dramatized by the play of light that, like a spotlight, picks out and highlights

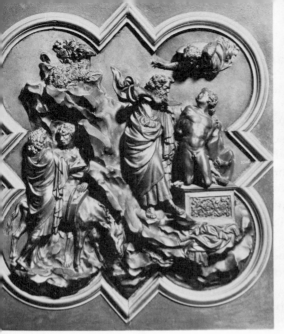

Fig. 4. Lorenzo Ghiberti,
The Sacrifice of Isaac.
Bronze. 1403. Florence, Bargello.
Photo: Alinari/Art Resource, Inc.

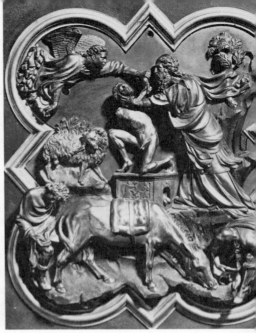

Fig. 5. Filippo Brunelleschi,
The Sacrifice of Isaac.
Bronze. 1403. Florence, Bargello.
Photo: Alinari/Art Resource, Inc.

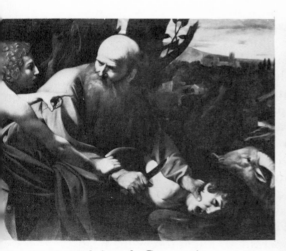

Fig. 6. Michelangelo Caravaggio,
Sacrifice of Abraham, c. 1599.
Oil on canvas. 104 x 135 cm.
Florence, Uffizi.
Photo: Alinari/Art Resource, Inc.

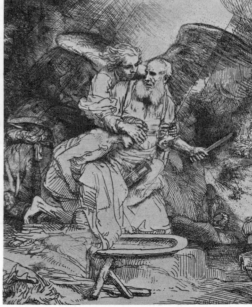

Fig. 7. Rembrandt van Rijn,
Abraham's Sacrifice. 1655. Etching.
The Metropolitan Museum of Art,
Bequest of Ida Kammerer
in memory of her husband,
Frederic Kammerer, M.D., 1933.

the shoulder of the angel and his beautiful hand with its commanding, long, pointing finger (a hand that Caravaggio has lifted out of Leonardo's *Madonna of the Rocks*).

The light falls fully upon Abraham's bald pate and forehead, creating deep shadows around his eyes and the left side of his head; the light falls whitely upon the upper arm and shoulder of the prone Isaac, and upon the side of his face, where the blunt, rough, and sunburned thumb of Abraham presses into the youthful flesh. Isaac's profile, his mouth wide-open and eyelids taut with terror, is adjacent to the head of the ram, with its expression of serene unknowing. The head of the beast and of the boy are related to each other in a kind of yin-yang opposition of related shapes and significances. The strong diagonal thrusts of the light from upper left to lower right, and the sudden contrasts of highlights and obliterating shadows, accentuate the immediacy and violence.

Caravaggio has involved the viewer in the event by bringing the three figures and the animal very close: the viewer becomes a witness at close range. Caravaggio's depiction of the great mythic story appears at first as a scene of violent murder, shorn of religious import. Is it the Olympian attack of the older generation falling, in a jealous rage, upon its own progeny?

If so, that is not all. Caravaggio has *lived* the story and imagined what *he* would experience if he were Abraham. Abraham had journeyed for three days with Isaac, knowing these to be his last days with his son, his only son, whom he loved: three long nights he had lain beside the boy, knowing the terrible command. In a rage of hatred of his task, self-hatred, and hatred of this beloved son, the father assaults his own flesh murderously.

When Rembrandt depicted the story more than fifty years later (Fig. 7), rather than involving us in the melodramatic action of the sacrifice, as Caravaggio did, he focuses the viewer's attention on Abraham's inward reaction. At the very moment of divine intervention, Abraham's hand is stayed. But Rembrandt depicts Abraham in the moment just before he comprehends that the terrible sacrifice must no longer be made. His face is grim and deeply shadowed as he turns unseeing eyes upon the angel. The angel embraces the old man as with one hand the angel stays Abraham's right hand, which holds the knife, and with the other releases Abraham's left hand, which covers the eyes of the kneeling Isaac. The innocent Isaac kneels obediently, his body pressed against Abraham's own. All other details—the two men and donkey in the distance, the landscape—are subordinate to the three figures—the angel, Abraham, and Isaac are locked together, the great, outspread wings of the angel balancing the truncated, pyramidal shape of their bodies.

Rembrandt's extraordinary etching is small in size but monumental in composition and profound in its interpretation of the theme. In the nineteenth century, Kierkegaard pondered the story and wrote of the sacrifice:

> Silently [Abraham] arranged the wood and bound Isaac, silently he drew the knife: then he saw the ram which God had chosen. He sacrificed it and returned home. . . . From that day Abraham grew old, he could not forget that God had demanded this of him. Isaac prospered as before, but Abraham's eyes were darkened and he knew joy no more.[10]

Rembrandt's Abraham, like Kierkegaard's, has darkened eyes that may never again know joy.

Rembrandt's interpretation of the Abraham and Isaac narrative is profoundly moving in the picturing of a range of complex emotions and of psychic states: we recognize our own humanity, that which we have experienced, though perhaps only partially and less profoundly. Yet the God-dimension is mysteriously present also for Rembrandt's *Abraham and Isaac*. It is in God's unseen presence that the terrible story unfolds. In all their humanity, Rembrandt's Abraham and Isaac yet live with a constant awareness of the divine dimension.

From Ghiberti and Brunelleschi to Rembrandt—a period of some two hundred fifty years—the artists whose works are included in this study depicted the ancient story in human terms, shorn of its liturgical significance. For these artists Abraham is not one of the great archetypal priests whose obedience foretells the sacrifice of Christ. Nor is he the patriarch whose descendants will be "as the stars of heaven and as the sand which is on the seashore," by whom "all the nations of the earth [will] bless themselves."[11]

For the Renaissance artists, and for Rembrandt, the visualization of the scene involves the moment of divine intervention, but as it would, or could, occur in their own lives. It is the Renaissance and baroque emphasis on the human father-son relationship, with its destructive force of love and hate inextricably bound together, that provides the background for George Segal's sculptures.

In 1960, Segal began to sculpt the human figure through life-casting figures of his friends and family. He worked out a technique of casting the face and figure in plaster in three sections: head, torso, and legs. These were covered first with petroleum jelly, then with Saran Wrap, and then with gauze soaked in Hydro-Stone. The sections, when dry, were removed and reassembled, and Segal reworked the surface with his hands. Since the model had to remain unmoving during the drying period, it was necessary for the positions the models took to be stable and capable of being sustained for up to thirty minutes. This latter fact led to an interesting result: the poses became those natural to the model, natural in his or her most inward and quiet moments. Segal's work is populated by a whole world of persons caught in attitudes of self-absorption, communing with themselves, often alone but not haunted by loneliness.

In 1973, Segal was invited to Israel to make a sculpture for Mann Auditorium in Tel Aviv. He chose the theme of the sacrifice of Isaac (Fig. 8). The commissioners of the private foundation were aware of the problems presented by the ancient biblical tale, and at first rejected the choice but finally approved. Of the inception of the sculpture, Segal wrote:

> My preparation consisted of rereading Kierkegaard's *Fear and Trembling*, that fevered six-time repeat of the trip to Moriah, with the contradictory tumble of Abraham's thoughts. I decided to leave out the Angel and the ram, and still the drama to a massive horizontal and vertical, with the knife just beginning to turn away from the body. All the emphasis is inside of Abraham's head.
>
> The figures are life size, a father and his real son posed. The rock is eight feet by nine feet, plaster cast from Jerusalem rock, which breaks into tiny slivers, a microcosm of a vast desert landscape.[12]

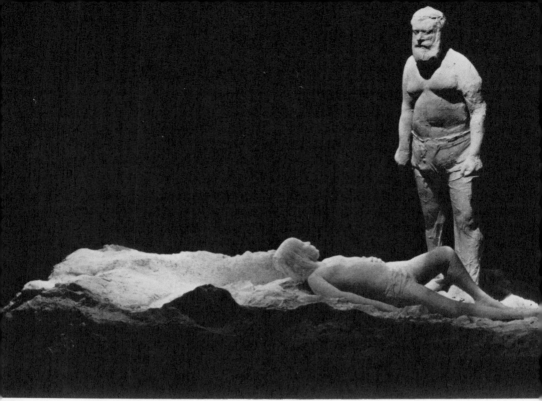

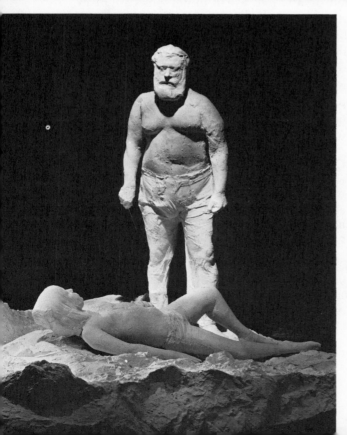

Fig. 8. George Segal,
Abraham's Sacrifice. 1973.
White Plaster 7 x 9 x 8½'.
The Mann Auditorium, Tel Aviv
Israel. Photo: Ran Erde.

In a previous trip to Israel, Segal had been tremendously struck by the barren desert landscape and its suggestion of religious ideas.[13]

In the Tel Aviv *Sacrifice of Isaac*, father and son are seen at the moment just after the words of the angel of the Lord, "Do not lay your hand on the lad or do anything to him; for now I know that you fear God, seeing you have not withheld your son, your only son, from me."[14] Abraham, a corpulent figure in blue jeans, stands seeming to sway forward slightly. He gazes down with unseeing eyes upon the recumbent Isaac. Isaac lies prone and relaxed, except for the forward tilt of his head, as he gazes unafraid at the grim face above him. Abraham's right hand, which holds the knife, hangs at his side, but the left is still clenched and tense.

Once completed and installed in Jerusalem, Segal's sculpture became the object of outraged comment. It shocked conservative Jews because Abraham, the great patriarch, the father of the nations, the noble man obedient to God's will in the ultimate test of faith, was represented as a paunchy Everyman[15] in blue jeans. Compounding the problem was the fact that the model was a well-known and colorful Israeli artist. An analogy for Christians would be if Segal had used Picasso as a model for Jesus.

On the other hand, for liberal Jews, who were against the conscription of their daughters and sons into the army, the sculpture was a problem because it showed a youth as obedient to, and as a victim of, the older generation, who would, in Israel, send the young off to war. Ironically, soon after the sculpture was installed the Yom Kippur War broke out.

As a result of the dissension over the sculpture, it was withdrawn from exhibition, then reinstalled, then withdrawn, then exhibited again. Only the passage of time will allow the debate over the sculpture to subside and the work's aesthetic power to assert itself over against the transitory negativities of the historical moment.

Segal was later commissioned by the Mildred Andrews Fund in Cleveland to create a memorial to the students killed in the 1970 confrontation with the National Guard that took place on the Kent State University campus. As Segal returned to the sacrifice of Isaac theme, five years after the Tel Aviv sculpture, it was with full knowledge of the power and ambiguity of the story.

A polarization between youth and age had taken place in the 1960s in America. The campus riots that started at Berkeley erupted at universities and colleges all over the country. With a dread inevitability came the terrible killing of four students at Kent State University on 4 May 1970. Those who saw the television reenactment of the event (in the spring of 1981) will have lived again the sprawling, untidy, unstoppable march of events leading up to the horror of those deaths.

Segal made the maquette for the Kent Statè sculpture (Fig. 9), but, on 28 August 1978, the university officials decided to reject the commissioned work and issued the following statement:

> The Isaac figure appears to be a male between twenty and thirty, unclothed except in athletic trunks . . . he kneels before Abraham in the posture of a supplicant, his hands bound before him. Abraham's right hand holds a knife. The inescapable first impression is that an older person is threatening to kill a younger person who is pleading for his life. . . . It was thought inappropriate to commemorate the deaths of four and wounding of nine others . . . by a statue which appears to represent an act of violence about to be committed.[16]

For the Kent State officials, the statue mirrored too closely the tragedy which it was intended to commemorate.

Segal's intention was, in fact, to go beyond a simple memorial to the slain students. It was his intention to comment on the psychological gulf that can exist between youth and age. Segal sees Abraham and Isaac as equally tragic figures, placed by destiny in a terrible impasse, and he insists that his work is 'a call for compassion and restraint.' "[17]

When Kent State officials withdrew the commission, Princeton University became the owner of the bronze cast made from the plaster maquette. It stands now adjacent to the apse wall of the chapel. In the Princeton *Sacrifice of Isaac* (Fig. 9), the father and son are seen at the moment of ultimate confrontation, before the divine intervention, and Abraham's drawn and rigid face looks down into the passionately pleading face of the young man. One is reminded of Caravaggio's painting, which represents the same moment in more violently melodramatic terms. Whereas Caravaggio's Isaac howls and struggles, Segal's Isaac appeals and pleads for his life.

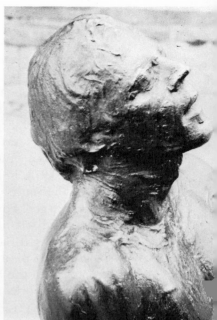

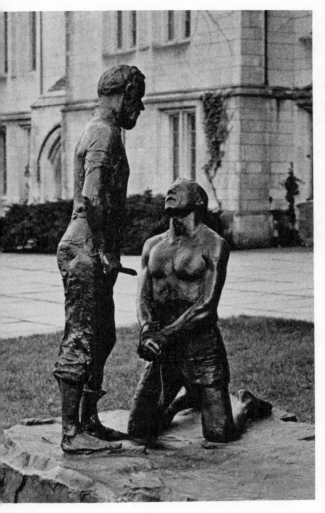

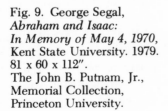

Fig. 9. George Segal,
Abraham and Isaac:
In Memory of May 4, 1970,
Kent State University. 1979.
81 x 60 x 112″.
The John B. Putnam, Jr.,
Memorial Collection,
Princeton University.

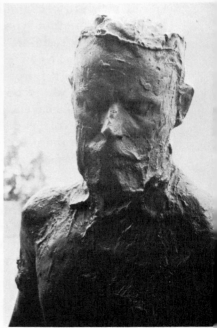

In the Princeton sculpture, Abraham is physically smaller than Isaac. The model for Abraham is a friend of the sculptor, "fortyish" of age, as Segal says. The Isaac is robust and larger, of bony and muscular frame. Were Isaac to stand, he would tower over Abraham. Physically, he could make Abraham cower. But psychically, Isaac hasn't a chance. A father's instruments of domination are more powerful than physical force, or the threat of the knife. In 1978, in a public-television film on his work, George Segal said the sculpture was about the moral problem of "older people in charge." For Segal, the focus in the Princeton sculpture is the clenched left hand of Abraham, wherein the horror of the deed that the right hand must accomplish is expressed.

Reviewing the plates, one sees that though the biblical story is the basis of both the San Vitale mosaic and of Segal's two sculptures, the two works have little in common. Whereas the mosaic makes of Abraham both the priest and the patriarch, Segal's Abraham is Everyman, both in the Tel Aviv and in the Princeton sculpture. Whereas the mosaic pictures the sacrifice of Isaac as part of a vast theological scheme that celebrates the eucharist and sees the obedient offering of the innocent Isaac as a prefiguration of Christ's offering of himself upon the cross, the Segal sculptures represent the event stripped of all such symbolic overtones.

Jewish in background but not in practice, Segal is not an heir to the Christian typology that traditionally interprets the events of the Old Testament as veiled and mysterious prefigurations of events of the New Testament. The Old Testament story concludes with the Lord's promise that because Abraham did not withhold his son, he would be blessed and his descendants multiplied "as the stars of heaven and as the sand which is on the seashore." Abraham's role as patriarch is delineated in these biblical verses. Segal's Abraham in the Tel Aviv sculpture possesses in his heavy figure a pervasive generative power appropriate to his patriarchal role.

In both sculptures Segal has eliminated all details except the two figures. By eliminating the angel of the Lord and the ram, which are symbolic of divine intervention, the resolution of the story is left in doubt. In the Tel Aviv sculpture, Abraham has just withdrawn the thrust of the hand holding the knife, but it is only upon careful examination of the sculpture that this becomes evident. In the case of the Princeton sculpture, the moment depicted is that of the intense confrontation before divine intervention.

Shorn of otherworldly references, Segal's sculptures quite intentionally involve us in the ambiguities and horror of the moment as it might occur in our own lives. In this, he is close to Caravaggio and remote from Rembrandt, whose embracing, sustaining angel in the 1655 etching is the bearer of divine deliverance. Segal has said his Tel Aviv sculpture was a call for compassion and restraint, and that the Princeton sculpture was about the moral problem of the older generation being in charge. It is the older generation that sent the younger generation to Vietnam, which lead to the student riots of the 1960s.

The Princeton sculpture goes beyond the topicality of a tragedy that all have participated in: it represents the primal generation gap and the terrible conflicts within the father-son relationship. This Abraham will return to Mount Moriah, like Kierkegaard's most profoundly imagined Abraham. Like Kierkegaard's Abraham, he will throw himself on his face, praying to God to forgive him for having wanted to sacrifice Isaac. Kierkegaard continues,

> Abraham frequently rode his lonely way, but he did not find rest. He could not conceive that it was a sin to have wished to sacrifice to God his most precious possession when he would have given his life many times over for the sake of his son; and if this *was* a sin, if he had *not* loved Isaac in this way, then he could not understand that it could be forgiven. Could any sin be more terrible? [18]

Isaac will live out a normal life with Rebecca in suburbia, but Abraham, guilt-ridden and possessed by self-doubt and God-doubt, will know no peace in this life.

Though both of Segal's sculptures of the sacrifice of Isaac have been controversial, their place among the significant works of art of our era is assured. Uniquely among twentieth-century sculptors, Segal has affirmed the dignity and worth of humankind. In his own words, all his sculptures "talk about the value of a single human being and the value of private thought and private response." [19]

When the Kent State tragedy has become a footnote in the history books of future generations, the Princeton sculpture will be seen in its human, biblical, and archetypal role. When Israel is no longer beset without and within, and the topicality of the identity of the model for the Abraham is blurred by passing time, Segal's *Sacrifice of Isaac* for Tel Aviv will surely find acceptance in the state for which it was made.

NOTES

1. For a scholarly and illuminating study of this theme in Judaic sources and art, see Josephine Milgrom, "The Akedah: The Binding of Isaac," Thesis, Graduate Theological Union, Berkeley, CA, 1978.

2. Walter Lowrie, *Art in the Early Church* (New York: Pantheon Books, 1947), p. 60.

3. Otto G. Von Simson, *Sacred Fortress, Byzantine Art and Statecraft at Ravenna* (Chicago: University of Chicago Press, 1948), p. 24.

4. Genesis 18:7.

5. Genesis 22:2.

6. Emile Mâle, *Religious Art from the Twelfth to the Eighteenth Century* (New York: Pantheon Books, 1949), p. 77.

7. Genesis 22:11–12.

8. Genesis 22:13.

9. "And Abraham circumcised his son Isaac when he was eight days old, as God had commanded him," Genesis 21:4.

10. Soren Kierkegaard, *Fear and Trembling and Sickness Unto Death* (New York: Doubleday, 1954), p. 28.

11. Genesis 22:17–18.

12. George Segal, in a letter to the author, 1 November 1976.

13. George Segal, in a conversation with the author, 10 February 1981.

14. Genesis 22:12.

15. Segal says that Abraham is Everyman and reports that he was greatly pleased when the Israeli model for the Tel Aviv sculpture, on seeing the finished maquette, said, "Abraham is our father and our mother" (Conversation with the author, 10 February 1981).

16. Martin Friedman and G. W. J. Beal, *George Segal: Sculptures* (Minneapolis: Walker Art Center, 1978), p. 84.

17. Ibid.

18. Kierkegaard, p. 28.

19. Christian Geelhaar, "Marriage Between Matter and Spirit," interview with George Segal, *Pantheon* 34 (July 1976), p. 237.

PART III

HISTORIANS OF RELIGION: ART IN RELIGIOUS TRADITIONS

10

The Origin and Use
of Images in India

ANANDA K. COOMARASWAMY

> It may be said that images are to the Hindu worshipper
> what diagrams are to the geometrician.
> Rao, *Elements of Hindu Iconography*, II, 28.

Few of those who condemn idolatry, or make its suppression a
purpose of missionary activity, have ever seriously envisaged the
actual use of images, in historical or psychological perspective, or
surmised a possible significance in the fact that the vast majority
of men of all races, and in all ages, including the present, Protestants, Hebrews, and Musalmans being the chief exceptions, have
made use of more or less anthropomorphic images as aids to devotion. For these reasons it may be not without value to offer an
account of the use of images in India, as far as possible in terms
of thought natural to those who actually make use of such images. This may at least conduce to a realization of the truth enun-
ciated by an incarnate Indian deity, Kṛṣṇa, that "the path men
take from every side is Mine."

   In explaining the use of images in India, where the method is
regarded as edifying, it should not be inferred that Hindus or
Buddhists are to be represented *en masse* as less superstitious than
other peoples. We meet with all kinds of stories about images that
speak, or bow, or weep; images receive material offerings and services, which they are said to "enjoy"; we know that the real pres-

Reprinted from *The Transformation of Nature in Art* by Ananda K. Coomaraswamy (Cambridge: Harvard University Press, 1934 [Dover edition, 1956]), pp.
153–69, 213–14.

ence of the deity is invited in them for the purpose of receiving worship; on the completion of an image, its eyes are "opened" by a special and elaborate ceremony.[1] Thus, it is clearly indicated that the image is to be regarded as if animated by the deity.[2]

Obviously, however, there is nothing peculiarly Indian here. Similar miracles have been reported of Christian images; even the Christian church, like an Indian temple, is a house dwelt in by God in a special sense, yet it is not regarded as his prison, nor do its walls confine his omnipresence, whether in India or in Europe.

Further, superstition, or realism, is inseparable from human nature, and it would be easy to show that this is always and everywhere the case. The mere existence of science does not defend us from it; the majority will always conceive of atoms and electrons as real things, which would be tangible if they were not so small, and will always believe that tangibility is a proof of existence; and are fully convinced that a being, originating at a given moment of time, may yet, as that same being, survive eternally in time. He who believes that phenomena of necessity stand for solid existing actualities, or that there can exist any empirical consciousness or individuality without a material (substantial) basis, or that anything that has come into being can endure as such forever, is an idolater, a fetishist. Even if we should accept the popular Western view of Hinduism as a polytheistic system, it could not be maintained that the Indian icon is in any sense a fetish. As pointed out by Guénon, "Dans l'Inde, en particulier, une image symbolique representant l'un ou l'autre des 'attributs divins,' et qui est appelée *pratīka*, n'est point une 'idole,' car elle n'a jamais été prise pour autre chose que ce qu'elle est réellement, un support de méditation et un moyen auxiliaire de realization" (*Introduction à l'étude des doctrines hindoues*, p. 209). A good illustration of this is to be found in the *Divyâvadāna*, Ch. XXVI, where Upagupta compels Māra, who as a *yakṣa* has the power of assuming shapes at will, to exhibit himself in the shape of the Buddha. Upagupta bows down, and Māra, shocked at this apparent worship of himself, protests. Upagupta explains that he is not worshipping Māra, but the person represented—"just as people venerating earthen images of the undying angels, do not revere the clay as such, but the immortals represented therein."[3] Here we have the case of an individual who has passed beyond individuality, but is yet represented according to human needs by an image. The principle is even clearer in the case of the images of the angels; the image *per se* is neither God nor any angel, but merely an aspect or hypostasis (*avasthā*) of God, who is in the last analysis without likeness (*amūrta*), not determined by form (*arūpa*), trans-form (*para-rūpa*). His various forms or emanations are conceived by a process of symbolic filiation. To conceive of Hinduism as a polytheistic system is in itself a naïveté of which only a Western student, inheriting Graeco-Roman concepts of "paganism" could be capable; the Muḥammadan view of Christianity as polytheism could be better justified than this.

In fact, if we consider Indian religious philosophy as a whole, and regard the extent to which its highest conceptions have passed as dogmas into the currency of daily life, we shall have to define Hindu civilization as one of the least superstitious the world has known. *Māyā* is not properly *de*lusion, but strictly speaking creative power, *śakti*, the principle of manifestation; *de*lusion, *moha*, is to conceive of appearances as things in themselves, and to be attached to them as such without regard to their procession.

In the *Bhagavad Gītā*, better known in India than the New Testament in Europe, we are taught of the Real, that "This neither dies nor is it born; he who regardeth This as a slayer, he who thinketh This is slain, are equally unknowing." Again and again, from the Upaniṣads to the most devotional theistic hymns the Godhead, ultimate reality, is spoken of as unlimited by any form, not to be described by any predicate, unknowable. Thus, in the Upaniṣads, "He is, by that alone is He to be apprehended" (cf. "I am that I am"); in the words of the Śaiva hymnist Māṇikka Vāçagar, "He is passing the description of words, not comprehensible by the mind, not visible to the eye or other senses." Similarly in later Buddhism, in the Vajrayāna (Śūnyavāda) system, we find it categorically stated that the divinities, that is, the personal God or premier angel in all His forms, "are manifestations of the essential nature of non-being"; the doctrine of the only reality of the Void (Behmen's "Abyss") is pushed to the point of an explicit denial of the existence of any Buddha or any Buddhist doctrine.

Again, whereas we are apt to suppose that the religious significance of Christianity stands or falls with the actual historicity of

Jesus, we find an Indian commentator (Nīlakaṇṭha) saying of the Kṛṣṇa Līlā, believed historical by most Hindus, that the narration is not the real point, that this is not a historical event, but is based upon eternal truths, on the actual relation of the soul to God, and that the events take place, not in the outer world, but in the heart of man. Here we are in a world inaccessible to higher criticism, neither of superstition on the one hand, nor of cynicism on the other. It has been more than once pointed out that the position of Christianity could well be strengthened by a similar emancipation from the historical point of view, as was to a large extent actually the case with the Schoolmen.

As for India, it is precisely in a world dominated by an idealistic concept of reality, and yet with the approval of the most profound thinkers, that there flourished what we are pleased to call idolatry. Māṇikka Vāçagar, quoted above, constantly speaks of the attributes of God, refers to the legendary accounts of His actions, and takes for granted the use and service of images. In Vajrayāna Buddhism, often though not quite correctly designated as nihilistic, the development of an elaborate pantheon, fully realized in material imagery, reaches its zenith. Śaṅkârācārya himself, one of the most brilliant intellects the world has known, interpreter of the Upaniṣads and creator of the Vedânta system of pure monism accepted by a majority of all Hindus and analogous to the idealism of Kant, was a devout worshipper of images, a visitor to shrines, a singer of devotional hymns.

True, in a famous prayer, he apologizes for visualizing in contemplation One who is not limited by any form, for praising in hymns One who is beyond the reach of words, and for visiting Him in sacred shrines, who is omnipresent. Actually, too, there exist some groups in Hinduism (the Sikhs, for example) who do not make use of images. But if even he who knew could not resist the impulse to love,—and love requires an object of adoration, and an object must be conceived in word or form,—how much greater must be the necessity of that majority for whom it is so much easier to worship than to know. Thus the philosopher perceives the inevitability of the use of imagery, verbal and visual, and sanctions the service of images. God Himself makes like concession to our mortal nature, "taking the forms imagined by His worshipers," making Himself as we are that we may be as He is.

The Hindu Īśvara (Supreme God) is not a jealous God, because all gods are aspects of Him, imagined by His worshippers; in the words of Kṛṣṇa: "When any devotee seeks to worship any aspect with faith, it is none other than Myself that bestows that steadfast faith, and when by worshipping any aspect he wins what he desires, it is none other than Myself that grants his prayers. Howsoever men approach Me, so do I welcome them, for the path men take from every side is Mine." Those whose ideal is less high attain, indeed, of necessity to lesser heights; but no man can safely aspire to higher ideals than are pertinent to his spiritual age. In any case, his spiritual growth cannot be aided by a desecration of his ideals; he can be aided only by the fullest recognition of these ideals as retaining their validity in any scheme, however profound. This was the Hindu method; Indian religion adapts herself with infinite grace to every human need. The collective genius that made of Hinduism a continuity ranging from the contemplation of the Absolute to the physical service of an image made of clay did not shrink from an ultimate acceptance of every aspect of God conceived by man, and of every ritual devised by his devotion.

We have already suggested that the multiplicity of the forms of images, coinciding with the development of monotheistic Hinduism, arises from various causes, all ultimately referable to the diversity of need of individuals and groups. In particular, this multiplicity is due historically to the inclusion of all pre-existing forms, all local forms, in a greater theological synthesis, where they are interpreted as modes or emanations (*vyūha*) of the supreme Īśvara; and subsequently, to the further growth of theological speculation. In the words of Yāska, "We see actually that because of the greatness of God, the one principle of life is praised in various ways. Other angels are the individual members of a unique Self" (*Nirukta*, VII, 4): cf. Ruysbroeck, *Adornment* . . . , Ch. XXV, "because of His incomprehensible nobility and sublimity, which we cannot rightly name nor wholly express, we give Him all these names."

Iconolatry, however, was not left to be regarded as an ignorant or useless practice fit only for spiritual children; even the greatest, as we have seen, visited temples, and worshipped images, and certainly these greatest thinkers did not do so blindly or unconsciously. A human necessity was recognized, the nature of the necessity was understood, its psychology systematically analyzed, the various phases of image worship, mental and material, were defined, and the variety of forms explained by the doctrines of emanation and of gracious condescension.

In the first place, then, the forms of images are not arbitrary. Their ultimate elements may be of popular origin rather than priestly invention, but the method is adopted and further developed within the sphere of intellectual orthodoxy. Each conception is of human origin, notwithstanding that the natural tendency of man to realism leads to a belief in actually existent heavens where the Angel appears as he is represented. In the words of Śukrâcârya, "the characteristics of images are determined by the relation that subsists between the adorer and the adored"; in those cited by Gopālabhatta from an unknown source, the present spiritual activity of the worshiper, and the actual existence of a traditional iconography, are reconciled as follows—"Though it is the devotion (*bhakti*) of the devotee that causes the manifestation of the image of the Blessed One (Bhagavata), in this matter (of iconography) the procedure of the ancient sages should be followed."[4]

The whole problem of symbolism (*pratīka*, "symbol") is discussed by Śaṅkarâcārya, Commentary on the Vedânta Sūtras, I, 1, 20. Endorsing the statement that "all who sing here to the harp, sing Him," he points out that this "Him" refers to the highest Lord only, who is the ultimate theme even of worldly songs. And as to anthropomorphic expressions in scripture, "we reply that the highest Lord may, when he pleases, assume a bodily shape formed of Māyā, in order to gratify his devout worshipers"; but all this is merely analogical, as when we say that the Brahman abides here or there, which in reality abides only in its own glory (cf. *ibid.*, I, 2, 29). The representation of the invisible by the visible is also discussed by Deussen, *Philosophy of the Upanishads*, pp. 99–101.

Parenthetically, we may remark that stylistic sequences (change of aesthetic form without change of basic shape) are a revealing record of changes in the nature of religious experience; in Europe, for example, the difference between a thirteenth-century and a modern Madonna betrays the passage from passionate conviction to facile sentimentality. Of this, however, the worshiper is altogether unaware; from the standpoint of edification, the value of an image does not depend on its aesthetic qualities. A recognition of the significance of stylistic changes, in successive periods, important as it may be for us as students of art, is actually apparent only in disinterested retrospect; the theologian, proposing means of edification, has been concerned only with the forms of images. Stylistic changes correspond to linguistic changes: we all speak the language of our own time without question or analysis.

Let us consider now the processes actually involved in the making of images. Long anterior to the oldest surviving images of the supreme deities we meet with descriptions of the gods as having limbs, garments, weapons or other attributes; such descriptions are to be found even in the Vedic lauds and myths. Now in theistic Hinduism, where the method of Yoga is employed, that is, focused attention leading to the realization of identity of consciousness with the object considered, whether or not this object be God, these descriptions, now called *dhyāna mantrams* or trance formulae, or alternatively, *sādhanās*, means, provide the germ from which the form of the deity is to be visualized. For example, "I worship our gentle lady Bhuvaneśvarī, like the risen sun, lovely, victorious, destroying defects in prayer, with a shining crown on her head, three-eyed and with swinging earrings adorned with diverse gems, as a lotus-lady, abounding in treasure, making the gestures of charity and giving assurance. Such is the *dhyānam* of Bhuvaneśvarī" (a form of Devī). To the form thus conceived imagined flowers and other offerings are to be made. Such interior worship of a mantra-body or correspondingly imagined form is called subtle (*sūkṣma*), in contradistinction to the exterior worship of a material image, which is termed gross (*sthūla*), though merely in a descriptive, not a deprecatory, sense.

Further contrasted with both these modes of worship is that called *para-rūpa*, "trans-form," in which the worship is paid directly to the deity as he is in himself. This last mode no doubt corresponds to the ambition of the iconoclast, but such gnosis is in fact only possible, and therefore only permissible, to the perfected Yogin and veritable *jīvanmukta*, who is so far as he himself is concerned set free from all name and aspect, whatever may be the outward appearance he presents. Had the iconoclast in fact attained to such perfection as this, he could not have been an iconoclast.

In any case it must be realized, in connection with the gross or subtle modes of worship, that the end is only to be attained by an identification of the worshiper's consciousness with the form under which the deity is conceived: *nādevo devaṁ yajet*, "only as the angel can one worship the angel," and so *devo bhūtvā devaṁ yajet*, "to worship the Angel become the Angel." Only when the *dhyānam* is thus realized in full *samādhi* (the consummation of Yoga, which commences with focused attention) is the worship achieved. Thus, for example, with regard to the form of Naṭarāja, representing Śiva's cosmic dance, in the words of Tirumūlar,

> The dancing foot, the sound of the tinkling bells,
> The songs that are sung, and the various steps,
> The forms assumed by our Master as He dances,
> Discover these in your own heart, so shall your bonds be broken.

When, on the other hand, a material image is to be produced for purposes of worship in a temple or elsewhere, this as a technical procedure must be undertaken by a professional craftsman, who may be variously designated *śilpin*, "craftsman," *yogin*, "yogi," *sādhaka*, "adept," or simply *rūpakāra* or *pratimākāra*, "imager." Such a craftsman goes through the whole process of self-purification and worship, mental visualization and identification of consciousness with the form evoked, and then only translates the form into stone or metal. Thus the trance formulae become the prescriptions by which the craftsman works, and as such they are commonly included in the *Śilpa Śāstras*, the technical literature of craftsmanship. These books in turn provide invaluable data for the modern student of iconography.

Technical production is thus bound up with the psychological method known as *yoga*. In other words the artist does not resort to models but uses a mental construction, and this condition sufficiently explains the cerebral character of the art, which everyone will have remarked for himself. In the words of the encyclopaedist Śukrâcārya, "One should set up in temples the images of angels who are the objects of his devotion, by mental vision of their attributes; it is for the full achievement of this yoga-vision that the proper lineaments of images are prescribed; therefore the mortal imager should resort to trance-vision, for thus and no otherwise, and surely not by direct perception, is the end to be attained."

The proper characteristics of images are further elucidated in the *Śilpa Śāstras* by a series of canons known as *tālamāna* or *pramāna*, in which are prescribed the ideal proportions proper to the various deities, whether conceived as Kings of the World, or otherwise. These proportions are expressed in terms of a basic unit, just as we speak of a figure having so many "heads"; but the corresponding Indian measure is that of the "face," from the hair on the forehead to the chin, and the different canons are therefore designated Ten-face, Nine-face, and so on down to the Five-face canon suitable for minor deities of dwarfish character. These ideal proportions correspond to the character of the aspect of the angel to be represented, and complete the exposition of this character otherwise set forth by means of facial expression, attributes, costume, or gesture. And as Śukrâcārya says further, "Only an image made in accordance with the canon can be called beautiful; some may think that beautiful which corresponds to their own fancy, but that not in accordance with the canon is unlovely to the discerning eye." And again, "Even the misshapen image of an angel is to be preferred to that of a man, however attractive the latter may be"; because the representations of the angels are means to spiritual ends, not so those which are only likenesses of human individuals. "When the consciousness is brought to rest in the form (*nāma*, "name," "idea"), and sees only the form, then, inasmuch as it rests in the form, aspectual perception is dispensed with and only the reference remains; one reaches then the world-without-aspectual-perception, and with further practice attains to liberation from all hindrances, becoming adept."[5] Here, in another language than our own, are contrasted ideal and realistic art: the one a means to the attainment of fuller consciousness, the other merely a means to pleasure. So too might the anatomical limitations of Giotto be defended as against the human charm of Raphael.

It should be further understood that images differ greatly in the degree of their anthropomorphism. Some are merely symbols, as when the Bodhi tree is used to represent the Buddha at the time of the Enlightenment, or when only the feet of the Lord are represented as objects of worship. A very important iconographic type is that of the *yantra*, used especially in the Śākta systems; here we have to do with a purely geometrical form, often for instance composed of interlocking triangles, representing the male and female, static and kinetic aspects of the Two-in-One. Further, images in the round may be *avyakta*, non-manifest, like a *lingam;* or *vyaktâvyakta*, partially manifest, as in the case of a *mukha-lingam;* or *vyakta*, fully manifest in "anthromorphic" or partly theriomorphic types.[6] In the last analysis all these are equally ideal, symbolic forms.

In the actual use of a material image, it should always be remembered that it must be prepared for worship by a ceremony of invocation (*āvahana*); and if intended only for temporary use, subsequently desecrated by a formula of dismissal (*visarjana*). When not in *pūjā*, that is before consecration or after desecration, the image has no more sacrosanct character than any other material object. It should not be supposed that the deity, by invocation and dismissal, is made to come or go, for omnipresence does not move; these ceremonies are really projections of the worshipper's own mental attitude toward the image. By invocation he announces to himself his intention of using the image as a means of communion with the Angel; by dismissal he announces that his service has been completed, and that he no longer regards the image as a link between himself and the deity.

It is only by a change of viewpoint, psychologically equivalent to such a formal desecration, that the worshipper, who naturally regards the icon as a devotional utility, comes to regard it as a mere work of art to be sensationally regarded as such. Conversely, the modern aesthetician and Kunsthistoriker, who is interested only in aesthetic surfaces and sensations, fails to conceive of the work as the necessary product of a given determination, that is, as having purpose and utility. Of these two, the worshipper, for whom the object was made, is nearer to the root of the matter than the aesthetician who endeavors to isolate beauty from function.[7]

NOTES

1. See my *Mediaeval Sinhalese Art* (1908), pp. 70–75.
2. Cf. G. U. Pope, *The Tiruvāçagam* (Oxford, 1900), p. xxxv.
3. Cf. the *Hermeneia* of Athos, § 445, cited by Fichtner, *Wandmalereien der Athosklöster* (1931), p. 15: "All honor that we pay the image, we refer to the Arche-

type, namely Him whose image it is. . . . In no wise honor we the colors or the art, but the archetype in Christ, who is in Heaven. For as Basilius says, the honoring of an image passes over to its prototype."

4. "It is for the advantage (*artha*) of the worshippers (*upāsaka*) (and not by any intrinsic necessity) that the Brahman—whose nature is intelligence (*cin-maya*), beside whom there is no other, who is impartite and incorporeal—is aspectually conceived (*rūpa-kalpanā*)," *Rāmôpaniṣad*, text cited by Bhattacharya, *Indian Images*, p. xvii. That is to say the image, as in the case of any other "arrangement of God," has a merely logical, not an absolute validity. "Worship" (*upāsana*) has been defined as an "intellectual operation (*mānasa-vyāpara*) with respect to the Brahman with attributed-qualities (*saguṇa*)."

5. Verses cited in the *Triṁśikā* of Vasubandhu; see *Bibliothèque de l'Ecole des Hautes Études*, fasc. 245, 1925, and Lévi, "Matériaux pour l'Étude du Système Vijñaptimātra," *ibid.*, fasc. 260 (Paris, 1932), p. 119.

6. The stage of partial manifestation is compared to that of the "blooming" of a painting. The term "bloom" or "blossom" (*unmīl*) is used to describe the "coming out" of a painting as the colors are gradually applied (Maheśvarânanda, *Mahârthamañjarī*, p. 44, and my "Further References to Indian Painting," *Artibus Asiae*, p. 127, 1930–1932, item 102).

7. Cf. my "Hindu Sculpture," in *The League*, vol. V, no. 3 (New York, 1933).

11

Foundations for a Religio-Aesthetic Tradition in Japan

RICHARD B. PILGRIM

In 1946, F. S. C. Northrop wrote in his book *The Meeting of East and West* that the traditional cultures of the Orient, perhaps more so than all other cultures, emphasized the aesthetic mode in experiencing, apprehending and living in this world. In a rather awkward but suggestive way, he spoke of this as "apprehending the undifferentiated continuum in and through the immediately apprehended differentiated continuum."[1] What he meant by this, and how it is manifested in a variety of Oriental cultures, takes up a good part of his book: to pursue it would take us here too far afield. However, in spite of the problems in his approach, there is something of merit in that it helps us understand "religio-aesthetic" in Japan.

Ma and Kū: Contributions to a Religio-Aesthetic Sensitivity

The central thrust of Northrop's argument seems to be that Oriental cultures, to a degree not known in Western cultures, place primary value on immediate, direct, intuitive, aesthetic experience of this multiple world as itself the primary mode of "knowing" or apprehending the world. Especially in the religious dimensions of these cultures, this mode of knowing not only apprends the immediately sensed world of "differentiated" objects and feelings, but—in and with that—the underlying "undifferentiated," sacred unity that empowers and is the ground for everything.

Furthermore, this immediate, aesthetic apprehension experiences the world as a continuum—whether understood as differentiated or undifferentiated. Direct experience, by its very nature, does not stop the flow of reality or distance the experiencing subject from its object. Time, space, and the world of differentiated things are not discrete, frozen entities but constitute an immediately experienced continuum rich with the fullness of Being. In such a view, "reality" is less some thing(s) or some description of things than direct, immediate, lived experience—an immediate, flowing "reality" that, as differentiated, is the deobjectified world of things, and, as undifferentiated, is the underlying Reality of all. By not being reduced to some *thing* or some description of things, it remains "no-thing" or "in between" the this/that, subject/object reality of discrete objects and distinguished things.

Such a mode of apprehending the world is expressed in much of Japanese culture, especially Japanese religion and art. One of the several foundations for a religio-aesthetic tradition in Japan is this tendency to find the fullness of Being in the immediate flow of the aesthetic moment—in what Shinto has sometimes referred to as living "in the midst of now" (*naka ima*). The aesthetic character of this is expressed in a heightened sensitivity to the beauty of things and to artistic creativity, while the religious character of it issues in religious expressions and religions. Such a sensitivity and art therefore carry religious meaning, and such religious expressions often have aesthetic meaning. This tendency is therefore one important aspect of what is referred to as a "religio-aesthetic tradition" in Japan.

This particular mode of apprehending the world has been expressed in at least two central ideas in Japan—one reflecting a more Shinto and indigenous viewpoint, and the other a more Buddhist one. The former relates to the term *ma* ("interval") and the latter to the term *kū* ("emptiness").

Ma

Ma is a complex term generally suggesting intervals or gaps in time and space. For example, it refers to a room as the space in between the various walls, or to a musical rest as an interval in the temporal flow of the music. Similarly, it can simply mean "between," thereby carrying a host of related meanings. While it is particularly important as an aesthetic and technical term in architecture, its roots lie in ancient Shinto ideas concerning the nature and signs of *kami* ("gods" or "sacred power[s]"). In that context, it referred to an in-between time/space into which the essentially formless *kami* energy (*ki*) or spirit (*mitama*) came to dwell temporarily and bring its benefits. As such, it was closely related to *kekkai* ("gap," "rip," "crevice") as the void into which *kami* came, and to *kehai* ("sign," "indication of presence") as the distinct atmosphere or indicator signaling this coming and leaving of *kami*. In this complex of associated ideas, *ma* came to be related not only to the space/time intervals in between things, but to the sensitivity to this atmosphere of ephemeral, temporary, spiritual presence. As one contemporary Japanese architect says:

> *Ma* is the way of sensing the movement of movement and is related to the term *utsuroi*. Originally, *utsuroi* meant the exact moment when the *kami* spirit entered into and occupied a vacant space. . . . Later it came to signify the moment when the shadow of the spirit emerges from the void. This sense of *kami's* sudden appearance . . . gave birth to the idea of *utsuroi*, the moment when nature is transformed; the passage from one state to another. The Japanese have earnestly attempted to grasp and to fix the emergence, the flowing, the movement along time into space. Here again we find a mode of thinking that merges rather than differentiates space and time. This interpenetration of time and space dominates the Japanese aesthetic.[2]

When seen in this way, *ma* suggests a mode of apprehending the world that places primary value on immediately experiencing the presence of *kami*—a "spiritual" rather than material presence that appears in between all space/time distinctions and transforms by fleetingly filling that in-between with sacred power. As "immediate experience," it places a premium on a heightened, intuitive, aesthetic sensitivity, both to the shadowy, fleeting, vague, and ephemeral atmosphere created by the coming and going of *kami*, and to the formless, in-between, essentially "void" character of Reality. Not unlike Northrop's formulation, it is a mode of apprehending the world in which the undifferentiated aesthetic continuum (called *kami*, in this case) is experienced in, with, and in between the immediately experienced differentiated continuum.

In this case, the differentiated continuum refers to the particular time, space, and setting into which *kami* comes. More specifically, it is the Shinto shrine and its environment. Rather continuously in Japan, this setting has expressed the underlying religioaesthetic experience or sensitivity of *ma*. The paradigmatic, but by no means only, example of this is the great shrine of Ise. This shrine and its surroundings, like many others, exude both aesthetic and religious character. It is a differentiated continuum comprised of the beauty of nature, the simplicity of architectural design, the purity and cleanliness of open spaces, and the subdued colors of natural wood and stone. The mode of experience that seeks to merge immediately and directly with the flow of things expresses itself in the beauty of form; the "aesthetic" as intuitive, direct experience becomes the "aesthetic" as the beauty of form. The mode of apprehending that values an experiential wonder about things (*mono-no-aware*) rather than a speculative one seems naturally to express itself in aesthetic and artistic form.

Of course, one would be remiss in leaving the impression that the Japanese aesthetic character of the differentiated continuum has been merely a result of a tendency to unitive, aesthetic experience. Other factors have certainly come into play. One of these that cannot be overlooked in a concern for the foundations of a religio-aesthetic tradition in Japan (and is generally related to a Shinto and/or indigenous viewpoint) is perception of the natural world itself as the embodiment and/or locus of sacred power (*kami*) and as paradisal. In Japanese mythology, the land itself is a creation of the gods, and a mirror image of the heavenly abode of the gods. Moreover, at a certain moment in the mythic past, those heavenly deities descended to take up residence in the natural world already populated by the earthly deities. This mythology, and the tradition of the sanctity and beauty of the land, lives on in Japan in the recurring and dominant cultural motif of aesthetic and religious sensitivity to nature. In short, and insofar as the land was a "land of natural affirmation" full of beauty and sacrality,[3] the differentiated continuum called nature was already a religio-aesthetic paradise—whether apprehended by direct experience or not. If one adds to this a tendency to value direct, intuitive experience "trained" to be sensitive to an in-between space and time where a deeper Reality is experienced, one finds a crucial foundation for a religio-aesthetic tradition in which the arts carry religious meaning and religion is fundamentally associated with aesthetic and artistic modes.

While the *ma* sensitivity has manifested itself throughout Japanese culture, for the most part it can be seen in an aesthetic of form that values the flowing, processing, transforming, transient, ephemeral, subdued, simple, clean, and "empty" character of things. The literal, descriptive, objective world—the differentiated world—is collapsed in direct, immediate experience. An aesthetic continuum emerges as an in-between Reality where time, space, and all things merge into one flowing moment. As quoted above, the Japanese have "attempted to grasp and fix the emergence, the flowing, the movement along time into space" in their art. As emphasizing the Reality of in-between, a *ma* aesthetic features expectant stillness and open space pregnant with possibility. As such, this aesthetic "was to pervade the structure of houses, literature, arts, and entertainment, and it has developed into the characteristic Japanese aesthetic of stillness and motion."[4] This pregnant space and expectant stillness is no mere emptiness in the Japanese arts—it is the "living room" of the spirit. "Space or *ma*, is the very foundation of Japanese aesthetics. Minute particles of *kami* as it were, fill that *ma*."[5]

One very specific example of this aesthetic "style" manifested in architectural design can be seen in the *engawa*, or the veranda/walkway surrounding many traditional Japanese homes. In a discussion of Japan as a "culture of grays," Kisho Kurokawa speaks of the *en* of *engawa* as related to both *ma* and *kū;* namely, as expressive of relational merging into "third worlds" of in-between reality. As he says:

> Perhaps the most important role of the *engawa* is as an intervening space between the inside and outside—a sort of third world between interior and exterior. Insofar as it sits in the shelter of the eaves, it may be considered interior space, but since it is open to the outside, it is also part of exterior space. The *engawa* is an outstanding example in architecture of what I call "gray space" or the intervening area between inside and outside. But the special significance of the *engawa* gray space is that it is not cut off or independent from either the interior or the exterior. It is a realm where they both merge.[6]

Ma sensitivity does not manifest itself merely in an aesthetic of form, however. It also importantly implies a whole mode of religio-aesthetic sensitivity and artistic creativity; that is, a religio-aesthetic mode of being in the world and especially of being an artist. The artistic/aesthetic expressions of a religio-aesthetic tradition imply a religio-aesthetic sensitivity and quality of experience. After all, the ability to express an in-between Reality in objective form depends almost necessarily on an ability to experience it. For this reason, most of the primary aesthetic categories of Japanese culture, starting with *mono-no-aware* and going on through to *yūgen* ("ethereal beauty") and *sabi* ("loneliness"), refer not only to objective, stylistic features in the arts, but also to a subjective "feeling tone" or atmosphere reflecting and demanding one's aesthetic/intuitive experience and sensitivity. One has to sense things in more intuitive, direct, and immediately aesthetic ways in order either to create or to appreciate the aesthetic/artistic world as it reflects the religious depths. As Kurokawa says, "All [later developments in the aesthetic tradition] attempt to express a condition, atmosphere, or spiritual quality rather than a material or concrete quality."[7] This is one of the two central ideas upon which the Japanese religio-aesthetic tradition rests.

Kū

The other central idea, both expressive of Northrop's formulation and foundational for a religio-aesthetic tradition in Japan, is *kū* ("emptiness," cf., *mu*, "nothingness"). This term is crucial to normative forms of Mahayana Buddhism that existed in Japan as early as the sixth century and developed well into the fourteenth century, when Zen Buddhism became important. Within a normative Buddhism, the term grows out of early Indian Buddhist ideals of the importance of realizing (directly experiencing, thereby "knowing") the mutually conditioned character of all things (*pratīya samutpāda*). This realization, together with the doctrinal expression of it, is the Truth (*dhamma, dharma*) for early Theravada Buddhism, and is called in Indian Mahayana Buddhism the realization of emptiness (*śūnyatā*). In both Theravada and Mahayana, however, it is described as a "middle way"—indeed, a way in between other ways. As the Buddha himself announced very early on:

> "Things exist": this, Kaccāyana, is one dead end. "Things exist not:" this, Kaccāyana, is the other dead end. Not approaching either of these dead ends the Truth-finder teaches *dhamma* by the mean: conditioned by ignorance are the constructions; conditioned by the constructions is consciousness; and on through the whole of the dependently arising elements of our world.[8]

Expressing this in another way the Buddha says that all questions about whether this is or this is not are not rightly put. Rather, he advises, awaken to the radically conditioned, desubstantialized, and "empty" character of things; and abandon all refuge in subject/object mental attachments. Only then can one "thoroughly know and see, as it were, the universe face to face."

In much of Mahayana this realization is called the realization of emptiness and is tantamount to enlightenment (*bodhi*) and true liberation (*nirvana*). Here, too, at least in one major sector, it is a "middle way" (*madhyamaka*) between subject/object modes of knowing that posit either is or is not, this or that, and a world of substantialized things. In this realization of in-between, things are emptied of their separate thingness. They are no-thing, or "nothingness" (*mu*), and are empty of separate existence. In this realization, the subject/object (or dualistic) world is collapsed in nondual experience. In this realization there is liberation and freedom from ego-consciousness and dualistic attachment.

Such an emptiness-realization bears no *necessary* relationship to "aesthetic," except, perhaps, as aesthetic refers to direct, unitive experience. Normatively and radically understood, it cuts through and across all particular forms of experience. As such, it is not quite the same as *ma*, nor is it quite appropriate to relate it to Northrop's aesthetic apprehension. However, while there may be no necessary relationship to aesthetic, certainly and at least in the hands of many Japanese, emptiness-realization became closely associated with a religio-aesthetic apprehension of the world in which both aesthetic experience as unitive, immediate, intuitive experience, and aesthetic experience as sensitivity to the beauty and wonder of things, was a primary means for being in touch with the deeper dimensions of Reality. This process culminated in developments within the Zen Buddhism of medieval Japan, and in the influences that Zen had on the artistic traditions of time.

Emptiness-realization (*kū*) became particularly associated with a tradition of immediate, aesthetic apprehension in the tranquil stillness of nature—a *ma* sensitivity now combined with Buddhist ideals of detachment and monastic seclusion. For many Japanese the realization of emptiness was the overcoming of ego and subject/object consciousness amidst the religio-aesthetic surroundings of nature. Not unlike *ma*, *kū* indicated a mode of experience that apprehended the undifferentiated aesthetic continuum in, through, and between the differentiated aesthetic continuum. Not unlike *ma*, *kū* also could not be separated from an affirmation of nature as a religio-aesthetic paradise of deep spiritual and aesthetic significance. In such a context, *kū* carried both religious and aesthetic meaning.

Examples of this more Buddhist oriented religio-aesthetic sensitivity are found throughout Japanese culture.[9] One particularly important and early example is to be seen in the twelfth-century monk-poet Saigyō. The religio-aesthetic ideal he strived for entailed the ideal of detachment from civilization and ego-consciousness, and that of becoming empty amidst nature. Out of such experience comes the best of his poetic creativity. The word that captures both the poetry's key stylistic feature and the nature of the experience out of which it comes is *sabi* ("loneliness")—a term that subsequently became a primary religio-aesthetic category in the Japanese tradition and pointed to a mode of apprehension in and through which the phenomenal world (of nature) is absolutely valorized and experienced in detached, impersonal, tranquil solitariness (or "loneliness"). It is emptiness-experience aesthetically appropriated within a tradition of nature as religio-aesthetic paradise. It is exemplary of what Ienaga Saburo has referred to in Japan as the "salvation provided by nature"; a salvation more inherently Japanese and more pervasive in Japan than the salvation provided by the religions themselves.[10] It is, as Shūichi Kato has said of the closely related term *wabi*, "none other than the aesthetic, sensuous expression of an awareness of the void."[11]

Sabi, like *wabi*, names and expresses the experience of emptying or collapsing subject/object consciousness amidst the de-

tached, aesthetic surroundings of nature. It is Buddhist emptiness-experience conditioned by a *ma* sensitivity to the undifferentiated, aesthetic continuum as manifested in, through, and
between the differentiated, aesthetic, continuum called nature
(and art). *Kū*, therefore, adds depth and breadth to a religio-
aesthetic tradition already highly sensitive to the immediacy of
lived experience in an aesthetic context as religious and salvific.
This leads Kurokawa to say, for example, *"en, kū,* and *ma* are all
key words which express the intervening territory between
spaces—temporal, physical, or spiritual—and they thus all share
the 'gray' quality of Japanese culture."[12]

This gray culture, which would certainly include a *sabi* and *wabi*
sensitivity and aesthetic style, permeates Japanese aesthetic principles, artistic forms, and many of the religions of Japan. Aesthetically or artistically, it might be best expressed as the attempt to
capture a fleeting white eternity (an empty or in-between moment) amidst the black of phenomenal, differentiated existence.
The great landscape paintings of China and Japan often suggest a
fleeting, tranquil moment in nature caught against the background of open space. The great poetic tradition of Japan suggests the importance of capturing the flow of immediate experience—with plenty of space in between the words for formless
Reality to shine through. The tradition of drama also shows this,
as the following comment by the great fifteenth-century Nō master Zeami Motokiyo indicates:

> Sometimes spectators of the Nō say, "The moments of 'no-ac-
> tion' are the most enjoyable." This is an art which the actor
> keeps secret. Dancing and singing, movements and the different
> types of miming are all acts performed by the body. Moments
> of "no-action" occur in between. When we examine why such
> moments without actions are enjoyable, we find it is due to the
> underlying spiritual strength of the actor which unremittingly
> holds the attention. . . . The actions before and after an inter-
> val of "no-action" must be linked by entering the state of mind-
> lessness [*mushin*] in which one conceals even from oneself one's
> intent. . . . The mind [of no-mind, or *mushin*] must be made
> the strings which hold together all the powers of the art.[13]

The moments of no-action are empty and still with a pregnant
fullness that bespeaks the deepest Reality. It is spiritual presence

that shines through, whether "minute particles of *kami* filling that *ma*" or "the aesthetic, sensuous expression of the Void."

Both *ma* and *kū*, therefore, are foundational modes of experience for a religio-aesthetic tradition, and both carry religious and aesthetic meaning. They are *not* everywhere understood or expressed in exactly the same way, nor are they everywhere manifested in similar aesthetic styles. However, in suggestive ways they both seem to echo the *Tao Te Ching:*

> Thirty spokes share one hub. Adapt the nothing therein to the purpose at hand, and you will have the use of the cart. Knead clay to make a vessel. Adapt the nothing therein to the purpose at hand, and you will have the use of the vessel. . . . Thus what we gain is something, yet it is by virtue of Nothing that this can be put to use.[14]

Art as Ritual Process

A rather different way to come at the foundations of a religio-aesthetic tradition in Japan is to consider the important relationship between art and religious ritual, and/or between artistic action and ritual action. Such a consideration involves both a concern for various art forms as either grounded in or closely related to ritual practices in the religions of Japan, and a concern for the nature of artistic discipline and creativity as itself a form of "ritual" practice. (Here, "ritual" is understood rather broadly as any specific actions that function religiously to make connection with that which someone considers transcendent, holy, sacred, or Real, and as that which transforms life in some significant way. Ritual is thus any particular action in which the religious dimension or character of experience is heightened.)

Ritual Art

The classic and paradigmatic example of art as related to religious ritual is found in one of the central myth sequences of ancient Japan. In this story, the great sun goddess, Amaterasu, has withdrawn into a cave after being frightened by certain taboo actions of her brother, Susanowo. As a result, darkness, death, and destruction reign, and the myriad gods of heaven gather to establish a plan for enticing her out of the cave. The plan of action chosen entails an elaborate gathering of sacred symbols and offerings (traditionally central to Shinto), the chanting of liturgical prayers, and the performance of a ritual dance by the heavenly shamaness Uzume. As the ancient myth describes it:

> Ame-no-Uzume-no-Mikoto bound up her sleeves with a cord of the heavenly *pi-kage* vine, tied around her head a headband of the heavenly *ma-saki* vine, bound together bundles of *sasa* leaves to hold in her hands, and overturning a bucket before the heavenly rock-cave door, stamped resoundingly upon it. Then she became divinely possessed, exposed her breasts, and pushed her skirtband down to her genitals.[15]

The immediate result of this rather singuar performance is said to have been laughter. Amaterasu, hearing this laughter with some curiosity, opened the rock-cave door to look out. As she did, the other gods enticed her out with further actions until light, life, and order were restored.

This is more than a quaint story. In one stroke it suggests very broadly the historic origins of much of human artistic endeavor in ritual and shamanistic practices, while more specifically for Japan it suggests a ritual art in early Shinto and folk-religious practices that has become a paradigmatic model for many of the traditional arts. It indicates, moreover, the vocation of the shaman in any culture as one who becomes a special vehicle for divine or sacred power and "knowledge," and acts this out in a variety of the artistic modes. Visual, literary, and performing arts are the stock and trade of the shaman. In *this* case, the shamaness is a dancer and the paradigmatic model for the performing arts of Japan. She is the one who takes on sacred power, and, through ritual art, dispels evil and fosters the transformation and renewal of life. To this day, the sacred music and dance of Shinto (*kagura*) "remembers" this mythic model, even though history has interceded to change the particular character and function of it. To this day, as well, other performing arts of especially traditional Japan somehow "remember" their historic roots in religious ritual and are even used on festival occasions as entertainment for gods and men.

These brief comments are intended to suggest the idea that much of the Japanese aesthetic sensitivity and artistic tradition is at least grounded in—if not continuingly related to—religious ritual of a more indigenous sort. Both Shinto and a broader folk religion of ancient Japan fostered the development of an artistic tradition that only later became separate or distinct from its religious roots. Even then, however, it tended to "remember" those roots and thereby contribute to a religio-aesthetic tradition in which art carried religious meaning.

Buddhism, however, also contributed to this general sense of artistic form serving distinctly religious and ritual purposes.[16] Buddhist iconography, painting, architecture, and music have all been important aspects of the arts of Japan, and most of these have served primarily religious functions in their original settings. For the early Japanese, for example, Buddhist statuary embodied rather directly and literally the sacred power ascribed to particular Buddhas or bodhisattvas enshrined in temples. Much of popular Buddhism still feels this way, and Buddha images remain religiously powerful for many.

In the more normative tradition of orthodox, sectarian Buddhism, however, the arts have also served important religious functions. All the way from the rich iconic/symbolic art of an esoteric Shingon Buddhism to the more "economic" iconoclastic/nonsymbolic art of Zen Buddhism, visual and performing arts have played a central role. A classic statement from the former suggesting the ritual centrality of art is given by the great ninth-century Shingon master Kūkai:

> The Dharma is beyond speech, but without speech it cannot be revealed. Suchness transcends forms, but without depending on forms it cannot be realized. Though one may at times err by taking the finger pointing at the moon to be the moon itself, the Buddha's teachings are indeed the treasures which help pacify the nation and bring benefit to people.
>
> Since the Esoteric Buddhist teachings are so profound as to defy expression in writing, they are revealed through the medium of painting to those who are yet to be enlightened. The various postures and *mudras* (depicted in *mandalas*) are products of the great compassion of the Buddha; the sight of them may well enable one to attain Buddhahood. The secrets of the sutras and commentaries are for the most part depicted in the paintings, and all the essentials of the Esoteric Buddhist doctrines are, in reality, set forth therein.[17]

As with painting, however, so also with sculpture, architecture, and music—all may serve important religious functions in the practice of Shingon, for here is a tradition that realizes the essentially formless nature of Reality, but also realizes the importance of form in the process of realizing this deeper Reality. To use Northrop's categories again, this is a tradition that emphasizes the importance of the differentiated continuum (here, art and symbol) as crucial "fingers" pointing to the moon of enlightenment—that is, to the undifferentiated continuum. Shingon is the paradigmatic case in Japan for a Buddhism that holds ritual art and religious art in central focus.

At the other end of at least one Buddhist spectrum, however, is Zen. Ostensibly, and in a good share of its tradition, Zen has suggested that one must be wary of fingers pointing to the moon lest the fingers be mistaken for the moon. This tradition in Japan has been suspicious of iconic and symbolic forms, as it has also been of doctrinal or verbal formulations of the Truth. Kukai and Shingon see the risk but are willing to take it; much of Zen is not. The result is a tradition that tends to break with the orthodox iconographic tradition, especially in statuary and painting.

However, this does not mean that Zen forsakes a ritual art, or an art that stands central to its expression, if not to its practice. A visit to any Zen temple or a quick look through a standard book on Zen's relation to the arts will immediately show otherwise. Zen's iconoclastic tradition has been aimed at the symbolic expression of Buddhist teachings and Buddhist realization; it has not been aimed at art per se. Zen's aesthetic sensitivity and artistic interest has simply found outlet in other ways and other artistic styles—particularly calligraphy, landscape painting, poetry, gardens, and the tea ceremony. For the most part, these art forms have not necessarily been central to the practice, as has been the case for Shingon, but have rather been important nonsymbolic or noniconic expressions of emptiness-realization. The emphasis in Zen art is on the direct and immediate expression or manifestation of Buddha-mind, not on the mediated meaning of a more symbolic art. Zen's story of its own origin in the teachings of the Buddha, after all, suggests precisely this. The essential transmission of the Truth from the Buddha to his main disciple is *not* traced through any particular scripture (as with other Buddhist sects), but through a nonverbal act of holding up a flower and smiling. With this act, Buddha's discipline achieved his own awakening, and the transmission took place. The Zen tradition of China and Japan has been relatively faithful to the spirit of this story; direct and immediate expression better manifests and transmits direct and immediate experience than does symbolic expression. Let the moon shine directly; do not risk obscuring it with fingers.

The concept of *kū* is also relevant here. Insofar as Zen fostered and accepted an understanding of emptiness-experience as closely related to aesthetic experience, the relation of Zen to the arts is drawn even more tightly. The arts became for Zen not only an appropriate expression but, in effect, a "natural" one. Aesthetic and artistic expression became the natural expression of a tradition that found the aesthetic central to the nature of its highest goals and to the atmosphere and environments of its practice. This rather Japanized, aestheticized understanding of *kū* is not necessarily the normative Buddhist understanding, but it prevailed in much of Zen nonetheless. The result is a tradition that was not only a patron of the arts, but produced them out of its own self-understanding and its own religious experience. In that sense, its art has been "ritual" art and inextricably religious. It is ritual not so much in the sense of particular practices designed to further the religious progress, but expressions that (ideally) directly manifest emptiness-realization. As such, Zen also contributes to a larger religio-aesthetic tradition in which artistic form is inextricably bound up with aesthetic/artistic form.

The Artistic "Ways"

Still another major factor in understanding the religio-aesthetic tradition in Japan is the important and recurring theme of artistic pursuits as "Ways" (*dō, michi*) of ultimate (or religious) significance. While the arts as Ways can sometimes merely refer to the tradition of a particular artistic form and practice, ideally and often the Japanese arts took seriously the spiritual or religious implications of the Way as it functions not only in Japan but also in China, where it was central (as Tao) to a whole Chinese religious understanding. In its ideal context in Japan, therefore,

> The *dō* in the field of art is a way of leading to spiritual en-
> lightenment through art; the *dō* consist here in making an art
> a means by which to achieve enlightenment as its ultimate goal.
> In the artistic *dō* . . . particular emphasis is laid on the pro-
> cess, the way, by which one goes toward the goal. To every stage
> of the way a certain spiritual state corresponds, and at every
> stage the artist tries to get into communion with the quintess-
> ence of art through the corresponding spiritual state, and make
> himself bloom in the art.[18]

This religio-aesthetic self-understanding in the arts arose particularly with the Buddhist-inspired poets of the eleventh and
twelfth centuries, but might even be traced (in part) back to a
more indigenous tradition of the craftsman as priest.

Later, however, and under the influence of Zen as well as the
Chinese traditions of landscape painting and calligraphy, the understanding of the arts as Ways both broadened and deepened—
eventually including all the visual and performing arts, and extending into both the martial arts and many of the crafts as well.
In many of these arts, the perfection of technique and form is
simply the beginning of a deeper art. The purpose is to go beyond
technique and form in disciplining body, mind, and spirit for a
deeper creativity—one which is both spiritually and aesthetically
based.[19]

Art is thus a kind of spiritual exercise, and its vocation a kind
of spiritual journey. Like many other spiritual practices in Japan,
it is considered a *shugyō*, or ascetic discipline in which concentrated practice seeks to press through to a deeper spiritual fulfillment. Much of what runs through all these arts—at least in their
religio-aesthetic ideals—is closely related both religiously and
historically to a *ma* and/or a *kū* religio-aesthetic sensitivity, which
underlie the ideals of these arts—an in-between sensitivity that
features unitive, direct experience understood both religiously and
aesthetically, and a sensitivity closely related to nature as a religio-aesthetic paradise.

Such a sensitivity, experience, or "mind" is called by Bashō,
for example, a "narrow" or "slender" mind (*hosomi*). Only a slender mind can slip in between the thingness of things, or in between the subject and its objects. As Bashō says, "When you are
composing a verse . . . let there not be a hair's breadth separat-

ing your mind from what you write. Quickly say what is in your mind; never hesitate at that moment."[20] "To 'learn' [in this art] means to submerge oneself within the object, to perceive its delicate life and feel its feeling, out of which a poem forms itself."[21]

Art as a religious Way, however, is only another way to discuss the fundamental issue of a religio-aesthetic tradition in Japan. Whether by *ma* or *kū* sensitivity, or by ritual process, these and other Japanese arts are often grounded in religio-aesthetic ideals, forms, and experiences. As suggested at the beginning of this essay, most often and most uniquely this involves an art that immediately manifests in form a kind of awareness that functions beyond subject/object awareness: namely, an "in-between" and/or "no-thing" experience rich with the flowing continuum of the immediate aesthetic awareness.

NOTES

1. F. S. C. Northrop, *The Meeting of East and West* (New York: Macmillan, 1946), pp. 315–58, 394–404.

2. Arata Isozaki, in *Ma: Space-Time in Japan* (New York: Cooper-Hewitt Museum, ca. 1979), pp. 36, 17.

3. A. O. Matsunaga, "The Land of Natural Affirmation: Pre-Buddhist Japan," *Monumenta Nipponica* 21, no. 1–2 (1966), pp. 203–09.

4. Seigow Matsuoka, in *Ma: Space-Time in Japan*, p. 56.

5. Arata Isozaki, in ibid., p. 47.

6. Kisho Kurokawa, "A Culture of Grays," *The I-Ro-Ha of Japan*, ed. Tsune Sesoko (Tokyo: Cosmo Public Relations Corp., 1979), pp. 5f.

7. Ibid., p. 16.

8. Translated in Lucien Stryk, ed., *World of the Buddha* (Garden City: Doubleday, 1968), p. 184.

9. See, e.g., Richard B. Pilgrim, *Buddhism and the Arts of Japan* (Chambersburg, PA: Anima Pub., 1981).

10. See Ienaga as discussed in William La Fleur, "Saigyō and the Buddhist Value of Nature," *History of Religions* 13, no. 3 (1974), pp. 232f.

11. Shūichi Kato, *Form, Style, Tradition* (Berkeley: University of California Press, 1971), p. 154.

12. Kisho Kurokawa, p. 10.

13. Translated in William DeBary, ed., *Sources of Japanese Tradition* (New York: Columbia University Press, 1958), vol. 1, pp. 285f.

14. Translated in D. C. Lau, *Lao Tzu: Tao Te Ching* (Baltimore: Penguin Books, 1963), p. 67.

15. Translated in Donald Philippi, *Kojiki* (Tokyo: University of Tokyo Press, 1968), p. 84.

16. See note 9.

17. Translated in Yoshihito Hakeda, *Kukai: Major Works* (New York: Columbia University Press, 1972), pp. 145f.

18. Toyo Izutsu, "Far Eastern Existentialism: Haiku and the Man of Wabi," *Philosophical Forum* 4, no. 2 (1973), pp. 43f.

19. Cf. note 9, and that author's "The Artistic Way and the Religio-Aesthetic Tradition in Japan," *Philosophy East and West* 27, no. 3 (1977), pp. 285–305.

20. Translated in Makoto Ueda, *Literary and Art Theories in Japan* (Cleveland: The Press of Western Reserve University, 1967), p. 159.

21. Translated in Makoto Ueda, *Zeami, Basho, Yeats and Pound* (The Hague: Mouton and Co., 1965) p. 38.

12

Judaism and Art

DAVID ALTSHULER AND
LINDA ALTSHULER

The Torah (Pentateuch) of the Hebrew Bible presents a curious paradox in describing God's attitude toward art and Judaism. On the one hand, the second commandment of the Decalogue declares,

> You shall have no other gods to set against me. You shall not make a carved image for yourself nor the likeness of anything in the heavens above, or on the earth below, or in the waters under the earth. You shall not bow down to them or worship them; for I, the Eternal your God, am a jealous God. . . ." (Exod. 20:3–5)

On the other hand, subsequent passages describe in detail an elaborate "tent of the presence," which the Israelites are to build as a cultic center for God's worship. God specifically designates Bezalel as the chief artisan for this project, saying, "I have filled him with divine spirit, making him skilful and ingenious, expert in every craft, and a master of design . . . for workmanship of every kind" (Exod. 31:3–5). Furthermore, the very ark of the covenant housed in the tent is covered, at God's command, by a golden cover flanked by two winged cherubim (Exod. 25:18–22, 37:6–9).

The biblical description of Solomon's temple shows it to have been elaborately decorated with figurative images (1 Kgs. 7:27–37, 8:6–7), and we may assume that such was the case as well when the temple was rebuilt after the Babylonian exile (Ezra 3:1–6:15).[1] Besides this self-contradictory set of written information, little evidence regarding the relations between art and Judaism has survived from the biblical era (down to the destruction of the Second Temple, in 70 c.e.).

Until this century, most writers have viewed the tent of the presence and the two temples as exceptions to the general rule that Jews, throughout their long history, shunned artistic endeavors out of respect for the Decalogue.[2] Thus Immanuel Benzinger, writing in 1903 in the authoritative *Jewish Encyclopedia*, opined:

> Such a command as that of the Decalogue . . . would have been impossible to a nation possessed of such artistic gifts as the Greeks, and was carried to its ultimate consequences—as today in Islam—only because the people lacked artistic inclination with its creative power and formative imagination.[3]

Thanks to many new discoveries and methodological insights of the past eight decades, Benzinger's view has given way to a new scholarly consensus, as expressed by Cecil Roth in the *Encyclopedia Judaica:*

> The meticulous obedience or relative neglect of the apparent biblical prohibition of representational art seems in fact to have been conditioned by external circumstances, and in two directions—revulsion or attraction. . . . Until the 19th century, the Jewish attitude toward art was in fact not negative, but ambivalent.[4]

Indeed, scholarship in this century has proven again and again that the history of Judaism is intertwined with the history of Jewish art; the study of each has been enriched by and is now inseparable from the study of the other.

Late Antiquity

The period from the rise of Christianity until the birth of Islam (in the seventh century) is often regarded as the classical age in the development of Judaism. It was during this time that Jews had to cope with the destruction of their state, the loss of their temple and its priestly cult, and the dispersion of their nation to hundreds of communities within the Roman Empire. These centuries saw Jews establish the home and the synagogue as centers for the ritual life of Judaism, and under the leadership of rabbinic sages the most important postbiblical documents of Jewish law, lore, and liturgy (Mishna, Talmud, Midrash, and Siddur) were compiled.

At this crucial juncture in Jewish history, Jews sought to maintain their special identity in a world very much unified by the cultural influence of Hellenism. Until very recently, scholars understood rabbinic Judaism mostly as a protest against the norms of Hellenistic universalism, particularly when the question of religious art arose. After all, Christians from the apostle Paul onward seemed more successful in synthesizing Judaism and Hellenism, and ultimately in winning the allegiance of Rome, than did Jews, whose two failed revolts against the empire led to disenfranchisement and deprivation.[5]

Three dramatic archaeological discoveries in the 1930s served ultimately to shatter scholarly consensus about rabbinic Judaism. In 1930, kibbutzniks digging irrigation trenches discovered the remains of a sixth-century synagogue from the ancient community of Bet Alpha. Much to the surprise of all, the synagogue floor was adorned with elaborate mosaic panels, one of which portrayed the zodiac complete with human and animal representations of the months and seasons, and with a figure like the Greek god Helios riding a chariot at the center. Just two years later, excavators unearthed a third-century synagogue in Dura Europos (now in Iraq), and there they found massive wall frescoes of biblical scenes, again with human forms that clearly are of Hellenistic style. Finally, in 1936 archaeologists explored third- and fourth-century burial caves at the Bet Shearim site in the Galilee, and amidst epitaphs of some of the most important ancient rabbis they found sarcophagi and walls decorated with Hellenistic symbols of the afterlife and, again, with human and animal forms.

Suddenly, assumptions about Judaic iconoclasm had to be revised, if not discarded altogether. The Bet Alpha mosaics—signed by Jewish artists—depict not only a zodiac, but also the hand of God reaching down to Abraham! In Dura, naked Egyptian princesses are portrayed fetching the infant Moses from the bulrushes, just a few feet away from the niche reserved for scrolls of the Torah! Such unprecedented and unpredicted discoveries led to fruitful scholarly analysis that has considerably revised previous views of rabbinic Judaism and, therefore, of the general relations between Judaism and Hellenism.

First of all, Judaism in its classical era now seems to have been far more pluralistic than was previously imagined. Norms regarding idolatrous imagery in one community, for example, may not have been shared by others. Second, far more widely and deeply than was previously thought, Jews must have shared in the Hellenistic cultural environment in which they lived. This conclusion has been fortified by new discoveries of mystical manuscripts and by careful reexamination of classical rabbinic texts. Finally, it is clear that for many Jews the worlds of religion and art were very much contiguous in late antiquity. Even in the synagogues in which they worshiped and in the chambers in which they were buried, artistic expression was an important vehicle for symbolic communication and the interpretation of history and destiny.[6]

The Middle Ages

Just as the synagogue and Jewish burial art of late antiquity reflects the stylistic canons of the Hellenized world in which the Jews lived, so, too, did Jews of the Middle Ages adapt the cultural tastes of their neighbors. Jewish art, like Jewish clothing, cuisine, and music, came to be as diverse as the myriad of environs in which Jewish communities were established. From the seventh to the eighteenth century, nearly the whole of world Jewry was divided into two main cultural orbits, living in countries dominated either by Christianity or by Islam. The former group, centered in Europe, are called Ashkenazim (from the Hebrew word for Germany); the latter, centered in the Middle East and North Africa, are called Sefardim (from the Hebrew word for Spain).

There is, then, no Jewish style per se. Rather, Jewish art from Italy will generally look more like contemporary Christian examples from that country than like work produced in the same period by the Jews of Morocco. Certain Jewish motifs do, of course, recur—lions of Judah, biblical characters or objects (e.g., the ancient temple or the Decalogue tablets), crowns (according to rabbinic formulation, representing the crowns of the Davidic monarchy, the priesthood, learning, and a good name). The menorah (now the symbol of the state of Israel) and the "Jewish star"[7] are common. However, even these symbols bear the distinctive styles of their provenance.

Jewish art of the Middle Ages is distinguished not so much by style or even by symbols, but by function. In religious documents, ceremonial objects, and synagogue architecture and decoration, the purpose of art is constant, namely, "beautification of the commandments." This expression signifies that art is not employed or enjoyed for its own sake, nor certainly as an object of worship. Rather, art enhances fulfillment of God's revelatory instructions to Israel, the Jewish people, bringing meaning and emotion to religious observance.

Unquestionably, the most distinctive variety of Jewish art is connected with scribal traditions.[8] Since ancient times, the Torah scroll has been hand-lettered on parchment; while never decorated or illuminated, this sacred text is often a work of great beauty, produced with care and treasured more than any other community possession. Other manuscripts customarily were illuminated and decorated. For example, the Passover Haggadah (ritual narrative)[9] and Purim Megillah (scroll of Esther)[10] often bore illustrations that helped to teach and celebrate their textual narratives. Perhaps most diverse and attractive of all Hebrew documents are Ketubot (Jewish marriage contracts),[11] which may include wedding scenes, flora and fauna, family coats of arms, and, most commonly, scenes of Jerusalem.

In addition to manuscripts, a considerable number of other ritual items developed that Jewish artisans sought to beautify in media from embroidery[12] to metalwork, paper-cuts to ceramics. Symbols of the Jewish home include the mezuzah (a doorpost amulet)[13] and mizraḥ (a plaque indicating direction of Jerusalem); ceremonial objects associated with daily worship are the tallit (prayer shawl) and tefillin (phylacteries). In synagogues, the most elaborate artistic efforts would be focused on the garments and the fine metal decorations often covering the Torah scrolls, and on the ark that housed them.[14] The weekly Sabbath and seasonal holy days, which commemorate both natural and historical events, all are associated with ritual objects. Perhaps the best-known and most commonly produced of these are lamps, wine cups, and spice containers, since the symbols of light, wine, and sweet fragrances are so often expressive of the holy. Finally, special moments in the lives of individuals also are ritualized in Jewish community observance. Swaddling clothes may be fashioned into a binder (wimpel) for a Torah scroll, while a beautiful chair in the synagogue might be reserved for the circumcision ceremony. The marriage canopy (ḥuppah) and ceremonial ring would be as beautiful as the community could afford, and even memorial lamps for the dead and burial society memorabilia inspired Jewish artisans in certain periods. In sum, Judaic worship extends to a myriad of home and synagogue occasions, and no such moment lacks implements whose artistic character may enrich piety.[15]

To this shorthand account of medieval Jewish manuscript and ceremonial art must be added, finally, mention of synagogue architecture.[16] Here, too, Jews adapted local styles, whether Roman basilicas, single- or double-nave Gothic and Romanesque models, domed wooden structures in seventeenth- and eighteenth-century Poland, or even a pagoda built in 1652 in Kai Feng Fu, China. Three features, however, were distinctive: the ark for Torah scrolls, a platform from which the scrolls were read, and a separate section—often a balcony—for women worshipers. The design of synagogues, moreover, commonly was limited by the fact that ordinances required them to be lower than the local churches. Since Jewish tradition requires that synagogues reach upward toward the heavens, floors often were sunk considerably below ground level. To avoid offending political and ecclesiastical authorities, elaborate decoration generally was restricted to interiors.

The scope of Jewish art in the Middle Ages thus was very broad. Unfortunately, however, relatively little of it survived the long centuries of discrimination and persecution that Jews endured. (The oldest synagogue—built in the eleventh or twelfth century—extant in modern times was destroyed by the Nazis.) Precious few examples of pre-sixteenth-century ceremonial objects or illuminated manuscripts have survived. Yet the heritage of art in Judaism persisted, until finally the eighteenth century brought at least a temporary improvement in the social and political circumstances of Jews in the West.

Modern Times

Three interrelated factors greatly limited access of Jews to artistic training in the Middle Ages. First, much European artwork was devoted to and supported by ecclesiastical institutions. Second, Christian intolerance did not allow many Jewish artists to enter guilds beyond the ghetto walls.[17] Finally, many Jewish communities were quite poor, and so the arts, like other endeavors, could not receive adequate funding. As a result, it was not until the so-called emancipation of the eighteenth century that Jewish artists truly could enter the modern world; therefore Jewish art of the Middle Ages often has more the quality of folk art than of fine art.

Since the French Revolution, the improved circumstances of Jewish life have radically altered both the scope and the aesthetic level of Jewish artistic expression. On the one hand, medieval traditions of manuscript illumination (with increasing emphasis on printed books), fashioning of ritual objects, and architectural designs of synagogues have blossomed in contemporary styles. However, many Jewish artists, now free to work independently of Jewish community sponsorship, have rapidly gained prominence in the larger modern-art arena. Some, like Amedeo Modigliani, Camille Pissarro, and Chaim Soutine, earned worldwide recognition for artwork that is devoid of Jewish content. Others, most notably Marc Chagall, treated both Jewish and more general themes.

Indeed, the advent of modernity seriously complicated attempts to isolate or define the nature of Jewish art.[18] This problem applies particularly to the work of Israeli artists, since their national and religious identities diverge as often as they overlap.[19] Yet both in Israel and in the Diaspora, the twentieth century has witnessed a dramatic new interest in the collection and analysis of Jewish art.[20]

Not until the end of the nineteenth century were the first Jewish museums founded in such European cities as Vienna, Hamburg, and Frankfurt; today such institutions are to be found in almost every major center of Jewish population. In addition to the important archaeological discoveries mentioned above, academic attention during this period has focused on a wealth of beautiful manuscripts that, until their recent publication, were tucked away in European libraries and general museums.[21] Thus, historians have benefited from the rediscovery of Jewish art, even as the conservation and exhibition of the remnants of this heritage have been taken up by museums and private collectors.

The academic study of Jewish art and its relation to the history of Judaism now is pursued earnestly in the United States, Israel, and Europe. Artwork serves as important evidence for the ethnographic analysis of Jewish communities that flourished briefly, only to disappear or be destroyed. Scholars of Christian and Islamic art now may explore comparative and contrasting tendencies in Jewish art from contemporary settings. Most crucially, though, a world of Jewish expression that reaches back to antiquity and to virtually every corner of the civilized world now has reemerged.[22]

NOTES

1. Yigael Yadin, ed., *The Temple Scroll (Hebrew Edition)* (Jerusalem: Society for the Exploration of Eretz Yisrael and its Antiquities, 1977), pp. 137–54, discusses the problem of describing the Second Temple in light of the newly published Temple Scroll of Qumran and other ancient texts. See also Joseph Gutmann, *The Temple of Solomon: Archaeological Fact and Medieval Tradition in Christian, Islamic and Jewish Art* (Missoula, MT: Scholars Press, 1976).

2. E.g., Solomon J. Solomon, "Art and Judaism," *The Jewish Quarterly Review* 13 (1901).

3. *The Jewish Encyclopedia*, s.v., "Art among the Ancient Hebrews."

4. *Encyclopedia Judaica*, s.v., "Art."

5. An early classic statement is Norman Bentwich, *Hellenism* (Philadelphia: The Jewish Publication Society of America, 1919). Important general revisions include Moses Hadas, *Hellenistic Culture, Fusion and Diffusion* (New York: Oxford University Press, 1959); Viktor Tcherikover, *Hellenistic Civilization and the Jews*, 2nd ed. (Philadelphia: Jewish Publication Society of America, 1961); Elias Bickerman, *From Ezra to the Last of the Maccabees* (New York: Schocken Books, 1962); and Martin Hengel, *Judaism and Hellenism* (Philadelphia: Fortress Press, 1981).

6. The most seminal and comprehensive work in this field is Erwin Goodenough, *Jewish Symbols in the Greco-Roman World*, 13 vols. (New York: Pantheon Books, 1953–68). See also Morton Smith, "The Image of God. . . ," *Bulletin of the John Rylands Library* 40, no. 2 (1958), pp. 473–512; Bernard Goldman, *The Sacred Portal* (Detroit: Wayne State University Press, 1966); Joseph Gutmann, *The Dura-Europos Synagogue, A Reevaluation 1932–1972* (Missoula, MT: Scholars Press, 1973); Benjamin Mazar et. al., *Beth She'arim*, 3 vols. (Jerusalem: Massada Press, Ltd., 1973–76); Jacob Neusner, *Early Rabbinic Judaism: Historical Studies in Religion, Literature and Art* (Leiden: E. J. Brill, 1975); and Herschel Shanks, *Judaism in Stone: The Archaeology of Ancient Synagogues* (New York: Harper & Row, 1979).

7. See *Encyclopedia Judaica*, s.v., "Magen David."

8. A good introduction is Bezalel Narkiss, *Hebrew Illuminated Manuscripts* (Jerusalem: Keter Publishing House, 1969). See also Joseph Gutmann, *Hebrew Manuscript Painting* (New York: George Braziller, 1978).

9. Late medieval and modern printed examples are surveyed in Josef Yerushalmi, *Haggadah and History* (Philadelphia: Jewish Publication Society of America, 1975).

10. See *Purim: The Face and the Mask* (New York: Yeshiva University Museum, 1979).

11. See David Davidovitch, *The Ketubah: Jewish Marriage Contracts* (Tel Aviv: E. Lewin-Epstein, 1979).

12. See *Fabric of Jewish Life* (New York: The Jewish Museum, 1977).

13. See Franz Landsberger, "The Origin of the Decorated Mezuzah." *Hebrew Union College Annual* 31 (1960), pp. 149–66.

14. See *Encyclopedia Judaica*, s.v., "Torah Ornaments."

15. On ritual objects, see, e.g., Joseph Gutmann, *Beauty in Holiness: Studies in Jewish Customs and Ceremonial Art* (New York: Ktav, 1970); Abram Kanof, *Jewish Ceremonial Art and Religious Observance* (New York: Harry N. Abrams, 1970); and David Altshuler, ed., *The Precious Legacy: Judaic Treasures from the Czechoslovak State Collections* (New York: Summit Books, 1983).

16. See Rachel Wischnitzer, *The Architecture of the European Synagogue* (Philadelphia: Jewish Publication Society of America, 1964), and Joseph Gutmann, *The Synagogue: Studies in Origins, Archaeology and Architecture* (New York: Ktav, 1975).

17. Cf. Mark Wischnitzer, *History of Jewish Crafts and Guilds*, (New York: J. David, 1965).

18. See, e.g., *Jewish Art: What Is It?* (New York: The National Council on Art in Jewish Life, n.d.)

19. The recent catalogue, "Artists of Israel: 1920–1980" (New York: The Jewish Museum, 1981) is a useful introductory text with a fine selected bibliography.

20. The standard reference is Leo A. Mayer, *Bibliography of Jewish Art* (Jerusalem: Magnes Press, 1969). Perhaps the most important recent development has been the founding of the *Journal of Jewish Art*, edited by Bezalel Narkiss (volumes 1–5 [1974–78] published in Chicago, by Spertus College; volumes 6ff., in Jerusalem, by the Center for Jewish Art of the Hebrew University).

21. See *Encyclopedia Judaica*, s.v., "Illuminated Manuscripts" and "Manuscripts, Hebrew."

22. Useful surveys include Cecil Roth, ed., *Jewish Art* (Greenwich, CT: New York Graphic Society, 1961), and Geoffrey Wigoder, ed., *Jewish Art and Civilization* (New York: Walker and Co., 1972).

13

An Islamic Perspective on Symbolism in the Arts: New Thoughts on Figural Representation

LOIS IBSEN AL FARUQI

Probably the most outstanding single feature by which the Islamic arts have been characterized is the rejection of figural representation. This essay will attempt to explain the reasons for that rejection and to identify and clarify the basic characteristics of Islamic art.

The tendency to abstraction has been prominent since the dawn of Islamic civilization in the seventh century c.e., and is attested to in the writings of Muslim authors, as well as in Orientalist descriptions and appraisals of the art of the Muslims. To be sure, there have been "exceptions to the rule"—in manuscript illustration, particularly in Persian, North Indian, and Ottoman Turkish art, and in animal and human figures occasionally found in works for private or domestic use. But such examples are few compared to abstract creations using geometric, calligraphic, or stylized floral motifs.[1] Even when figures of plants, animals, or humans have been used in Islamic art, they have been denaturalized and arranged in ways that make them appear more as elements of design than as representations of earthly and living creatures.

Many hypotheses have been suggested for this tendency to abstraction in Islamic art. These include the arguments that figural art is categorically forbidden by the Qur'ān[2] and the ḥadīth literature;[3] that it results from an inherent fear of idolatry on the part of the early Muslims;[4] that it is an effect of the influence of early converts to Islam from Judaism;[5] or that it was a negative reaction generated by the sense of inferiority which the early Muslims supposedly felt when they encountered Byzantine figural art.[6]

None of these hypotheses provides a true and satisfying explanation for the rejection of figural art in the wide historical and geographic expanse of Islam. None accounts for the breakthrough in aesthetic expression accomplished by the Muslim peoples. This breakthrough in the arts was too important, too novel, too creative to be a mere conformation to condemning injunctions, to the fear of idolatry, outside influences, or jealousy. This was not merely a negative reaction; it was a positive development of a whole new vocabulary of artistic materials organized under new methods of stylistic and structural combination.

We must therefore try to explain this phenomenon in a more satisfying way. Let us step back from the problem, first of all, and ask ourselves some important questions. What does a work of art do? How does it fulfill its function?

Functions of the Work of Art

Over the centuries, philosophers, aestheticians, psychologists, art historians, critics, and artists have made many attempts to understand art and its role in human life and thought. There seems to be little disagreement that the arts can be defined as symbolic statements of ideas, using sensory stimulus to make their presentation. But there has been wide disagreement on the kind of statements that the arts embody, on the kind of truth they convey. The varied theories of the meaning of art seem to fall within three general categories: (1) "humanistic" theories, which deem art to be a statement about humanity or some aspect of human life, (2) "naturalistic" theories, which describe artistic meaning as an intuition of truth about the natural world, and (3) "transcendent" theories, which describe art as a means of conveying an intuition about divinity.

1. One important example of the humanistic view is the theory of Friedrich Schiller, which we shall call "dichotomist." Schiller describes beauty in art as achieved through an oscillation between two antagonistic human functions: the "sensuous impulse" and the "formal impulse."[7] These two impulses compete within man, ever seeking to achieve a balance, but never reaching a last-

ing stability or equilibrium. Neither is wholly good or wholly bad. Both are, in fact, necessary and desirable for the competitive situation, in which neither sensuousness nor rationality should overpower its opposite. According to Schiller, artworks should present an aesthetic statement that reveals the importance of this balance between the two forces of human nature.

In the works of Susanne Langer,[8] we find a different kind of a humanistic art theory, the "subjective" view. As in the dichotomist theory of Schiller, humanity and man are seen here as the "measure of all things." Art is described by Langer as comprising forms symbolic of human feelings. This emphasis on the subjective human emotions accords well with post-Romantic expressionist thought (e.g., Croce, Cassirer, and their followers), and has indeed been described as an "expression" theory of art.[9]

Other types of humanistic meaning-in-art theories could be cited. All of them argue that humanity contains the "seeds," the forms, the source of artistic meaning.[10]

2. Among the "naturalistic" theories, I have grouped those that treat nature or the natural world as the main focus and source of artistic symbolism. One group of writers of the naturalistic category—the "formalists"—believe that in nature (rather than in the human being, as in the humanistic theories) the artist and his culture find the universal forms that are represented in art. These forms are seen as governing life and the whole universe. To perceive these forms, whether consciously or unconsciously, and to represent them in aesthetically rendered structures is the task of the artist—painter, sculptor, author, dancer, or composer. "The formal relations within a work of art and among different works of art consist of an order for, and a metaphor of, the entire universe."[11] Nature impresses form upon itself in such a way, these writers maintain, that both organic and inorganic life can be characterized as objectifying symbols, as beautiful forms or designs. Art is thus emphatically nature-based and nature-rooted. By becoming a metaphor for the forms of the universe, the formalists maintain, the work of art helps man achieve a mental and spiritual adjustment to the mystery of his existential situation.[12]

Another aesthetic theory that falls within the naturalistic category is that of Plato, who regarded art as an imitation of nature or, in the case of music, of moral moods.[13] Nature, in turn, was in his view a concrete, though never perfect, instantiation of the realm of "ideas." Though these ideas, or ideal forms, exist outside of space and time, in a kind of transcendent realm, Plato's theory remained bound to the cultural environment of ancient Greece. As such, it is nature-based. The ideas themselves seem more projections of the natural world or idealizations of its phenomena than intuitions of an independent or self-realizing realm.

Also implied in Plato's writings, though not expressed specifically as an aesthetic theory, is the idea that, while certain arts are described and condemned as improper art, another kind is possible and desirable that incorporates symbolizations of ideals beyond the natural world. If this line of thought is pursued to its logical conclusions, art should carry a deeper significance, which would make it an embodiment of those principles of unity and harmony that exist beyond perceived reality.[14] Since Plato's works do not include a conscious theory of art's relation to transcendent principles, Platonic theory stands squarely within the naturalistic category.

3. The third category of theories explaining aesthetic significance or import are those which maintain that the chief function of a work of art lies in its ability to communicate a view or intuition of transcendence. Here again, art attempts to disclose an intuition of reality; but with transcendence theories, reality is not conceived as based in human existence or in nature. Instead, transcendence theories regard finite motifs and subject matter as subtly disclosing a view of a reality that reaches beyond the natural world. They are based on the idea that reality is governed by factors that are neither represented in, nor completely explainable by, nature and the human intellect.

Aestheticians in various cultures have expressed transcendence theories on aesthetics in ways that accord with their particular religio-cultural base. For Indian culture, there are many writers who have seen art as a way of disclosing and understanding the Hindu notion of the transcendent.[15] According to Paul Tillich, who speaks from a Christian context, art strives to communicate ideas about "ultimate meaning, the most profound apprehension of reality."[16]

The Islamic art materials themselves, as well as the basic ideology determining Islamic culture, preclude a humanistic or naturalistic understanding of Islamic art. However, Islamic art does seem peculiarly suited to a transcendence theory. According to the Muslims, every aspect of their culture must be seen as somehow determined by the uniquely Qur'ānic and Islamic monotheistic doctrine of *tawḥīd*. This doctrine regards Allah, or God, as a being of utterly transcendent nature, as the Creator Who has a hand in nature but Who is completely distinguishable from His creation. No facet or aspect of human existence or the natural world is properly identifiable with Him. Neither can He be pictured or represented in any way. This view of transcendence is found in the Qur'ān, in the *sunnah*, or "example," of the Prophet Muḥammad, as well as in the legal, literary, and scientific writings of every period of Islamic history. The Muslims have indeed been "obsessed" with *tawḥīd*, and have wished to bring every aspect of their existence into conformity with it.

It would seem likely then that a similar influence of *tawḥīd* is to be found in the Islamic arts. For the Muslim, the aesthetic realm, the beautiful, is that which directs attention to Allah. It is this permeating factor, then, of Islamic being—rather than scriptural or prophetic directives, Jewish influence, fear of idolatry, or jealousy of Byzantium—that has put the stamp of Islamicity on the Islamic arts and molded them into a recognizable unity. It is only through an Islamic transcendence theory of aesthetic meaning that we can explain the nature of Islamic art in general, and the rejection of figural representation in particular.

If Islamic thought maintains that God, or Allah, is so utterly non-nature as to preclude His representation, the absence of any visual form standing for God in this culture is to be expected. But this is a negative characteristic of Islamic art resulting from *tawḥīd*. It draws attention to that which is *not* in the art—i.e., the representation of God—but it fails to explain the positive dimensions of the effect of *tawḥīd*—i.e., to explain that which *is* in the art. The fact that God is not to be represented does not automatically and inevitably lead to the character of Islamic art as we know it. The Jewish people also proscribed the representation of God, but they did not produce a Judaic equivalent of Islamic art.

The Islamic work of art is a symbolic statement, as is all art; for it attempts to make a sensory representation of an important idea not evidenced to the senses. Yet Islamic art must make use of art symbolism in ways that conform to and enhance its particular message. Let us examine how this is done, first by defining the different levels of aesthetic symbolic meaning, and then by showing how Islamic art exemplifies those meanings.

Three Levels of Aesthetic-Symbolic Statement

There are three levels of symbolic statement, or of meaning, that can be evidenced in a work of art: (1) the explicit, (2) the literally symbolic, and (3) the implicit. A particular culture or a particular work may evidence a preponderant use of one, or it may utilize two or even all three levels. The explicit level of symbolism, as far as the visual arts are concerned, is that which depicts characters, objects, actions, scenes, and motifs, whether they appear in painting, sculpture, wood carving or ceramics. It includes the subject matter, or "surface content," of the work. These elements vary significantly from one culture to another, or even from one period to another within a single culture.

The literally symbolic content makes use of a particular figure, object, or scene to arouse in the mind of the initiated spectator a remembrance or an intuition of another object, figure, or an idea that is conventionally associated by that culture with the sensory image. Aesthetic symbolism of this type substitutes an abbreviated visual, aural, or kinetic "clue" for a much wider and deeper intellectual idea.

Both of these levels, the explicit and the literally symbolic, make up the materials which are generally included in the "iconography" of art. This branch of artistic knowledge is often described as embodying the "content" or "import" of art, as opposed to its "structure" or formal aspects.

The third type of aesthetic symbolism is generally not included in iconographic studies. I have called this implicit symbolism, for it is a less specific, an implied category of aesthetic statement. It is to this category that we must assign those features of any art that relate to the way in which the materials of the explicit content and the literally symbolic content are combined in product or performance. Implicit symbolism includes those elements that are generally subsumed under the designation "style," as well as those that constitute artistic "form." "Style" denotes here the manner or mode of expression. It includes the details of the combination of artistic motifs and figures. "Form," on the other hand, refers to the overall structure of the artwork. Style and form have often been regarded as being extrinsic to the content or import of a work of art. Such a view fails to take account of the symbolic meanings evidenced by these elements. Characteristics of structure, along with explicit and literally symbolic elements, can all be shown to be determined by and expressive of the basic ideology of a culture.[17] Not only the subject matter, the iconography, of the artwork is determined by those deepest convictions of a culture and people; equally affected are the style and form, that is, the implicit symbolism. The very interrelatedness of content and structure makes them difficult and even impossible at times to separate in a work of art.[18] In fact, one might say that form itself is, in a deeper sense, a conveyer of content rather than an antithesis to it. This is exactly what we mean when we consider the implicit level as representative of meaning. The way in which the subject matter of a work of art is structured is itself indicative of the message conveyed.

The Work of Art in Islamic Culture

Explicit Symbolism

Since the Islamic work of art attempts to disclose an intuition of *tawḥīd* and its concomitant premises through the aesthetic organization of words, figures, sounds, and movements, explicit content for the Muslim artist is never involved with a depiction, however stylized or abstracted, of God Himself. That is categorically disapproved by the religion and the culture. Even to depict living figures from nature, though never intended to represent God, is regarded as futile as a way of eliciting contemplation of transcendence and the truths embodied in *tawḥīd*. The beautiful, the significant in art, therefore, is for the Muslim not an aesthetic portrayal of humanity or human attributes, as humanistic theorists have maintained. It is not a symbolic statement of the truths of nature, as naturalistic theorists argue. Instead, this transcendence-obsessed culture sought, through the creation of the beautiful, to stimulate in the viewer or listener an intuition of, or an insight into, the nature of God and of man's relation to Him.

Given this goal, the Islamic visual arts found explicit symbolism which involves scenes or figures from human, divine, or apotheosized life as utterly unsuited to its projection of the message of *tawḥīd*. Such elements of subject matter were not suitable for drawing the mind of the viewer toward contemplation of *tawḥīd*. Explicit symbolism in Islamic culture instead involves abstract or stylized motifs (especially geometric, calligraphic, and denaturalized figures) in intricate patterns and designs.

Literally Symbolic Symbolism

In describing the motifs of the Islamic visual arts, we must be careful not to think of them as carriers of that kind of literally symbolic meaning that the motifs from another art tradition may evidence. No figure or form is invested with the cultural relationship to other objects or ideas that is the province of literal symbolism. In fact, this type of symbolic expression is singularly absent in the Islamic arts. It is equally absent in other areas of Islamic culture. There are no sacraments to provide religious symbolization, no priesthood to play a symbolic role. Ablutions, postures of prayer, and religious rituals such as fasting and pilgrimage are functional rather than symbolic in their derivation and meanings. They are described as commands of God, not as the carriers of the esoteric or hidden significance that outsiders have been inclined to attribute to them.

In the arts, the lack of literal symbolism is equally evident. In architecture, the parts of the mosque, *madrasah,* or dwelling are consistently functional rather than symbolically significant. The minaret fulfills an important need for a high place from which the muezzin's call to prayer can more easily be heard. It has no symbolic significance. The dome of a mosque is not regarded as an aesthetic representation of heaven, as it has been in Christian iconography. It is simply a successful building device for roofing a large prayer area. The blues of the Persian ceramic domes express no hidden literally symbolic meanings; they result instead from the existence in the area of particular raw materials that make that color easy to produce.[19] The crescent moon came late to Islam—more as a symbol identifiable with the Ottoman Empire than with Islam and the Muslims. It was assigned to a Muslim context by non-Muslims who carried the sign of the cross as their identification. It has never been seriously considered as a symbol of Islam by the Muslims themselves.

It is only among the mystics of Islam (the Sufis) that we encounter that predilection of mystics of any religious background: to view every object, person, and activity as a symbol for something absent, hidden, or esoteric. This tendency runs counter to orthodox interpretations of *tawhīd*, which refuse to allow any figure or element of nature to stand for the divine, and which argue for an unequivocal distinction between nature and the divine. Attempts have been made to explain the art works of Islamic culture as manifestations of Sufi mystical ideas[20]—for example, to understand the honeycomb dome of the Alhambra as symbol of the universe, the single-spiked medallions on the margins of a Qur'ānic page as pointers toward God,[21] the sphere as the "symbol of the Spirit (*ar-Rūh*) emanating from the ungraspable point of Being,"[22] blue as "the color of the Infinite."[23] Such interpretations that judge the products of the whole Muslim *ummah*, or community, by ideas held by only a particular segment of it are bound to lead to misconceptions. Since there is little that distinguishes the aesthetic products of the Sunnī Muslim from those of the Shī'ī, those of the mystic from those of the nonmystic, those of one sect from those of another, an interpretation of the Islamic arts must be grounded on an aesthetic theory that fits all Muslims. With this requirement, the second level of symbolism, the literally symbolic, cannot serve for an understanding of Islamic art, for it is applicable to only a particular bent of mind within Islamic thought and religious life.

Implicit Symbolism

It is on the third level of meaning or content—that designated here as implicit symbolism—that Islamic art presents its most important category of symbolic expression. It is here that elements of style and structure, rather than iconographic features, subtly reveal meanings. In fact, it is these aspects of the aesthetic products of Islamic civilization that seem most revealing of its expression of meaning. It is in the stylistic and formal characteristics, rather than in explicit or literally symbolic content, that we find the crucial characteristics of Islamic art. A great variety of motifs and subject matter have been utilized by Muslim artists over the centuries, motifs that may have been common to other traditions. But the organization of these motifs has been unique and consistent. Whether calligraphy, geometric patterns, floral motifs, or even stylized human and animal figures are used, the result is unmistakably Islamic. The type of motif and the subject matter, then, even with the distinctive qualities of these elements, do not make the Islamic work of art. Far more crucial in determining that accord with the cultural and religious whole, with the desired orientations and meanings, are the modes and methods of treating those elements (style) and the overall organization of the artwork (form).

If the Muslim artist could not convey an intuition of *tawḥīd* through naturalistic representations, what would be a suitable aesthetic vehicle for his ideology? If we are to judge by the empirical evidence—the heritage of Islamic art from all periods and regions—we must conclude that the Muslim artist found this vehicle in the creation of patterns that suggest infiniteness as a quality of transcendence. If ultimate beauty was not-human and not-nature, the artist sought inspiration in the transcendent realm. But the transcendent realm, by Islamic definition, could not be depicted by images from nature. The Muslim artist, therefore, sought to express the nonrepresentableness, the inexpressibility, of the divine; and in this pursuit he created structures in the visual arts, music, and literature to suggest infinity. Islamic art has commonly been represented as an art of the "infinite pattern."[24] It is now our task to draw attention to the most significant elements of that structure which Muslim artists used to create such patterns.

A structural analysis of an Islamic work of art reveals many important characteristics that relate to style and form. Let us focus attention on two of the most important ones for style and two that relate to form.

STYLE

The first of these prominent features of an Islamic work of art is the smallness of the elements of the compositional motifs. The

Islamically oriented artist, in expressing the idea of *tawḥīd*, instinctively chooses motifs that lend themselves to his message. Since his goal is not naturalistic portrayal, reduction of size is never a negative aspect. In fact, it enhances the infinite pattern by forcing the viewer to concentrate on the details of the composition. It attracts the mind of the spectator to follow the unfolding of the design. The tiny flowers executed in enamel, the miniature geometric shapes on a carved or inlaid table, the detailing of an architectural calligraphic inscription—all of these are indicative of the preference the Muslim artist holds for small "building blocks" or "modules" from which to build his beautiful patterns.

A second stylistic feature of the Islamic work of art is its complicated and intricate combination of the chosen motifs. The designs of Islamic art move the eye and the mind with a proliferation of complicated and interrelated details. Each movement, each change of direction within the pattern, catches the eye of the viewer and draws him persistently on to new areas in its effort to generate the series of tensions and relaxations that the viewing of the pattern entails. Movement increases as the spectator is caught up in the aesthetic activities and encounters the numerous figures and combinations that make up the design. Then, as one unit is comprehended, with the corresponding release of aesthetic tension, contemplation of another complementary unit or segment is begun. A third, a fourth, . . . a hundredth may follow, in actuality or in the mind of the spectator; for the Islamic pattern carries the implication of never-ending continuity.

This implication of infinite continuity can seldom be generated, and certainly is not enhanced, by simplicity. An uninterrupted straight line can, of course, be projected across the canvas or the facade of a building. A single figure can fill a framed area. Though the line does not end within the boundary of the artistic composition, though the single figure carries an impression of largeness, neither of them conveys an aesthetic impression of infinity. It is only with the breaking up of the line or the figures, with the repetition and continuing variation of internal units, with their intricacy and complication of treatment, that the implicit symbolic message is realized.

FORM

The first of the two important characteristics of form which reveal the subtle message-carrying of implicit symbolism is the prevalence of divisions. The Islamic work of art has a disjunct organization. It is not viewed as a unit with a single or dominant focus for attention—such would not suggest an infinite pattern. Instead, whether executed in wood or stone, in paint or stucco, in words, tones, or even in the three-dimensional plans of buildings and complexes, the Islamic aesthetic creation captivates the mind with a series of units or modules. These internal units may be identically repeated to make up the total composition, or they may reappear in varied form. In both cases, the internal divisions of the work are essential to the sense of continuing and never-ending pattern.

The field of a carpet never contains but a single medallion. The pattern of that angular or rounded shape must occur in full or partial repetition in other locations on the central zone if the design is to provide the "significant form"[25] of Islamic culture. Carved, inlaid, or painted decorations reveal numerous internal compartments that make up the overall design. Even the calligraphic design can be representative of this disjunct quality of the Islamic work of art. Similarly, the Alhambra palace, built for a Muslim ruler of fourteenth-century Granada, has no one point of aesthetic and functional focus. Instead, it comprises a series of courtyard complexes, each containing a number of rooms surrounding an open court or garden. No one of these takes precedence over another. Even the domed chamber mosque becomes, in Muslim hands, an embodiment of disjunct structure.[26]

The Islamic work of art can be characterized as embodying still another feature that participates in its "significant form." This is its combination of the internal units into "successive modular combinations."[27] The Islamic infinite pattern is not simply a series of modules; it is instead a more-or-less intricate, multileveled combination of the various divisions within the design. The abstract or stylized motifs, for example, are combined, on the first level, to produce a composite unit or module. This module, in turn, is combined with repetitions of itself or other modules into a still larger pattern. An extensive or very complicated design could encompass even more complex successive combinations.

Sometimes the extremities of these levels of combination are physically emphasized by strapwork, border designs, or contrasting colors and materials. At other times, the extent of the successive combinations is less clearly delineated and the viewer must search carefully for the various organizations presented by the design. The possibility for new "views" continues to the very extremities of the artistic field. Even there, with the cutting of the pattern before its completion, the design hints at a larger field of vision and at other combinations. These combinations are to be supplied by the viewer as he continues the pattern for as long as his imagination can support him. When the point of collapse is reached, the Muslim viewer can only exclaim, "Allahu Akbar!" ("God is the greatest!"). He has, through this aesthetic process, gained an intuition of the infinity which characterizes transcendence.

Summary

The symbolic content of Islamic art is molded and determined by the transcendence doctrine of Islamic culture known as *tawḥīd*. This ideology furnishes the meaning substrate for Islamic art, as well as shapes the presentation of that meaning in reference to all three levels of aesthetic symbolism. *Tawḥīd* determines the type of explicit content, that is, the subject matter and motifs of this art. The rejection of figural art and the adherence to abstraction and stylization in Islamic art, therefore, result not from legalistic injunctions from within the society, nor from outside influences. They are instead the result of an internal demand of the culture's ideology. Islamic art displays little concern for literal symbolism, since the Islamic notion of transcendence is so sharply contrasted to the world of man and nature. Literal symbols from nature were never suitable for Muslims in their representations of ideas about transcendence. *Tawḥīd* also has determined the implicit content of the Islamic work of art by inducing Muslim artists to evolve a vast repertoire of stylistic and structural techniques for the creation of infinite patterns. Small and intricate detailing, division into modules, and organization into successive modular combinations constitute basic characteristics which make the work of art from that culture "Islamic."

NOTES

1. See the illustrations of Derek Hill and Oleg Grabar's *Islamic Architecture and Its Decoration: A.D. 800–1500* (Chicago: The University of Chicago Press, 1964), in which, of 527 photographs of architectural sites and decoration, less than a handful include representations of living creatures.

2. The Qur'ān is the Holy Scripture of the Muslim peoples, disclosed by Allah to the Prophet Muḥammad in the seventh century. This series of verbatim communications to mankind were committed to memory by Muḥammad and his followers and subsequently recorded. The revelation contains no injunctions against figural art.

3. This vast body of literature contains the anecdotes and sayings from the life of the Prophet Muḥammad, which were painstakingly collected, verified, and recorded during the first two centuries of the Islamic period. Here we do find negative statements regarding figural art (see Muḥammad ibn Ismaʻīl al Bukhārī, *Ṣaḥīḥ al-Bukhārī*, ed. Muḥammad Muḥsin Khān, 7 vols. to date [Madīnah: Islamic University, 1971–], vol. 1, pp. 226–27; vol. 7, pp. 540, 543–47). Other passages seem to have made the acceptance or rejection of art works with figures dependent on the use made of them (*Ṣaḥīḥ*, vol. 7, p. 542). Therefore, this hypothetical explanation for the rejection of figural art in Islamic culture does not escape equivocation.

4. The Jews and early Muslims have even been accused of having a special fear of iconolatry as a result of the "fact" (*sic*) of the Semite's "tendency to deify the symbol itself . . ." (Frithjof Schuon, *The Transcendent Unity of Religion*, trans. Peter Townsend [New York: Harper and Row, 1975], p. 72). Thomas Arnold disparagingly writes that the image is for the Muslim "a kind of *double*, injury to which will imply corresponding suffering to the living person" (Thomas W. Arnold, *Painting in Islam* [New York: Dover Publications, 1965], p. 11). No doubt, such undocumented statements evidence a lively chauvinism that sees the culture of which they speak as primitive and superstitious.

5. Arnold, *Painting in Islam*, p. 10; K. A. C. Creswell, "The Lawfulness of Painting in Early Islam," *Ars Islamica* 11–12 (1946), pp. 165–66; Henri Lammens, "L'Attitude de l'Islam primitif en face des arts figurés," *Journal Asiatique*, 2nd ser., 6(1915), pp. 274–79. This argument defies the statistical realities of the early conversions: the number of converts from Judaism to Islam in that period was minimal compared to the number of converts of non-Jewish background. In addition, many more Jews had become converts to Christianity. Christianity had even closer ties than Islam with Jewish teachings, since the Torah was incorporated as the first five books of the Christian Old Testament, yet Jewish influence on Christian art has been negligible. The so-called "influence" of Jewish converts on Islamic art seems to rest more on a correspondence of aesthetic premises in the two traditions than on "influence."

6. Oleg Grabar, *The Formation of Islamic Art* (New Haven: Yale University Press, 1973), pp. 88–89. This theory perplexes even its author (p. 99), so he falls back on the chauvinistic argument that the Muslims were unable to free themselves from a primitive fear of the magic that operates in nature! Such a belief would constitute, in Islam, the greatest of sins (*shirk*, or "associationism"). See Qur'ān 4:48, 116.

7. Friedrich Schiller, *On the Aesthetic Education of Man*, trans. Reginald Snell (New Haven; Yale University Press, 1954), pp. 64–67. See Curt Sachs, *The Commonwealth of Art: Style in the Fine Arts, Music and the Dance* (New York: W. W. Norton, 1946), for another "dichotomist" theory, in which the author uses the terms "pathos" and "ethos."

8. Susanne K. Langer, *Philosophy in a New Key* (Cambridge, MA: Harvard University Press, 1942); idem., *Feeling and Form: A Theory of Art* (New York: Charles Scribner's Sons, 1953).

9. Albert Hofstadter, *Truth and Art* (New York: Columbia University Press, 1965), pp. 15–21.

10. See Hofstadter, *Truth and Art*, where he defines art as "the articulation of human being" (p. 86) or "a piece of human existence" (p. 72).

11. Henri Focillon, *The Life of Forms in Art*, trans. Charles Beecher Hogan and George Kubler (New York: George Wittenborn, Inc., 1948), p. 2.

12. Herbert Read, *The Origins of Form in Art* (New York: Horizon Press, 1965), p. 79.

13. Plato, *The Republic*, X:595–602; III, 398–400.

14. Bernard Bosanquet, *A History of Aesthetic*, 2nd ed. (London: Allen & Unwin, Ltd., 1904), pp. 30–32.

15. See, for example, Mulk Raj Anand, *The Hindu View of Art* (Bombay: Asia Publishing House, 1957); Ananda K. Coomaraswamy, *The Transformation of Nature in Art* (Cambridge, MA: Harvard University Press, 1934); Radhakamal Mukerjee, *The Cosmic Art of India: Symbol (Mūrti), Sentiment (Rasa) and Silence (Yoga)* (Bombay: Allied Publishers Private, Ltd., 1965); O. C. Gangoly, *Indian Art and Heritage*, comp. and ed. A. Goswami (Calcutta: Oxford Book and Stationery Co., 1957).

16. Quoted in James Luther Adams, *Paul Tillich's Philosophy of Culture, Science and Religion* (New York: Harper and Row, 1965), p. 80.

17. See Langer, *Feeling and Form*, chap. 4; Erwin Panofsky, *Studies in Iconology* (New York: Harper Torchbooks, 1962); and Paul Tillich, *Masse und Geist*, passage trans. and quoted in Adams, *Paul Tillich's Philosophy*, pp. 90–93. All contain statements on the symbolic content of structural characteristics.

18. Langer, *Feeling and Form*, pp. 51–52.

19. Donald N. Wilber explains the existence of the blue tiles as perhaps due to the fact that "the copper compound used to produce the light blue glaze was available at so many places and was so easily worked to separate the glazing material from the ore," *The Architecture of Islamic Iran: The Il-Khānid Period* (Princeton: Princeton University Press, 1955), p. 65.

20. Examples can be found in Titus Burckhardt, *The Art of Islam* (London: World of Islam Festival Publishing Co., Ltd., 1976); Schuyler Camman, "Symbolic Meanings in Oriental Rug Patterns," *The Textile Museum Journal* 3, no. 3 (1972), pp. 5–54; idem., "Cosmic Symbolism on Carpets from the Sanguszko Group," *Studies in Art and Literature of the Near East in Honor of Richard Ettinghausen*, ed. Peter J. Chelkovski (Salt Lake City and New York, 1975), pp. 181–208; Martin Lings, *The Quranic Art of Calligraphy and Illumination* (London: World of Islam Festival Trust, 1976); and Schuon, *The Transcendent Unity*.

21. Lings, *The Quranic Art*, p. 73.

22. Burckhardt, *The Art of Islam*, p. 76.

23. Lings, *The Quranic Art*, p. 76.

24. Ernst Grube, *The World of Islam* (New York: McGraw-Hill, 1966), p. 11.

25. This expression is used by Susanne K. Langer to designate symbolism conveyed through formal characteristics; she credits Clive Bell with coining it (Langer, *Feeling and Form*, p. 32).

26. Lois Ibsen al Faruqi, "The Aisled Hall and the Dome Chamber—Their Use in Islamic Culture," *Islamic Culture* 50, no. 3 (1976); pp. 155–67.

27. Lois Ibsen al Faruqi, "The Suite in Islamic Culture and History," *The Concept of the Suite in the Islamic Near East*, ed. J. Pacholczyk, in press.

14

The Sacred and the Modern Artist
MIRCEA ELIADE

The Quest for the Unrecognizable Sacred

Ever since 1880, when Nietzsche first proclaimed it, people have been talking a great deal about the "death of God." Martin Buber asked recently whether this is a question of a genuine "death," or simply of the eclipse of God—the fact that God is no longer in evidence, that he is no longer responding to the prayers and invocations of man. Nevertheless, it does not seem that his rather optimistic interpretation of Nietzsche's verdict is able to assuage all doubts. Certain contemporary theologians have recognized that it is necessary to accept (and even to assume) the "death of God," and are trying to think and to build on the basis of this fact.

A theology based on the "death of God" can give rise to exciting debates, but for our purposes it is only of subsidiary interest. We have made allusion to it to recall the fact that the modern artist encounters a similar problem. There is a certain symmetry between the perspective of the philosopher and theologian, and that of the modern artist; for the one as for the other the "death of God" signifies above all the impossibility of expressing a religious experience in traditional religious language: in medieval language for example, or in that of the Counter-Reformation. From a certain point of view, the "death of God" would rather seem to be the destruction of an idol. To acknowledge the death of God would thus be equivalent to admitting that one had been taken in, that he had been worshiping just a god and not the living God of Judaeo-Christianity.

Reprinted from *Criterion*, Spring 1964, pp. 22–24.

Be that as it may, it is evident that, for more than a century, the West has not been creating a "religious art" in the traditional sense of the term, that is to say, an art reflecting "classic" religious conceptions. In other words, artists are no longer willing to worship "idols"; they are no longer interested in traditional religious imagery and symbolism.

This is not to say that the "sacred" has completely disappeared in modern art. But it has become *unrecognizable*; it is camouflaged in forms, purposes and meanings which are apparently "profane." The sacred is not *obvious*, as it was for example in the art of the Middle Ages. One does not recognize it *immediately* and *easily*, because it is no longer expressed in a conventional religious language.

To be sure, this is not a conscious and voluntary camouflage. Contemporary artists are by no means believers who, embarrassed by the archaism or the inadequacies of their faith, do not have the courage to avow it and who thus try to disguise their religious beliefs in creations which appear to be profane at first glance. When an artist recognizes that he is a Christian, he does not dissimulate his faith; he proclaims it according to his own means in his work as, for example, Rouault has. Nor is it difficult to identify the biblical religiosity and the messianic nostalgia of Chagall even in his first period, when he peopled his paintings with severed heads and bodies flying upside down. The ass, a messianic animal, *par excellence*, the "eye of God" and the angels were there to remind us that the universe of Chagall had nothing in common with the everyday world—that it was in fact a sacred and mysterious world such as that which is revealed during childhood. But the great majority of artists do not seem to have "faith" in the traditional sense of the word. They are not consciously "religious." Nonetheless we maintain that the sacred, although unrecognizable, is present in their works.

Let us hasten to add that this is a question of a phenomenon which is generally characteristic of modern man, or more specifically of man in Western society: he wants to be, and declares himself to be areligious—completely rid of the sacred. On the level of everyday consciousness, he is perhaps right; but he continues to participate in the sacred through his dreams and his daydreams, through certain attitudes (his "love of nature," for example), through his distractions (reading, theater), through his nostalgias and his impulses. That is to say, modern man has "forgotten" religion, but the sacred survives, buried in his unconscious. One might speak, in Judaeo-Christian terms, of a "second fall." According to the biblical tradition, man lost after the fall the possibility of "encountering" and "understanding" God; but he kept enough intelligence to rediscover the traces of God in nature and in his own consciousness. After the "second fall" (which corresponds to the death of God as proclaimed by Nietzsche) modern man has lost the possibility of experiencing the sacred at the conscious level, but he continues to be nourished and guided by his unconscious. And, as certain psychologists never stop telling us, the unconscious is "religious" in the sense that it is constituted of impulses and images charged with sacrality.

We are not about to develop these few remarks about the religious situation of modern man here. But if what we are saying is true of Western man in general, it is *a fortiori* still more true of the artist. And this is for the simple reason that the artist does not act passively either in regard to the Cosmos or in regard to the unconscious. Without telling us, perhaps without knowing it, the artist penetrates—at times dangerously—into the depths of the world and his own psyche. From cubism to tachism, we are witnessing a desperate effort on the part of the artist to free himself of the "surface" of things and to penetrate into matter in order to lay bare its ultimate structures. To abolish form and volume, to descend into the interior of substance while revealing its secret or larval modalities—these are not, according to the artist, operations undertaken for the purpose of some sort of objective knowledge; they are ventures provoked by his desire to grasp the deepest meaning of his plastic universe.

In certain instances, the artist's approach to his material recovers and recapitulates a religiosity of an extremely archaic variety that disappeared from the Western world thousands of years ago. Such, for example, is Brancusi's attitude towards stone, an attitude comparable to the solicitude, the fear, and the veneration addressed by a neolithic man towards certain stones that constituted hierophanies—that is to say, that revealed simultaneously the sacred and ultimate, irreducible reality.

The two specific characteristics of modern art, namely the destruction of traditional forms and the fascination for the formless, for the elementary modes of matter, are susceptible to religious interpretation. The hierophanization of matter, that is to say the discovery of the sacred manifested through the substance itself, characterizes that which has been called "cosmic religiosity," that type of religious experience which dominated the world before the advent of Judaism and which is still alive in "primitive" and Asiatic societies. To be sure, this cosmic religiosity was forgotten in the West in the wake of the triumph of Christianity. Emptied of every religious value or meaning, nature could become the "object" *par excellence* of scientific investigation. From a certain viewpoint, Western science can be called the immediate heir of Judaeo-Christianity. It was the prophets, the apostles, and their successors the missionaries who convinced the Western world that a rock (which certain people have considered to be sacred) was only a rock, that the planets and the stars were only cosmic *objects*—that is to say, that they were not (and could not be) either gods or angels or demons. It is as a result of this long process of the desacralization of Nature that the Westerner has managed to *see* a natural object where his ancestors saw hierophanies, sacred presences.

But the contemporary artist seems to be going beyond his objectivizing scientific perspective. Nothing could convince Brancusi that a rock was only a fragment of inert matter; like his Carpathian ancestors, like all neolithic men, he sensed a presence in the rock, a power, an "intention" that one can only call "sacred." But what is particularly significant is the fascination for the infrastructures of matter and for the embryonic modes of life. In effect we might say that for the past three generations we have been witnessing a series of "destructions" of the world (that is to say, of the traditional artistic universe) undertaken courageously and at times savagely for the purpose of recreating or recovering another, new, and "pure" universe, uncorrupted by time and history. We have analyzed elsewhere the secret significance of this will to demolish formal worlds made empty and banal by the usage of time and to reduce them to their elementary modes, and ultimately to their original *materia prima* (Cf. *Myth and Reality*, Harper and Row, 1963). This fascination for the elementary modes of matter betrays a desire to deliver oneself from the weight of mortal form, the nostalgia to immerse oneself in an auroral world. The public has evidently been particularly struck by the iconoclastic and anarchistic furor of contemporary artists. But in these vast demolitions one can always read like a watermark the hope of creating a new universe, more viable because it is more true, that is, more adequate to the actual situation of man.

However, one of the characteristics of "cosmic religion" both among the primitives and among the peoples of the Ancient Near East is precisely this need for periodically annihilating the world, through the medium of ritual, in order to be able to recreate it. The annual reiteration of the cosmogony implies a provisory reactualization of chaos, a symbolic regression of the world to a state of virtuality. Simply because it has been going on, the world has wilted, it has lost its freshness, its purity and its original creative power. One cannot "repair" the world; one must annihilate it in order to recreate it.

There is no question of homologizing this primitive mythico-ritual scenario to modern artistic experiences. But it is not without interest for us to note a certain convergence existing between, on the one hand, repeated efforts at destroying traditional artistic language and attraction towards the elementary modes of life and matter and, on the other hand, the archaic conceptions which we have tried to evoke. From a structural point of view, the attitude of the artist in regard to the cosmos and to life recalls to a certain extent the ideology implicit in "cosmic religion."

It may be, furthermore, that the fascination for matter may be only a precursory sign of a new philosophical and religious orientation. Teilhard de Chardin, for example, proposes to "carry Christ . . . to the heart of the realities reputed to be the most dangerous, the most naturalistic, the most pagan." For the Father wanted to be "the evangelist of Christ in the universe."

PART IV

PHILOSOPHERS
AND THEOLOGIANS:
REFLECTIONS
ON ART

15

Can Art Fill the Vacuum?

LANGDON B. GILKEY

Unfortunately, the fortunes of art and those of religion seem to rise and fall together, and that means that both are at a low ebb today. The regal, wealthy church of the medieval and Renaissance epochs was a more enthusiastic and generous patron of art than are modern banks, stock brokers, or the space industry in their present-day affluence; and certainly the church was more hospitable to the artist than are the disinfected classrooms, laboratories, and library stacks of modern universities. Unhappily, the day of organized religion being at the center of things has long since passed.

When in present-day culture conservative religion comes to social and political power—as has recently happened—it seems able, like its declared enemy communism, only to produce conformity in dress and morals, kitsch in art, and the American Way of Life in theology! Great acclaim for spiritual art, like that for many forms of greatness, is as rare in our day as is the unexpected relation of Alexander Calder to Braniff Airways. With this brief introduction, we are in sight of the vacuum in our present life to which I wish to speak.

Ours is a *technical* culture. What does that mean? We know how to do things, and we know "scientifically" how to do them; we are, or want to be, experts, competent. But more, it means that *what* we want to know how to do is how to do things. Our culture is expert at producing experts, competent in producing competence. What we are interested in is how to do things; what we *admire* is *how* to do things—to be an *expert* in knowledge, a

This essay is a revision of a commencement address delivered to the School of the Art Institute of Chicago, 17 May 1981.

technologist in operation, an *executive* in business, an *administrator* in political life and even in an academic department or a church.

Knowledge is for us expertise or competence, a *skill*, as we say; what *knowing* does for us is to give us increased, and in the end unlimited, skills. Education at all levels is there only to provide us with skills; that is why we support it, and why we go to school; any subject that does not result in a useful skill is for us not a real subject. Thinking is for us a skill that is useful for competing, for doing things better, for "making it." Even religion is for our age a skill or technique, helping us, if one sincerely tries it out, to become more successful in all we are trying to do.

A technical culture is voracious, devouring; it consumes all the other nontechnical aspects of culture by turning everything into a skill, a knowledge of how to do it, a *means*. Only art remains resistant—and then finds itself bought to decorate a gadget so as to sell the gadget better, or bought as an investment, better and safer than prime real estate!

What we are to do, and *why* we are to do it are queries thus pushed far to the side or left quite out of account. What all these instruments are *for*, what the *worth* of all this doing is, are forgotten matters, unpondered as if they were no longer questions at all. Our society generates tremendous rational and spiritual power, vast energies of thought, tons of words. But the highly trained and very expert *rational* power of the society, and the *spiritual* power of the society, its morals and religion, all seem bent on the production and glorification of instruments, creating effective, efficient, and competent *means* for doing something. If, however, all our joint energies, brains, and work are given to produce or refine some means for some further end, and if that future end never comes, or if, when it comes, it turns out to be worthless, *then* these energies, this thinking, and this work have been misspent, and a culture devoted entirely to them has a vacuum at its heart.

One significant role, or gift, of art is to enhance direct, immediate experience. It so reshapes immediate experience as to make it suddenly an end, an end in itself, as Aristotle put it; or as modern reflection has put it, an *event* of intrinsic worth, that is an event which, in and of itself, in and through its own taking place, creates immediate and experienced *meaning*. Artistic talent can, to be sure, be used also as an instrument—to beautify an object or spruce up an ad so as to sell something else—as can religious piety. But for art in itself, in its role as *art,* the "meaning stops here." It is a reality in itself, for itself. Whether it be a classic painting or sculpture, an ordinary object rendered into art, an assemblage of stray objects, we look at it as it *is,* as it presents itself. The event of our encounter is for itself, a significant enjoyment, an experience of seeing, here, at this moment. And we are deepened, refreshed, challenged to reorder ourselves, to see in a new way our world and ourselves—we are re-created. Here is a point, an end, a stopping place.

This event of enhancement is not "subjective" any more than a technical instrument is subjective; for, after all, every means is a means only as an instrument of our subjective purposes. An encounter with a work of art is an interaction, an interaction of the presence of that work and of ourselves into this new creative event, the enhancement of our experience, of our being, and of our world. Without these events of enhancement, the enhancement of direct experience, nothing we do makes sense. Instruments and means, preparing and making ready, fixing it up, getting it set, tuning it up, even of the finest stereos and autos, *all* are means to enhanced experience or else they are worthless. This is the first and utterly essential role of art and the artistic: to re-create ordinary experience into value, into enhanced experience; to provide the ends— the deep, immediate, present enjoyments—for which all instruments exist and from which alone they receive their point. When an event that we label art thus stops the heedless flow of time in an enhanced moment, a moment of new awareness or understanding, a moment of intense seeing and of participation in what is seen, then (as the Zen tradition has taught us) the transcendent appears through art, and art and religion approach one another.

Probably unintentionally art has, or frequently has had, a quite other but equally significant role. Sometimes this is intentional, sometimes not; but when it is there, it is of vast creative power. This is the role of art in making us see in *new* and *different* ways, below the surface and beyond the obvious. Art opens up the truth hidden behind and within the ordinary; it provides a new entrance into reality and pushes us through that entrance. It leads us to what is really there and really going on. Far from subjective, it pierces the opaque subjectivity, the *not* seeing, of conventional life, of conventional viewing, and discloses reality.

The most obvious example of this is what we can only call *outrage* in works of art: outrage at the *dehumanization* of persons, at the *emptiness* of persons and of their roles in life, at the *inhumanity* of men and women to others, at the grotesque *misshapenness* of people and of their behavior, at the wanton *suffering* that is universal. Here art is not so much providing the ends essential to a technical culture; rather is it uncovering the emptiness, the distortion, and the demonic cruelty of such a culture. Quite possibly artists feel subjectively that they are merely being "hard," "honest," "realistic," or possibly ironic and humorous—"laughing at the absurdity of life," as we like to put it—and they probably are right. But the work itself, and the event it creates in relation to us, *itself* manifests outrage, and this shines through every line and color—as, for example, in German Expressionism, Picasso's *Guernica*, in a lot of Chicago imagists, and in much punk art. Art enhances direct experience; it also tears off the mask covering ordinary experience to expose its disarray, its disastrous waywardness, its betrayals, its suffering. Here it has—possibly unconsciously—a "prophetic role," denouncing the culture it lays bare. And inescapably this is a *moral* and often a *political* role. An example from recent experience has been the unexpected power that folk music exhibited in the civil rights and the anti-Vietnam movements. Here a form of passionate art—*not* political or moral theory or even reformist preaching—led this mighty moral movement to political victory. What was revealed in and by those songs, and by the events of their being sung and being heard, was not subjective at all: what was revealed or exposed was the *reality* of a segregated, bloated, and imperialist culture that called for exposure and transformation. The need for that same role exists as much now as then—and art can be its most effective warrior, which is, incidentally, why Russia—and much of the American moral majority—is so afraid of contemporary art. When art thus condemns present reality in the name of humanity and justice and seeks for its transformation, it becomes itself the vehicle of the transcendent and approaches the religious.

Art, however, provides more than negative images of ordinary reality. It gives us most of our creative images of ourselves, our world and our relations to one another. Human life is lived in and through symbols that shape and guide us in all we are and do: symbols of nature, symbols of ourselves—who we are, what we can be, what we ought to be—symbols of our community and society, symbols of the sacred that permeates all. Works of art set these symbols into images; through them we can *see* ourselves and our world, possibly for the first time. "In art we find ourselves and lose ourselves at the same time," said Thomas Merton.[1]

Art is bitterly iconoclastic; it opposes the phony, the empty, and the outrageous in life; thus does it ruthlessly demolish the dead wood of convention—and thus does it search for new images of the strange reality of nature, of ourselves, and of the sacred amid which we live. It fills the vacuum of our present vague and empty images of ourselves and of reality. Like religion, it re-creates by offering a set of symbols of our own being, of community, and of the sacred. Like religion, it heals and re-creates as well as cuts and cauterizes; it is essential to every culture, and especially to a technical culture.

If all of this—and this is a lot—makes up the role of the artist in a technical culture, one can understand the inevitability of the artist as an *outsider,* as condemned to be on the boundary rather than in the comfortable, powerful, or acclaimed center of a culture's life. Artists have few of the traits that the culture emphasizes, applauds, or rewards: they are not experts; their importance is not that they know how to do anything useful to anyone but other artists; they don't make instruments for anyone else's use, or even make money or jobs for others. They say: Stop, look and *see* what is real, and *be.* In our rushing world, no one has time for this. Moreover they must and do participate in the suffering of the culture, live themselves within its sense of loneliness, emptiness, and aimlessness, experience outrage at its inhumanity, its infinite pain and despair—*if* they are to uncover, under its conventional and smooth surfaces, the stark reality of alienation. Kierkegaard once asked, "What is a poet?" And he answered that a poet is an unhappy man who in his heart harbors a deep anguish, but whose lips are so fashioned that the moans and cries that pass over them are transformed into ravishing music.[2] The artist must be inside the culture to feel its wounds and its hurt, and yet enough outside, alien from it, to recognize these as *outrages* and to shape them creatively into *new* images less untrue to our reality.

In our present culture, the artist is merely ignored; in other cultures (for example, in Russia) he or she is ostracized, oppressed, and expelled as dangerous to the culture's efficiency and unity—as artists really are! Like so-called religious persons, artists *can* adapt their work so that it merely celebrates current forms of power, so that it merely sanctifies our technical advances, our affluence, our dominance—and assures us that we are still Number One, as does official Soviet art. By this means, however, art will only enlarge the vacuum rather than fill it. If it is to be *art* and to fulfill its great task, it will move to the boundary, even to the outside—but by that it can re-create the world!

NOTES

1. *A Thomas Merton Reader*, ed. Thomas P. McDonnell (New York: Image Books, 1974), p. 387.

2. There are many ideas in these remarks that are indebted to Aristotle, John Dewey, Hans Georg Gadamer, Paul Tillich, and Diane Apostolos-Cappadona; the reference to Kierkegaard is from *Either/Or*, vol. 1, p. 1.

16

Artists and Church Commissions: Rubin's *The Church at Assy* Revisited

JOHN DILLENBERGER

The last four decades have witnessed the emergence of several church buildings for which distinguished artists have done works, ranging from the church of Notre-Dame-de-Toute-Grâce in Assy, France, for which artists were beginning to be commissioned in 1939, to St. Peter's Lutheran Church, New York City, for which Louise Nevelson's sculptural works create the entire environment of the Erol Beker Chapel, completed just over a year ago. Between these stand such European churches as the Chapel of the Rosary at Vence, France; the church Corbusier designed at Ronchamp, France, and the rebuilt cathedral at Coventry, England. In the United States, we would single out for special attention the Breuer designed University Church of St. John the Baptist, Collegeville, Minnesota; the Roofless Church at New Harmony, Indiana; the ceramic sculpture for the Newman Chapel at the University of California, Berkeley, by Stephen de Staebler; Lippold's Baldacchino for St. Mary's Catholic Cathedral, San Francisco; and the Rothko Chapel, Houston, Texas. If stained glass were included, we could stretch the number by adding the Presbyterian Church in Stamford, Connecticut, and the Community Church in Pocantico Hills, New York.

Viewed as a whole, the group is not significant in size. The period of the nineteenth century as a whole, together with the early twentieth century, did not witness a significant number of at-

Reprinted from *Art Criticism* 1, no. 1 (Spring 1979): 72—82.

tempts to utilize distinguished artists. In the United States, we can think of the decorative works of the late Neo-Gothic revival and the works of artists such as John LaFarge at Trinity Church, Boston, and the Church of the Ascension, and St. Thomas in New York City. Compared to the Medieval period, in which architecture, artifact and art coalesced in common cultural aspirations, the number of significant commissions is few, and the setting, of course, is entirely different.

Not surprisingly, most of the important departures in the last decades occurred in Roman Catholic churches, or with the influence of particular Roman Catholics, clerics or laypersons, and to a lesser extent, of individuals within the Episcopal and Lutheran traditions. The Roofless Church, at the site of the nineteenth-century Utopian community started by Robert Dale Owen, is in fact the result of the vision of Jane Owen, and the Rothko Chapel in Houston, Texas, of Dominique de Menil. In fact, from Assy to St. Peter's, one can only conclude that the projects happened because particular individuals were persistent in their determination to commission distinguished artists and architects.

Nothing happens, of course, without the initiating decision of individuals; but it is a matter of decisive difference as to whether or not their decisions reflect or have the support of, the community or culture at large; or whether they reflect only the vision of these individuals and the works of art and architecture come into being in indifferent or potentially hostile environments. Certainly the projects here mentioned fall into the second category. A pattern of individual initiatives may indeed start new directions. The question we will not be able to escape is whether that is in fact true of these instances as a whole.

In the case of the Church at Assy and several other churches noted (excepting Ronchamp and Coventry, Breuer's Chapel, and to some extent, New Harmony), the buildings are more significant for the works of art than for the architecture. During the same period, Protestantism and Judaism did indeed commission a few distinguished architects, such as Pietro Belluschi, Frank Lloyd Wright, and Louis Kahn. Protestantism, with its accent on auditory rather than liturgical or sacramental space, is conscious of forms, but uninterested, uneducated, or suspicious of the sensuous nature of the visual arts of painting and sculpture. Protestantism has lived so long without the visual that the loss of that human and spiritual resource is not even recognized as an issue.

Both the lack of numbers of significant church commissions and the special nature of these we have mentioned raise the critical issue of the relation of religion, the artists, society, and the church in our time. Paradoxically, there is more widespread interest in the visual arts than has been true in generations. This is reflected both in a genuine widespread interest in seeing and owning works of art, and in the attendance records for museum extravaganza exhibitions. That fact, too, testifies to the divorce of the church from the arena of patronage, though it once was one of the great patrons of the arts.

The evidence does not indicate a return to such patronage by the church directly. Though the Catholic Church has belatedly started a collection of twentieth century religious art, the Vatican has been the recipient of gifts of works of art rather than the commissioner and patron who actively shapes a notable collection. Thus, the whole wing devoted to contemporary religious art is for the most part filled with banal, or safe works which are not at all representative of the leading artists of our time. When one considers the Vatican's historic treasures, the contrast is all the more startling.

The United Church of Christ, noted for its interest in promoting the arts generally, has not been as imaginative in the visual arts as in the other arts. Yet, this church body is the recipient of a major collection of art by black artists. In short, churches seem to have joined the general wave of interest in the visual arts, without returning to, or advancing toward, their significant inclusion in church structure and liturgical life. The result is that the arts are among the activities in which individuals participate, and which may diversify and enrich what they already know. But in that context, the arts do not transform human existence, except peripherally or accidentally, and they are not essential to the human spirit.

Protestant history has left the churches, either with no art at all, or with art as the illustration or confirmation of what was considered safely known and knowable on other grounds. It seems that the misuse or abuse of the power of art led, not to the correction of those abuses, but to limitations of the nature and use of art for the church. The inherent processes of art were diminished at the point of the central, critical power of art, when issues of faith were involved. Thus, the visual arts, when expressing the integrity of their own process, were superior when these works were produced outside the life of the church, even when the same artist was the creator. In many instances, the pressure of the church and synagogue led to an internalization in the psyche of the artist to the extent that artistic freedom and creative competence diminished when faith issues were involved. The works of the Roman Catholic Rouault, for instance, are more interesting and profound when clowns and prostitutes were depicted, than when he dealt with religious figures, and the Christ. It follows that the mere commissioning of artists by the church is not enough. Indeed, the issues of the competence, vitality, freedom, and spiritual perception of the artist are essential ingredients, which, in the twentieth century, are only tenuously related to the faith conviction and shape of the liturgical, believing life of the church.

Not only has the churchly cultural ambience of the middle ages disappeared; the psychic posture which depresses the sensuous vitalities remains an ingredient of our culture. That is why some of the great art produced for the church in our time has come from non-believers, or those residually related to the life of the church. That fact, as the history of the Church at Assy indicates, can become a new source of problems. In the seventeenth century, the issue arose, can the non-regenerate do good theological work. The answer was, if there are enough regenerate around.

That problem and its answer reflected a recognition that the leading and dominant orientations of the culture were at that time still basically Christian, but that other perceptions were beginning to be powerful enough to demand attention. In our time, the problem is more complicated, for single leading orientations no longer exist. Perceptions have become multiple or pluralistic, while the church has lived for some time without an awareness of the sensual as a powerful force in the visual arts. Today, many of the perceptions needed and absent in the church are being formed afresh by the artists themselves. That intensifies the issue as one moves from the virtual divorce of the two to new potential alliances and possibilities. From Assy and Vence to the Rothko and Nevelson chapels, that issue is both threat and possibility. Indeed, there is considerable discussion these days as to whether paintings reflect, or essentially may purvey spiritual or religious conceptions. Hilton Kramer of the *New York Times* and Thomas Messer, Director of the Guggenheim Museum, can write and talk in such terms, particularly in regard to the paintings of Mark Rothko. That development does not solve the problem for the church, particularly when its own perception of the content of a work of art is dependent upon particular iconographic recognitions. That problem was particularly acute at Assy, as was its opposite, that the accepted iconographic content presented problems as executed, partly because of the modernism of the style and partly because in the eyes of the Vatican, there seemed to be a connection between the modern mode and the lack of Christian faith, or faith in any form, among many of the artists.

William S. Rubin in his definitive book, *Modern Sacred Art and the Church of Assy* (Columbia University Press, New York and London, 1961—based on a doctoral dissertation completed in 1958), provides us with a full account of the commissions, the response of the Vatican, and his own, I think, misdirected, and therefore overly pessimistic conclusions about art and the church. For the reader unfamiliar with the church as Assy, a list of the works done by the various artists is essential and is here provided.

Fernand Léger	*The Virgin of the Litany*-1946 Mosaic on the Facade.
Georges Rouault	*Christ aux Outrages*-1939 Stained Glass.
	Le Grand Vase-1946–1949 Stained Glass.
	Christ of The Passion-1946–1949 Stained Glass.
	Le Petit Bouquet-1946–1949 Stained Glass.
	Saint Veronica-1946–1949 Stained Glass.

Jacques Lipchitz   *Notre-Dame-de-Liesse*-1948–1955
Bronze.

Marc Chagall   *Crossing of the Red Sea*-1952–1957
Ceramic Mural.

Psalm 42
Plaster Bas-relief.

Angel with Candelabra
Stained Glass.

Angel with Holy Water
Stained Glass.

Henri Matisse   *Saint Dominic*-1948–1949
Ceramic Mural.

Georges Braque   *Tabernacle Door*-1948
Metal Bas-relief.

Pierre Bonnard   *St. Francis of Sales*-1943–1946
Oil on Canvas.

Jean Lurçat   *The Apocalypse*-1945
Tapestry.

Germaine Richier   *Crucifix*-1948–1949
Bronze.

A cursory glance at the subjects will confirm that there is no iconographic scheme related to the liturgy and the theological scope of the church's affirmations. Indeed baptism alone is represented among the sacraments. Narrative scenes, so prominent in earlier churches, are absent. The subjects were determined by the individual artists in conversation with Canon Jean Devémy, to whom had been entrusted the plan of the building, and Father Marie-Alain Couturier, who in light of association with Devémy, took over the general schematic development at the end of the Second World War.

For Couturier, the Church at Assy represented the possibility of bringing the talents of the great artists in relation to the church once again. Hence, starting with the artist, an individualistic rather than liturgical scheme was followed, though many of the saints depicted are associated with healing, thus emphasizing this theme.

The Church at Assy was created precisely to meet the needs of the many sanatoriums being built in the area. It seems strained, however, when Rubin remarks that the "iconographic and stylistic discontinuity is not out of harmony with the more individualistic, less group-oriented religious experience of the convalescents at Assy" (p. 39). More central, from our perspective today, is whether the individual works, without a consistent iconographic scheme, provide a religious ambience, susceptible to and encouraging of, the life of faith; or, has the church become merely a museum?

Rubin's conclusion about Assy was that it was the product of a temporary alliance between liberal priests, artists, and the French Left; that it has a lack of liturgical integrity; that most of the artists had anti-religious orientations; that there is a lack of new artistic discoveries at Assy; and that the Vatican officially opposed it. His pessimistic conclusion follows if one expected an entirely new relation between the artists and the church as a result. An anomaly, as Rubin calls the Church at Assy, may be instructive, and indeed, of considerable significance, when times and history change. One could make the point that the anomalies of the past are as instructive to the future, and occasionally much more so, than the continuities of history.

Father Couturier knew precisely what he was doing, using the confluences, indeed the anomalies of his time, to full advantage. Couturier knew that acceptable Catholic theory manifested itself in poor works of art, that pious artists produced banal works. On this point, he had to stand against even those who had helped to revitalize both theology and the arts, such as Jacques Maritain, who believed that Christian art could only be done by Christian artists. Modern art, so despised in the 50's by the Vatican, reflected the church's rejection of unfamiliar artistic styles, inevitably, in the Vatican's view, associated with the modern, unbelieving age. Hence, the dogmatic connection made by the hierarchy between the artist's style and his unbelief meant that the art at Assy would automatically be rejected. Couturier, on the other hand, believed that the reemergence of significant art in relation to the church, indeed, sacred art, would emerge only when significant artists were employed. That direction was focused by Couturier in his taking over the review, *L'Art sacré*, and in his vision of the Church at Assy as his laboratory. Of course, his personal involvement in the arts, the temporary alliance between the left and the church among artists and intellectuals, the role of liberal priests and worker-priest movement, made possible Couturier's achievement. That this coalition did not last may be less significant than that it gave a moment in which Couturier could produce what would no longer be possible, once the strange coalition collapsed and Vatican pressure intensified.

Among the first of the artists to be asked to create art for Assy was Rouault, a devout Catholic, who at the age of seventy had not yet had a single Catholic commission. Eventually five of his paintings were translated into stained glass, two figures of Christ, two floral designs symbolizing the prophetic imagery of Isaiah, and Saint Veronica as another Christ type. Hence, all five are Christological in intention, exhibiting greater unity than Rubin noted. The Virgin, according to Rubin, is more important in Assy than is Christ, being central in a large mosaic on the facade by Léger, in a sculpture by Lipchitz, in a window, and in Lurçat's tapestry. But it is also conceivable that Rubin draws the conclusion he does more from what he knows of the role of the Virgin in Catholic history at the time, than from the actual works of art at Assy which place Mary's role alongside Christ, not necessarily in hierarchical order or in a specific context of ascendency.

The fact that Rouault was Catholic did not divert criticism from the Catholic right. His work was considered devoid of beauty, full of agony, individualistic and private rather than communal. But the major attack was reserved for others. Granted that Lurçat's apocalyptic tapestry, based on the twelfth chapter of the Book of Revelation, is non-traditional in its delineation of Paradise and the apocalypse, with its Dragon, the Woman and the Archangel Michael, the fact is that this was not the real issue. Lurçat was a Marxist, hence an unbeliever and communist. He had agreed only to do the tapestry out of his friendship for Couturier. Léger, too, who did the brilliant, colored mosaic on the facade wall, *The Virgin of the Litany*, was suspect because he had programmatically announced that the materialism of his own work was a substitute for the sentimental and outmoded representations in the church.

Less controversial but yet troublesome were the works by two Jews, Lipchitz and Chagall. While believing that Judaism and Christianity were linked like no other two religions, Lipchitz, in his sculptural creation of the Virgin, with its tear shaped form, showing Mary with the dove descending, and the lamb, nevertheless was insistent that he not be misunderstood. Hence, on the back of the sculpture—both on the one at Assy and the one which Jane Owen secured for New Harmony, appear the words: "Jacob Lipchitz, Jew, faithful to the religion of his ancestors, has made this Virgin to foster understanding between men on earth that the life of the spirit may prevail."

Chagall's context, in contrast, is more ambiguous. Sought after as a potential Catholic convert, Chagall, though proud of his Jewish heritage, professed no religious propensities of his own apart from the poetry of all religions. His ceramic wall in the Baptistry, the *Crossing of the Red Sea*, can be interpreted as an Old Testament paradigm of the New, but his crucifixion within it, like his other crucifixions, in intention reflects the suffering of all, and of the Jew in particular, in the human world. Agony and joy, pieces of the world that reflect both, are juxtaposed in unfamiliar patterns of incandescent power.

More troublesome to Rubin apparently than to the Catholic Church was Bonnard's *Saint Francis of Sales*, which in Rubin's eyes is a weak work, inappropriate to the artist whose private world of gardens, friends, hills and coastline represented in his art, had nothing in common with a subject about which initially he knew nothing at all, and for which he at first had no personal sympathy. But the color of his palette and the unanticipated juxtaposition of contrasting scales provide a congenial setting for the saint and saintly values. Rubin is more positive about Matisse's *Saint Dominic*, which was modelled upon the one he was doing for the chapel of the Rosary at Vence. Here, too, the head has no features, but the power of the Saint Dominic lies in the turned head. In the instance of Matisse, Rubin, too, wants us to be clear that Matisse had no religious inclinations except as his attitude toward painting might be defined as religious. Rubin's position is obviously over against those who interpreted Matisse's association with Vence as a religious conversion. The problem remains, why that question should loom so large from all sides.

Not surprisingly, when one considers the centrality of the crucifixion in Christian life and thought, Germaine Richier's *Crucifix* became the focus of the most violent attacks. Herself an atheist, Richier nevertheless became involved in the project to the extent of confessing that for her "unconscious things of a unique kind were being translated" (p. 16). The body of Christ suggestively emerges from the cross, not uncharacteristically resembling the craggy and weathered wood of her sculpture in general. The form of the *Crucifix* was so offensive to the hierarchy and some of the congregation, that the words of the condemnation were tags of rejection, rather than explanations of error or inadequacy.

The history of the next years is familiar enough. The *Crucifix* was ordered removed, the hold of the conservatives increased, and Rome increasingly attacked modern art, identifying it with all the modern forces the church opposed, within and without its life. The worker-priest movement, considered the source of many of problems with which we have dealt, was suppressed, and the role of the Dominicans was side-tracked. In that confusing history, theologians and philosophers like Maritain and Marcel were themselves on the wrong side. The hoped-for mutual alliance had corroded on the one side through the increasing independence of the leading artists, and on the other, by the increasing conservatism of the church, in which Tridentine conceptions of beauty and purity were reasserted in a world moving in quite opposite directions. Considering the two diverging movements, the surprise is not that Assy failed to create a future, but that it happened at all, that it survives as a monumental anomaly prodding us with issues we can now more peacefully address. The Catholic Church, too, has abandoned the stand of the 50's. Vatican II has changed all that, and the selection of a Pope from a communist country has lately defanged even the traditional responses.

In spite of the fact that Assy possesses no liturgical or theological harmony, and that the artists who executed its works were not believers—a fact that Rubin seems to think the church has a right to ask—and that some of the artists did better work elsewhere, Assy stands for a church rich in artistic perception. Surely its non-traditional riches are to be accepted rather than mundane artistic productions that follow the liturgical calendar or a specific theological agenda. There are, of course, those in the church who prefer the latter choice.

Rubin's sympathies for traditional subjects is surprising, since when it comes to the art itself, his comments are rather formalistic even as art criticism, not to say devoid of social or theological meaning. Rubin has defined the French theological direction, including its social setting, and the negative Vatican response; he has discussed how the individual works were commissioned, and whether they are good or bad; but in his book the particular works of art and their context never meet. Rubin never tells us, for instance, whether Germaine Richier's *Crucifix* is a work of artistic and religious perception, valid in its own right, or whether it is congruent or not-congruent with theological insight. That penchant for formalistic non-meaning, in which a work of art stands only on canons of its own, narrows the horizons of art itself. Art for social or illustrative purposes represents the opposite extreme. Surely great art meets artistic canons, but has multiple suggestive, contextual perceptions and meanings beyond its formal character as art. For that reason, Assy is more significant than Rubin thought, even if all that he says concretely is true.

During the western period of so-called Christian civilization, the artist and faith convictions were not issues. The artist, too, participated in the faith, and his or her particular talents brought such transcendent beauty to their art that even we, who may not share the same faith, are still left in wonder. Art expresses, and then, transcends as art, timebound convictions. When the free, natural alliance of faith and artistic talent no longer continues, the diverging sensibilities and perceptions ignore each other or engage in sporadic conflict. For much of reformed Protestant history and for Catholicism from Trent to Vatican II that situation was fairly pervasively true. In our own time, the perceptions of the artists and the church rarely coincide. Fewer western artists today are probably materialists or communists than was true at the time of Assy. It is not inconceivable that their perceptions may have had a profundity of passion and depth, however directed, which the church had lost in the defensiveness of a past that no longer breathed vibrantly. That depth, indeed, may be evident even in works where the subject matter was foreign. Surely that is the meaning of what Germaine Richier said about her work on the *Crucifix*.

Many artists today view their own work as converging in the grandeur of humanity, i.e., in terms of worth, spirituality, transcendence, ultimacy, even in the midst of sameness, tragedy, or destruction. Abstract Expressionism surely had that sublime intention, expressing depths no longer conveyed in the recognizable subjects of either art or religion. That is why the Rothko paintings and the Rothko Chapel encompass us, making us reflect, meditate, no matter from which tradition or non-tradition we may come. They reach us where traditional symbols no longer do.

That loss may also be an opportunity. The early church baptized the vital perceptions around it, joining contemplation, thought and action. In time, it, too, could create its own language for art, its own vitalities and forms. That, too, may happen again. It is surely an overwhelming experience to see Richard Lippold's shimmering, exquisite, wire metal construction, the baldacchino over the altar in St. Mary's Cathedral, San Francisco. Our memory of history may let us see in it, as Jane Dillenberger remarked, the dome of heaven of the Early Christian baldacchinos or the Christ in Majesty of the Eastern Church. Historic realities, not historic memories, I submit, create great art. Hence, we move, not from traditional baldacchinos, or their equivalent, to Lippold. But sensing and experiencing the power of what this baldacchino is, we may see historic memories in new ways and be open to fresh perceptions and formulations.

17

The Aesthetic Dimension in Theology

THOMAS FRANKLIN O'MEARA

Entering a fifth-century basilica or a Gothic cathedral, we have a specific experience of church architecture and of ecclesial community. We look not only at the architecture but into the being of the church. Aisle and apse define an era culturally and historically. At the service of theology, an aesthetic vision poignantly portrays the history of the church in its forms: ecclesial institutions and theological formulas parallel the history of art.

My theme is not the visual illustration of ecclesiology or Christology through the arts, but the suggestion that the aesthetic illustrates human theological interpretation of divine revelation.[1] The aesthetic modality is a basic fact of experience. Aesthetics can describe religion, revelation, faith, and thinking-about-faith with a strength and clarity equal to the categorical style ("categorical" in both the Aristotlelian and Kantian sense). Theologians should examine the potentiality of an aesthetic description. For some time, the accepted foundation of theology has been logic and reason or concepts and words which reveal ultimate structures of meaning. The aesthetic intuition of ineffable presence in reality, of subjectivity surrounding the object and penetrating to its depth, does not presume that theology or life is mainly word, syllogism, myth, or symbol. Theology can flow from an encounter with and a grasp of revealing mystery in a manner analogous to the production and appreciation of art. The human personality not only in religious expression but also in thoughtful reflection on belief in a revealing God perceives mystery in an aesthetic way, where insight and emotion strive for immediacy.

The theologian observes the cultural scene and discerns that words have dominated contemporary theology, a trend parallel to the rule of software and computer programs in today's technological world. Transcendental hermeneutics has frequently reduced the rich inheritance of idealism to words, rendering biblical words linguistically attractive or nonthreatening rather than uncovering new perspectives on the reality of salvation history.[2] As this word-oriented approach today withdraws somewhat from fundamental theology and accepts a more modest role in biblical exegesis, the radical deconstruction of language challenges anthropology and literary criticism.

The Roman Catholic personality and vision do not rest easily in verbal expressions. Catholicism's glory and scandal are found in its commitment to and insistence on reality.[3] What shocked Karl Barth in the *analogia entis* is the Catholic determination to find and to hold—and to see—the human and the divine together. This Paul Tillich called the "Catholic substance"; it aims at sacramental transparence to the divine but sometimes reaches only one or another form of idolatry. The finite and the infinite, nature and tradition, what we call the revelation of mystery or the presence of grace, blend in the varied levels of a changing culture.

The single greatest task of twentieth-century Catholic theology, especially since Vatican II, was to develop theology from the point of view of the evolving self. The temporary synthesis of Roman Catholicism and Romantic idealism accomplished in the early nineteenth century was represented. Basic contemporary thought forms are not those of the thirteenth and the seventeenth centuries, and the thought forms of the modern person and culture are irrevocably subject-oriented. The names of Luther and Descartes, Kant and Marx, Klee and Schoenberg, lead modern culture ever deeper into the realm of the self. The Roman Catholic ethos, however, cannot abandon the affirmation of an independent reality in revelation even as it explores the individual and collective subjects and their creative encounter with what we call revelation. The intuitive mode of human engagement typical of the world of art suggests a mode of subjectivity that not only rejects the technocracy of words but which unleashes, bestows, and discloses the more of Presence.

A Nineteenth-Century Union: Aesthetics with Religion

A single ship or an iceberg against a vast sky of white and blue; a solitary person sitting on the edge of the Hudson River or the North Sea; two companions on a path in the German forest or the American wilderness—these were among the common visions of nineteenth-century Romantic art. Romantic painters used blue, white, and gold light to bring together the self with the mysterious world of nature.[4] The aesthetic was visually transformative and disclosive.

In 1794, at the age of nineteen Friedrich Schelling observed in one of his first publications that the full implication of Kant's thought had been drawn by Fichte. If the self was active enough to create space and time, did not the self produce all that was the non-self?[5] This full mastery of each personality over reality corresponded to the personal and political freedom offered by the French Revolution. In the new presentation of consciousness, the most profound theory joined the most radical praxis to liberate the infinite and the finite and all their modalities.

Schelling did not remain long with Fichte's consistent if radical position. The new natural sciences of chemistry and electricity, and the new Romantic movement in the arts, led him to posit a dialectic between the highly productive self and the pulsating, mysterious network of structure—nature—in his first system. In 1800, Schelling intended to show that nature and spirit were united ultimately in an aesthetic act of consciousness: the imagination. Imagination pervaded both matter and spirit; and joined them to each other. Spirit intends to be concrete and specific, while nature releases its own *Geist*. In art, Schelling saw the unity of human self-consciousness and free intelligence with objective matter. Through the imagination, which is inventive and creative, the mind's consciousness of universals joins with the particulars of the material universe. The resulting artwork is both real and ideal as it presents and symbolizes the union of spirit and nature. The freedom and power of art does not consist in ideal pictures at the edge of emptiness but in a total interpenetration of diverse and opposite elements. Art is a tension of reality and image, abstraction and emotion.[6] Art is passion moderated by beauty, and matter grasped by intellectual spirit.[7] Art links not only form and matter but subject and object, freedom and necessity; these last two dialectics are the horizon of all of Schelling's thought.

"Beauty is the infinite presented in the finite."[8] Schelling sought the quintessence: he wanted both the ideal and the real. The German word for the activity of the imagination, or aesthetic power, is *einbilden* ("to form into one"). The transcendental has room for both the absolute and the finite as art presents both structures of the absolute: *Geist* and *Natur*. Aesthetic intuition sees the interplay of both while the artwork presents them concretely. The artist patterns a work after the activity of the Absolute, whose cosmos is also art. For Schelling, creation, art, and revelation search the same world.[9] The absolute, whether in universal or individual consciousness, does not so much objectify as manifest. In manifestation, the revelation of the ideal in the real takes place, and this is the highest activity and ultimate ground of every object.[10]

Until Schelling's first system, in which philosophy ended in art, the philosophy of art was a treatment of artworks as objects for a section of philosophy or a view of aesthetic perception as a function of epistemology. With Schelling, art became the paradigm of being and production. "Art reflects for us the identity of conscious and unconscious activity. Their tension is infinite. . . . The basic character of art is a consciousless infinite."[11] Art has a multidialectical nature, as its stands at the intersection of the revelation of consciousness and the world of nature. Along with religion and philosophy, art gives access to what is the enduring question in Schelling's philosophy: Why does the Absolute objectify itself? Why is there not simply nothing?

Art is a reflection of the primal unity of the absolute out of which, in freedom and necessity, the variety and development of objectivity has flowed. Art does justice to both sides of the dialectic: it begins in turmoil and it ends in peace. In his study of imagination during the Enlightenment and the Romantic era, J. Engell elegantly describes Schelling's goal:

> Schelling uses many pairs to clarify the nature of the two poles
> connected by the imagination. On the one side are infinite form,
> matter in its particular and concrete manifestation, the individ-
> ual, nature, and works of art. This pole includes a beautiful
> tropical fish, Saturn's shadow cast on its own rings, and the

Apollo Belvedere. On the other side are infinite being, spirit in
a universal or abstract mode, the race or type, the mind of God,
and the mind of man. This is where God broods over the face
of the waters, where the Logos of Saint John speaks, and where
souls feel what Buddha calls Nirvana. The "productive power,"
apparently nothing in itself, is the power that creates all things.
More dramatically, it is the power to make galaxies out of a
seeming vacuum, worlds out of stellar dust, and the *Last Supper*
from dyes and wet plaster. Only by exercising this pervading
creative spirit in both man and nature, only by re-attaining a
pre-established harmony, can perception and reality, the ideal
and the real, work through each other and become one.[12]

Schelling maintained that science is not capable of producing
the universal theory. Science remains particular and intent upon
a group of elements or powers, while art is intuition, and an insight of genius, into the whole. In a drama or a sculpture, one
finds not just the part but the totality, both the real and the ideal.
Schelling compared the absolute and its revelation to a play-
wright involved in the play with the players. Such revelation must
be immanent, subtle, and ongoing; otherwise, both the divine life
and human freedom would end.[13]

In 1800, Schelling wrote that art is the only true and full
expression of the new philosophy, which was idealist and developmental (an "objective idealism").

The real world develops entirely from the same primal composition which gives rise to the world of art. It is to be viewed as
one great whole, and is, in all its individual products, depicting
the one Infinite. . . . Aesthetic intuition is simply transcendental intuition become objective, and so it is obvious that art is
the only true and eternal organon and document of philosophy,
ever speaking to us of what philosophy cannot depict in external form, namely the unconscious elements in acting and producing, and their original identity with consciousness. Art is
paramount to the philosopher, precisely because it opens to him,
as it were, the holy of holies, where burns in eternal and original unity, as in a single flame, that which in nature and history
is rent asunder, that which in life and action, no less than in
thought, must forever fly apart.[14]

For Schelling, art is not the special evocation of the solitary
genius but a realization of the life of absolute consciousness. It is

an access to the structure of reality—past, present, and future. Art, like philosophy, is revelation. The triad of religion, art, and philosophy has become one manifestation in Schelling's systems where electromagnetism explicates sculpture and Christianity, and all describes the history of the objectification of the absolute spirit.[15]

Art and Revelation

Through their respective uses of light, Raphael and Rembrandt offer two different theologies on their canvases: different views of human nature, the world, and sin, as well as differing views of grace emerge (in art, light signifies grace). The details of Raphael's backgrounds are luminous and rich, for light is in the air and air is in the landscapes. In Renaissance art, the tragedy of suffering humanity does not overwhelm, as the colors of light exuding from both nature and grace separate and unify. The vibrant emotions and the linear corporality of the High Renaissance are serenely present in Raphael's art. Optically spacious, Raphael's *Stanze* are balanced, thoughtful contemplations of the harmonic and salutory springs of antiquity and Christianity.

Rembrandt's visual Calvinism presents another theology, as succeeding levels of darkness frame and proclaim the single space of light: Jesus as the Christ. Even the light surrounding Jesus as preacher and crucified has a source outside the canvas in the totally transcendent God. Shadows of browns and blacks intrude upon John and Joseph of Arimathea at the cross—nothing escapes sin except the divine Word.

After Rembrandt, art became increasingly secular. The attempts of the Romantic naturalist Caspar David Friedrich to insert crucifixes into pantheistic landscapes did not modify the trend toward impression and expression. Whether in art or theology, the explicitly supernatural, when presented in objects, seemed only to block grace from human vision. In the early twentieth century, Wassily Kandinsky sought "the inner necessity of *das Geistige*."[16] At the moment of triumph for subjective art, he perceived a shift toward an epoch of great spirituality in which the dimension of spiritual revelation would be revealed. Kandinsky's *Compositions* and *Improvisations* were not a surrender to decoration or solipsism but an attempt to let absolute spirit appear in forms: to let the holy disclose itself in a precise arrangement of tone, color, and line. Echoing Schelling's last system, Kandinsky wrote of abstract art:

> I realize that this view of art is Christian and at the same time it shelters within itself the necessary elements for the reception of the "third" revelation, the revelation of the Holy Spirit.[17]

The similarity in thought of Kandinsky, Franz Marc, and Paul Klee to Rudolf Otto and Martin Heidegger is inescapable. Art in the twentieth century is not a flight from all objectivity into nihilism and atheism but the piercing into the horizons of holiness, transcendence, or sin, which lie within and beyond every objectification. For Heidegger, the subject-object dichotomy could be overcome by viewing Being as a process of disclosure and covering through history. Art was Being's illustration.

Theologians, like artists, strove to get beyond the landscape of simplistic salvation history, where biblical and supernatural objects were strewn. Paul Tillich's "symbol" and Rudolf Bultmann's "myth" have their cultural sources not in the technology of the postmodern world but in nineteenth-century aesthetics and philosophy. Tillich's and Bultmann's disciples forgot the aesthetic source of their subject-oriented theology and reduced revelation to a technology of linguistics constructed upon the principles that nothing could exist (or be credible) outside of nature and secularity. Reflection upon aesthetic perception helps the contemporary theologian to rediscover the objectivity of divine revelation within the horizons of human subjectivity.

Consider the New Testament, whose forms are rarely those of logic and law. These texts, and the Jesus they record, teach through imagination's forms: parables, stories, paradoxes, confrontations, dramas, hymns, gospels, and letters. In Luke, Jesus explains that his *doxa* could only come through both passion and resurrection (24:26). In Philippians, Jesus, though in the *morphe* of God, has lived in the schema of the human person (2:6ff.). Romans proclaims Jesus to be the *ikon* of God (8:30). The New Testament Jesus is an individual person who is at the same time a depth barely plumbed by his followers (John 21:25; Ephesians

3:18f.). The Word Incarnate, from the infinity of the Logos, reveals itself as man through the very limitations and characteristics of Jesus ben Joseph. They are the channels not of finite failure but of revelation. Jesus is viewed from different perspectives by a variety of people: sign of Jonah, suffering servant, savior of the people, fountain, son of God, son of man, vine, Logos, and bread. Varied, even contradictory interpretations are possible as with a work of art.

The Aesthetic Dimension in the Theology of Hans Urs von Balthasar

The Swiss Roman Catholic theologian Hans Urs von Balthasar has observed carefully and extensively the aesthetic dimension in New Testament theology.[18] Influenced both by the German idealists and by the Calvinist theologian Karl Barth, Balthasar concluded that the various presentations of Jesus and his message are not rational systems or clusters of existential myths but images giving limited accesses to the always greater reality of Jesus; accesses that are revelatory in their art form and real in their captivating, colored concreteness.

In 1961, Balthasar began to publish a theological system entitled *Herrlichkeit* ("Glory").[19] Its seven volumes were original, not only in elegance of style and extent of ambition, but in their format. *Herrlichkeit* was an aesthetic theology explaining the Christian faith through the leitmotiv of the visual arts. The system did not simply point out Christian themes in works of art or show parallels between theology and painting. Rather, the expression and reality of Christianity were interpreted as realized in a given style of art.

This theological system of aesthetics did not neglect the concern of Schelling: consciousness and creation as aesthesis. In his first volumes, Balthasar compared the Christian faith with aesthetic enjoyment and contemplation. The system moved beyond the interplay of our consciousness of subject and object in the aesthetic mode to revelation as object, i.e., as art. Our consciousness receives revelation in the way that a drama or a mosaic mirrors subjectivity; the people and events in the history of God's reign appear in a pattern similar to the way artworks enter our mind and emotions. This was not to imply that revelation is a symbol rather than a reality, but that the reality of Jesus Christ was both hidden and disclosed, and that the kingdom of God preached by Jesus employs a variety of forms to exist around and within us as something believed and encountered.

Christ is portrayed in the New Testament as God's *ikon* or *logos* not because he is fragile and docetic, but because he is infinite. Balthasar has philosophic and theological precedents to support his interpretation of revelation as a polychrome work of art. He arranges the Old and the New Testament around biblical motifs such as "image," "glory," and "form." The central volume on Jesus Christ has aesthetic horizons, not dogmas, for its principles and develops them to include their shadow side, their opposite: e.g., incarnation (crucifixion), glorification (hiddenness and opacity), and awe and praise (social and personal emptiness). Jesus' self-interpretation is ambiguous and may end in an aesthetic form. The underlying revelation of Jesus Christ is that God's plan for us, his "glory" in us, includes contradiction, suffering, failing, and death.

Human Faith, Divine Revelation, and the Aesthetic

Figures as diverse as Schelling and Balthasar have suggested an intersection of faith and revelation that occurs in emotion and insight. The style of human faith and divine revelation resembles the aesthetic. Not simply irrational faith or analytic reason are possible meeting points but imagination provides a milieu that is both receptive and interpretive. The aesthetic pattern is: *intuitive* (seeing is its exemplary function); *immediate;* and *born* forward in *emotional* experience. Analogous to the artist, the believer seeks through the words and events of revelation an openness through objectivity toward a further reality. The interplay of subject and mysterious presence (which, as grace, exists on both sides of the subject-object encounter) happens in the style of an encounter. As with the arts, faith is a seeing: a perceiving of likeness and then a perceiving of distance and difference. This is mediated through the emotions and images that open to ecstasy.

The faith-revelation experience, like the artistic one, gives not a single but a double access: one into the self, and the other to "the holy." For example, when I attend the symphony, my psyche is stimulated by the music and lets the bottom drop out. Then the experience regroups vision and emotion to lead me to something "more" mediated by art.

Enduring art is not merely self-productive or self-interpretive. Nor is aesthetic experience only subjective and existential. The demythologizing-existential model of theology has proven to be ultimately not an aesthetic model but a technological one. Art, like revelation, is a liturgy of the "More." As the ideal-presence increases through the intensity of the aesthetic-mystical experience, the intervening object declines in perceived centrality and the two powers intermingle: self and further presence. Paul Ricoeur writes:

> To summarize, poetic language is no less *about* reality than any other use of language but refers to it by the means of a complex strategy which implies, as an essential component, a suspension and seemingly an abolition of the ordinary reference attached to descriptive language. This suspension, however, is only the negative condition of a second-order reference, of an indirect reference built on the ruins of the direct reference. This reference is called second-order reference only with respect to the primacy of the reference of ordinary language. For, in another respect, it constitutes the pri-mordial reference to the extent that it suggests, reveals, unconceals,—or whatever you say— the deep structures of reality to which we are related as mortals who are born into this world and who *dwell* in it for a while.[20]

Conclusions

There are several consequences for fundamental theology when it takes seriously the quality of access found through the aesthetic experience.

First, fundamental theology sees in art a sustenance of two domains: subjectivity and objectivity. The aesthetic act is productive. The forms of art are not the object of perception but the medium. Similarly, in faith and theology, the text, the law, the liturgy, and the church building are not the object but the medium. Art's particular relationship to cognition and emotion allows it to lay claim to immediacy. Religious immediacy may be an aspect of consciousness, not of analysis, and mature awareness of revelation invites the objectless pondering of grace. The realm of immediacy as found in mysticism is traditionally seen as a development of faith, grace, and life.[21] So both revelation and theology follow an aesthetic pattern. Therefore, the goal of theology is not model-substitution but contemplation as openness to disclosure through life and presence.

Second, fundamental theology explains how areas of Christian faith and life can be enterprises of the imagination. As productive consciousness gives structure to knowledge, theology arranges and draws out the new, creative correlations of revelation within culture. Although the medium can be legal, logical, and verbal forms, it is primarily intuitive. Theological creativity is neither an emptying of language nor an arbitrary projection of meanings. Like revelation, art aims at the transcendent but is realized in history. Art is ultimately not theoretical; it withers under too intense a hermeneutic. Theology is the discernment of the presence of the "More" amid sin and grace. Like art, when theology is only a symbolism, it is empty—devoid of prophetic, existential, and spontaneously transcendent dimensions, and ready to be passed over quickly. While finite form is the medium for both grace and art, the identification of meaning with symbol spells not the birth but the death of art and faith in the contemporary world.

Third, in the arts, we find a presentation of the fundamental pattern of our existence: joy mixed with tragedy. There is a negative aesthetic: pain and limitation. The scriptural theme of life out of death is also an artistic truth. The ultimate critique of everything is suffering, and each suffering is ultimately the messenger of death. Contradiction and negation are presence and glory. Every human life, not just Jesus Christ's, like every artwork, has the quality of chiaroscuro: the beautiful is glimpsed with the sharp lines of finitude, the limits of negation, and the shadows of apophasis.

In their union of the aesthetic-mystical and the real-divine, these ideas about the aesthetic dimension in theology stand in a long tradition reaching from Origen to Pseudo-Dionysius to Meister Eckhart to Schelling to Heidegger. For them, human finitude and change are not hopeless and punishing shipwrecks but clearings for revelation. Even nothingness—which in our century seems at times to be the lord of the world—has its own dignity, reality, and dark glory.

NOTES

1. Much of the past discussion on art and theology was limited to the theory of aesthetics, particularly medieval aesthetics, and failed to grasp the synchronicity existing at times between artistic media and theology and philosophy. The Aristotelianism of Jacques Maritain and Etienne Gilson, along with their rejection of cultural historicity and the legitimacy of the post-Kantian world, made it inevitable that they would miss the mutual expression of a *Zeitgeist* in arts and humanities. By 1945, on the other hand, the French Dominicans Regamey and Courturier saw the new modes of presence of the holy in modern art, and Paul Tillich observed similarities to Rudolf Otto, Rainer Marie Rilke, and Martin Heidegger.

2. John Dillenberger criticizes the "total victory" of meaning and arrangement in language over other experiences and human processes in the role of religious analysis and expression. "The Diversity of Disciplines as a Theological Question: The Visual Arts as Paradigm," *Journal of the American Academy of Religion* 48 (1980):235.

3. "The act of faith ends not in a statement but in a reality. We form statements only to have knowledge of things by them; this is true of the sciences, and also of faith," *Summa Theologiae*, II-II, q.1, a.2, ad.2. On the necessity of correcting the modern *Wendung zur Idee* with life and history and of achieving a balance of "subject" and "field," cf. Bernard Lonergan, *Method in Theology* (New York: Herder and Herder, 1972), pp. 144f.

4. Cf. John Wilmerding, *American Light: The Luminist Movement, 1850–1875* (Washington: The National Gallery of Art, 1980); William Vaughn, *German Romantic Painters* (New Haven: Yale University Press, 1981); and Barbara Novak, *Nature and Culture* (New York: Oxford University Press, 1980).

5. "Fichte was an event . . . a flash of lightning. . . . For him everything was through and for the ego. Fichte took the autonomy Kant gave to human actions and expanded it into theoretical philosophy," Friedrich Schelling, *Grundlegung der positiven Philosophie*, ed, H. Furhmans (Turin, 1972), pp. 177, 180.

6. *Kunstgeschichtliche Anmerkungen*, in *Samtliche Werke* (*SW*) (Stuttgart: Cotta, 1856–61), 9:159.

7. Schelling, *The Philosophy of Art* (London: Chapman, 1845), pp. 2, 9, 18. This is the only work of Schelling fully translated into English during his lifetime. Cf. the new edition with commentary from L. Sziborsky (Hamburg: Meiner, 1981).

8. *System of Transcendental Philosophy* in *SW* 3:620.

9. Ibid., pp. 610, 601. "History as a whole is a progressive, gradual self-disclosing revelation of the absolute. So one can never indicate in history particular places where the mark of the providence of God himself is visible. For God never *exists*, if the existent is that which presents itself in the objective world; if he existed in such a way, then we would not be. Rather, he continually reveals himself," (p. 603). On Schelling's philosophy of art, two works stand out: X. Tilliette, *Schelling. Philosophie en devenir* (Paris: Vrin, 1970), and D. Jähnig, *Schelling. Die Kunst in der Philosophie* (Pfullingen: Neske, 1969).

10. *Zur Geschichte* in *SW* 10:117.

11. *System, SW* 3:619.

12. J. Engell. *The Creative Imagination: Enlightenment to Romanticism* (Cambridge: Harvard University Press, 1981), p. 3.

13. *System, SW* 3:623, 601.

14. Ibid., p. 627. For various reasons the idea of art as the point of union of the subjective and objective fades from Schelling's thought after 1804 as his philosophy undergoes modifications drawn from Hegel and Jakob Boehme. Still, art perdures, appearing with new vigor as the core of the late philosophy in "myth" and "revelation." Myth is the result of the human dialectic, work not of a single genius in stone and color but of a group of people within the history of consciousness, which is, as a product, also the history of religion. For Schelling, mythology is the revelation of the absolute and the collective consciousness of a people, and becomes the ultimate expression of the ideal in the real (*SW* 11:241ff.). Engell describes the change in Schelling, when religion becomes more explicit after the move to Munich in 1804, as one from imagination to love. "Increasingly he identifies the two principles of God no longer as reason and creative imagination but as reason and love. The oneness of God, working through love, brings about creation itself. Imagination is a form of love because it involves escaping from self and becoming involved in the world. To this end the whole of creation is God's act of love. Christ is a promise and symbol of that love" (p. 327). We should recall, too, that the church in the last pages of Schelling's final *Philosophie der Offenbarung* is a work of art.

15. *SW* 10:118.

16. W. Kandinsky, *Uber das Geistige in der Kunst* (Munich: Piper, 1912), p. 104. Jähnig observes two distinct worlds of art linking the twentieth century to the world of Romantic idealism. One, continuing *Sturm und Drang*, saw art as poetry: this was the philosophic world of Hegel and Schopenhauer, the musical world of Schumann, Wagner, and Schoenberg, and the painterly world of Friedrich and Kandinsky. The second world, the child of classicism, saw art as architectonic, a tension and a life between creativity and form: this was the world of Goethe, Schiller, Novalis, Kleist, Haydn, Mozart, Beethoven, and Schubert. This second style is closer to the baroque than to its sibling, and perdures in Delacroix, Cézanne, van Gogh, and Renoir. *Schelling's Philosophie der Kunst*, 2, p. 172.

17. Cited in *Modern Artists on Art* (New York: Prentice-Hall, 1968), p. 81.

18. Hans Urs von Balthasar, *Herrlichkeit*, I (Einsiedeln: Johannes, 1961), pp. 25ff.

19. Von Balthasar intends to compose three theological systems, each based upon one of the transcendentals: the beautiful, the good, and the true. While the third (as yet unwritten) would be a logic, the first two arrange Christian revelation around aesthetics (*Herrlichkeit*) and a second art form, drama (*Theodramatik*). "Dramatics is agogics, teaching as action, and in the relationship between life and stage the border between both fades. So in the action of God with humanity the border between the agent and the spectators is lifted. The human person is not a spectator but a co-player in God's drama. . . . Naturally, in this theodrama the stage is God's. What he does remains the decisive content of the play . . . and so viewing revelation as a drama remains image and simile." "Zwischen Aesthetik und Logik," *Theodramatik*, I, *Prologomena* (Einsiedeln: Johannes, 1973), p. 18. Aiden Nichols, O.P., develops a similar quest into the features of art and aesthetic perception for a model serving a theology of revelation. He observes the artwork as mediating between artist and viewer: this happens through the mediation of signs, and human beings are led to an awareness of ultimate and personal values but as manifest in concrete life. "The Artwork and Christian Revelation," *The Art of God Incarnate* (New York; Paulist Press, 1980), pp. 105ff. Cf. also, von Balthasar, "Offenbarung und Schönheit," *Skizzen zur Theologie*, I (Einsiedeln, 1960).

20. Paul Ricoeur, "The Metaphorical Process as Cognition, Imagination and Feeling," *Critical Inquiry* 5 (1978), p. 153. Cf. Bernard Lonergan, *Insight* (New York: Longmanns, 1958), p. 185.

21. For Thomas Aquinas the highest human activity was not metaphysics or theology but psychic life touched by the Holy Spirit's charism of wisdom. Wisdom is intuitive, experiential, surpassing knowledge and understanding in its emotionally driven, immediate communion with that which faith accepts and reason ponders analytically. Interestingly, for an illustrative analogy to wisdom, Aquinas chose art. Cf. *Summa Theologiae*, II-II, q.45, aa.1,3; q.45, a.2; I, q.14, a.8; cf. T. Gilby, *Poetic Experience* (London: Sheed and Ward, 1934).

18

Art and Ultimate Reality

PAUL TILLICH

It is a great and unexpected honor that I have been asked to give an address in a place which for years has been for me a favored oasis within this beloved city of New York. It is an unexpected honor; for I am far from being considered an expert in the visual arts—or in any other art. I could accept the invitation to speak here only because the Museum planned a series of "Art *and*" lectures, the first of which was to be "Art and Religion." It is the religious angle from which I am asked to look at the visual arts. This means that I must do it as a theologian and a philosopher.

A disadvantage of such an approach is obvious. One must conceptualize and generalize, where intuitive penetration into the particular creation is the first and all-determining task. It is well known that many artists feel uneasy if their works are subsumed to categories; nevertheless, art criticism is as necessary as literary criticism. It serves to guide one to the point where the immediate intuitive approach to the particular work can occur. Attempts at conceptualization like the following should be judged in the light of the demand to make such criticism finally superfluous.

The series of the *"Art and"* lectures was supposed to begin with the lecture on art and religion, but it does not. Instead, I intend to speak about art and ultimate reality, a subject which, although including religion, transcends by far what is usually called religious. Ultimate reality underlies every reality, and it characterizes the whole appearing world as non-ultimate, preliminary, transitory and finite.

Reprinted from *Art and the Craftsman: The Best of the Yale Literary Magazine, 1836–1961*, ed. J. Harned and N. Goodwin (New Haven: Yale Literary Magzine, 1961), pp. 185–200.

These are philosophical terms, but the attitude in which they originally have been conceived is universally known. It is the awareness of the deceptive character of the surface of everything we encounter which drives one to discover what is below the surface. But soon we realize that even if we break through the surface of a thing or person or an event, new deceptions arise. So we try to dig further through what lies deepest below the surface—to the truly real which cannot deceive us. We search for an ultimate reality, for something lasting in the flux of transitoriness and finitude. All philosophers searched for it, even if they called change itself the unchanging in all being. They gave different names to ultimate reality expressing in such names their own anxieties, their longing, their courage, but also their cognitive problems and discoveries about the nature of reality. The concepts in which ultimate reality is expressed, the way philosophy reached them and applied them to the whole of reality fills the pages of the history of philosophy. It is a fascinating story just as is the history of the arts in which ultimate reality is expressed in artistic forms. And actually, they are not two histories. Philosophical and artistic expressions of the experience of ultimate reality correspond to each other. But dealing with such parallels would trespass the limits of my subject.

The term "ultimate reality" is *not* another name for God in the religious sense of the word. But the God of religion would not be God if he were not first of all ultimate reality. On the one hand, the God of religion is more than ultimate reality. Yet religion can speak of the divinity of the divine only if God *is* ultimate reality. If he were anything less, namely, *a* being—even the highest—he would be on the level of all other beings. He would be conditioned by the structure of being like everything that is. He would cease to be God.

From this follows a decisive consequence. If the idea of God includes ultimate reality, everything that expresses ultimate reality expresses God whether it intends to do so or not. And there is nothing that could be excluded from this possibility because everything that has being is an expression, however preliminary and transitory it may be, of being-itself, of ultimate reality.

The word "expression" requires some consideration. First, it is obvious that if something expresses something else—as, for instance, language expresses thought—they are not the same. There is a gap between that which expresses and that which is expressed. But there is also a point of identity between them. It is the riddle and the depth of all expression that it both reveals and hides at the same time. And if we say that the universe is an expression of ultimate reality, we say that the universe and everything in it both reveals and hides ultimate reality. This should prevent us from a religious glorification of the world as well as from an anti-religious profanization of the world. There is ultimate reality in this stone and this tree and this man. They are translucent toward ultimate reality, but they are also opaque. They prevent it from shining through them. They try to exclude it.

Expression is always expression for someone who can receive it as such, for whom it is a manifestation of something hidden, and who is able to distinguish expression and that which is expressed. Only man within the world we know can distinguish between ultimate reality and that in which it appears. Only man is conscious of the difference of surface and depth.

There are three ways in which man is able to experience and express ultimate reality in, through and above the reality he encounters. Two of these ways are indirect; one of them is direct. The two indirect ways of expressing ultimate reality are philosophy—more specifically, metaphysics—and art. They are indirect because it is their immediate intention to express the encountered reality in cognitive concepts or in esthetic images.

Philosophy in the classical sense of the word seeks for truth about the universe as such. But in doing so, philosophy is driven towards explicit or implicit assertions about ultimate reality.

We have already pointed to the manifoldness of such concepts, and "ultimate reality" is itself one of them. In the same way, while trying to express reality in esthetic images, art makes ultimate reality manifest through these images—the word image, taken in its largest sense, which includes lingual and musical figures.

To be able to show this concretely is the main purpose of my lecture, and here I feel supported by the self-interpretation of many artists who tell us that their aim is the expression of reality.

But there is the third and direct way in which man discerns and receives ultimate reality. We call it religion—in the traditional sense of the word. Here ultimate reality becomes manifest through ecstatic experiences of a concrete-revelatory character and is expressed in symbols and myths.

Myths are sets of symbols. They are the oldest and most fundamental expression of the experience of ultimate reality. Philosophy and art take from their depth and their abundance. Their validity is the power with which they express their relation of man and his world to the ultimately real. Out of a particular relation of this kind are they born. With the end of this relation they die. A myth is neither primitive science nor primitive poetry, although both are present in them, as in a mother's womb, up to the moment in which they become independent and start their autonomous road. On this road both undergo an inner conflict, similar to that in all of us, between the bondage to the creative ground from which we come and our free self-actualization in our mature life. It is the conflict between the secular and the sacred.

Usually secular philosophy is called simply philosophy, and art simply art; while in connection with the sacred, namely, the direct symbols of ultimate reality, philosophy is called theology, and art is called religious art. The creative as well as destructive consequences of this conflict dominate many periods of man's history, the most significant for us being the five hundred years of modern history. The reduction of these tensions and the removal of some of their destructive consequences would certainly come about if the decisive point in the following considerations were established.

That decisive point is this: the problem of religion and philosophy as well as that of religion and art is, by no means confined to theology and religious art; it appears wherever ultimate reality is expressed through philosophical concepts and artistic images, and the medium through which this happens is the stylistic form of a thought or an image.

Styles must be deciphered. And for this one needs keys with which the deciphering can be done, keys which are taken from the very nature of the artistic encounter with reality. It is not my task to point to such keys for the deciphering of styles in general, or of the innumerable collective and personal styles which have appeared in history. Rather, I shall indicate those stylistic elements which are expressive for ultimate reality. The best way to do this is to look at the main type in which ultimate reality is shown in the great manifestations of man's religious experience. They express in a direct way the fundamental relation of man to ultimate reality, and these expressions shine through the artistic images and can be seen in them.

On this basis, I suggest distinguishing five stylistic elements which appear, in innumerable mixtures, in the great historic styles in East and West, and through which ultimate reality becomes manifest in works of art. After the description of each of these elements, I want to show pictures as examples, without discussing them concretely, and with the awareness of the contingent, almost casual, character in which they were chosen, for many technical reasons.

The first type of religious experience, and also the most universal and fundamental one, is the sacramental. Here ultimate reality appears as the holy which is present in all kinds of objects, in things, persons, events. In the history of religion, almost everything in the encountered world has become a bearer of the holy, a sacramental reality. Not even the lowest and ugliest is excluded from the quality of holiness, from the power of expressing ultimate reality in the form of here and now. For this is what holiness means, not moral goodness—as moralistically distorted religions assume. There is actually no genuine religion in which the sacramental experience of the divine as being present does not underlie every other religious utterance.

This enables us to discover the first stylistic element which is effective in the experience of ultimate reality. It appears predominantly in what often has been called magic realism. But because of the non-religious meaning of the term, magic, I prefer to call it *numinous* realism. The word numinous is derived from the Latin *numen* (appearing divinity with a divine-demonic quality). It is *realism* that depicts ordinary things, ordinary persons, ordinary events, but it is numinous realism. It depicts them in a way which makes them strange, mysterious, laden with an ambiguous power. It uses space-relations, body stylization, uncanny expressions for this purpose. We are fascinated and repelled by it. We are grasped by it as something through which ultimate reality mysteriously shines.

Much primitive art has this character. It does not exclude other elements, and this is most conspicuous, for its greatness has been rediscovered by our contemporary artists who have been driven to similar forms by the inner development of their artistic visions. These visions have received different names. In the development of cubism from Cezanne to Braque, at least one element of numinous realism is present. It is present in the stylo-metaphysics of De Chirico and in the surrealism of Chagall. It appears in those contemporary painters and sculptors who unite the appreciation of the particular thing with cosmic significance they ascribe to it.

All this is the correlate to religious sacramentalism. It shows ultimate reality as present here and now in particular objects. Certainly, it is created by artistic demands, but intended or not, it does more than fulfill these demands. It expresses ultimate reality in the particular thing. Religiously and artistically, however, it is not without dangers.

The religious danger of all sacramental religion is idolatry, the attempt to make a sacramentally consecrated reality into the divine itself. This is the demonic possibility which is connected with all sacramental religion. The artistic danger appears when things are used as mere symbols, losing their independent power of expression.

It is difficult to draw the line between an artificial symbolism and the symbolic power of things as bearers of ultimate reality. Perhaps one could say that wrong symbolism makes us look away from one thing to another one for which it is a symbol; while genuine symbolic power in a work of art opens up its own depths, and the depths of reality as such.

Now I should like to mention a group of pictures which, without special interpretation, shall give you a concrete idea of what I mean about the predominance of this first stylistic element.

Since it was difficult to find among the innumerable examples of primitive art one that was especially more significant than another, I have chosen the "Figure," as it is called, by the sculptor, Lipchitz. Please do not forget, however, that it is a stylistic element which is predominant, not a special type.

Next we have Klee's "Masque of Fear" where we find a very similar expression, the stylized presence of ultimate reality in terms of awe, which belongs to all human relations to ultimate reality.

Again, another Klee—"Child Consecrated to Suffering."

Then a Cezanne—"Still Life." About this I must say something which goes back to my earliest encounter with the visual arts immediately after I came out of the ugliness of the First World War and was introduced to modern art by a friend, Dr. Eckhard V. Sydow, who wrote the first book on German expressionism. At that time I came to the conclusion that an apple of Cezanne has more presence of ultimate reality than a picture of Jesus by Hoffman (which can now be found in the Riverside Church of this city).

Next we have Braque—"Man with Guitar," which also shows elements of reality which otherwise are not seen, and in which elements of ultimate reality show through as foundations of the surface which never appear in reality on the surface.

Then we have Chagall—"I and the Village," and again it is the individual things to which I want to draw your attention as in the stylization, the color, the lines, the relationship, and something I would like to be able to mention at greater length—the two-dimensionality which is not superficial but one of depth. All these express what I called presence of ultimate reality.

Then De Chirico—"Melancholy and Mystery of the Street." This and similar pictures are especially near to my heart, not only because I am interested in depth psychology, in which things like this appear as dreams or as nightmares, but because at times I think all of us become estranged from ordinary reality; and this estrangement produces a new encounter with dimensions of reality otherwise unseen.

Miro—"Composition." Now here you have nothing left but the surface: nevertheless, these elements embody a power of being which you never would find in surface reality in the same way.

Next is a picture with a funny name, which no one whom I asked, including myself, understood. It is by Tanguy, and the puzzling title is "Mama, Papa is Wounded." But I think these forms express something of the potentialities which are in reality but which never come to the surface without the realizing mind of the artist.

Now I come to a Gabo entitled "Spiral Theme." This and a few others express something very important to me, namely, the possibility that man's power of technical transformation of nature and of scientific penetration into the ultimate elements of nature is thus able to produce still another way of manifesting the creative ground of reality.

And the same in this. This is by Lippold and is called "Full Moon, Variation 7." The variation expressed in these lines is a new understanding of something which has appeared in man's mythological thinking for ten thousand years. The symbol of the moon is a goddess, and here the mathematical structure brings the same fundamental motif into another kind of expression.

Related to the sacramental type of religion and at the same time radically going beyond it is the mystical type. Religious experience tries to reach ultimate reality without the mediation of particular things in this religious type. We find this type actualized in Hinduism and Buddhism, in Taoism and Neo-Platonism. And, with some strong qualifications, in some places in later Judaism, Islam, and Christianity. It can undergo a transformation into a monistic mysticism of nature under the famous formula of the God of Nature. In it God is equated with nature—with the creative ground of nature which transcends every particular object.

We find this in ancient Asia as well as in modern Europe and America. Correlate to this religious type is that stylistic element in which the particularity of things is dissolved into a visual continuum. This continuum is not a grey in grey; it has all the potentialities of particular beings within itself, like the Brahman in Hinduism and the One in Neo-Platonism or the creating God in Christianity as they include within themselves the possibility of the whole world. The continuum contains tensions, conflicts, movements. But it has not yet come to particular things. They are hidden in a mere potential state. They are not yet actual as distinguishable objects; or if so, they shine through from afar as before creation.

We find this in Chinese landscapes in which air and water symbolize the cosmic unity, and individual rocks or branches hardly dare emerge to an independent existence. We find it in the background of Asiatic and Western paintings, even if the foreground is filled with figures. It is a decisive element in the impressionist dissolution of particulars into a continuum of light and colors. Most radically it has been carried through in what is called to-day, non-objective painting. For instance, the latest decade of American painting is dominated by it. Of course, one cannot show ultimate reality directly, but one can use basic structural elements of reality like line, cubes, planes, colors, as symbols for that which transcends all reality—and this is what the non-objective artists have done.

In the same period in which Eastern mysticism powerfully enters the American scene, American artists have deprived reality of its manifoldness, of the concreteness of things and persons, and have expressed ultimate reality through the medium of elements which ordinarily appear only in unity with concrete objects on the surface of reality.

Here also the dangers must be seen. The sacred emptiness can become mere emptiness, and the spatial emptiness of some pictures indicates merely artistic emptiness. The attempt to express ultimate reality by annihilating reality can lead to works in which nothing at all is expressed. It is understandable that as such a state in religion has led to strong reactions against the mystical type of religion, it has led in art to strong reactions against the non-objective stylistic elements.

And now I should like to give you examples of pictures of this second stylistic element.

First is the Japanese artist, Ashikaga—"The Landscape." This shows a pantheistic nature—trees and rocks barely emerging out of the whole.

Tai Chin, where it is even more powerfully expressed.

Klee—"Equals Infinity." The word infinity here expresses this going beyond of concrete reality.

Seurat—"Fishing Fleet," where the individual things are there, but they hardly dare to become fully individual.

Kandinsky's "Improvisation." I remember when I was once sitting in a house in Berlin in the 20's, there was a Kandinsky similar to this. It was really a liberation for me to be freed from the individual things and to be in a realm which at that time was very near to my own religious thinking.

Then, finally, Jackson Pollock's "No. I," and I must say I found it difficult to evaluate him, but since seeing some of his very best pictures at the Brussels Exhibition, I have become very much reconciled with this fullness of reality without a concrete subject matter.

Like mysticism, the prophetic-protesting type of religion goes beyond the sacramental basis of all religious life. Its pattern is the criticism of a demonically distorted sacramental system in the name of personal righteousness and social justice. Holiness without justice is rejected. Not nature, but history becomes the place of the manifestation of ultimate reality. It is manifest as personal will, demanding, judging, punishing, promising. Nature loses its demonic as well as its divine power. It becomes subject to man's purposes as a thing and a tool. Only on this religious basis could there arise an industrial society like that in which we are living.

If we now ask what stylistic element in the visual arts corresponds to such an experience of ultimate reality, we must answer that it is "realism" both in its scientific-descriptive and in its ethical-critical form. After nature has been deprived of its numinous power, it is possible for it to become a matter of scientific analysis and technical management. The artistic approach to this nature is not itself scientific but it deals with objects, prepared as mere things by science. Insofar as it is artistic creation, it is certainly not imitation of nature, but it brings out possibilities of seeing reality which enlarge our daily life encounter with it, and sometimes antecedes scientific discoveries.

The realistic element in the artistic styles seems far removed from expressing ultimate reality. It seems to hide it more than express it. But there is a way in which descriptive realism can mediate the experience of ultimate reality. It opens the eyes to a truth which is lost in the daily-life encounter with reality. We see as something unfamiliar what we believed we knew by meeting it day by day. The inexhaustible richness in the sober, objective, quasi-scientifically observed reality is a manifestation of ultimate reality, although it is lacking in directly numinous character. It is the humility of accepting the given which provides it with religious power.

Critical realism is predominantly directed to man—personally, socially, and historically, although the suffering in nature is often taken into the artistic expression of the ugliness of encountered reality. Critical realism, as, for instance, given by Bosch and Brueghel, Callot and Goya, Daumier and Ensor, by Grosz and Beckmann, shows ultimate reality by judging existing reality. In the works of all those enumerated, it is the injustice of the world which is subject to criticism. But it is done in works of art, and this very fact elevates critical realism above mere negativity.

The artistic form separates critical realism from simple fascination with the ugly. But of course if the artistic form is lacking, it is distorted reality and not ultimate reality that appears. This is the danger of this stylistic element as it also is of some kinds of merely intellectual pseudo-criticism, to succumb to a negativity without hope.

Now it would be good to look at pictures with this third element.

I never really saw the ocean, which I know and love very much, until I saw Courbet's "Wave."

Next there is the very radical "Self-Portrait With Death" by Corinth.

Then two Americans. Hopper—"Early Sunday Morning." Very fascinating for me, because it is based on experiences of the emptiness of reality and the sharp contours coming out of it.

And then the Sheeler "Classic Landscape," which shows things which are in themselves of no significance but which show reality in a way which was hidden to us before.

Now I come to the critical group. First we have Goya—"What Courage"; standing on a heap of corpses.

Then social caricature, and there is a title by Goya also—"Till Death She Will Beautify Herself."

Then something about nature. Daumier's "A Butcher." The life of man dependent on this distortion of the natural realities.

Dix—"War," which made him famous. The trenches of the First World War, of which I unfortunately have a good knowledge—and he was right.

And finally George Grosz—"Metropolis." Here you have the most radical form which also shows the dangers of it; the perhaps solely negative form of criticism.

The prophetic-critical type of religion has in itself the element of hope. This is the basis of its power. If the element of hope is separated from the realistic view of reality, a religious type appears which sees in the present the anticipation of future perfection. What prophetic hope expects is affirmed as given in forms of perfection which the artist can produce in the world of images. The self-interpretation of the Renaissance as society reborn was particularly conducive to this attitude. But it had predecessors, for instance, in the classical period of Greece, and has been followed in our modern period by attempts to renew this stylistic element.

As a religious attitude it can be called religious humanism which sees God in man and man in God here and now, in spite of all human weakness. It expects the full realization of this unity in history and anticipates it in artistic creativity.

The artistic style expressing it is usually called idealism, a word which is in such disrepute today that it is almost impossible to use. It is worse than criminal if you are called an idealist. But not only the word, the concept itself was under harsh criticism. In the period in which the numinous, the descriptive and the critical-realistic element dominated the whole development, the idealistic tradition was despised and rejected. In spite of the innumerable religious pictures that it produced, it was seen as unable to mediate ultimate reality. I myself shared this mood. The change occurred when I realized that idealism means anticipation of the highest possibilities of being; that it means remembrance of the lost, and anticipation of the regained, paradise. Seen in this light, it certainly is a medium for the experience of ultimate reality. It expresses the divine character of man and his world in his essential, undistorted, created perfection.

But more than in the other stylistic elements, the danger which threatens artistic idealism must be emphasized: confusing idealism with a superficially and sentimentally beautifying realism. This has happened on a large scale, especially in the realm of religious art, and is the reason for the disrepute into which idealism, both word and concept, has fallen. Genuine idealism shows the potentialities in the depths of a being or event, and brings them into existence as artistic images. Beautifying realism shows the actual existence of its object, but with dishonest, idealizing additions. This danger must be avoided as we now come to attempts to create a new classicism. I am afraid that this warning is very much apropos.

Now for this stylistic element, let us look at some of these pictures, old and new.

There is Francesca—"Queen of Sheba" and "Solomon."

And there is Perugino—"Courage and Temperance." Here you see the anticipation of human fulfillment even in the title of these pictures.

Next is the idealization of paradise in a Poussin "Landscape."

In Ingres—"Study for the Golden Tiger"—we have again memory and anticipation just as I said about this kind of style; it is the style of the paradise. But we have it also in more recent painters. We have it in the blue period of Picasso under the title "Life." Tragedy is present, but in the background, and the fulfillment is shown in the form.

And finally, we have it in the form of "Dream," which is most adequate perhaps in Rousseau. It is all-idealizing anticipation of essential fulfillment, but not beautifying.

Now I come to my fifth and last stylistic element. The great reaction against both realism and idealism (except numinous realism) was the expressionistic movement. To which religious type is it correlated? Let me call it the ecstatic-spiritual type. It is anticipated in the Old Testament, it is the religion of the New Testament and of many movements in later Church history; it appeared in sectarian groups again and again in early Protestantism, in religious Romanticism. It appears in unity and conflict with the other religious types. It is marked by its dynamic character both in disruption and creation. It accepts the individual thing and person but goes beyond it. It is realistic and at the same time mystical. It criticizes and at the same time anticipates. It is restless, yet points to eternal rest.

It is my conviction as a Protestant theologian that this religious element, appearing everywhere as a ferment—and in many places highly developed—comes into its own within Christianity.

But our problem is, how does this type express itself in the visual arts? Which stylistic element corresponds to it? I believe the expressionist element is the artistic correlative to the ecstatic-spiritual type of religious experience. Ultimate reality appears "breaking the prison of our form," as a hymn about the Divine Spirit says. It breaks to pieces the surface of our own being and that of our world. This is the spiritual character of expressionism—using the word in a much larger sense than the German school of this name.

The Church was never happy with ecstatic movements. They seemed to destroy its sacramental foundation. Society today has not been happy with the great expressionist styles in past and present because they have broken and are still breaking through the realistic and idealistic foundations of modern industrial society. But it is just this that belongs to the manifestation of ultimate reality. Expressionist elements are effective and even dominating in many styles of past and present. In our Western history they determine the art of the catacombs, the Byzantine, the Romanesque, most of the Gothic and the Baroque style, and the recent development since Cezanne.

There are always other elements co-operating, but the expressionistic element is decisive in them. Ultimate reality is powerfully manifest in these styles, even if they disregard symbols of the religious tradition. But history shows that styles which are determined by the expressionist element are especially adequate for works of art which deal with the traditional religious symbols.

But we must also mention the dangers of the expressionist elements in our artistic styles. Expression can be understood as the expression of the subjectivity of the artist, just as in the religious field, the spirit can be understood as an ecstatic-chaotic expression of religious subjectivity. If this happens in religion, ecstasy is confused with over-excitement; and over-excitement does not break through any form and does not create anything new. If a work of art expresses only the subjectivity of the artist, it remains arbitrary and does not penetrate into reality itself.

And now let us recall some examples in a final group of pictures.

Van Gogh—"Hills at St. Remy."

Munch—"The Scream."

Derain—"The London Bridge."

Marc—"Yellow Horses." I must tell you something about this painting. I was Professor at the University of Berlin in the years

1919 to 1924 and opposite the University was a modern museum in an old Imperial palace, and while I was lecturing on ancient Greek philosophy and comparing Parmenides and Heraclitus and others with the pictures of the modern artist, there were fist fights going on on the opposite side of the street. The fighting was between the lower petty bourgeoisie and the intelligentsia, and these fist fights at that time were a preview of what would happen later on under Hitler when the petty bourgeoisie became the dictatorial power in Germany. And for this reason, these horses of Marc have a tremendous symbolic meaning for me for this was one of the paintings I had been discussing at that time.

This is Schmidt-Rottluff—"Peter and Fishermen." I am not sure of exactly how it is translated. You see much of the typical, very rough kind of German expressionism.

Now in the next one you also see the religious aspects in it—Heckel's "Prayer."

Nolde—"Pentecost." And I must confess that some of my writings are derived from just this picture, as I always learned more from pictures than from theological books.

And, finally, Nolde—"Prophet."

The main point in the discussion of the five stylistic elements which can become mediators of ultimate reality has been to show that the manifestation of the ultimate in the visual arts is not dependent on the use of works which traditionally are called religious art. I want to conclude with a few remarks about the nature of such works and their relation to the five stylistic elements discussed.

If art expresses reality in images and religion expresses ultimate reality in symbols then religious art expresses religious symbols in artistic images (as philosophical concepts). The religious content, namely a particular and direct relation of man to ultimate reality, is first expressed in a religious symbol, and secondly, in the expression of this symbol in artistic images. The Holy Virgin or the Cross of the Christ are examples. In this relation it can happen that in the work of art as well as in the encounter with it, the one of two expressions may prevail over the other one: The artistic form may swallow the religious substance, objectively or in personal encounter. This possibility is one of the reasons for the resistance of many religious groups against religious art, especially in a devotional context. Or the religious substance may evoke pictorial products which hardly can be called works of art, but which exercise a tremendous religious influence. This possibility is one of the reasons for the easy deterioration of religious art in its use by the churches.

The avoidance of both shortcomings is a most demanding task for religious artists. Our analysis of the five stylistic elements may be useful in this respect.

Obviously, the stylistic element which we have called numinous realism is an adequate basis for religious art. Wherever it is predominant in the primitive world, the difference between the religious and the secular is often unrecognizable. In the recent forms of numinous realism the cosmic significance of works under the control of this element is obvious, but it is hard to use them for the highly personalistic stories and myths of the religions of the prophetic type.

The mystical-pantheistic element of artistic styles resists radically the attempt to use it for the representation of concrete religious symbols. Non-objective art like its mystical background is the elevation above the world of concrete symbols, and only symbols of this elevation above symbols can be expressed in artistic images.

Descriptive and critical realism, if predominant in a style, have the opposite difficulty. They can show everything concretely religious in its concreteness, but only if united with other elements can they show it as religious. Otherwise, they secularize it and, for example, make out of Jesus a village teacher or a revolutionary fanatic or a political victim, often borrowing sentimental traits and beautifying dishonesty from the distortions of the idealistic style. This is the seat of most religious *Kitsch*.

Another problem is religious art under the predominance of the fourth stylistic element, the anticipating one. Anticipation of fulfillment can, of course, most easily be expressed through figures of the religious legend and myth. But one thing is lacking. The estrangement of the actual human situation from the essential unity of the human with the divine, the reality of the Cross which critical realism shows in its whole empirical brutality, and which expressionism shows in its paradoxical significance. Because this is lacking even in the greatest works under the predominance of the idealistic style, it can become the other source of *Kitsch* in religious art.

The expressionistic element has, as already indicated, the strongest affinity to religious art. It breaks through both the realistic acceptance of the given and the idealistic anticipation of the fulfilled. And beyond both of them it reaches into the depth of ultimate reality. In this sense it is an ecstatic style-element, expressing the ecstatic character of encountered reality. Nobody can overlook this ecstatic element in the great religious art, however different the combination of this element with the other stylistic elements may be. To show the ecstatic-spiritual character in the expression of ultimate reality in the many great periods of religious art in East and West is a task to which the ideas of this lecture could only lay the foundation. It is enough if they have done this and made somehow visible the manifestation of ultimate reality through the different stylistic elements which appear in different relation to each other in all works of the visual arts.

19

The Religious Classic and the Classic of Art

DAVID TRACY

If we allow the experience of any classical work of art to provide some guidelines for an entry into the conversation of the religious classics, then we find certain rubrics worth nothing. The interpreter of the religious classic, like the interpreter of all classics, enters with some preunderstanding of those questions and responses named "religious." As an individual with a particular temperament, effective history, needs, hopes, desires and fears, the interpreter enters with some personal preunderstanding of what religion is. One's personal temperament (in William James' sense) and tradition, along with the major situational focus for the fundamental questions of existence, provide the primary focus of that preunderstanding. Yet no individual interpreter lives as a sheer individualist. Rather each lives in some relationship—either unconscious or conscious, trusting or rejecting—of the history of the effects, influences and interpretations of the religious dimension of a culture. For some, a particular church tradition may have principally formed that history. For others, some minor or major secularization of a religious tradition—as with the Romantics and their secular successors—may prove the principal carrier of the tradition. Some particular method of interpretation that the interpreter has learned to trust may prove the foremost carrier of the tradition itself as the tradition enters, via the method, into one's preunderstanding of "religious" issues.

More usually, some combination of these distinct, sometimes

Reprinted from *The Analogical Imagination* by David Tracy (New York: Crossroad, 1981), pp. 167—68.

conflicting, sometimes complementary carriers of the tradition will emerge to help form the interpreter's initial preunderstanding of religious questions and responses. Especially when the reality of the tradition is united to some powerful personal sense of the limit-situations to the everyday, or the limit-questions to science, art and morality, the preunderstanding of the prospective interpreter of the religious classics is likely to prove more fully alert—intelligent, sensitive, open, critical, responsive—to the possibilities for existence disclosed in the religious classics. Nothing so concentrates the mind, Doctor Johnson once observed, as the thought that one is to be hanged in the morning. Analogously, nothing so concentrates the attention of the prospective interpreter of the religious classics as a powerful sense of some focussed situational experience of a fundamental question for existence—death, trust, anxiety, wonder, loyalty to a cause greater than self, radical contingency, meaninglessness, wonder, joy, love.

With some preunderstanding of religion (due to some preunderstanding of those fundamental questions) and with some experience (either negative, positive or ambivalent) of a particular religious tradition and its diverse carriers, every interpreter approaches the religious classic—now trusting, even eager, now wary, skeptical, suspicious. At this juncture, rather than describing the whole spectrum of conflicting interpretations of the religious classics, I will now attempt to articulate one major, indeed classic approach—an approach that I have found to be the most adequate one. I cannot fully defend that adequacy here. For the moment, therefore, let us formulate the belief as a proposal for the appropriate preunderstanding for an interpreter of religion, not as an already warranted conclusion but as an "if-then" proposition still in search of its warrants.

The approach is this: If one is guided by a sense for those fundamental questions, if guided as well by that great modern tradition of interpretation of the *sui generis* character of religion ranging from Schleiermacher through James, Otto, Søderblom, von Hügel, van der Leeuw, Scheler, Wach, Eliade and Tillich, the interpreter is likely to find relative adequacy in the kind of interpretations of the appropriate responses to the religious classics described in different, sometimes conflicting ways by these great modern phenomenologists of the *sui generis* character of religions.

For example, despite the difficulties, even occasional bizarreness, of Rudolph Otto's neo-Kantian schematisms and his demand for a religious "a priori," the kind of experience of "the holy" which Otto classically delineated is still a fitting description of the kind of realized experience (to employ my own language) that a genuine religious classic often does elicit.

More exactly, the kind of claim to attention that a religious classic, *as religious*, provokes is a claim that discloses to the interpreter some realized experience bearing some sense of recognition into the objectively awe-some reality of the otherness of the whole as radical mystery. The genuinely religious person (James' "mystics" and "saints"), it seems, do experience that reality of mystery as the reality of the holy bearing overwhelming and life-transformative force.

From many phenomenological (i.e., descriptive) accounts of that experience, the same sense—now usually in more muted, more mediated-as-interpretative tones—is available to the prospective interpreter of the religious classic. For the religious classic elicits in the interpreter, by the very power of its ownmost claim to attention, a heightened awareness of the reality of what Otto named the "numinous." The interpreter is unlikely to be struck dumb with the kind of amazement familiar to the classic religious persons, the saints, prophets and mystics. And yet the interpreter cannot but sense in any religious classic the force of the claim by a power not one's own. Anxiety in any particular preunderstanding of the fundamental questions may yield, however momentarily, to an awe, or, at the limit, a dread disclosed in that *tremendum* claim. Wonder and the trust in any preunderstanding may yield to the enticing, evocative, even seductive *fascinans* power in that same reality. Yet what seems most likely to account for these experiences of anxiety, wonder and trust becoming their intensified (as explicitly religious) analogues—awe and dread (for anxiety), love and ecstasy (for wonder and trust)—save the claim evoked by the religious classic itself?

In a manner analogous to that of any later dismissal of the realized experience of the work of art, we may upon reflection become skeptical and suspicious of the original experience of the religious classic. We may even have good reasons for that later suspicion. It is, for example, difficult in a post-Freudian age to take William James' relatively innocent account of the "unconscious" at face value. Yet does a difficulty with James' theory of the unconscious (a theory proposed to explain a religious experience that was first described phenomenologically) allow us to call into question his original phenomenological description of religion? In any conflict of interpretations one primary criterion of relative adequacy endures: whether the experience being interpreted is itself acknowledged and described as it appears to consciousness. Most of us have relatively little interest in theories of music formulated by the tone-deaf, or theories of painting formulated by the color-blind. Most of us possess relatively little interest in aesthetic theories which discount the actual experience of the work of art.

Some interpreters of religion make the directly analogous suggestion that what we need above all in any adequate interpretation of religion is a phenomenology of the religious experience *as* religious. An interpreter need accept neither Schleiermacher's Romantic, indeed sometimes effusive language, nor James' own "over-beliefs," nor Otto's schematism, his analysis of the "irrational," nor his faculty-of-divination language, nor von Hügel's particular understanding of mysticism, nor Søderblom's or van der Leeuw's classification systems, nor Wach's Romantic hermeneutic and metaphysical "decision," nor Scheler's "nonformalist" claims, nor Tillich's formulation of religion as "ultimate concern," nor Eliade's particular formulation of the dialectic of the sacred and the profane to see and accept what unites these otherwise diverse, often even conflicting interpretations of the religious phenomenon: the insistence that the first responsibility of the interpreter of religion is to describe the experience itself as it appears to consciousness. The description, itself necessarily an interpretation, must attempt to develop interpretative categories that fit the realized experience ranging from a sense of resonance to a full-fledged shock of recognition. Some realized experience is the response of the religious person to the religious classic and is often the initial response of the phenomenological interpreter of the religious classic to the same, now mediated, event of disclosure.

Since I have not found persuasive reasons to deny this seemingly obvious but widely challenged insistence posed by the phenomenological interpreters of the *sui generis* character of religion, I will align myself with that tradition and attempt an interpretation of the religious classic. If one desires the warrants for that alignment, I can only recall that they are the same kind of warrants as those provided for interpreting the work of art: to begin with some description of the realized experience of art or religion; to allow the focus upon the response to provide the central clue for understanding the object or work being responded to, followed by methods of explanation for the modes of expression internal to that work and the vision of reality disclosed by and in that work. Any attempt at *relative* adequacy to an interpretation of the reality of art or religion would seem to demand some kind of phenomenological, hermeneutical approach. Moreover, if the fuller model for hermeneutics described above is also allowed (the model not of *Verstehen* alone but of the dialectics of understanding-explanation-understanding), then the further conversation with all legitimate methods of explanation—methods that correctly develop the understanding or even confront or challenge it—should also be encouraged in the process of interpretation.

But if those methods of explanation are finally reductionist ones (for example, Malinowski's functionalist method as distinct from Geertz's functional one), then one will, of course, still be likely to learn something of real importance (e.g., the functional interactions of religion and society in Malinowski). And yet these methods will also be likely to be described as relatively inadequate—because unable or unwilling to account for the *sui generis* character of the initial religious response—by claiming that religion is "nothing but" a product of society, neurosis, that its "origins" are exclusively in animism, totemism, magic, etc. To state this position is, of course, not to warrant it. For that, only the multidisciplinary conversation among competing and conflicting hermeneutics of retrieval and hermeneutics of suspicion would prove sufficient. Yet to state the position may at least serve the function of clarifying the kind of positive warrants entailed: the warrants that any claim to relative adequacy must provide some initial description of the religious phenomenon that is hermeneutically appropriate to a realized experience of the phenomenon under investigation.

On those grounds, the tradition of the phenomenological interpretation of the *sui generis* character of religion, from Schleier-macher through Eliade, seems the clearest candidate among competing traditions of interpretation for relative adequacy. The more speculative elements in that tradition of retrieval (like the analogous speculative elements in the "origins" of religion in "totemism" in the distinct positions of Durkheim and Freud) are easy enough to spot and thereby to bracket. What warrants that tradition of interpretation, however, is not its more speculative moments (like Otto's schematism of James' search for origins in the unconscious). Rather its major warrants lie in its insistence that the first moment of interpretation of religion should be a phenomenological one appropriate to the *sui generis* character of an explicitly religious response. From that response, as from the response to art, all else follows. To understand and explain that response, all methods, all readings, all conflicts of interpretation should be geared.

With that tradition of interpretation of the *sui generis* character of religion, therefore, we enter the conversation with the religious classics at great risk. For we may find that our present mode of being in the world is disclosed as either inauthentic, spent, finished—or disclosed as confirmed beyond any hope for confirmation; we may find some manifestation of another style or ethos of living bearing the redescriptive power of a manifestation that this is what reality itself in its sheer actuality is, along with the prescriptive force of a demand that our present mode of living be changed. We may also recognize that if this particular religious classic is genuinely a classic then we should free ourselves to experience the dialectic of the classic: the dialectic of respect and critical freedom that allow us to be caught up in the dialectic of the fundamental questions and answers, the subject matter of the classic itself. We should allow for the possibility that an *event* of truth as both disclosure and concealment may happen.

No more than in experiencing the genuine work of art should we become merely passive. But we do need minimally to move beyond the enslaving self-consciousness of those who cannot play any game, enter any conversation, allow any disclosure into the critical freedom and receptivity of the real conversation partner, the authentic player, the responsible self. On the side of critical freedom, we must, of course, remain open to the possibility that we will discover that this conversation is really misnamed. For religion may prove a classic expression, but not really of some limit-of reality. Rather religion may prove to be a classic expression of morality (as with Braithwaite) or of cosmology (as with Huxley) or of poetry (as with Santayana). We must remain open to the possibility that the conversations of the religions are not merely risky, but fatal, poisonous. Then we must leave this sick and resentful game and enter—with Freud, Nietzsche, Marx, Feuerbach—into another classic conversation with alternative, postreligious visions of a promised wholeness and the whole. Yet we must also be open to the possibility that the conversation elicited by the religious classics is, on the other side of both critique and suspicion, a public conversation open to all responsible thinkers: a conversation with classics whose event-like character may liberate the interpreter for and to the whole and to a wholeness which cannot be achieved. Yet religion can be experienced, received and understood as event, gift, even what Christians name grace.

It might also be noted that even if the religious character of the classical religious expressions is denied, the event character of true disclosure and concealment implied in its classical status will yet endure—as Santayana articulated in his cryptic dictum that "poetry is religion that supervenes upon life; religion is poetry that intervenes in life," and as any secular person can and ordinarily does experience, with or without the aid of Henry Adams, in experiencing the event of Chartres.

However, if the experience of the religious classic is what it claims for itself—a genuine manifestation of the whole from the reality of that whole itself—then we may surmise that every religious classic will bear the essential characteristic of all genuinely religious experiences as limit-experiences. The religious classic, if really religious, will at the very least disclose a limit-to experience distinguishing religion from morality, science, art and politics. The religious classics of a living religious tradition will also disclose an event of manifestation by the whole of a limit-of, ground-to, horizon-to experience—in sum, an authoritative-be-cause-classic expression of the whole that promises a wholeness to life. The testimony to some dialectical experience of the whole expressed in the religious classics will not prove available *as* religious to either the heteronomous or the narrowly autonomous consciousness, i.e., to all who refuse to enter and be caught up in and played by the conversation, the game of the religious classic itself. To either the autonomous or the heteronomous self, another game is going forward, one wherein the religious classics are simply out there, external to and under the rule of my subjectivity. That subjectivity and its present worldview and that alone will determine whether I extrinsically will accept, in heteronomous obedience to authoritarian norms—or extrinsically reject, in autonomous obedience to the norms of a finally technical reason—any claims to truth in the religious classic. In what Tillich named a theonomous consciousness in a person, a society or a culture, however, another possibility beyond heteronomy and autonomy occurs: the risk of interpreting the world of the religious classic and studying its claims to a truth of an event-like manifestation of the whole—that event of self-manifestation by the power of the whole which Christians and Jews name "revelation."

As with the experience of all classics, by entering the world of the religious classic, the interpreter enters an intensification process that promises and promotes experiences of both participation in reality and distancing from reality. Unlike the experience of nonreligious classics, in the religious classics this common intensification process is itself intensified to the point of a transgression of the usual limits of both participation and nonparticipation in the whole. Beyond even the intensification process of all limit-to experiences, the religious classic expresses the power of a manifestation of a "limit-of" experience, an experience of a self-manifesting power, an eruption of both radical participation and nonparticipation in the whole.

Authentic religious experience, on the testimony of those all consider clearly religious, seems to be some experience of the whole that is sensed as the self-manifestation of an undeniable power not one's own and is articulated not in the language of certainty and clarity but of scandal and mystery. The religious person does not claim a new control upon reality but speaks of losing former controls and experiencing, not merely affirming, a liberation into a realm of ultimate incomprehensibility and real, fascinating and frightening mystery. When religious persons speak the language of revelation, they mean that something has happened to them that they cannot count as their own achievement. Rather they find themselves compelled to honor that realized experience as an eruption of a power become self-manifestation from and by the whole in which, by which, and to which they live. They employ language like "liberation," "emancipation," "wholeness," "salvation" to articulate the conviction elicited and empowered by that experience itself. That conviction, that faith, takes many forms: ethos and worldview are radically united; wholeness in life has come not as personal achievement but as gift from the whole: above all, how one ought to live is ultimately grounded in what reality itself is.

In the religious intensification of the common experience disclosed in all major classics religious persons often describe themselves as being caught up in and by the power of this manifestation to the point where they both radically participate in the whole while yet, with equal radicality, are distanced from the whole. Religious awe in the face of mystery involves both real anxiety, sometimes even dread, and the real fascination of love and ecstasy. The "mystics" and "saints" do not speak as if the experience they describe were merely a limit-to experience, nor even one adequately captured by some limit-language like that of "limit-of," "horizon-to," "ground-to." Rather they ordinarily employ an irretrievably dialectical language to express the character of their experience of this limit-of. The language of John of the Cross, for example, is both disclosive and dialectical in the poetry while seeming contorted, forced, broken, almost useless in the Scholastic conceptual language employed in some of his commentaries on the experience. The poetic language seems appropriately disclosive of the kind of intensely religious dialectical experience he describes; the intellectualist Scholastic language of his tradition seems to break apart every time he attempts to articulate the mystical experience through it. The testimony of the genuinely religious is that this manifestation, this revelation, does not disclose the certainty of a clarity and a control but the reality of a power at once *tremendum et fascinans*. The event of revelation does not seem to disclose only our radical participation in the whole. The event conceals that participation with equal radicality—precisely as a participation in a realized experience of the whole as radical mystery both disclosing and concealing itself. The reality of mystery is, after all, experienced and understood as mystery only on the other side of the breakdown of the clarity of the everyday.

For such dialectical experience, dialectical speech like silence may prove the only relatively adequate form of expression. The tributes to silence by mystics in all traditions might well lead the rest of us to distrust all our attempts to translate their dialectical experience of participation-nonparticipation, clarity-obscurity, comprehensibility-incomprehensibility, disclosure-concealment of the whole. Silence may indeed be the final and most adequate mode of speech for religion. And yet silence is possible as silence only to a speaker. The mere existence of religious classics should alert any interpreter that, whatever else these strange expressions are, they are, precisely as expressions—whether in the texts of the mystics and the theologians, the styles of life of the saints and witnesses, the imagery of the icons, the founding symbols of the tradition, the events of religious history—all finally discourse. We must interpret them.

A further clue to the genuinely religious character of all religious classics as expression may be found in the analogies of the religious classic to other classics, more exactly to the positive and negative functions of distanciation involved in all classic expressions. Insofar as we strive to communicate through expression the meaning of any experience, we always distance the said from the saying, the noema from the event of noesis. Through the levels of the word to the sentence, the paragraph, the genre of the work as a whole and the style of authorial presence in the *oeuvre,* the same positive function of distanciation for producing a communicable meaning through an appropriate expression occurs. Where the originating experience is real but minor, the form will ordinarily prove fully adequate to express the meaning, as in the existence of those "minor classics" distinct from both period pieces and major classics. Where the original experience of participation and alienation in reality is major, the form—both the genre and the style—will be relatively adequate for the expression of the meaning: partly tentative, partly a matter of design, partly a matter of accidents and fate become destiny in the masterpiece. With the major classics, the form somehow works to the point where the expression assures both the permanence of the meaning and allows a fullness, even an excess of meaning that is always in need of reinterpretation, even by the author.

If the religious experience of participation-nonparticipation in the whole is as radical as I have claimed for the intensified (as both limit-to and limit-of) and the thereby intrinsically dialectical experience of an event grounding all religious expression, then it follows that the process of distanciation common to all classics will also be intensified in the case of classic religious expressions. Since expression occurs, the same positive role of distanciation occurs; even the silence of the mystic is an expression of a meaning produced by a speaker. Since the originating experience whose meaning is expressed via distanciation in classic religious texts is also the result of an intensification process into a particular route that the subject both engages in and lets happen, since that religious experience is the radical one of both participation-nonparticipation in the whole's manifestation of itself, the religious expression (by means of genre and style in texts and images, by means of style in lives, ritual and events) will always prove at best only relatively adequate to the experience of a gifted, graced self caught up in a power not its own.

In principle, classic expressions other than the religious may find some adequate form: in minor classics with relative ease; in major classics with varying degrees of tentativeness, unsteadiness, accident, flaws, unsurety. In principle, the religious classic expression cannot find an adequate form. For the whole experienced as radical mystery is experienced as giving itself in the religious response. The whole, in manifesting itself, is also experienced as freeing the real self of the respondent to its true freedom: a freedom where the self's new ethos is experienced as grounded in reality itself—a reality both disclosed and concealed as the whole by the power of the whole. Any religious experience of participation-nonparticipation in that whole remains a dialectical one incapable in principle of full adequacy: a principle expressed even in the best finite, dialectical religious forms. The giftedness of the event of manifestation can be evoked or elicited for others through the production of relatively adequate forms. Yet the reality granting that sense of giftedness can never be expressed adequately.

Since the respondent's sense of radical mystery points to but does not encompass the reality of the whole, the sense of mystery will include experiential elements of both a *fascinans* and a *tremendum* character. That sense of mystery reexperienced as event from the whole will take the respondent beyond all alternative realized experiences of the classic works of art, beyond the good and evil realities of ethics, and beyond the powers of expression possible to any finite human being caught up in a disclosure of the infinite by the infinite.

The intensification process involved in the experience of participation-nonparticipation in the whole seems to force the genuinely religious person to an experience of awe beyond anxiety, an experience of radical reverence beyond wonder, an experience of fascination, even terror, beyond both trust and alienation. That same process elicits its dialectical opposite: a radicalized sense of existential estrangement in the light of the event-ful, gifted presence of real mystery. So too the same kind of intensification process occurs on the side of expression for the religious classic to impel all modes of religious expression—classic texts, persons, images, rituals, myths, symbols, events. Yet the process disallows any idolatrous suggestion that any of these expressions is adequate to the event itself. As symbols, religious symbols do participate in that reality to which they point. As intrinsically inadequate symbols, religious symbols bear their own internal demand that idolatry be disallowed and their own internal hints that they too must finally be broken to allow the event to occur.

An adequate religious expression seems, therefore, impossible. We are left with a search for what at first sight sounds disappointing: a search for relatively adequate forms of religious expression. We are left, in sum, with the religious classics—where the form expresses both the necessity and the reality of a human response to a reality that cannot finally be adequately expressed. In the religious classics more clearly even than in any other classics, the interpreter will note that the expression itself must be as dialectical as the originating experience. At best religious expression can hope for relative adequacy. Even Bernini in his classic "Saint Teresa in Ecstasy" would claim no more. More to the point, perhaps, Teresa herself in her classic writings claims far less. The relativity of religious expressions must always be open to new negations as novel forms are discovered and new religious experiences occur. Its relativity must be open above all to the negations needed when the form tries to replace both the experience and the reality whose meaning the form serves only to disclose. In every religious tradition, forms evolve, break, disappear, reappear as the dialectics of religious expression enters the dialectics of a religious tradition. Consider, for example, the history of religious art. As one example, the Baroque, in its greatest expressions in Rubens or Bernini, astonishingly works as *religious* art and works largely by means of negations and shock to evoke wonder and affirmation. In lesser hands, the intrinsically dialectical character of the strangely exalted yet self-negating religious and artistic Baroque confidence lives no more. Then one finds merely the dazzling virtuosity of form attempting to live on its own, ripped from its religious roots and trying to redress that loss through the ever more ingenious, undialectical experiments of Rococo virtuosi.

To enter the conversation of the religious classics through real interpretation, therefore, is to enter a disclosure of a world of meaning and truth offering no certainty but promising some realized experience of the whole by the power of the whole. That world affords no technically controlled comprehensibility yet it does release the self to the uncontrollable incomprehensibility of an experience of radical mystery.

The mystery elicits, even empowers the religious self to believe that how we ought to live (for the Jew and Christian, with compassion, in justice and in love, in righteousness) is grounded in the fundamental nature of reality itself. That mystery evokes a sense of freedom that is at the same time a gift; a command to live that empowers even as it commands. That mystery begins to be sensed in the wonder, anxiety and fundamental trust of our earlier experiences of a religious dimension to all reality. That sense of mystery is intensified as it transforms the self's initial experiences of wonder, anxiety and trust by a response to the stark otherness of the religious reality disclosed in the religious classic. For the religious person, wonder, anxiety and trust yield in the religious experience to awe, sometimes even rapture and dread, the sense of giftedness disclosed by pointing to the enveloping, self-manifesting whole in which we live and move and have our being. That same sense of radical giftedness both fascinates and frightens as it shocks and transforms the self to believe what one dare not otherwise believe: that reality is finally gracious, that the deepest longings of our minds and hearts for wholeness in ourselves, with others, with history and nature, is the case—the case granted as gift by the whole; the case expressed with relative adequacy determined by the intrinsic inadequacy of every classic religious expression. The appeal of any religious classic is a nonviolent appeal to our minds, hearts and imaginations, and through them to our will. Its authoritative status is not, therefore, the violent appeal to obedience demanded by authoritarians in all religious traditions. These latter, in fact, have lost the sense of the only authoritative, nonviolent appeal that any religious classic or any religious tradition faithful to its ownmost vision can possess. For religious authoritarians replace the nonviolent appeal of the authoritative religious classics with their own distortions of those realities into ideological demands forced upon a heteronomous will. The damage done to the cause of the religious classics by authoritarian distortions and their seeming capture of the religious classics as their property is incalculable. Fortunately, the religious classics themselves can be counted on always to challenge those distortions at the root.

Nor will the world of the explicitly religious classics domesticate the earlier common human experiences of a religious-as-limit-to dimension to the everyday so that it becomes the false security of one more ideology or worldview. Rather interpretation of the world of the religious classics can actually intensify that limit-to experience by liberating it from its troubled confines through some experience of the limit-of reality: a disclosure of an event of manifestation of the whole by the power of the whole. The religious classic will demand of all those caught up in the interpretation of its world that its religious subject matter—its fundamental questions and responses upon my present relationship to the whole—be openly addressed. To allow for the world of the religious classics is in the end to allow for a world of meaning and truth disclosing the truth of the paradigmatic, the classical, the extraordinary. Every religious classic expresses an event of a "limit-of" reality that has the full force of a power finally liberating us from ourselves, summoning us to and by a power not our own. The interpretation of religion, like the interpretation of art, lives by its ability to risk a genuine response to the classics.

20

Question: When Is Religion Art?
Answer: When It Is a Jar.

T. R. MARTLAND

I

Of course, the title of this essay comes from the familiar pun: "When is a door not a door? When it is ajar." But this is not to suggest that the issue of religion and art is nonsense. Puns do make sense, religion and art make sense, and so does religion as art. They make that special kind of sense that we might call a jarring sense.[1]

But what does a jarring kind of sense mean? That depends upon what we mean by a jar. So far as doors are concerned, ajar means to be slightly open. But what makes the pun a pun is that when we write it as two words, a jar signifies a wide-mouthed container. Thus our pun goes in two directions, toward "slightly open" but then back again to the wide-mouthed container.

We who are concerned with religion and art also have a pun going. It, too, is related to the slightly open aspect of ajar. Religion and art open us to something. To what? Ah, this is a false move. It is more fruitful to go in the other direction and ask, open us out *from* what? The reason for this is that while there is an opening to, it is not something with which we can deal until art and religion take us there. By this I mean to simply expand upon Wallace Stevens's reaction to a critic's comment that "Mr. Stevens's work does not really lead anywhere." Stevens responded, "This is not quite the same thing as 'get' anywhere."[2] Stevens's point was that art (and, we add, religion) "gets somewhere" and thus requires a going along, a "getting with it," whereas activities that "lead somewhere" imply a detachment, a pointing to rather than a participating in something. He says as much in the opening section of "The Man with the Blue Guitar":

> The man bent over his guitar,
> A shearsman of sorts. The day was green.
>
> They said, "You have a blue guitar,
> You do not play things as they are."
>
> The man replied, "Things as they are
> Are changed upon the blue guitar."
>
> And they said then, "But play, you must,
> A tune beyond us, yet ourselves,
>
> A tune upon the blue guitar
> Of things exactly as they are." [3]

My point then is that since it is impossible to talk about a something to which art and religion lead or point until we get there—until we listen to the tune beyond us, played on the blue guitar—we who want to understand the meaning of religion's (and art's) slight openness might more fruitfully consider art's (and religion's) relationship to that something from which they claim to free us or open us out from. It is this alone that we have in common, artist and nonartist, religious and nonreligious.

There is more. Ajar suggests not only a slight openness out from where we have been but also a discordance that comes from leaving it behind. Doors ajar sometimes jar. Here is implied something unsettling, even disagreeable. That which jars upsets the previously set situation. To jar is to make manifest something unexpected, thus to shock. Puns jar. To say they do is to emphasize the unsettledness they cause, the conflict they engender with what has gone before. To say that Géricault's realistic studies of the macabre are jarring is to say that they upset us, we who were previously settled down in a certain way.

So where are we? To say that religion is art when it is a jar is to play with the slight openness of ajar, the slight openness from that in which we were previously enclosed, the unsettling dimension of a jar, and all of the time to include a back-and-forth punlike switch to the wide-mouthed container. If we simply forget the pun, to say religion is art when it is a jar is to say religion is art when it opens us up to new ways of seeing things that are upsetting from the perspective of the old way of seeing things.

Thomas Kuhn helps to clarify how this jarring, upsetting kind of sense actually works. I suggest that Stevens's distinction between "lead" and "get" is also implied. Kuhn observes that it is one thing to write about the process from the outside or from a distance. This allows the author to be a witness to the process leading somewhere. Yet it is another thing to write about a process from within and to focus upon its openness and ambiguity, at best to be a witness to its getting somewhere. The distinction itself is not difficult to defend. The first approach is similar to writing your autobiography when things have settled down and become clear. From this perspective it is clear which leads you developed in your life and allowed to be productive. The second way of writing is similar to composing your autobiography as you are involved in your life, writing a diary perhaps, of necessity depicting all of the ambiguous leads available, all of the moves made, because at this moment you do not know which ones will turn out to be productive.

Kuhn identifies the detached former depiction with textbook histories of science and the involved latter situation with the way science actually works. Whereas the former depicts the process of doing science as a slow onward-and-upward development from childish beginnings to eventual mastery, the latter sees it rather as a continuous presentation of potential turning points or revolutions, each calling for the community's decision to accept it so that it may "get" some place, and in turn for the community's decision to reject a currently held theory that is incompatible with it. If the decision is to accept the new theory, or paradigm, a transformation of the old world follows, a jarring kind of transition takes place: from paradigm, to paradigm in crisis, to a new paradigm "from which a new tradition . . . can emerge," a transition which, Kuhn goes on to note, "is far from a cumulative process, one achieved by an articulation or extension of the old paradigm. Rather it is a reconstruction of the field from new fundamentals. . . . When the transition is complete, the profession will have changed its view of the field, its methods, and its goals."[4]

II

An example of this jarring sort of transition occurring in art is the eighteenth-century shift from baroque to rococo to neoclassicism. The transformation was so far from being a cumulative process, one achieved by articulation or extension, that by the time neoclassicism took over, the inventiveness of the baroque and the elegance of the rococo were considered "licentious decadence," offending the canons of good taste, to be forgotten and ignored— in essence, to be jarred right out of existence.

This example is especially interesting because the shift also reflected itself in religious taste as that taste is reflected in religion's judgments concerning the artistic treatment of religious source material. The shift occurred when "licentious" came to mean a lack of moral rather than stylistic restraint and "decadence" came to suggest a falling away from the standards of morality instead of a falling away from mere fashionable formulas. The process took only a little more than a hundred years. These moral associations came so to dominate nineteenth- and twentieth-century England and English-speaking North America that Bernini's baldacchino in Saint Peter's, with its massive combination of architecture and sculpture, its dramatic contrasts of materials and colors, of light and dark—the very epitome of a spirit dedicated to stir and reinforce Christians in their faith and to move heretics to reunite with the church—now became vulgar and irreligious to the eyes of a new generation, and the undulating columns variously copied from those originally incorporated into the high altar of Old Saint Peter's and traditionally believed to have come from Solomon's temple itself, now became obscene and profane.

A more fully argued example is Kenneth Clark's historical study of the nude. His study makes it clear that the nude is not a mechanical illustration of the naked body, that its history in art is not of an ever moving articulation or extension of a more and more realistic depiction of what already exists, but rather its history is an ever changing process of shapes that the artist imposes. In fact, one of his overarching observations is that "the nude makes its first appearance in art theory at the very moment when painters begin to claim that their art is an intellectual, not a mechanical, activity."[5] By so observing, he not only affirms the need for a community to accept an idea before it can "get" some place (the nude could only appear in a history when the community was prepared to accept it), but he also affirms the idea that art imposes—the nude is a jarring imposition on what it is, not merely an extension of it.

We conclude, then, that both examples witness to a new imposition. Although with neoclassicism, as the name suggests, it was a renewed imposition, what was imposed was forceful enough to deliver its content, and this is what is important. In both examples what was delivered was forceful enough to make them events in themselves, paradigms all, powerful enough to demand with Kuhn a "reconstruction of the field."

James Ackerman will help us to finish our discussion on how art jars. In harmony with our earlier discussion about religion and art opening us out *from* something, he insists that "evolution in the arts should not be described as a succession of steps toward a solution to a given problem, but as a succession of steps away from one or more original statements of a problem." He adds, "what actually motivates the process is a constant incidence of probings into the unknown, not a sequence of steps toward the perfect solution."[6] Elsewhere he acknowledges Kuhn's idea of the need for the community's decision to go along: he observes that "the biases and ideology of the time and place and the critic-historian's education and social class inevitably impose themselves. Choices that guide every aspect of the discussion of art, such as the kind of art found worthy of attention, the framework established for the discussion . . . and the particular works selected for consideration are determined by value criteria."[7] Ernest Gombrich observes that it is a false move (his word is "immature") to consider "the development of style, of modes of representation . . . as the result of organic growth." Rather, art grows by dint of the "institution's" acceptance, by "social factors, what we may term the attitudes of the audience, the style or the trend."[8]

III

Religion also jars, it also imposes that which demands a reconstruction of what has gone before. When the transformation is complete those who profess will have changed their view of the field, of its methods and goals. Zen, for one, is full of examples of such transformations. We ask: "What is the meaning of Bodhidharma's coming from the West?" and we are told: "The Cypress tree standing in the garden." More important, other religions do this as well.

The most jarring example I know is the story that Ramakrishna approvingly tells about Vyâsa. By all accounts, Vyâsa was a holy man and was recognized as such. It seems that he was about to cross the Jamunâ River when the Gopis, or shepherdesses, arrived to do likewise. But there was no ferryboat.

> They asked Vyâsa, "Lord, what shall we do?" Vyâsa replied: "Do not worry, I will get you across the river: but I am very hungry. Can you give me something to eat?" The Gopis had with them a quantity of milk, cream, and fresh butter. He consumed them all. The Gopis then asked, "What about crossing the river?" Vyâsa stood near the edge of the water and prayed: "O Jamunâ! As I have not eaten anything today, by that virtue I ask Thee to divide the waters, so that we can walk across Thy bed and reach the other side." No sooner did he utter these words than the waters parted and the dry bed was laid bare. The Gopis were amazed. They thought, "How could he say, 'as I have not eaten anything today,' when just now he has eaten so much?"[9]

Certainly this is an incredible story. Vyâsa's boldness, bordering upon chicanery, his willful flouting of the laws of sensible behavior and of the very meaning of intelligible discourse, is striking. Nevertheless Ramakrishna approves of his behavior, otherwise he would not have repeated the story in such an affirmative context.

What are we to make of it? Ramakrishna provides us with our clue. After he presents his story he comments that the failure of the Gopis was that they did not see that Vyâsa's prayer "was proof of firm faith; that Vyâsa had the faith that he did not eat anything. . . ." If Ramakrishna is correct, the facts are these: Vyâsa ate; Vyâsa had faith that he did not eat. Vyâsa had faith, and so it was according to that faith. Vyâsa prayed that the waters be divided, and so it was according to that prayer. Vyâsa's faith, Vyâsa's prayers, did something. They imposed themselves upon old situations, and henceforth there is a reconstruction of what has gone before.

Perhaps this explains Vyâsa's blatant directness, even his hint of mocking the previous limits of behavior and reality. There is a kinship with D. H. Lawrence's impetuous declaration: "Damn my impudence. . . . But I don't want to write like Galsworthy nor Ibsen, nor Strindberg nor any of them, *not* even if I could. We have to hate our immediate predecessors, to get free from their authority."[10] This strident revulsion from the authority of past masters, like Vyâsa's flouting of the limits of the old reality, is a most powerful way of letting us know that these previously established limits of expression and understanding are of no final consequence. To put it positively, those changes or accomplished things that came about because of what Vyâsa did *are* of consequence, that is, they are of the sort which impose that which demands a reconstruction of what has gone before. Thus I suggest that the story of Vyâsa's faith and mendacity tells us that, so far as religion is concerned, man's previous views of the "field," of "all this" (*sarvam idam*), is nothing (*māyā*), it is akin to beads strung on a string, the string of religious activity (*karma*). In one sense, all is illusion; in another sense, all is effect. With religious activity we have at once a jarring total annihilation and a new imposition.[11]

Let me cite an example from Christianity. It is that affirmation made in A.D. 325 at Nicaea, in which God the Son is declared to be *homoousios* ("of one stuff") with God the Father, in effect a declaration that the Son is not merely similar to the Father from whom he proceeds, but is identical to him. This is a far more significant example of religion's jarring kind of sense than is the Vyâsa story, one no less preposterous for those who look out from the old way of seeing things.

Its jarring effect is made clear by Hilary of Poitiers, who proclaimed in his defence of Nicaea that its decision was rooted in "a firm faith [which] rejects the captious and useless questions of philosophy," that it "does not confine God within the terms of ordinary understanding, nor does it judge of Christ . . . according to the elements of the world."[12] He is almost saying that the jarring effect of declaring the Father and the Son to be one is proof of its validity. And he does not hesitate to affirm the corollary: the heretical Arian and Sabellian alternatives are guilty of articulating or extending the old paradigm, they are attempts to incorporate the Christian experience into the context of the rational limits established by our previous world view rather than an acceptance of the Christian experience as a revolution or overthrow of that previous world view. In effect, Arius and Sabellius insisted upon a Christianity that makes sense in the world. Arius rightfully moans, "We are persecuted because we say, 'The Son has a beginning, but God is without beginning.' For this we are persecuted . . . and you know the rest."[13]

Hilary's criticism thus comes to this: Arius and Sabellius still live in their old worlds. Their religious arguments are beads strung on a string of old standards, old paradigms, and they fail to see that these paradigms are no longer valid. They fail to see that "a devout faith is found where there is also a natural ignorance."[14] Tertullian sounds the battle cry: "What has Jerusalem to do with Athens, the Church with the Academy, the Christian with the heretic? Our principles come from the Porch of Solomon, who had himself taught that the Lord is to be sought in simplicity of heart. I have no use for a Stoic or a Platonic or a dialectic Christianity. After Jesus Christ we have no need of speculation, after the Gospel no need of research."[15] Hilary sums up the attack well: the problem of Arius and Sabellius, he tells us, is that "they measured the omnipotent nature of God by the weakness of their own nature . . . [they] confined infinite things within the boundaries of their own power of comprehension and made themselves the judges of religion."[16] In effect, they refused to let religion jar, and therefore never achieved a proper understanding of what he calls the "evangelical" faith.[17]

There are lighter examples in Christianity. From the large and popular corpus of medieval miracles ascribed to the Virgin Mary there is the seemingly inconsequential story of an abbess who, in spite of her disciplined hand over her community, "fell into wantonness" and conceived a child. Her vindictive sisters were quick to notice her pregnancy, and denounced her to the bishop. The abbess implored the Virgin to help her. The Virgin responded and whisked away the child. The bishop arrived, discovered nothing, and rebuked the nuns for their slander.[18] Notice the similarity of this story to the Vyâsa one, even in tone. I suggest that of which Ramakrishna has made us aware in the first case is in fact valid for all three examples: Vyâsa ate, the bishops at Nicaea operated in a rational world, the abbess slept with her page, yet we are told in each case through the imposition of a later religious act that the previous situation is now reconstructed, that which was is no longer the way it is.

In stories such as this last one about Mary, which emphasized a religious abrogation of the old rules, there is often a suggestion of the equally important point that religion causes a transformation by imposing a new view of the field. For example, we are told later that the abbess has learned her lesson, that by her appeal to the Virgin she has never lost her faith—sure enough, the child one day became a bishop himself. But this is not always the case. Sometimes the flouting of the old structure stands alone.

> When Teng Yingfeng was about to die in front of the Diamond Cave at Wutai, he said to the people round him, "I have seen monks die sitting and lying, but have any died standing?" "Yes, some," they replied. "How about upside down?" "Never seen such a thing!" Teng died standing on his head. His clothes also rose up close to his body. It was decided to carry him to the burning ground, but he still stood there without moving. People from far and near gazed with astonishment at the scene. His younger sister, a nun, happened to be there, and grumbled at him, saying, "When you were alive you took no notice of laws and customs, and even now you're dead you are making a nuisance of yourself!" She then prodded her brother with her finger and he fell down with a bang. Then they went off to the crematorium.[19]

Sometimes the transformation is deliberately ignored.[20] But admittedly, these instances are rare. Most examples that emphasize the jarring annihilation of the past are in a context which itself at least implies a shift from an old reality to a new one. A quick case in point is that recent declaration of Paul VI and Athenagoras II to "remove from memory the sentences of excommunication [between Eastern and Western Christianity] . . . and [to] commit these excommunications to oblivion."[21] Here is a perfect example of religious leaders acting on the understanding that they, as religious leaders, have the ability to upset or unsettle worlds inherited and to effect in their place a new and changed world.

For a religious example of a different sort, one more in keeping with our previous example of the history of the nude, there is the history of Krishna. It, too, is not an ever ascending process to a more and more satisfying depiction, this time of what is in the *Mahabharata*, but rather its history is an ever changing process of insights imposed on the text at different times. For example, from the tenth to the twelfth century the function of Krishna changes, from his having been born solely to kill a tyrant and rid the world of demons to having been born to impose impassioned adoration of God as the most valid way to achieve salvation. It is not that the facts as given in the *Bhagavata Purana* are disputed; rather, it is their emphasis and viewpoint that are changed. Radha, the Gopi, comes to the fore and Rukmini, his wife, is relegated to the background. As I said, Krishna's chief function is now, with Radha's help, to declare passion as the symbol of the final union with God.

Here again we have a new imposition forceful enough to deliver its content, forceful enough to demand a reconstruction of the field, to establish a new understanding. There is a jarring, too, perhaps less severe than that occurring to Teng Yingfeng's laws and customs or to the Patriarch's memories, but this may be because the emphasis is not so much on doing away with the old as it is on imposing the new. As Vyâsa prayed and the waters parted, so the faithful listen and the tales of Radha's passion for Krishna, her willingness to commit adultery, express their intense longing for God.

IV

We should not be too surprised by findings such as these. Transformation, or that jarring kind of sense which does away with old structures and understandings, has always been the latch on the door to religion. Think of the common religious rite of initiation, confirmation, bar mitzvah. But we have said enough. Religion and art are activities that open their followers out from an inherited way of seeing things, from an inherited structure of reality, and "get" them into a new way of seeing things, into a new world. They upset. They jar. They impose. They reconstruct the world with new fundamentals. When the transformation is complete those who have gone along will have changed their view of the field, of its methods and goals.

What is so significant about all of this? It is that to continue to think of religion as an attempt to deal with the empirical world is to ignore a good bit of the evidence. In all, it suggests a more complicated picture. Religion does not deal with what is, it creates what is. Buber is correct: "Creation is not a hurdle on the road to God, it is the road itself."[22] Religion, like art, imposes. When is religion art? It is art when it jars us out of one world and into another. As Clifford Geertz said, the world in which we are "provides not evidence for their [religions'] truth but illustrations of it."[23]

NOTES

1. Religion is art when it is a jar. Although religion remains religion and art remains art, when religion is a jar and art is a jar religion is what art is, a jar. On the other hand, if we think that by pointing out that religion jars and that art jars we can therefore formally conclude that religion is art, we commit the fallacy of undistributed middle, i.e., men swim, fish swim, therefore men are fish. My procedure is not deductive but rather what Stephen Toulmin calls a "working logic," or, better, what John Dewey calls "experimental logic." Our model for inquiry comes from law, not mathematics.

2. Wallace Stevens, *Letters of Wallace Stevens*, ed. Holly Stevens (London, 1966), p. 863.

3. *The Collected Poems of Wallace Stevens* (New York, 1969), p. 165.

4. Thomas S. Kuhn, *The Structure of Scientific Revolutions*, 2nd ed. (Chicago, 1970), pp. 84–85.

5. Kenneth Clark, *The Nude* (Princeton, 1956), p. 366.

6. James S. Ackerman, "Style," *Art and Archaeology*, ed. James S. Ackerman and Rhys Carpenter (Englewood Cliffs, NJ, 1965), pp. 174–75.

7. James S. Ackerman, "On Judging Art Without Absolutes," *Critical Inquiry*, 5, no. 3 (Spring 1979), p. 469.

8. E. H. Gombrich, *Meditations On a Hobby Horse* (London, 1963), pp. 36, 43.

9. Ramakrishna, *The Gospel of Ramakrishna* (New York, 1907), p. 306.

10. D. H. Lawrence, *The Letters of D. H. Lawrence*, ed. James T. Boulton (Cambridge, 1979), I: 509.

11. Dare I suggest an affinity here with Odysseus, whose most famous quality was his guile and craftiness? Athena reminds him in a not-at-all challenging way that "Deceit and artful tales are dear to you from the bottom of your heart" (*Odyssey*, 13.295). In fact, Homer tells us it runs in the family. His maternal grandfather, Autolycus, "surpassed all men in thievishness" (*Odyssey*, 19.395–97).

12. Saint Hilary of Poitiers, *The Trinity*, trans. Stephen McKenna (New York, 1954), I, 13, p. 14.

13. "Letter of Arius to Eusebius of Nicomedia," *Christology of the Later Fathers*, ed. Edward Rochie Hardy (Philadelphia, 1954), p. 330.

14. Saint Hilary of Poitiers, op. cit., XII, 53, p. 539.

15. Tertullian, "The Prescriptions Against the Heretics," *Early Latin Theology*, ed. S. L. Greenslade (Philadelphia, 1956), p. 36.

16. Saint Hilary of Poitiers, op. cit., I, 15, p. 15.

17. Hilary is correct, but the *truth* of the evangelical faith is another matter. All religions jar. But not everything that jars is true. In other words, to recognize a religion's jarring is necessary, but not sufficient, to win the day. See my discussion of "Verification" in *Religion As Art* (Albany, 1981), pp. 133–58.

18. Johannes Herolt, *The Miracles of the Blessed Virgin Mary*, trans. C. C. Swinton Bland (London, 1928), miracle no. 24, pp. 42–43 (cited in Marina Warner, *Alone of All Her Sex* [New York, 1976], p. 277).

19. Cited in R. H. Blyth, *Oriental Humour* (Tokyo, 1959), p. 93.

20. See, for example, the story about the thief in Hwui-Li, *The Life of Hiuen-Tsiang*, trans. Samuel Beal (London, 1911), IV: 145.

21. Hilery Ward, *Documents of Dialogue* (Englewood Cliffs, 1966), p. 257.

22. Martin Buber, *Between Man and Man*, trans. Ronald Gregor Smith (New York, 1965), p. 52.

23. Clifford Geertz, *Islam Observed* (New Haven, 1968), p. 98.

21

Art, Religion, and the Elite: Relfections on a Passage from André Malraux

NICHOLAS WOLTERSTORFF

In André Malraux's *The Voices of Silence*, this striking passage occurs:

> The gestures we make when holding pictures we admire (not only masterpieces) are those befitting precious objects; but also, let us not forget, objects claiming veneration. Once a mere collection, the art museum is by way of becoming a sort of shrine, the only one of the modern age; the man who looks at an *Annunciation* in the National Gallery of Washington is moved by it no less profoundly than the man who sees it in an Itlian church. True, a Braque still-life is not a sacred object; nevertheless, though not a Byzantine miniature, it, too, belongs to another world and it is hallowed by its association with a vague deity known as Art, as the miniature was hallowed by its association with Christ Pantocrator.
>
> In this context the religious vocabulary may jar on us; but unhappily we have no other. Though this art is not a god but an absolute, it has, like a god, its fanatics and its martyrs and is far from being an abstraction. . . .
>
> From the Romantic period onward art became more and more the object of a cult. . . .

These are penetrating and insightful remarks. Perhaps they make some of us feel a bit uneasy. But Malraux has here put his finger on one of the fundamental ways in which paintings function in our society. Similar remarks can with equal propriety be made about the other arts. Though the "vocabulary may jar on us," art functions religiously for us.

It is indeed a function, a social role, of which Malraux is speaking, not the content of art. From his examples one can see that a work of art may function religiously even though its content may not be, in any straightforward way, religious. Naturally that does not mean that one cannot *also* speak of the religious *content* of art in society. I am myself presuaded that one cannot understand the arts of the twentieth century without noticing that over and over our artists (e.g., Mondrian, Kandinsky, Rothko, Motherwell, and Barnett Newman) have attempted to compose "objective correlatives" to their mystically religious feelings and convictions. One can follow Tillich in noting the "fittingness" between certain styles of art and certain types of religion. But this is neither what Malraux has in mind nor what I wish to examine. Malraux speaks of the *functioning* of art in our society with the suggestion that artworks function for us rather like cultic objects.

Malraux is not speaking of art that *actually* functions in some cult, nor of ecclesiastical art. His eye is on the art to be found in our museums and art galleries. Though it may have originally functioned as ecclesiastical or cultic art, it is now divorced from ritual function. Such art, Malraux suggests, functions nonetheless religiously for us.

"The gestures we make when holding pictures we admire . . . are those befitting . . . objects claiming veneration." Who is the *we* here? Who are the people for whom art functions religiously? It is tempting to answer, simply and straightforwardly, "we in our society." But that would be incorrect. It is clear from Malraux's discussion that it is the art of our museums (the *high art* of our society) that he has his eye on. This is the art that acquires that religious function which Malraux suggests. And the truth is that most people in our society pay no attention to high art. They never enter museums, concert halls, reading rooms, or theaters. They know nothing, and are content in knowing nothing, of an *Annunciation*, a Braque still life, or a Byzantine miniature.

The fact that not all members of a society are engaged by high art is not of much importance. What is important is that those thus engaged belong to a distinct social stratum and subgroup of our society. Specifically, they are the *cultural elite*. The religious functioning of *high art* in the lives of the *cultural elite* is Malraux's topic. This "religion" is a religion of the cultural elite in which the objects functioning in quasi-cultic fashion are works of high art. (This is not to deny that popular art may also function religiously for certain people. But the dynamics of that seem to me quite different, and will not enter into this essay.)

A fundamental feature of Western society is the presence of a massive deposit of works of art separated by stretches of space and time from the societies in which they were originally produced, and having at best a peripheral function in our own society. Culture is in good measure separated from society. The music of Notre Dame de Paris of the thirteenth century, the altarpieces of Jan van Eyck, the poetry of Chaucer—these works have been pulled loose from their originating societies and preserved so as to be available to us in ours. For many of us, art constitutes an extremely important dimension of our lives. Yet it must be admitted that most art could disappear without any significant alterations in our society. A certain segment of the "culture industry" would perforce be gone, but otherwise things would go on much as before. Most members of society would work and spend their leisure time exactly as they do now. And we would still have art: there would still be popular music, businesses would still inveigle us with advertising art, and magazines and books would still include illustrations.

Within this massive cultural deposit, and its contemporary extension, we find our works of high art. Yet these works constitute only a component within this deposit. Among the works to be found in that deposit are also works of "primitive" art—art from traditional societies. Yet no one would regard, for example, the masks from the New Hebrides as works of high art—even though now and then they are taken from their accustomed resting places in our ethnological museums and displayed in our art galleries. How then are we to pick out works of high art from this deposit of cultural artifacts?

I suggest that *history* is the fundamental clue. High art is art which has a history of a certain sort. The qualification "of a certain sort" is necessary. For the art of traditional societies also displays a continuity of artistic influence. Admittedly, in most cases there are too many "missing links" in the sequences and too little information about provenance for us to be able to trace these interior stylistic histories. Consequently, ethnological museums are generally content to specify the place and approximate date of origin. But we can be sure that there is a continuity of influence. For though artistic imagination is operative in traditional societies, most art in traditional society is produced by *modeling*. The artist models his work on that of his predecessors; that is why his works bear the mark of stylistic continuity with his predecessors.

What differentiates the art of traditional societies from the high art of our own society is just that the former is *traditional* art and the latter is not. One of Max Weber's great contributions to sociological theory was the development of his thesis that the fundamental difference between traditional societies and modernized society consists in the replacement of tradition by *rationalization* as the preeminent determinant of action. In traditional societies, that part of human action which is not merely routine and habitual is, for the most part, shaped by "how things have always been done." One marries as marrying is done, one farms as farming is done, one draws water as water is drawn, and one paints as painting is done. We in our society act differently. In great measure our actions, when not merely habitual, are determined not by tradition but by rational reflection on what would be the "best" way to achieve our ends and implement our principles. Action thus determined is what Weber called "rationalized" action.

I would suggest that the replacement of tradition by rationalization also characterizes the work of *artists* in the West. These artists are not content to make things in the traditional way. They do not compose the way composing has always been done, nor do they paint the way painting has always been done. They search for better ways of making and doing. They exhibit rationalized action. No doubt it sounds strange to speak of artists, along with technologists and bureaucrats, as engaging in rationalized action. And we must not ignore the fact that rationality in art has a different character from rationality in technology. Yet there can be no doubt that artists are no more guided by tradition than are the rest of us—perhaps less so.

What gives birth to high art is a special kind of reflection, a special type of rationalization. Though the artist may reflect on how to make an altarpiece that better serves the devotional function of altarpieces, this is not what makes his work high art. High art arises not when the artist begins to reflect on the intended social function of his artifact, but when he begins to reflect on the style of the artifact itself and on its manner of representation—when he begins to pursue ways of making that artifact and modes of representation that are (in his judgment) preferable to those presented to him by his predecessors. More precisely, it arises when this reflection is conducted in artistic dialogue with his predecessors. High art arises when the artist neither follows routinely in the footsteps of his artistic predecessors, merely modeling himself on their endeavors, nor when he simply ignores his predecessors (if that is possible), but when he allows what they have done to *suggest* new artistic and stylistic problems and challenges for himself. High art is art which in this way feeds on and incorporates its own history. High art is art which has in this way come to historical self-consciousness.

The high-art artist is usually a person of divided loyalties. Normally, he will have in mind some intended public function for his work. In the past, those intended public functions were much more diverse than they tend to be today. The intended public function for contemporary artists is usually perceptual contemplation. They make things for us to listen to, look at, read. There are exceptions, however: Stravinsky composed his *Mass* for use in the Catholic liturgy.

Whatever social function the artist intends his work to fulfill, he has his eye on that artistic deposit of which he is the inheritor. He allows that deposit to suggest to him his own project. He enters into stylistic dialogue with it. His hope is that he can contribute something significant to that ongoing artistic dialogue. No doubt, he usually hopes that people will enjoy his work; but he also hopes that that very same work will occupy a significant place in the stylistic dialogue of himself with his predecessors and of his successors with him. Sometimes these two goals nicely complement each other. But the history of art is filled with examples of tension. The artist finds his public uncomprehending; alienation follows. High art is suspended uneasily between its intended public use and its contribution to that autonomous cultural deposit.

Two or three clarifying points are in order here. High art is art produced out of stylistic dialogue with artistic predecessors. But we must not conclude that the artistic roots of high art are to be found solely in the high art of the past, coupled with the imagination of the artist confronted by those works. Repeatedly we find that the artistic imagination is shaped by art that falls outside the stream of high art. Bartók, for example, was influenced by the folk music of his native Hungary. Moreover, Western society is not the only society with a tradition of high art. China has such a tradition, as does India; and so did ancient Greece and Rome. The presence of such a tradition in a society will always be a matter of degree. It is massively present in our society, as it is in Chinese society. But the bronzes made for the royalty of the Benin tribe of Eastern Africa also represent a tradition of high art, albeit a short-lived and not very elaborate tradition.

I have suggested that only a segment of our society pays any attention to the high art of our society. Nobody is without art in his life. But most people find that they can do well without Beethoven, Rauschenberg, Rodin, or even Shakespeare! Within this segment of those who do engage themselves with high art, various subgroups can be distinguished. There are artists who contribute to the expansion of our society's body of high art. There are performers who bring alive previously composed works. There are critics who attempt to guide the public into an understanding of works of high art. There are teachers who aim to induct young people into one or another part of the deposit. There are people who work at preserving and recovering works from the past. There are people who engage in the merchandising of works.

Where, amidst all these subgroups, are we to find that group which best fits our vague concept of the cultural elite? I would suggest that the cultural elite consists not merely of those who have some sort of commerce with high art but of those whose own taste in the arts runs, to a significant degree, toward the high art of our own or some other society. Such a person may also find certain non-high art to his taste. What makes him a member of the cultural elite is that he finds the perceptual contemplation of high art to be, for him, a rewarding experience. And what makes it appropriate to call that group an elite is that the group is limited in its membership, and there is pervasive in society the attitude that its taste in the arts is finer, nobler, more elevated, than that of those who find nothing rewarding in high art.[1]

"The gestures we make when holding pictures we admire . . . are those befitting . . . objects claiming veneration," says Malraux. To step into the new East Wing of the National Gallery in Washington is to be reminded at once of those great shrines of Christendom, the medieval cathedrals. And to observe the hushed tones and reverential attitudes of those who trudge through those halls is to be put in mind of a procession through the ambulatory of one of those cathedrals. The veneration of bones and sticks and cloths connected with the saints has virtually disappeared from our society. The authenticity of all such objects is suspect to us; and even if it were not, we prefer our religious devotion to be less attached to artifacts. Malraux's suggestion is that this *type* of veneration has not disappeared from our society without trace. Instead, works of art have replaced relics.

It will be helpful at this point to introduce some elements from Max Weber's typology of religion, in particular his distinction between *ascetic* and *mystical* religions. These types of religion Weber sees as species of what he calls "salvation religions." Their origins lie in the emergence of a prophet who apprehends the everyday world as in some way evil or meaningless, and who accordingly preaches a meassage of salvation from this undesirable world.

> To the prophet, both the life of man and the world, both social and cosmic events, have a certain systematic and coherent meaning. To this meaning the conduct of mankind must be oriented if it is to bring salvation, for only in relation to this meaning does life obtain a unified and significant pattern. . . . The conflict between empirical reality and this conception of the world as a meaningful totality, which is based on a religious postulate, produces the strongest tensions in man's inner life as well as in his external relationships to the world.[2]

The way of "asceticism" and the way of "mysticism" are the two fundamental ways to relieve this tension.

Ascetic religion is that form of religion in which the believer, confronted by an evil or meaningless reality, struggles to transform the world and/or himself so as to bring the world and/or himself closer to the demands of God. In the face of an undesirable world, God is understood as issuing commands to the believer. And the believer then acts as an obedient instrument of God, struggling to suffuse the world with actions of obedience. Weber saw ascetic religion as profoundly activist and rationalized in character.

> The person who lives as a worldly ascetic is a rationalist, not only in the sense that he rationally systematizes his own personal patterning of life, but also in his rejection of everything that is ethically irrational, esthetic, or dependent upon his own emotional reactions to the world and its institutions. The distinctive goal always remains the alert, methodical control of one's own pattern of life and behavior. This type of inner-worldly asceticism included, above all, ascetic Protestantism, which taught the principle of loyal fulfillment of obligations within the framework of the world. . . .

The mystic withdraws from the world so as to approach God. Instead of aiming to be an instrument of God, he aims to become a vessel of God. Instead of ceaselessly engaging in the ethical struggle to reform himself and the world, he turns toward God to find rest. Contemplation is his mode of access; putting the world out of mind is its necessary accompaniment.

> But the distinctive content of salvation may not be an active quality of conduct, that is, an awareness of having executed the divine will; it may instead be a subjective condition of a distinctive kind, the most notable form of which is mystic illumination . . . as the end product of the systematic execution of a distinctive type of activity, namely contemplation. For the activity of contemplation to succeed in achieving its goal of mystic illumination, the extrusion of all everyday mundane interests is always required.

Common to asceticism and mysticism is the refusal to affirm the world as it is. Both see the world as laced with evil, meaninglessness, and inferiority. Yet their responses to this apprehension are profoundly different. The ascetic "feels himself to be a warrior in behalf of god, regardless of who the enemy is and what the means of doing battle are." Mysticism, by contrast, "is primarily the quest to achieve rest in god and in him alone. It entails inactivity. . . ." Weber suggests that it is best to speak of asceticism as a *rejection* of the world, and of mysticism as a *flight* from world. He says,

> From the standpoint of a contemplative mystic, the ascetic appears, by virtue of his transcendental self-maceration and struggles, and especially by virtue of his ascetically rationalised conduct within the world, to be forever involved in all the burdens of created things. . . . The ascetic is therefore regarded as permanently alienated from unity with god, and as forced into contradictions and compromises that are alien to salvation. But from the converse standpoint of the ascetic, the contemplative mystic appears not to be thinking of god, the enhancement of his kingdom and glory, or the fulfillment of his will, but rather to be thinking exclusively about himself. Therefore the mystic lives in everlasting inconsistency, since by reason of the very fact that he is alive he must inevitably provide for the maintenance of his own life.

It should be obvious that the religion of art described by Malraux is structurally akin to Weber's *mystical* religion. There is no god whose obedient instrument one is called to be. There is no ethical struggle to suffuse the world with the actions of obedience in a way that would sacralize one's ordinary experience. The dynamics are all the opposite. One departs from the ordinary world, and by way of contemplation one seeks to come into touch with something higher, better, and nobler.

What makes it possible to adopt this mystical stance toward high art is the relative independence of high art from all social functions—other than that of leisured contemplation. A work of high art may in fact have, or have had, some social function other than that of contemplation. But its service of that function does not exhaust its worth. In the eyes of the cultural elite, the social function does not constitute its main worth. It has a worth *independent* of however it may once have functioned—a worth that *transcends* the function and *abides* amidst the change of social institutions and functions. Independent, transcendent, and abiding in worth—it is these qualities that make possible the function of high art as an object of mystical religion. And it is the absence of these qualities in, for example, advertising art, that obstructs the taking of such art as objects of mystical veneration. Advertising art, with few exceptions, is totally embedded in its intended social function.

To observe the presence of these qualities in high art—or at least, the presumed presence—makes it *possible* to treat these works with veneration. But it does not yet explain why there are those in our society who *do in fact* venerate them. Possibility is not actuality. For people *actually* to take the step of adopting this religion of art they must see their immersion in high art as salvific from the ills of their own ordinary existence. The powers of this god must correspond to the apprehended ills of life in society. More is needed for the emergence of a mystical religion of salvation than just some relatively independent component of society which incorporates values perceived as nobler and more abiding than those to be found in society generally. Immersion in that component must be seen as saving us from what we discern as our fundamental ills.

It is not difficult to discern what members of the cultural elite typically find absent from society but present in high art, and what it is that leads them toward the step of adopting toward art the attitudes characteristic of mystical religion. Most fundamental is that people sense in art an *expressiveness* that they find missing in their ordinary social transactions. The result of our society's departure from tradition is that we have constructed a society pervaded by abstractness and alienation. We live by rules and regulations. Where once personal loyalties and institutional allegiances constituted the fundamental texture of society, now impersonal procedures and instrumental calculations constitute that texture. We work for wages within large, bureaucratically organized institutions. Neither what we produce nor the circumstances under which we produce it is expressive of ourselves.

In art we sense that something different takes place. The high-art artist is not part of some production line in which he has no voice and to which he must submerge his personality. True, the demands of social function still press down upon him. Yet to a great extent he is free to make as he desires to make and to give expression to his deepest self. It is no accident that the themes of expression and freedom resound through all modern writing on the arts. The very freedom and expressiveness that we find missing in ordinary life we find present in high art.

Perhaps also we sense in high art a different and refreshing form of rationality at work. The artist, along with the rest of us, no longer takes tradition as the preeminent determinant of his action. He engages in what Weber called rationalized action. But the form of rationality prominent in the work of our high art artist is different from that prominent in our society. The technologist and the bureaucrat have certain goals in mind—goals dictated by society or goals they have imagined. In light of their knowledge of natural, social, and psychological laws, they struggle to discover and to implement means for achieving these goals. Such means/end thinking is not wholly absent from the arts; but certainly it is not prominent. Prominent in the work of the artist is rather the imagining of new kinds of objects and of new kinds of activities. His struggle is not so much to find and implement means for achieving ends but to find ends that will satisfy his own demands. Relatively little of the musician's struggle goes into finding instruments and methods of playing those instruments that will produce the sounds he has imagined. Moreover, the artist, in his struggle to devise images and compose artifacts, in good measure does not do his thinking in terms of the conventions of language and the conceptual schemes that language expresses, but in terms of similarities and fittingnesses and eidetic resemblances that, for the most part, he feels and senses and intuits without ever bringing them to conceptual self-consciousness.[3] In art, intuition takes precedence over conception.

I suggest that it is such differences that often lead the cultural elite to see immersion in high art as salvific of what they apprehend as the sorrows of life in present-day society. It goes without saying that those who are adherents of some religion, in the strict sense of the word "religion," will regard this quasi-mystical "religion" of high art as an illusion. Art, they will insist, cannot save us from the root of evil; it is not the Absolute. My own conviction is that they are correct in that protest. But I am also persuaded that if, in their own vision of human existence, they fail to give adequate place to the artistic heritage of mankind, to this flowering of our creaturely potential, they will over and over drive people away from their religions. For there are those who cannot say no to the arts of mankind. There are those whose nature responds so deeply to this heritage that if forced, by the spokesmen of the religion in which they have been reared, to choose, they will, with sorrow, suffering, and anger, depart from home for a far country.

NOTES

1. Here I have explained the concept of the *cultural elite* by making use of the previously explained concept of *high art*. This reverses the order of explanation from that which I adopted in my *Art in Action: Towards a Christian Aesthetic* (Grand Rapids, Michigan: Eerdmans Publishing Co., 1980). There I took the concept of the cultural elite as being clear enough for my purposes, and explained high art as the art used pretty much exclusively by the cultural elite in a given society. I have several reasons now for preferring the present strategy of explanation, the chief being that I no longer think that we come to these matters with a clear initial grasp of the concept of our cultural elite.

An excellent sociological discussion on the nature of social elites, and a history of the use by sociologists of the concept of an elite, is to be found in T. B. Bottomore, *Elites and Society* (Baltimore: Penguin Books, 1964). There are those who would say that my concept of a cultural elite is still theoretically deficient, insisting that this particular group of people must be understood merely as part of a larger group that constitutes a *class* in Marx's sense. For one of the most recent and vigorous developments of this thesis, see Alvin W. Gouldner, *The Future of Intellectuals and the Rise of the New Class* (New York: The Seabury Press, 1979). I think that it can plausibly be argued that the "technical intelligentsia" of our society, as Gouldner calls them, constitutes a class in Marx's sense. But I think it is profoundly dubious that they *plus* the intellectuals (and the cultural elite) constitute a class.

2. Max Weber, *The Sociology of Religion*, trans. Ephraim Fischoff (Boston: Beacon Press, 1964), p. 59. Subsequent quotations are from this edition, pp. 168–71.

3. Cf. part 3, chap. 2 of my *Art in Action;* and part 6 of my *Works and Worlds of Art* (Oxford: Oxford University Press, 1980).

PART V

RELIGION AND ART: INTERDISCIPLINARY VISION

22

Painting As Theological Thought: The Issues in Tuscan Theology

JOHN W. DIXON, JR.

No special insight is required, given the context of modern scholarship, to recognize that specific languages shape our thought. What is much less commonly asserted is that systematic thought can occur in languages other than the verbal.

More is involved than simply extending the language of theology. It is, rather, a matter of determining the structures by which men have defined their relation to the world and responded to their apprehension of the manifestation of the divine. To do theology is not to know God in a particularly modern way, but to respond to God in the weight and structure and movement of a given language. The propositional language of traditional theology is a great imaginative achievement and part of the discipline and nourishment of the spirit of man. But it shapes thought by the specificities of its location (German as against English) and by the generality of its form (the structured action of Indo-European grammar); neither of these aspects represents the whole of human experience. Things which are talked about are things of curiosity, of argumentative interest, but they are not operative in the experience of men. It is only as the experience of the sacred becomes embodied, takes shape in those structures that can in turn shape the nervous system that they work rather than standing as specimens in a logical museum.

It should not be necessary to validate the Tuscan enterprise. A

An earlier, more expanded version of this essay appeared in *Humanities, Religion and the Arts Tomorrow*, edited by Howard Hunter (New York: Holt, Rinehart and Winston, 1972), pp. 134–56.

certain priority in the arts has been generally granted to Tuscany, but so long as the arts were peripheral in an enterprise to which propositions were central this was of no great moment. Such energy of imagination manifested over nearly five centuries points to a decisive act of the human intellect. It was the Florentines who shaped the primary imaginative acts of the western world for half a millennium. Perhaps, in a search for theology's definition, it would be well to turn away for a time from the Germans to those of another race and language.

All things have a history, and creativity is never creation from nothing, but a response to all that has been inherited. The enterprise of Tuscan theologians, their formal and structural response to their part of God's creation, was acted out in a particular landscape, in the shapes of a particular city, within the habits of mind and images of order generated in a particular history. What came to them was, above all, a particular sense of wall surfaces, a particular sense of the function, within the economy of devotion, of sacred objects that defined man's relation to the holy.

I

Italians grew up in the consciousness of the Byzantine icon. This is one of their circumstances that worked most constructively on the imagination, for the icon is a singular enactment of the relation between the human and the divine, and thus is a theological act of the highest importance. It is not an ordinary image. It is the point of agreed encounter between man and God. In function, it was not just for contemplation or instruction, it was an instrument of prayer. The sacred is present in the icon, not as the god inhabits the idol but as that to which the Lord comes.

This is not the only definition of the function of the sacred image. The canonical definition in the Western church was laid down by Pope Gregory the Great: the image is an aid and direction to devotion. It is a reminder of that to which devotion is rightly given, and it is, therefore, the occasion but not the instrument of the devotional act.

Under the pressure of Byzantine authority, Western art, in Italy at least, had small chance to develop its concern with the pedagogical and with the narrative that inspires devotion. It is precisely here that the issues that concern me are formulated and a specifically Tuscan theology begins to take shape.

Tuscany was a distinct region of the spirit before it was a political unit, and the revival of Western art was an affair of the Pisans Nicolo and Giovanni before it was of the Florentines or the Sienese. But it was in Florence and Siena that the final shaping of the issues took place.

Giotto and Duccio stand at the beginning of Tuscan theology, and they stand together on the definition of the issues, however diverse their fate. Giotto is perhaps a little short of Leonardo and Rembrandt as a household word but is, nonetheless, known in honor and most fervently loved. Duccio is known and honored by the specialists but beyond that known and somewhat patronized by those with a taste for the exotic. They do not divide subsequent history between them. Duccio had a few artistic heirs, the Lorenzetti, Simone Martini, finally the cold frenzy of Giovanni de Paolo and Sassetta. Beyond that even the tradition of his native town belongs to the Florentines. Giotto bestrides the next half millennium of the Western mind as few men ever have. Only Paul and Augustine, among the verbal theologians, so dominate history as did this man. I speak not only of artistic thought; I speak of the shaping of the imagination, that power in men that defines and forms our experience of the world. Later doctrines were shaped in other quarrels, but the shape of those quarrels was fixed in the image of order laid down by Giotto.

Although less well-known than Giotto, Duccio faced the same issues, and today we can turn to him for the merit of his answer now that five hundred years' work have used up what Giotto taught us to do.

The unit of all critical investigation is the individual work of art. The theological reference is the image of order embodied, incarnated, in the individual work. It is this image of order that determines the choices the artist makes in his contention with his material; it is the embodied image, the organizing principle of the individual work, that shapes the structural imagination of those who see it, including the artist who has had his imagination reshaped in his struggle to bring to life a work of art out of his medium's resistance to the imposition of ideal order.

It is a cliché of historical criticism that Duccio is, of all the great Italians, the closest to the Byzantine. Certainly, the Byzantine derivation is obvious. Elegant and eloquent linear rhythms, figures reduced to two-dimensionality, the iconography of the presentation. Against this cliché—again rightly—Giotto is represented as the revolutionary figure who places his figures in a real if limited space, who created solid, massive, three-dimensional persons, who interlocked them in precisely felt dramatic action.

These things are true, and very importantly true. Yet there are things, particularly in Duccio, that go beyond the cliché.

Duccio is not the culmination of the Byzantine style in Italy; he is a true Tuscan and his awareness of the issues in Tuscan theology is as profound as Giotto's.

It is perhaps true that prior to the work of the fourteenth-century Tuscans, the sense of personality was absent from art. Since drama is enacted only by persons, since dramatic action is by definition the interaction of persons with moral weight and the power of choice, then dramatic action does not exist without personality. Personality hardly exists outside Christian art. Individuality is the distinctiveness of appearance that belongs to a particular and specific person. Greek art had the sense of moral force that is of the essence of the person but basically saw it embodied in the human type. Roman art had, in its portraiture, one of the most intensely individualized of all arts but with rare (but important) exceptions did not infuse the individual shapes with the moral gravity of true personality.

The Christian artist could not make his forms fit his faith immediately. He used inherited forms and developed a symbolic speech of remarkable flexibility and authority. Byzantine art built up a symbolic vocabulary that could make manifest a wider range of states of the soul than had been present before.

Individuality in Western art was not the work of the Italians but the great anonymous sculptors of the French Gothic cathedrals. But there each individual participates in the peace of God radiating from the Christ figures of the trumeau.

Even so great a work as the *Bamberg Rider* is defined more nearly as a role than a person. He is the embodiment of one of the greatest dreams of the Middle Ages, the Christian king. The great Florentine, Donatello, also showing a warrior, demonstrates by contrast the possibility of complex humanity as identical with role and status. The *Bamberg Rider* lives in the vision of his purpose, his role not simply on earth but in the final dream of God's order. In Giotto and Duccio, for the first time in the history of art, we find depicted the fully developed person acting to some moral purpose toward coherent and understandable ends.

Artistic drama is not the imitation of the externals of an action, which would be no more than illustration. It is a making manifest, for good or evil, the moral purpose of human acts. To this end several artistic instruments are available to the artist. For both Giotto and Duccio the basic instrument is gesture, the expressive act and attitude that reveals the inner moral purpose. Procedurally this means the most intense and precise observation of human conduct and attitude. True gesture is unattainable as a general idea, a general principle. It depends rather on the most intense immediacies of relation to life as it is experienced.

In both men the sensitivity of gestures is such that they could, and, in the order of humanity, should, constitute a lifetime of study. In the Arena Chapel, Anna, with infinite tenderness, touches the face of Joachim returning. Equally, too, the great arch encloses the figures, the circle wraps their upper bodies together. Gesture is Giotto's principal dramatic instrument, but composition serves as well. Joachim is expelled from the temple with the coarse repelling gesture of the priest's inverted hand; Joachim resentfully looking back while lovingly holding the rejected sacrificial lamb. But he is also thrust into emptiness, an emptiness so unprecedented that historians were convinced for years that there must have been a figure painted there but which undeniably is Giotto's sign of the loneliness of rejected man. Another example, one of the finest of all, is the *Noli Me Tangere*, with Mary reaching out in infinite longing, and Jesus simultaneously moving away, holding her off, blessing her with infinite compassion and love.

Duccio's gesture is every bit as precise, every bit as revealing. Judas avidly grasps after the money and the whole group huddles conspiratorially, the only such congestion of a group on the whole *Maesta*. Or Joseph braces himself on the ladder while he holds the limp dead body that falls from the sorrowful emptiness above the cross.

Yet it is perfectly evident that Giotto and Duccio differed in their handling of the figures making these gestures, and in that difference lies the clue to their differing purposes and the seeds of the further development of theological work in Tuscany. Usually the difference is presented in terms of the greater density of Giotto's figures, the fuller space, the greater range of the action. But these ideas do not go far enough, for such devices are means and not ends, language but not what is said by means of the language, forms but not the content that is inherent in and inseparable from the form. It is not even enough to point out the intense awareness of the human drama in each one, for this again is pedagogy and not a complete analysis. For these works function so differently that the same dramatic material, even a concern for the same issues, takes us in very different directions.

Giotto's interest in not in tangibility as such. It is, indeed, a startlingly new world he offered for contemplation, a newly imagined world that changed the optics of the Western imagination. But there is no evidence to suggest that such formal matters were at the center of his concern. Rather, he seems to have sought to translate the drama into the statics of our body's existence as well as the dynamics of its interrelations. The tangibility of this gesture and action is such that our body responds in kind. The weight is our weight, the action is a disposition of our own flesh. Therefore, since in the painting both weight and action, the proportion and rhythms of the event, are manifestations of the moral relation inherent in the event, then our participation in the structure and dynamics trains us to the motivating act. Devotion is not contemplation but participation. It is thus active and not passive, transformative and not simply confirmatory.

Duccio, on the other hand, starts not only with as profound a grasp of the dramatic structure, but also with as great a sensitivity to the physicality of the acts; no man is truly a Tuscan if he does not have these two as fundamental to his imaginative language. But he does not seek the tangibility that compels the worshiper into participation. He seeks a visual form that is the symbolic equivalent of the action. The grasping hand is placed with absolute precision exactly where the hand should be placed but it does not truly grasp. It is an abstract curve that is the visual equivalent, or the symbol, of the grasp. The figures are disposed in positions proper to the participation in the action but the rhythm of their placement makes a counterpoint to the drama.

Rhythm in Giotto is always submissive to the drama, an enhancement of it as well as instrumental to it. Rhythm in Duccio is appropriate to the drama but independent of it, thus establishing a personality for the picture that is other than the immediacies of the event. The event is transfigured into something else.

Duccio's painting has one of the richest surfaces to be found anywhere in painting. The gold background is the setting, the deep rich colors set into it. The colors are absolutely pure, subdued in saturation to be sure that no color is detached from the integral surface. The enclosing lines are fine and sinuous like the intricate wires of the jeweler.

There is no atmosphere, which is to say in a narrative that there is absolute clarity of atmosphere. Where earlier works occupy only a symbolic space, Duccio's works have a real sense of space; the clarity of forms, the unimpeded and unqualified clarity of color, can only signify an absolute purity of atmosphere. Since each form in this purity of atmosphere has complete clarity, each form becomes a jewel for entranced observation.

Thus, the moral drama, the pure Tuscan element of the work, is not, as in Giotto, reproduced in the body of the observer. It is modulated into a different realm of being. The coherence and intensity of rhythmic structure, the quality of color and line, transfigure the intensely realized moral act. Instead of the transformation of the worshiper's life on this earth, the worshiper is caught up into a new realm. He does not see the vision of the heavenly city. Rather, it is his own life that is figured in the sacred drama— the emotions, the motives, the physical response of a life on this earth that is held away from the solidity of the earth and so becomes a true ecstasis that is of the substance of genuine mysticism.

What Giotto and Duccio share, then, is the concern for the life of man in its moral dimension and the expressive attitude of the body—the gesture—that is revelatory of the quality and character of the moral act. They share, too, the analytical and calculated intelligence that makes them so responsive to the particularities of human acts as well as so able to construct a work of art that makes their grasp of the dramatic moral act manifest.

This is the same intelligence that made possible the other Florentine achievements: precise observation, yet penetration through surface appearances to the forces that give structure to the elements of surface appearances. The Florentines created the study of history and politics, not because they chronicled information, but because they understood what held that information together.

Thus they established the context in which Tuscan theology worked out the problem around which later solutions congested. Where they differ is the direction in which they took this moral drama. Duccio moved it into the realm of the mystic vision, Giotto into the dimensions of this earth.

This kind of statement is rhetoric made possible only by the fact that Giotto's spatial vision dominated Western thought until the end of the nineteenth century and the reformation we identify with the name of Cézanne. Because Giotto so shaped our imagination we take that shape of space as normative, just as we take as normative those structures of systematic propositions that have been built in the intellectual framework that Giotto designed.

What most decisively differentiates Giotto from Duccio in the Tuscan enterprise is his choice of artistic instrument. Duccio worked in the traditional medium of egg tempera, Giotto primarily in fresco. Tempera made possible the extraordinary richness that is so important to Duccio's vision. Fresco provides something else again.

These differences are not simply two ways of making a painting. They are two fundamental modes of thought, two ways of being-in-the-world. Fresco does not happen to be just a painting on a convenient and relatively permanent support. It is the energizing of a wall which is itself a determinant of the imagination. Even in his tempera panels, Giotto so ordered his colors that his painting had the breadth of form characteristic of fresco, where his basic thinking was done.

What I have pointed to already is enough for a theological revolution: the transformation of figures from being symbols of pathos, pointers to devotional response in the worshiper, into figures of moral density and muscular control, with gestures as revelations of inner feeling and moral relation. Yet this is not specific to fresco. The substance of fresco is the congestion of weight onto the surface of the wall.

A wall is an act of the imagination, not simply when it is enclosure, but when it encloses and gives shape to meaningful space. A wall is the boundary of our private selves and can take the shape of our image of order. It is also the shaping edge of corporate space, giving body to the image of the common self held by the community whose vision, through the agency of the master builder, has shaped the space. When such a wall is fittingly frescoed, its meaning has been translated into human drama, and the emotional life which was contained by the walls is caught up onto the sustaining surface of the wall to be transfigured in the sacred story. The wall is two-dimensional. The great achievement of Giotto (himself a builder) was the energizing of this two-dimensional plane by affirming it and then extending it back into the represented space. The drama is enacted at the juncture of the real space and the represented space. It was the taking up of the third dimension into thought.

It is not just the third dimension that Giotto uses; it is the third dimension cut to the measure of man. The space is clear and intelligible, movement in it is free and orderly. The pictures are unprecedentedly large, thus relating the pictorial space closely to the actual space of the spectator. The mystery and magic of Duccio is wholly absent. The worshiper, his imagination stunned and overwhelmed by Duccio, here feels a different exhilaration. He stands apart from the picture, at what can later be called "the point of view." Icons are objects in our world, lacking depth and a spatial existence of their own. Giotto's paintings go back from a fixed surface and create a new world which the worshiper now contemplates from within his own space. Thus is the worshiper's individuality clearly established while it is enhanced by his participation in the dynamics of the picture. With Giotto, there is never any separation of the worshiper and the world of the picture, since it is the life of the worshiper that is taken up onto the wall and there transformed. But when, as it were, the worshiper took a step or two back from the wall and became the spectator rather than the worshiper, then the attitude was secularized. The spectator became detached from the world with the result that science became possible, as did the form of theology that finds its work possible in detachment from that which is being accounted for by its uncommitted and involved technique.

In Giotto's work, the several movements of the spirit are muted into harmony and for this reason so many who come to the Arena Chapel have the sense of coming home. This is the shape of our corporate life before the modern revolution. Only a few people have been able to respond deeply to the entranced vision of Duccio. Rather, it is the radiance of the moral act in Giotto that shaped the European theological imagination, but the moral act is radiant not just in itself but on the surface of the wall. Attention to the moral act alone eventually produced the novel, and later secular psychology. With Giotto the integrity of the wall is never lost, even when it is simply the sustaining context of the moral drama.

Duccio's space is clearly very unlike Giotto's, but it is not sufficient simply to identify this difference. Let us, therefore, look comparatively at Giotto's and at Duccio's representation of the same subject, the "Entry into Jerusalem."

Giotto's handling of the subject is in harmony with his general structural principles. The spatial setting is three-dimensional but decisively cut off immediately behind the figures and thus subordinate to the action. The city gate is too large to be merely symbolic but too small to be a true gate; after all, people are more important than gates. Jesus is high to the left of center; the ass's neck and head lead across, while the blessing gesture is isolated in the open center. The congested rhythm of the apostles crowds in from the left. The crowd spills out of the gate in a falling rhythm that ends in the prostrate figure spreading his robe, a rhythm characteristically syncopated by the figure drawing back in awe. Nature is present, but instrumental only. All is concentrated on the drama, fairly simple in this case but nonetheless profoundly realized. The act of the entry is made manifest, along with a variety of responses to it, but the dominant element is the majesty of the figure of Jesus.

With some complexities, Duccio's space in some of the panels is relatively straightforward, clear, cubic, concise, and adequate without being obtrusive. Where the emotional tone of the subject suggests a different treatment, space is treated in unusual ways. The most remarkable of all is the panel depicting the entry.

Unlike Giotto's treatment, space here is not simply an instrument, but is an actor. The painting is formally flatter than Giotto's, but symbolically much deeper. The road zigzags up the surface of the panel rather than back into depth, but the symbolic movement begins in a field, goes across a road, another field, an expanse of city to a cathedral dome.

In Giotto's painting the point of view is low, moving toward the actual position of the spectator in the chapel and enhancing the majesty of the central figure. The point of view in Duccio's is manipulated in a shockingly sophisticated manner. At first it appears to be high, somewhat above the middle of the panel. We look down on the road, at least partially into the orchard beyond the road, and up to the arches of the gate. But we also look up to the lower surface of the lintel of the doorway in the foreground. Actions of all figures are as intelligible as they would be were we standing immediately in front of them at whatever level they are.

Scale is manipulated to the same purpose; the figures just in front of the gateway are larger than the ones close to Jesus, their heads as large as the head of Jesus himself, who is much closer to the spectator's position. Thus, in moving from left to right, the spectator moves from the foreground into the group at the gate and is prepared to enter.

At this point I become aware that I am no longer dealing with the vagaries of medieval perspective, or even with the emotional manipulation of space in the Byzantine icon. Instead, there is a highly sophisticated manipulation of surfaces for a peculiarly devotional purpose. Objects and persons alike are defined in faceted surfaces that are angled against each other in a complex pattern that may remind the modern observer of the structured facets of cubism. But instead of the profound structural purpose of cubism, ordering is here a trap for devotional meditation. The glance of the spectator slides from plane to plane, back into the symbolic space to the temple, out again to the figure of Jesus, who is crowned by the temple yet reaches it only through the life of the city.

Since the picture is full of allusions to the experienced world and the circumstances of our common life, the origin of our response is the awareness of this world. But appearances are embedded into the intensity of color structure and the complexity of spatial organization—the common life is transfigured into the uncommon life of a spiritual event. There is no weight to figures or tangibility to stone, so the holy event floats like a mystical vision; yet the entrapment of vision is so complete that the serious spectator cannot extricate himself from his participation in the event. Thus the icon to which Duccio is so closely linked is carried still farther away from its appointed task and into a distinctly Western vision. This is no longer the occasion for prayer or the instrument of prayer. It is itself an act of devotion trapping not only the conscience but the optical consciousness of the spectator into a singular act of involvement with the deepest structures of the faith. From this the worshiper returns into his own circumstances not so much better informed about the nature of the common life as prepared to see the ordinariness of things radiant with the faith.

It is, perhaps, symptomatic of the special nature of Duccio's work that it appears on the back of a great altarpiece and was usually seen only by priests. Giotto's is on the walls of a chapel, accessible to all. Here there is no entrapment but complete openness. Space is structured without ambiguity. Movement is measured and weighty, determined by the mechanisms of the body, so the worshiper participates in both adoration and blessing and learns in his own flesh, not in his argumentative mind, what it means to bend in adoration of the holy. As he moves slowly through the chapel he experiences in his own bodily dynamics a full range of human acts incarnating the holy history. The event is distant from him and independent of him, resting serenely in the shallow space carved by the paint on the clear and integral wall. Simultaneously it is working in his flesh and in the rhythm of his movement. Those who take Giotto seriously do not go back into their world like the disciples blinking on their return from the Mount of the Transfiguration or from the Museo del Duomo of Siena. They go back into a clarified world, a world of weight and substance, of intelligible relations among things, where people move in the integrity of intelligible moral purpose, whether good or evil. The response to Duccio is ecstasy. The response to Giotto is joy.

It is perhaps not surprising that Duccio's work was so unfruitful. The occasion was not Duccio's but Giotto's. There was a formal range to Giotto that created problems still alive in the early years of the twentieth century. There was a moral complexity and depth hardly yet available to intellects formed on philosophy and literature rather than art.

Yet, even so, the world since Cézanne has moved away from Giotto. Space is no longer so clearly rational nor morality so intelligible. The spectator must participate in the artwork, be trapped in its ambiguities, and make parts of it in his own entranced response. Thus, surprisingly, Duccio, uninfluential since the sixteenth century, becomes again a leader by making manifest the process of involvement of optics with devotion. He outlines the process whereby intelligence is itself transformed into prayer.

II

Giotto works on the sensibility of the spectator by making the work of art something other than the spectator, although related to him in a distinctive way. In doing so he created a pictorial world that impinges uniquely on the world of the spectator but is nonetheless a different world.

Giotto's figures have weight and density, they move according to both anatomical and psychological logic, and they act in the context of discernible moral purpose. Whatever Giotto's intention, whatever the experience of the original participants in his work, it was inevitable that the work of art developed an increasing distance from the spectator, and, finally, even from the artist.

Clearly, this separation is essential to the writing of true history as true history has been defined since the time of the great Florentine historians. Clearly, too, it is false to the world. There is no sense in which "I" can be defined as over against my world; I am a part of it, shaped by culture and environment.

This detachment of the "I" from the world, the subject from the object, was the indispensable first step in the Western intellectual enterprise; because of it all sorts of things have been accomplished that could not have been accomplished otherwise. But the price had to be paid, and we are beginning to pay it now.

The price was the reifying of process. All human experience is ebb and flow. In the moment we are involved in it by an intricate network of relations, in time we are involved in it as change, flow, process. To objectify any part of experience is to excise it from the flow. In the reifying of process, things or events are cut loose from relations, fixed permanently in the amber (or plastic) of scholarly language. This *works* in the Arena Chapel; part of the extraordinary power of the paintings is to be located precisely in the suspension of the moment, compelling the entranced attention to absorb somatically the moral structure that is the supporting skeleton of the painted forms. It no longer works.

So far as Giotto (or any artist) is concerned this is both liberation and limitation. Giotto did not paint for me. He painted for men of the fourteenth century. This either has nothing to do with cultural relativism or it is the only true meaning of cultural relativism. The besetting sin of the modern intellect, and, as a result, of modern pedagogy, is the conviction that the thing divorced from this relation and suspended in scholarly plastic is "in fact" the thing itself. Where pedagogy should try to put the student into the process, it concentrates on the presentations of these mythical things.

Giotto was a particular man, shaped by a particular culture and working within it. Those who participated in his work were trained to the same cultural speech as Giotto was. They were not twentieth-century men; they knew nothing of Rembrandt or Picasso or, for that matter, Niels Bohr. Consequently, what they saw in the Arena Chapel is very different from what I see. We are different people. The artwork is not a thing working in a certain way on equally objectified persons; we cannot define the work as it was and is and ever more shall be. The artwork is a term in a relation that involves the artist and the participant. Change the participants and, while the physical substance of the work is not changed, it is not just a manipulation of language to say that it is a different work. The work of art is not a thing but a function and a relation. The relation originates in the physicality of the work and is shaped by the material structure of the work and is inseparable from it, but the physical separability of the material should not suggest that it can be separated in our understanding.

Thus I can never be sure how the work of art worked for fourteenth-century observers. Nor am I obliged to assume that the way it worked then is authoritative today. It certainly works for me as I have described it, and my description can be confirmed by the experience of others. Once I am freed to experience the work as though it had been done for me, for our time, I can then experience it in the knowledge that fourteenth-century men were not only profoundly different from me but profoundly the same; they are men with bodies shaped as mine, responding to the world as mine does. Thus my dialogue is not only with Giotto but with them. I cannot know that they responded according to my analysis; neither can I know that they did not.

Thus the paintings are not a function and relation simply in one dimension. Rather, there is a three-way relation: Giotto and his spectators (or participants); Giotto and us; the fourteenth-century participants and us. The error, the false step, in traditional criticism is the presumption that somehow a work can be isolated from this functional relation and presented in itself. An artwork *is* these relations, it is not simply a thing that functions differently in different situations.

In traditional formal analysis, the unstated assumption is directed toward the "being" of the artwork, that this is what the artwork "is." What I have tried to define is how the paintings "work." Participation in a painting is not a mystical, visionary, undefinable experience. A painting works in a certain way because it is made in a certain way. My response to the way it is made is in good part a consequence of my history and nature, so I can never extract myself—or better, my self—from the analysis. Analysis is always reciprocation, dialogue, discourse, intercourse, wherein the self, or all the participant selves, and the work of art are mutually defined.

A history of art should be and must be an intricate, careful thing—and a most consequential thing, for it should be a history of consciousness. Art does not simply reflect consciousness but shapes it. What is needed here is the sense of the continuous line of Giotto's heritage; whatever the several traditions from Giotto to Cézanne, a painting is an illusory world over against the spectator (at some point in the development, no longer a participant). Pictures function very differently at different times (this difference is the subject matter of the study of art history), but they share the character of being on the other side of the painting surface, a created world that is other than the spectator, and—crucially—in various ways subservient to him.

The objectivity of nature was vital to the growth of science. Now science itself comes to know that the resulting scientific knowledge is not simply part of the truth but a misshapen truth. Not only art but mystic communion gives another part of the truth, but also a different modality of truth, which is not different from science and to be added to it, but is, in ways we do not yet know, inseparable from scientific truth. The question really is, whether the Western scientific enterprise is to be denied and reversed or whether it can be restored to wholeness. This is a metaphysical question but also a methodological one and therefore political and social.

At some point along the way science became the determinant of man's consciousness. Science grew out of the consciousness shaped by art; as science falters in face of its own destructive products, art may be the only resource for putting the divided consciousness together again.

All this is the background against which "modern art" (which I regard as starting with Cézanne) must be understood. As is true with all developmental artistic styles, the whole development is implicit from the beginning, and what artists successfully do is twofold: they develop the implications of the original stylistic idea and they translate the original form into the new vocabulary in order to maintain the purity of the original effect. Every act shapes the consciousness of those who participate in it. Participants become, therefore, different persons, no longer able to receive the originating work in the same way. Preservation of the canonical effect requires a new form that does for the new consciousness what the originating form did for the old. This process can be truncated by the appearance of an overpowering new idea or it can be exhausted in the failure of the rejuvenating imagination, or the changing forms can modulate into a distinctively new effect.

Cézanne stands, as all such men, including Giotto, do, as the fulfillment of the old tradition as well as the initiator of the new. The pictured world is still palpably three-dimensional and solid. Yet it is no longer beyond the picture plane, but translated into it. Nothing is permitted to disrupt the surface of the painting; the wall that Giotto energized into drama returns as the controlling plane of painting. Suddenly the painting is no longer subservient to the spectator, but is an object in his presence. Much, if not most, of the intensely emotional protest against modern art arises from pride offended at the loss of this subservience, and from a sense of being crowded. A modern work of art is not over there beyond the frame, but obtrudes into the room.

The drama that was the substance of Renaissance painting and a constant presence in post-Renaissance art has been ruthlessly excised from the painting. But it has not been excised from the painting act, the painting relation, for the drama is very much present, quite transformed. The painting is so clearly the product of a high intellectual act that to experience a Cézanne is not simply to experience an encounter with Provence or an encounter with a painting. It is to experience the creative intelligence of the artist. There is a creative intelligence behind every work of art, but usually that intelligence is absorbed into the work. It is very nearly only in Western art that the intelligence of the artist is so publicly present and so clearly at work solving an artistic problem. With Cézanne this extraordinary presence of the artist in his dramatic interaction with his material becomes one of the factors participating in the extraordinary complex of relations that make up a Cézanne painting.

The surrealistic-expressionistic tradition owes little to Cézanne, but the rest of modern art is a working out of the themes he designated. The cubist tradition pursued the problem of interaction between represented space and the integral picture plane. Non-representational art pursued the same problem while sacrificing the assistance or freeing itself of the burden of association with the world of our common life. That world appears, violently and obtrusively, in the mislabeled "pop" art style. The presence of the artist is variously established, from the cool remoteness of Mondrian to the passion of the action painters, who make of their own creative act both the subject and the occasion for the painting. But constantly the painting is an object established in the intimate presence of the spectator, carrying intensely the dramatic presence of the artist (even when, as often happens, that presence is trivial, frivolous, or indulgent).

One of the major movements of the 1960s comprises a series of works that apparently go to the other extreme. All signs of the artist's personality are effaced. As nearly as possible all action and all hierarchy within the work are abolished. Sculpture becomes pure geometric forms, color is brought to the same value level to prevent any effect of space or modeling, space and drama are expelled. The work of art is reduced to pure objecthood, often without any inherent interest at all. Indeed, the artist works hard to cancel out "interest," that is, any sensuous quality or any complex of internal relations that can give pleasure or direct our attention in time. The work is totally manifest in the instant of first viewing, it deliberately eschews anything that can hold the attention of the spectator.

At the same time, the work functions in the attention of the spectator, for it is very difficult to ignore it. These artists are given to big works that cannot be evaded, that intrude into the consciousness of the spectator.

Some critics have interpreted these new works as the beginning of a new style and, therefore, of a new consciousness. I do not hold to this interpretation; a style (or any human attitude) is human through its negations as much as through its affirmations. These new works do not appear at some generalized period in the history of man; they appear in the context of a culture in which men are surfeited with moral or structural exhortation. They appear precisely in a culture that has worn out the work of Giotto. They so exactly reverse everything that Giotto and his successors have tried to do.

They deny inherent interest and involvement. They are ostentatiously anonymous. They avoid all drama, all development, space and three-dimensionality, everything, in short, that has concerned Western artists. And by the denial, they affirm the absence of what they are denying.

Here is the artistic statement of the death of God.

It is not "a" concept of God that has died, it is the very concept of having a concept of God that has died. There is no point in trying ingeniously to reformulate a concept of God; there is no language left to do more than make an idol in memory of the lost God. "The death of God" is as good an idol as any other but it is no more than that. Despite the dogmatism of some (but not all) theologians, the statement has no status as history or description. It is no more than a working instrument to contend with the particularities of a situation.

The minimal art of the 1960s; the color painting of Stella, Louis, Olitski, and the art of many others, make this same affirmation. They are not affirming vacuity or meaninglessness. They are affirming that something once alive is now dead. In so doing they are working very precisely in the methodological tradition of Western art.

The main point of this essay has been to elucidate the way in which two great artists directed the consciousness of worshipers to particular, if different, devotional ends. In the minds of Duccio and Giotto this appears to have been a conscious (if probably not verbalized) purpose. There was no question of whether God existed. It was a matter of shaping consciousness to the proper (orthodox?) reception of God. It is possible, even necessary, to speak of this body of material as "Tuscan theology," with the full intention of making clear that both the language and the issues are those of painting, not of propositional systems.

No such "theological" interpretations can be offered for the modern material, for its use is very different. Yet its procedures are not all that different, for its explicit (now at least partially verbalized) intention is to have an effect on the consciousness of the spectator. "Have an effect" rather than "shape," because to shape something is to be in a moral or dramatic relation to it, a relation and a responsibility that these artists have rejected. Rather, consciousness is thrown back on its own resources, undetermined by the work of art. This art is (as, of course, all art is) unintelligible outside its own history. It is the affirmation of the death of that history or, perhaps, of the present exhaustion of that history.

For the moment, the history of Western art is exhausted, and some of the most creative artists are giving themselves over to the task of doing more than denying that tradition or affirming its death. They are compelling consciousness to be aware of itself in a way that man has never achieved before. I have always felt that "the world come of age" was a singularly arrogant phrase, as though even the greatest of our predecessors were children, and we are mature. Many of our predecessors have been a good deal more self-aware than that. What is, however, granted to us or imposed on us is, so far as I know, unprecedented—the consciousness of consciousness itself; the awareness of the instruments of our awareness, even the instruments of that self-aware awareness; the symbolic means men have used for the construction of their own integrity.

The history of man has been a history of his generation of symbolic structure for coping with experience, and of his eventual defeat in the failure of his structures. We are involved now in the common and traditional process of the collapse of inherited structures. Yet, history is not cyclical; there is something to be salvaged from that process, and the first thing to salvage is the understanding of the process itself.

POSTSCRIPT

This paper is drastically abridged from its original version. As a result, qualifications are lost and the argument is more baldly assertive than it should be. Nuance is lost, transitions are more abrupt than I like, and some important parts of the argument have been eliminated. In the interest of economy of space, appearances, and continuity of reading, the customary elision marks have been eliminated.

My case for "Tuscan theology" has been pressed further in three papers: "The Drama of Donatello's David," *Gazette des Beaux Arts* (January 1979); "The Medici Chapel as a Resurrection," *Southeastern College Art Conference Review* (1976); and, "Michelangelo's Judging Christ," *Studies in Iconography* (1983). The methodology for criticism has been examined at greater length in "Art as the Making of the World," *The Journal of the American Academy of Religion* (March 1983).

23

Theological Reflections on an Image of Woman: Picasso's *Girl before a Mirror*

MELINDA WORTZ

Western culture in the twentieth century has often been described as spiritually bereft. Virtually every belief system and ideology—economic, political, psychological, philosophical, and theological—has been shattered and subjected to attempts at restructuring. The situation is not altogether negative, however. The historical/critical consciousness of the nineteenth century has enabled our acceptance of pluralism and of the validity of multiple world views. As John Cobb has suggested:

> The results are that many traditional Christian beliefs, practices and experiences can be reaffirmed, but now in such a way that their truth and reality do not oppose the truth and reality of what is affirmed in the study of other traditions. This affirmation of the reality of highly diverse experiences and the truth of highly diverse convictions is essential to pluralism.[1]

Pluralism is the *affirmation*, not merely the toleration, of various traditions. Pluralism is absolutely mandatory for our physical survival in today's world. It is a world view implied by the early twentieth-century artistic revolutions, such as Cubism, which are seedbeds for theological analysis and insight.

In analyzing Pablo Picasso's painting *Girl before a Mirror* (1932; Museum of Modern Art, New York), I will use a methodology derived from Edward Hobbs's trinitarian theology. Hobbs elucidates the three *personae* of God (Son, Father, and Spirit) in terms of responses to the three negative encounters of human existence.

The first—the Christ encounter—is characterized as *exposure:* specifically, the exposure of our true nature, with its hypocrisies, pretensions, and bogusness. The appropriate Christian response to this "no" encounter with our deepest selves is an affirmative one, a "yes" saying that is possible only through the *judgment* and *redemption* of the Christ encounter, which results in a turning around of consciousness. This turning around brings forth a freedom from enslavement to the past, with the consequent ability to be alive in the present and open to the future. The opportunity to turn negations into life, goodness, and affirmation through encounters with the three *personae* of God is the very heart of the Christian understanding of the meaning of existence.

The second *persona* of God (Creator/Father) is encountered in the ultimately conditioned nature of human life. The perception of life's limitations as a confrontation with creatureliness, finitude, or limitations is experienced as depressing and intolerable. The appropriate Christian response is one of gratitude for the undeserved gifts of life and creation. This act of affirming the conditionedness of human existence creatively transforms the very conditions of daily life and allows for participation in the process of creation.

The *persona* of God as Spirit, or need-giver, manifests the third negative encounter: the needs of others. As before, we can respond either negatively or affirmatively to the call of the Spirit for need-fulfilling. Perhaps, we are too busy with "important matters" to respond to the unexpected needs of strangers or to the unseen starving millions, or to the everyday needs of our families. The Christian response to these situations is affirmation. As love is given in response to human needs, we participate in a relationship: love is experienced by both giver and receiver. Through this reciprocal exchange of love, we find grace and build community.[2]

Preliminary Analysis

Picasso's painting *Girl before a Mirror* depicts two vertically aligned, slightly larger than life female figures, one apparently an image of the other as reflected in a mirror. Stylistically, the painting is abstract, although some condensed representational references to the female body can be discerned. During his early Cubist period (1908–12), Picasso restructured objects in order to present multiple views of the same image in a manner that would be impossible in the natural world; this device is evident in the simultaneous views of profile and full face of each figure in this painting. In contrast to the geometric fracturing and restructuring of form that characterized Picasso's analytic Cubist period, here his approach to form is curvilinear. The round, circular forms serve to emphasize those parts of the female anatomy, the breasts and the womb, that are associated with fertility, procreation, and nurture. The artist's use of form reflects a celebration of sensuality as well as an intellectual dissection and reordering of the way things look.

Picasso's abstract language reflects a radical departure from a long tradition in Western art: the Renaissance revival of Greek thought, which manifested itself in the skillful two-dimensional replication of the naturalistic appearances of figures in space. His use of color and space is also at odds with a common understanding of the natural order; for example, a whole spectrum of colors, not a relatively homogeneous skin tonality, are present in the faces. Picasso's use of paint does not suggest the varying textures of hair, skin, or fabric, but paint's own material reality. Individual sections of the painting contain little modulation of color from light to dark, a device that traditionally suggests the volume of objects and their presence in the different spatial planes of foreground, middle ground, and background. In this painting, most forms are separated from one another by strong black outlines whose contours are filled with relatively flat color. The overall flat patterning of the composition affirms the actual nature of the materials with which Picasso is working—the paint and the two-dimensional surface of the canvas. This is in marked contrast to the traditional Renaissance notion of a painting as a window on the world—a fictive world of realistic-looking forms existing in space.

Picasso's use of form and compositional format may not correlate with our preconceptions of the natural order; however, his painting is not lacking in coherent structure. It is held together by a rhythmic repetition of abstract motifs in which the curvilinear forms of the human figures are played off against the more angular patterns of diamonds and stripes. The relatively uniform high saturation of color in this painting works to emphasize its flat patterning.

A final contradiction between what is ostensibly being depicted and what we see is the variance in appearance between the girl and her reflection in the mirror. Instead of a mirror image, the reflection looks like an entirely different figure in terms of facial features, color, and the appearance of body and hair. The extended arm of the girl outside of the mirror reaches across the glass and its reflected image in a gesture that seems to embrace them, as if welcoming the dark side of her psyche (in a Jungian sense). At the right-hand edge of the mirror her hand appears to be outside the glass, while at the left it appears to be transparent, a part of the reflected image. In other words, the arm seems to be existing simultaneously in two different spatial planes, just as the plane of the face is seen both in profile and full view.

Here, Picasso "achieves a metamorphosis of the traditional vanity (or 'Vanitas') image, in which a woman looking in the mirror sees herself as a death's head; here, the figure with a double head is reflected as a somber-faced but voluptuous image."[3] Such a transformation of a traditional art-historical theme, from the emphasis on temporality and death to the celebration of sensuality and fecundity, has important theological implications. Many theologians, including Hobbs, Cobb, and Pannenberg, have emphasized that bondage to the past is ultimately a form of sin, as the Christian Gospel calls for release of our ties to the past in order to turn around our consciousness for hope in the future.

The preceding remarks have concentrated on the literal, or overt, subject matter of Picasso's painting; that is, the formal characteristics of shape, color, composition, space, and the objects that are being depicted. This level of analysis is what Noam Chomsky would call the surface structure of an artwork or what Hobbs would refer to as the "object matter" of a painting. This kind of analysis is important as a preliminary stage for a consideration of Chomsky's deep structure, or of Erwin Panofsky's iconology, or of what I consider to be the underlying philosophical or theological subject matter. To understand this deeper level of meaning, the painting must be considered in relation to its historical context.

Theological Analysis

Picasso's life spanned a complex period of revolution—political, social, and conceptual. National boundaries had been broken down and reestablished several times during this period. The social structure had been profoundly shattered by two waves of change in the process of production and consumption: first, the evolution from a largely rural and agrarian world population to a highly industrialized one; and, second, the transition from an industrialized society to an electronic one. Major conceptual shifts occurred: for example, in physics, an understanding of the world as composed of discrete, solid objects was transformed into one of a continuous process of exchange between matter and energy. Similarly, in psychology, Freud's suggestion that the human psyche is more complex than the conscious mind and that human beings are motivated by unconscious drives has had enormous impact.

In these new conceptual paradigms of physics and psychology, it is apparent that reality has no fixed entities or unchanging truths: all experience and understanding is the product of continuously shifting interrelationships. In other words, the contemporary world view of reality is of a multifaceted, polyvalent, relational, and relativistic situation; the same pluralistic world view can be seen in Picasso's paintings. The simultaneity of forms that traditionally occupy different spatial planes, the interpenetration and overlapping of forms, and the commitment to analyze and restructure the appearance of things are elements of Picasso's work that express the twentieth-century understanding of the universe as pluralistic rather than as a rationally ordered and coherently functioning machine. In contrast, the beautifully proportioned Renaissance figure fully articulated in space incorporates a vision of "man as the measure of all things," of man in control of a rational universe.

In *Girl before a Mirror* Picasso's encounter with the conditionedness of creation is evident in his use of flat forms rather than the representation of deep space on the two-dimensional surface of the canvas; his style reflects an acceptance of the given nature of the painterly medium. In the so-called "realistic" tradition of Western art, from the Renaissance to the nineteenth century, the two-dimensional limitation of the painting's surface was transcended by linear and atmospheric perspective, which created the illusion of deep space on a flat surface. Both responses to the limitations of the painting medium can be seen as theologically appropriate, as a mode of saying yes to the givenness of creation. The replication of the outer appearance of things, however, embodies a belief in their reality—a world view that is not universally held in the twentieth century.

The first *persona* of God, as Christ, the revealer of our false perceptions of ourselves, is indicated in the dichotomy between the images of the girl outside and inside the mirror. The reflected image is different, but not altogether of another order; it shares similarities of scale and configuration with the figure outside the glass. In response to the exposure of the discrepancy between what we think we are and what we are revealed to be, we have two options: (1) to reject the unanticipated image of what we are, or (2) to admit the reality of an unfamiliar or contradictory image, let it go, and then face the future with hope. The latter affirmative theological response allows for creative transformation.

In Picasso's painting, there is no hierarchical relationship between these two images: they are equal in scale, color, value, and compositional placement. Picasso offers no value judgment of their relative worth. Similarly, we cannot judge our own worth, either in terms of our own actions or in comparison to the actions of others. It is not our role to act as judge or redeemer, but rather to surrender to those encounters and their potential for a turning around of consciousness in the *persona* of Christ.

The metaphor of a mirror as a means for revelation is found in the New Testament (James 1:23–26), where those who look at their reflections are urged to be doers not just hearers of the Word. Glass as a metaphor for the nature of human existence is indicated in Saint Paul's description of how we see "through a glass darkly." Only in our encounters with God can we see clearly.

The encounter with the third *persona* of God as Spirit, or needgiver, is indirectly evidenced as Picasso represents the confrontations of a female figure with her own image in a mirror. His emphasis on the sexual and nurturing aspects of the female form might be interpreted as an affirmation of the human potential for relationality.

In considering the iconology, or total meaning, of Picasso's painting, I come to the question of intentionality. Obviously, Picasso did not intend to paint theologically, at least in terms of the surface structure of his statements. However, there is more to the world than meets the eye, and the deep structure of thought and language is not always conscious. If the theological process is understood as a questioning of the ultimate meaning of our encounters with each other and with the universe, Picasso's art is a theological enterprise, regardless of his intentions.

In a relativistic universe, a major task for theological and philosophical inquiry is the breaking of conceptual boundaries that we use to judge and separate ourselves from one another and from the encounter with God. Picasso's works are exemplary in their continuous challenging of inherited attitudes, materials, and techniques. If we can apply this vision of liberation from the past and openness to the future as expressed in Picasso's painting and Hobbs's theology, we are closer to salvation through an affirmation of pluralism and a willingness to participate actively in the creation of the kingdom of God.

NOTES

1. John Cobb, *Christ in a Pluralistic Age* (Philadelphia: The Westminster Press, 1975), p. 27.

2. For a more detailed account of Edward Hobbs's theology, see his "A Theology of Visual Art," which was the second lecture of the Jane and John Dillenberger Endowment for the Visual Arts, Graduate Theological Union, December 1981.

3. William Rubin, ed., "Pablo Picasso: A Retrospective." Exhibition catalogue (New York: Museum of Modern Art, 1980), p. 277.

24

Berdyaev and Rothko:
Transformative Visions

ROGER WEDELL

Almost without exception, discussions of Mark Rothko mention his statement that, for good painting, "the subject is crucial and only that subject matter is valid which is tragic and timeless."[1] Unfortunately, few have ventured beyond quotation of that phrase and brief allusions to the tragic nature of the human condition. Such allusions misunderstand both the intent and the outcome of Rothko's statement.

The writings of Nicholas Berdyaev pertaining to theology and art have also received scant attention. They have been dismissed as unorthodox statements by an unsystematic and flamboyant mind. Granted his self-acknowledged departures from Christian tradition into gnosticism, his work undertook to reinvigorate human life with the paradoxical senses of the transcendent creative spirit and the immanent creative spirit.

Both of these men incorporated into his spirituality an understanding of art as theological discourse and revelatory event. Berdyaev wrote frequently and eloquently of the co-mingling of art, the creative enterprise, and the divine. His most concerted effort at describing this co-mingling came in a book translated under the title *The Meaning of the Creative Act*. It was, in itself, an expression of the experience of comingling, the essence of which he saw as eschatological: though the product of an artist's creativity is confined to this world of imperfect objectification, the initial creative impulse originates from "God's claim on and call to man."[2] This discrepancy between impulse and object Berdyaev calls the tragedy of art. But the created object carries within itself a glimmer of its origin, and, just as it emerges from contemplation on the part of the artist, so by contemplation a viewer may apprehend something of that original creative art. By contemplation Berdyaev means an active engagement, not a passive receptiveness.[3]

With Mark Rothko, we must *look more* and read less, for in his art, especially the paintings for the Houston Chapel, we have the representation of his experience of the co-mingling of art and the divine, the created objects of a creative act. By placing these works in the world, Rothko provides us with the opportunity to experience through contemplation his vision, and, if not to share it, at least to be confronted with the possibility of an art of the spirit, even in twentieth-century America. The seeming failure of Berdyaev to capture the vision in words is shared by Rothko's attempts with paint, until the Houston series.

It is the active participation of the viewer with the work of art that completes the dialogue. In the moment of its inception, the work of art proceeds from the inner life, or spirit. This is the creative act, according to Berdyaev. This is the heritage of Rothko's art. In translating this moment of insight into an object to be shared with others, as occurs with any translation from one language to another, something is altered. Alteration also occurs in the translation from object to viewer. Such diverse persons as John Dewey, Jacques Maritain, and Wassily Kandinsky have argued for an integral act of communication from inner life to inner life by way of the work of art. Our knowledge of the intricacies of this mode of communication is growing. With Rothko, Berdyaev, and others, there remains the creative act, which, by the spiritual nature of its origin and power, remains beyond our intellection.

Rothko's struggle with subject matter for his painting was lifelong, culminating in the fourteen paintings now in the Houston Chapel. In his 1938 work *Subway Scene*, the human condition is the real subject, the subway station only the momentary environment; here a label "tragic" for the human condition is appropriate. The total isolation of the figures, not only as characters in a drama, but as forms in a geometric abstraction, is unyielding. Later, his fascination with ancient myths resulted in a series of works bearing names of mythical figures and stories. Even his biomorphic works of the 1940s, such as *Poised Elements* (1944) and *Entombment I* (1946), indicate his continuing struggle for the simple presentation of the complex subject. But none of these representational forms was able to convey his experience of the tragic and timeless subject. He abandoned representational forms and participated in the birthing of the New York School, abstract expressionism. His *Number 10* (1950) and *White Center* (1957) show a gradual simplification of form that resulted in his signature works where two or three rectangular clouds of color appear superimposed on a large monochrome ground. In details of these mature works, the wispy edges of his rectangles are visible: only in such details do we discern the artist's hand in the brush work. At a distance of just several feet, such human marks disappear, are absorbed, and we are left with fields of rich color that radiate light from a hidden inner source. Such a loss of the human imprint is one characteristic of a unitive art, and such a yearning for the absorption of the human into something larger than human is one characteristic of a unitive religious configuration.[4]

The fourteen paintings by Rothko for the Houston Chapel are the quintessential statement of a unitive spirituality in art, and are, therefore, among the best examples of creativity as delineated by Berdyaev. We can be thankful that recent adjustments in the lighting of the paintings allows them more nearly to present themselves as intended. Originally conceived as a chapel for a Roman Catholic university, the so-called Rothko Chapel now stands in the vibrant crossroads of ecumenicity. The floor plan of the chapel indicates the original intention. The roughly octagonal form is a clear reference to early Christian buildings, particularly baptistries, and even more specifically to the Torcello baptistry, a building for which Rothko had a fondness. The shallow apse was to have included a tabernacle. The abandonment of sectarian ties has permitted far more flexible use of the chapel.

Though only fourteen canvases were to be hung in the chapel, Rothko painted eighteen for the commission. The extra canvases were to allow some choice in the final disposition of the commission. The number fourteen, though, was always settled. Jane Dillenberger reports that the artist briefly considered numbering the canvases one through fourteen, a reference to the traditional stations of the cross. Such a reference was too specific, and the particular reference unsuitable to this series, so the idea was dropped.[5] Of the fourteen canvases, nine are grouped in threes with clear allusions to Christian triptychs. These groupings are on the wall of the pseudo-apse and the two walls perpendicular to it. Four of the remaining pieces hang on walls forming an inscribed square. The fifth work, narrower than the other single pieces, hangs on the back wall and, unless one turns for a final look at the interior, is the last canvas viewed when leaving the chapel.

It is clear that these paintings indicate a shift in Rothko's work. With the exception of the central panel of the apse triptych, these works do not have the inner luminosity of the earlier mature works. It is true that as one sits with them and contemplates them, a certain radiant warmth is slowly perceived, but the dark maroons and purples do not affect us as did the previous vibrant, saturated colors. The structure of the works is different, too. Gone are the soft edges reflecting the frame, and in their place are firmer bands that become frames. Or, there is no edge at all, and the monochrome ground moves all the way across the canvas. Also, Rothko has quelled the dramatic pulsation of color and form evident in the earlier pieces. Such activity frustrated his attempts at visualizing the unitive experience. The change in palette and structure can be seen in their infancy in the Harvard murals and in the Four Season's series, most of which are now in the Tate Gallery. Disturbed by the public's acceptance of his work as decorative, Rothko sought to remove these aspects from his work so that we would be forced to deal with the subject matter. In this way, he simplified the presentation of the most complex subject, that of the inner life, or spirit, of individuals, and the relationships between that spirit and a transcendent wholeness, or unity. With the Houston series we can no longer revel in color or light. If we are to revel at all, it must be in the unitive experience, both artistically and spiritually. With these works we are initially thrown back upon ourselves and our own experience. If we venture into active contemplation, become involved with these paintings, and are able to look within ourselves deeply enough, then we, too, engage in the creative act, that primal spiritual act which Berdyaev identified as eschatological, or transformative.

The creative act as eschatological is the key to Berdyaev's understanding, not only of art, but of human experience. The creative act as eschatological is the tragic and timeless subject that Rothko sought to present in his paintings. In his book translated under the title *Dream and Reality*, Berdyaev writes:

> The creative act . . . strikes at the root of the egocentric, for it is eminently a movement of self-transcendence, reaching out to that which is higher than oneself. Creative experience is not characterized by absorption in one's own perfection or imperfection: it makes for the transfiguration of man and of the world; it foreshadows a new Heaven and a new Earth which are to be prepared at once by God and man.[6]

He is careful to continue the qualification that created objects are the imperfect embodiment of the creative act. Because of our slavery to necessity, to the power of the external and symbolic world, our attempts at the real transformation of the world through the creative act are doomed to failure. But the failure is absolute only if the artist is so controlled by the lash of necessity and objectification that the product is altered by the intention that it be merely an object for aesthetic consumption. The artist who lives with the spiritual understanding of the fallen nature of the present time and world, and who gives vent to the "real" creative spirit within and without, contributes to the actual transformation of the world-as-it-is into the world-as-it-shall-be, contributes to the realization of the kindgom of God.

The Houston paintings are the powerful results of Rothko's journey into the unknown. While working on them he wrote, "The magnitude, on every level of experience and meaning, of the task in which you have involved me exceeds all my preconceptions. And it is teaching me to extend myself beyond what I thought was possible for me."[7] His own experience of the creative act became clearer and more profound as he proceeded. Years earlier he had removed images from his painting. Now he worked at presenting his own contemplation of the infinite in the simplest manner possible. The juxtaposition of the apse triptych, especially the central panel, and the narrow panel on the back wall heightens the sense of transfiguration that Rothko sought to present. The back panel is a black ground edged with deep maroon, while the front panel is lighter and more inviting. Rothko had in mind, not the iconography, but the meaning of last judgment and celestial vision, again referring to the Torcello church.[8] Both relate to the transformation of the present into the qualities of the future. This is the timeless subject with which Rothko had struggled.

In regard to the reception of these paintings, the tragedy is two-fold. First, there is the inability to manifest perfectly in any object the unitive spirituality that Rothko shared with Berdyaev and out of which he created; second, there is the apathetic response of viewers to the call to contemplation. Their nonengagement eliminates them from the creative act and so inhibits the ultimate transformation of self and world.

Rothko and Berdyaev exhibit parallel concerns, and in Rothko's art we see them and are drawn into their actuality. His art is his dialogue with the spirit, and as we enter into the dialogue, the art becomes a manifestation of theological discourse. His art must be contemplated to be seen, and the seeing is a revealing of divine purposes for individuals and world. By way of contemplation on the part of artist and viewer, the art releases into the world the creative spirit that transforms self and world and proceeds toward the infinite. Rothko once commented, "I don't express myself in my painting. I express my not-self."[9] In this context, it is the not-yet-self that is expressed along with the movement toward the achievement of self in the transcendent unity. Contrary to what some have written, Rothko's art is not religion, nor is it the content of faith. Art, the physical manifestation of the creative act for artist and viewer, is a partner in the achievement of ultimate divine purposes. The vision of Rothko and Berdyaev is the transformation of the world-as-it-is into the world-as-it-shall-be.

NOTES

1. A famous letter to *The New York Times*, 13 June 1943, sec. 2, p. 9, was signed by Mark Rothko and Adolph Gottlieb. It was later learned that Barnett Newman had collaborated on the project.
2. Nicholas Berdyaev, *Dream and Reality*, trans. Katherine Lampert (New York: Macmillan, 1951), p. 220.
3. The term "contemplation" is a technical term developed and used by Berdyaev. He uses it in speaking about any creative act, but especially when talking about art as a manifestation of the creative enterprise of the divine-human. By contemplation, he means an active engagement of the viewer with the work of art.

Such engagement requires an attitude of openness to the work and of an inward searching of ourselves.

4. The term "unitive" emerged at the 1975 meeting of the Society for Arts, Religion, and Contemporary Culture, when Joshua Taylor initiated a conversation based on what he discerned as two distinct religious configurations which have influenced twentieth-century art. Alongside the "unitive" is placed the "communitive." The communitive configuration approaches spirituality as a matter of human compassion and human interrelationships, while the unitive seeks after an absorption of the individual self into a perfect order beyond self and erases the lines of individuality. Neither configuration is understood as more religious or more spiritual than the other, but such diverse patterns of religious experience have consequences in art conceived of and produced in a spiritual context. Among the consequences is the presence or absence of the hand of the artist. The neoclassical sculpture of Hiram Powers *Eve Tempted* is indicative of the unitive configuration, the will to form. Emil Nolde's expressionist piece *The Last Supper* is indicative of the communitive, the will to fellowship. Berdyaev and Rothko are here understood as seekers after the unitive experience, both spiritually and artistically. See Doug Adams, "Insights from 'Three Perspectives on the Religious and Aesthetic Imagination,'" *Seedbed* 3 (June 1975), pp. 1–3.

5. Reported in Lawrence Alloway, "Residual Sign Systems in Abstract Expressionism." *Artforum* 12 (November 1973), pp. 39–40.

6. Berdyaev, *Dream and Reality*, p. 210.

7. David Snell, "Rothko Chapel—The Painter's Last Testament." *The Smithsonian* 2 (August 1971), p. 52.

8. The Torcello mosaics are of the Last Judgment and a celestial Madonna and Child. The former is at the entrance and the latter is in the apse. One is impending doom, while the other is eternal salvation. Rothko has contrasted these same qualities in his two axial paintings in the Houston Chapel.

9. Comment by Rothko to Harold Rosenberg, reported in Donald Goddard, "Rothko's Journey into the Unknown." *Art News* 78 (January 1979), p. 37.

25

Theological Expressions Through Visual Art Forms

DOUG ADAMS

Much discussion of visual art and religion has focused on works that are religious in subject matter. This iconographic preoccupation suggests that visual art be read as literature and ignores the distinctive forms of painting or sculpture. Theologians need to look carefully at visual art forms: color, shape, line, size, and texture. This essay focuses on the less obvious but no less profound expression of theology through visual art forms. The contributions of Paul Tillich and Joshua Taylor to the analysis of the religious significance through art will be evaluated and extended to contemporary art.

Paul Tillich advanced the discussion of "theology and the arts" by noting that some art is strongly religious in style even though it is not religious in subject matter, and conversely, that some art is not religious in style even though it is religious in subject matter. Tillich distinguished religion in the larger sense ("being ultimately concerned about one's own being, about one's self and one's world, about its meaning and its estrangement and its finitude") from religion in the narrower sense ("having a set of symbols . . . divine beings . . . ritual actions, and doctrinal formulations about their relationship to us"[1]). The larger sense of religion is communicated in style and the narrower sense is communicated through subject matter.

Tillich distinguished four categories of relation between religion and visual art. First is a style expressive of no ultimate concern and a content without religious subject matter. The second is religious in style and nonreligious in subject (for example, Picasso's *Guernica*, where "we do not cover up anything, but have to look at the human situation in its depth"[2]). Third is a nonreligious style with religious subject matter (for example, Raphael's *Madonna and Child* or *Crucifixion*). The fourth category has both a religious style and a religious subject (for example, Grunewald's *Crucifixion* in the Isenheim Altarpiece, where the style as well as the subject expresses human finitude).

For Tillich, religious style is the style of biblical faiths as prophetic. As Abraham Joshua Heschel reminds us, the prophet's central concern is "the plight of men. . . . God Himself is described as reflecting over the plight of man, rather than as contemplating eternal ideas."[3] Tillich's earlier definition of religion in the larger sense resonates with Heschel's description of prophetic concern. There is a possible Protestant or Northern European bias in Tillich's definition: rough-edged forms may be seen not only in much Protestant theology but also in Northern European art, from the ancient Celtic through Grunewald to twentieth-century German expressionism. Perfected forms are more prevalent in Roman Catholic theology and in Southern European art, from the ancient Greek through the Italian Renaissance to twentieth-century abstraction.[4]

Early twentieth-century German biblical scholars, by whom Tillich was influenced, overstated the case when they identified the prophetic as the true biblical faith and classified the priestly tradition as corruption. Both traditions are parts of the biblical faith and are difficult to understand apart from each other. One might argue that biblical faiths are more prophetic than priestly and resonate more with asymmetrical than symmetrical forms (and thus are represented in expressionist painting rather than in classical or neoclassical painting). The priestly concern for form leads to symmetrical art where all is sustained in harmony and order, while the prophetic concern for reform leads to asymmetrical art where new percussive ingredients disorder our previous conceptions of proper form. The repetitions of initially asymmetrical forms eventually strike the viewer as symmetrical, so artists who continue to resonate with biblical faith are those who incorporate surprising new ingredients in their work. While Christian art may contain both priestly and prophetic forms, the latter are nearly absent in church, where they should predominate.

Joshua Taylor clarified these categories of how visual forms express theology. Taylor saw a parallel of the prophetic in an art form he called "will to fellowship," or "communitive": art that makes us aware of individual persons and our relationships. Figurative or not in subject matter, the work's style (for example, van Gogh's expressionism) makes us aware that a person with a body painted this image and makes us aware of ourselves as distinct bodily individuals who can relate with others but never totally become one with them. In contrast, the priestly form is called a "will to form" and "unitive" (for example, classical or neoclassical works); it makes one oblivious to persons as one is drawn beyond into perfect unity. Both "priestly-unitive" and "prophetic-communitive" art forms are religious, but they correspond to different understandings of religion: "unitive" corresponds to the Eastern religious concern for unity with eternal ideas and absorption into immortality and oneness; "communitive" corresponds to a Western religious concern for community and resurrection of the body, with each individual persisting as a distinct part in the world.

Taylor's unitive form is illustrated in the neoclassic sculptures of Hiram Powers, in William Blake's *The Morning Stars* (from Job), Piet Mondrian's *Tableau I*, Wassily Kandinsky's *Fuge*, Barnett Newman's *Vir Heroicus Sublimis*, and Josef Albers's *Homage to the Square*. In these works, there is a sense of completion and definition that removes one through such precise forms to a sense of order beyond that normally seen. These works "allow you to be in harmonious spheres, to join in . . . with a larger order without describing it. With a power of transport, such works seem to come from nature; but the artist uses the senses as only the means to spiritual unification by the discovery of perfect designs."[5] The very precision of the works removes them from visual reality in this will to form.

Taylor's examples of the communitive forms ranged from Millet's *Sower* to Heckel's *Zwei Menschen in Freien*, Van Gogh's *La Berceuse*, Nolde's *Last Supper*, and deKooning's *Woman, Sag Harbor*. These works "never allow you to separate yourself from others and human kind—never allow us to forget we are members of a physical race." There is a refusal to organize a unity eliminating reference to selves: looking at these works one "never forgets

that they are hand painted . . . that an artist expressed himself"
in this will to fellowship.[6]

Taylor noted that neither the unitive nor the communitive is
more spiritual than the other: "both are religious and concerned
for religious values. But the religious values are not simply differently described means to the same end. They are two different
means serving two different religiously described ends."[7] In response to Taylor's presentation, Ted Gill correlated Taylor's distinctions between unitive and communitive forms in art to Emil
Brunner's distinctions between Eastern and Western religions:

> Emil Brunner used to describe this distinction in the history of
> religions and theology as the distinction between those who
> reach for union and those who look for communion: those who
> look for some melding of the spirit with some enveloping whole
> as over against those others who want always to maintain iden-
> tity in the presence of and in the vibrant confrontation with
> other integrities. The unitive, he always thought, were eastern
> religionists; and we protestants were communionists. Another
> way to describe the same thing is the difference between im-
> mortality of the soul and resurrection of the body—with the
> immortality of the soul and its adherents not necessarily look-
> ing to a merging (but the whole teaching tilts toward everyone
> finally being sucked into a mush of divinity and losing detail
> and outline). . . . Dr. Brunner remarked that his favorite paint-
> ing was in the Vatican and was the Creation of Michelangelo.
> God isn't touching Adam: that's the separate, the persistent,
> idea.[8]

I suggested to Taylor that his categories might mislead one into
associating mystical experience exclusively with the unitive and
not with the communitive, which would be viewed instead as the
realm of social concern. He responded that there may be mystical
experience with either form; but these would be two different
types of mystical experience.[9]

As Western artists become influenced by Eastern religions, one
may note shifts from communitive to unitive art forms. Or, such
shifts may originate in the artist's own odyssey. Mark Rothko's
works reflect this shift. Many of his works of the 1950s present
two sensuous pulsating abstract fields of color that prevent an
experience of a unitive sensibility as the viewer is engaged first

by one color field and then by the other. He styled such works "tragedy."

But in his canvases for the Rothko Chapel (1971), he eliminated such finite and communitive sensibility. One may experience the unitive sensibility in those wall-size works in very dark shades of purple and brown that initially seem black. While Rothko viewed the communitive forms as tragic because they prevented one from experiencing the unitive, the negation of the unitive experience is often associated with God's activity in Western religions. Realizing oneself to be a finite creature with limited capabilities is a corollary of acknowledging God to be Creator and Christ to be Judge and Redeemer.[10]

Taylor's examples and expressions of the communitive are an advance over Tillich's discussion, which makes prophetic forms appear exclusively related to broken forms of suffering and pain. Taylor showed that prophetic forms are related to finitude and are not necessarily all painful. If one desires the unitive experience of the infinite, then communitive forms could be perceived as disruptive, tragic, and even painful. But if one desires the communitive experience, then many prophetic forms could be perceived as affirmations of our humanity, which we are to enjoy and not escape. For instance, in many of Van Gogh's brighter works, there is a tactile quality in the expressiveness of rough lines that makes me aware of my own body; but there is nothing painful about that awareness.

A viewer's experiences, attitudes, and expectations affect what is seen or experienced in any artwork. There will be differences in evaluating works as unitive or communitive. Taylor acknowledged part of this problem: "The response to art as religious experience is as profound and as religious as the understanding of the person who looks at it makes it."[11] The same person may experience and evaluate an artwork differently at different times. In contrast to Taylor's classification of Albers's squares as unitive, Harold Rosenberg noted that Albers considered them to be "a vibrant struggle between tones of color." But Rosenberg continued,

> I looked around the room of fourteen paintings and three of them look as though they are ready to start a fight; and the other eleven are just sitting there square on square. And then if

I come around two days later, they may all be sitting there; and none of them are jumping up and making any noise at all. And some other time, three other paintings may be hot. . . . Good thinking in modern art is that you can't always get it.[12]

In Albers's works, the lines and shapes evoke a unitive sense while the conflicting colors evoke a communitive sense. Through colors that eventually burn out our visual perception of them, a work becomes communitive by revealing our perceptual limitations.

Time spent looking at a work may reveal it as communitive when it originally looked unitive. Some of Barnett Newman's works are immediately sensed as communitive, for the rough-edged black zips that run down the vertical canvases prevent any unitive experience, as in his *Stations of the Cross*. But in other Newman works, the zip down the canvas appears to be straight-edged and admits a unitive experience, until one has looked at the line a long time and discovered a subtle curve or roughness at the bottom of the zip, a feature that disrupts the unitive relation with the work. Yet other works by Newman, such as the eighteen-foot-wide *Vir Heroicus Sublimis* are classified by Taylor as unitive; for even after a long viewing of that large red painting with its small hard-edged vertical zip, the unitive experience is maintained. An artist may do both unitive and communitive works.

Tillich's and Taylor's discussions have helped us see theological expressions through visual art forms in terms of line, shape, color, and texture. Size may also communicate theological expressions, as evidenced by Christo's *Running Fence* (1976). Running twenty-four miles across Marin and Sonoma counties in northern California for two weeks, the artwork evoked strong communitive sensibilities. In viewing the work (made of white nylon, eighteen feet high, suspended by steel girders, and extended twenty-four miles), one became aware of one's own limitations and needs to interact with other persons of different dispositions. The viewer's finitude was stressed by the twenty-four-mile size: the whole work could not be seen from one place. Required to drive and periodically walk on a day-long trip to view much of the fence, one became more conscious of one's own body.[13] Since the fence ran across dozens of jurisdictions including numerous privately owned farms, the viewer not only was made aware of the different political entities (with their different policies for approaching the fence) but also became acquainted with a number of farmers, some of whom did not allow one to cross their land to view the fence as it ran down a gully or behind a barn. Another dimension of one's finitude was made evident when one was surprised as the artwork appeared from behind a hill or out of a previously unnoticed valley.

Building the artwork revealed the interrelations of many distinct political entities. In process art, seeing these interrelations is a part of the art experience. As they tried to support or oppose the fence's construction, many persons realized for the first time not only the different political jurisdictions in which they lived but also the different views held by their neighbors. The litigation over the fence made evident the profiles of different persons and groups in the communities; and the several years of planning revealed individual characteristics of different farmers and political jurisdictions as different settlements were made with each of them. For instance, breaks in the fence were designed to accommodate the primary travel routes in each farm or political jurisdiction. This accommodation made explicit what may have been only tacitly known.

Through communitive form, Christo's *Running Fence* expressed a theology resonant with the biblical prophetic forms as outlined by Tillich and Taylor. The artwork occasioned the awareness of one's own body and finitude as well as the recognition of other distinct individuals and groups. The work surprised the viewer and taught that one cannot separate oneself from others. But prophetic forms, and Christo's *Running Fence*, call us to see more than clear reflection on our present forms and the forms of others.

Taylor spoke of the "will to fellowship." Heschel noted the tenderness and hope at the heart of the prophetic: the pathos of God.[14] Repent so that the crooked may be made straight, so that the barren places may bear fruit, so that Jacob may stand, for he is very small. The fence brought together individuals who would otherwise have remained unknown to each other. Even after the fence had been down for five years, one could not drive or walk along that stretch of northern California without remembering the wider possibilities for fellowship that *Running Fence* revealed.

NOTES

1. Paul Tillich, "Existentialist Aspects of Modern Art" in *Christianity and the Existentialists*, ed. Carl Michelson (New York: Scribner's Sons, 1956), p. 132.
2. Ibid., p. 138.
3. Abraham Joshua Heschel, *The Prophets* (New York: Harper and Row, 1969), p. 5.
4. Jane Dillenberger suggested the contrasts between these forms in the first lecture of the Jane and John Dillenberger Endowment for the Visual Arts at the Graduate Theological Union, Berkeley, 25 February 1981: "Michelangelo vs. Grunewald: A Study of Northern and Italian Sensibilities at the Time of the Reformation."
5. Joshua Taylor presented these views to the Society for the Arts, Religion, and Contemporary Culture meeting in New York (Spring 1975), as reported in Doug Adams, "Insights from Three Perspectives on the Religious and Aesthetic Imagination," *Seedbed* 3, no. 3 (June 1975), pp. 1–3.
6. Ibid., p. 2.
7. Ibid.
8. Ibid.
9. Examples of the communitive mystical experience where there is no complete merger into one are discussed not only by Martin Buber in *I-Thou* but also by Russian Orthodox theologian Vladimir Lossky in *The Mystical Theology of the Eastern Orthodox Church*.
10. Edward Hobbs outlined this theological interpretation in the second lecture of the Jane and John Dillenberger Endowment for the Visual Arts at the Graduate Theological Union, Berkeley, 18 December 1981. Melinda Wortz discerned the presence of this theological analysis in the visual arts as a formal response to Hobbs's presentation.
11. Adams, p. 2.
12. Ibid., p. 3.
13. A quality of pilgrimage demanded by an artwork is increasingly common in contemporary art; e.g., Walter DeMaria's "Lightning Field" (1978). See Melinda Wortz, "Walter DeMaria's 'The Lightning Field,'" *Arts Magazine* 54, no. 9 (May 1980), pp. 170–73.
14. Heschel, pp. 7, 12.

PART VI

BIBLIOGRAPHIES

Sources for the Study of Christianity and the Arts

JOHN W. COOK

The arts have always been an essential aspect of the language of the Christian tradition and today there is no corporate act of worship by any group of Christians that does not appropriate some aspect of the arts to enact its praise and prayer. A critical sense of what the Christian tradition has intended in its artistic expressions and what it intends today can serve the study of Christianity. While the arts involve many forms and media, I am concerned here with sources for the study of the visual arts.

Since students of theology and religion have had less experience studying art and architecture than the traditional theological disciplines, it may be helpful to make some suggestions concerning content and method. The discipline of art history has produced a wealth of valuable resources for religion and theology. The strength of the art-historical discipline for religion and theology lies in the methods and sources it has made available. With precision and scrutiny, art historians have for some time been delving into primary documents (visual and verbal) of the Christian faith.

The materials listed in this bibliographic survey illustrate how the visual media of art and architecture relate to and participate in the story of Christendom, past and present. This is an abbreviated list, an introduction to the range of insights available in the visual arts to students of religion and theology.

Our study of the world of the New Testament and the nature of

An earlier version of this essay appeared under the title "Theology and the Arts" in *Theology Today* 34 (April 1977): 45–51.

the early church is enriched when we include the witness of Early Christian art. An excellent introduction is available in André Grabar's *Early Christian Art* (Princeton University Press, 1980 [1968]), and a broader view is presented in the highly readable, if abbreviated, study by Edward Syndicus under the same title, *Early Christian Art* (Hawthorne Books, 1962). The best set of illustrations of the Christian witness in catacomb fresco painting is found in Pierre du Bourguet's *Early Christian Painting* (Viking Press, 1965). His introductory essay contributes to our appreciation of the liturgical background of these remarkable paintings.

The most valuable recent publication concerning the relationship of Early Christian art to the Late Antique world is the collection edited by Kurt Weitzmann entitled *Age of Spirituality* (The Metropolitan Museum of Art, 1979). This volume is the catalogue of the exhibition held at The Metropolitan Museum of Art in the winter of 1977–78 on Late Antique and Early Christian art from the third to the seventh century. The articles and excellent illustrations contribute to our understanding of the visual arts of the early church in their historical and cultural setting, with contributions from many eminent scholars; the bibliography is the best and most up-to-date available in a single volume today. This volume, in combination with Frederik van der Meer's *Atlas of the Early Christian World* (Nelson, 1958)—in which illustrations from the art of the early church are presented with translations of relevant ancient texts—gives an insightful picture of the life of the early Christians.

Our understanding of the meeting places and practices of the Early Christian house churches is informed by house-church (*tituli*) excavations in Rome and in the small town of Dura-Europos, in Asia Minor. A summary of the findings concerning the meeting places of the young Christian communities in Rome is given in the opening chapters of the remarkable book by Richard Krautheimer, *Early Christian and Byzantine Architecture* (Penguin Books, 1965). The complete and meticulously detailed reports of the evidence from ancient Rome are available in the large folio volumes by the same author, *Corpus Basilicarum Christianarum Romae* (Pontif. Istituto di Arch. Cristiana, 1937 and following).

The earliest house church known today from physical evidence is a renovated private home that became a gathering place and center of worship in the first half of the third century at Dura-Europos. Its full story is beautifully told in Carl Kraeling's *The Christian Building* (J. J. Augustin, 1967). A more elaborate and sumptuous building at Dura-Europos, the Jewish synagogue, is interpreted in Carl Kraeling's *The Synagogue* (KTAV Publishing House, 1979). A summary of scholarship on the synagogue was published in a series of articles edited by Joseph Gutmann under the title *The Dura-Europos Synagogue: A Re-evaluation (1932–1972)*, (The American Academy of Religion, 1973). For a general introduction to the study of this town and its art, see Ann Perkins's *The Art of Dura-Europos* (Oxford University Press, 1973).

When the church emerged in its more public forms, after the Peace of the Church at the beginning of the fourth century, the monumental Christian basilica structures in centers like Rome, Constantinople, and Jerusalem, illustrate a dramatic shift in the ecclesial needs and self-understanding expressed in architecture. This astonishing story is reported in the above-mentioned works by Krautheimer. One of the most surprising parts of the story is about the buildings that Constantine's architects constructed in Jerusalem around the places accepted as the sites where Christ was crucified, buried, and resurrected. Kenneth Conant's "The Holy Sepulchre" (*Speculum*, volume 31, pp. 1–48) is a good introduction. A more recent interpretation of the archaeological as well as literary evidence is Charles Coüasnon's *The Church of the Holy Sepulchre in Jerusalem* (Oxford University Press, 1974).

The mosaics, sculpture, and architecture in the splendidly preserved monuments of fifth- and sixth-century Ravenna, Italy, provide a spellbinding chapter in the artistically creative language of the Christian faith. The complexity and beauty of this art records an essential chapter and reflects a rich, faithful tradition. Get a glimpse of it in Otto von Simson's *The Sacred Fortress* (University of Chicago Press, 1948), Spiro Kostof's *The Orthodox Baptistery of Ravenna* (Yale University Press, 1965), Giuseppi Bovini's *Ravenna Mosaics* (New York Graphic Society, 1956), and the relevant sections of André Grabar's *The Golden Age of Justinian* (Odyssey Press, 1967).

The production of Bibles, liturgical books, and theological texts resulted in such masterpieces of Christendom as the Book of Kells, the Utrecht Psalter, numerous books of hours, and other amazing illuminated manuscripts. A good one-volume introduction to the history of illuminations is available in David Diringer's *The Illuminated Book* (Philosophical Library, 1958). An excellent commentary, beautiful color plates, and a bibliography are to be found in Kurt Weitzmann's *Late Antique and Early Christian Book Illumination* (George Braziller, 1977).

The history of illuminated manuscripts in the Christian tradition relates necessarily to the early monastic movements because the scriptoria of the monasteries were responsible for book production in the Middle Ages. The nature of medieval monastic life is reflected today in the remains of architectural monuments that embody so much of that legacy, and a few studies of that architectural history probe the significance of those forms and the faith they house. Wolfgang Braunfels's *Monasteries of Western Europe: The Architecture of the Orders* (Princeton University Press, 1972) enlightens our understanding in that it presents thorough scholarship, reproduces excellent plans and photographs, and translates original texts that help us to evaluate the monuments within the range of ideas that created them. In that regard, the soon to be published series of papers entitled *Monasticism and the Arts*, edited by Timothy Verson, John Dally, and myself, can serve as an excellent complement to Braunfels's study.

Three recent works on three different medieval monasteries make major contributions to the study of Christianity, and each illustrates in its own way how these works of art embodied a tradition. Kenneth Conant's many years of research on the monastic community at Cluny is published in *Cluny, les Églises et la Maison Du Chef de L'Ordre* (Medieval Academy Press, 1968). G. Forsyth and Kurt Weitzmann's *The Monastery of Saint Catherine at Mount Sinai* (University of Michigan Press, 1973) is the only study in English that makes that remarkable place available through its art. Of course, one of the great publishing events of the 1970s was Walter Horn's *The Plan of St. Gall* (University of California Press, 1980). This elegant three-volume study is the product of a life's work and shows how a rare medieval architectural plan can be a primary source concerning Carolingian religious sensibilities.

Too often, studies of religion generally, and of Christianity specifically, neglect the Byzantine world. The mysteries of Byzantium and Eastern Orthodoxy tend to intimidate rather than inspire. However, a wealth of new material is available, especially about the religious significance of Byzantine art and architecture. Thomas Mathews's *The Early Churches of Constantinople, Architecture and Liturgy* (Pennsylvania State University Press, 1971) is a model for seeing how archaeological evidence reveals a community's context for worship. Cyril Mango's *Sources and Documents of Byzantine Art* (Prentice-Hall, 1972) is actually a sourcebook in the history of doctrine. Our fascination with the Byzantine icon is substantially informed by the following studies: Gervase Mathew, *Byzantine Aesthetics* (John Murray, 1981 [1969]); Leonid Ouspensky and Vladimir Lossky, *The Meaning of Icons* (Mowbray Press, 1981 [1969]); Eugene N. Trubetskoi, *Icons: Theology in Color* (St. Vladimir's Seminary Press, 1980 [1973]); and Leonid Ouspensky, *Theology of the Icon* (St. Vladimir's Seminary Press, 1978).

The architecture of the Byzantine tradition is summarized in its earlier stages in Krautheimer's volume on Early Christian and Byzantine architecture. See also Heinz Kähler's *Hagia Sophia* (Praeger, 1967), Cyril Mango's *Byzantine Architecture* (Abrams, 1976), and T. Mathews's *The Byzantine Churches of Istanbul* (Pennsylvania State University Press, 1976).

The richest development of religious art in Western civilization is represented by the Gothic cathedrals. Seldom have the arts carried so much of the religious mentality of an age, or sought to embody such spiritual significance. Otto von Simson's *The Gothic Cathedral* (Princeton University Press, 1974 [1956]) and Emile Mâle's *The Gothic Image* (Harper Torchbooks, 1958) convincingly interpret the sources. Two publications of translated documents of the time suggest the role of the arts in the church of the Gothic era: Erwin Panofsky's *Abbot Suger* (Princeton University Press, 1979 [1946]) and Paul Frankel's *The Gothic* (Princeton University Press, 1960). The flavor of the period is uniquely captured in Henry Adams's beautifully written *Mont-Saint-Michel and Chartres* (Princeton University Press, 1981 [1905]). Adams's breadth of sources and personal insight make the volume especially relevant to studies of the age of faith.

The strength of the Christian tradition in the Italian Renaissance has been neglected in light of the overwhelming emphasis on classical sources in Renaissance humanism. However, the

Christian story is an essential aspect of the Renaissance: see Peter and Linda Murray's *The Art of the Renaissance* (Oxford University Press, 1963). Studies of the individual artists of this period are especially important. James H. Stubblebine's *Giotto: The Arena Chapel* (Norton, 1969) is a set of documents and essays about Giotto's great cycle at Padua of the life of Christ. Masaccio's work, and the influence of the reformer Savonarola on the work of Botticelli are fascinating illustrations of Christian responses in the arts. Especially poignant are studies of Donatello and Michelangelo. See, for instance, Frederich Hartt's *History of Italian Renaissance Art* (Abrams, 1969), Charles de Tolnay's *The Art and Thought of Michelangelo* (Pantheon Books, 1964), and Charles Seymour, Jr.'s *Michelangelo: The Sistine Chapel Ceiling* (Norton, 1972).

An excellent introduction to the Renaissance in the North is Otto Benesch's *The Art of the Renaissance in Northern Europe* (Harvard University Press, 1967 [1945]). Significant to the artistic and religious attitudes at the beginning of the Reformation is Wolfgang Steckow's *Northern Renaissance Art 1400–1600* (Prentice-Hall, 1966). The central figure of Albrecht Dürer comes alive in Erwin Panofsky's *Albrecht Dürer* (Princeton University Press, 1948). The story of one of Christianity's most important works of art is told in Georg Scheja's *The Isenheim Altarpiece* (Abrams, 1969), a beautifully illustrated and documented interpretation of Matthias Grunewald's masterpiece. The role of the arts in the Reformation is discussed in A. G. Dickens's *Reformation and Society in Sixteenth-Century Europe* (Harcourt, Brace and World, 1966), and although a great deal remains to be clarified about Reformation iconography, a valuable study and model of scholarship is Charles Garside's *Zwingli and the Arts* (Yale University Press, 1966). The best study of the relationship between the arts and Reformation theology is Carl G. Christensen's *Art and the Reformation in Germany* (Wayne State University Press, 1979), a well-researched book with theological depth and an excellent bibliography.

The Counter-Reformation responded to the Reformers vigorously through the arts. The visual arts in the service of architecture and altars burst forth in the Counter-Reformation as if they were essential to the enterprise. Baroque art forms became a language for the intentions of the Roman Catholic Church, and the church's patronage of the arts was at an all-time high. See Rudolf Wittkower and Irma Jaffe's *Baroque Art: The Jesuit Contribution* (Fordham University Press, 1972), Rudolf Wittkower's *Art and Architecture in Italy, 1600–1750* (Penguin, 1958), Germain G. Bazin's *The Baroque* (Norton, 1978 [1968]), and the comparative study concerning Catholic piety and the arts in Robert T. Petersson's *The Art of Ecstasy: Teresa, Bernini and Crashaw* (Atheneum, 1970). One of the best studies of high-baroque art in the Christian context is John Rupert Martin's *Rubens: The Antwerp Altarpieces: The Raising of the Cross and the Descent from the Cross* (Norton, 1969).

Many sources for the study of baroque art in the life of the church are readily available, and although this apparently opulent era is often out of favor today, it demonstrates a powerful use of decorative art forms born of a particular Christian point of view.

The story comes together and reaches new heights in Rembrandt. W. A. Visser't Hooft's *Rembrandt and the Gospel* (Meridian Books, 1960) gives the essential points, and Jakob Rosenberg's *Rembrandt, Life and Work* (Phaidon Press, 1968 [1948]) is the best one-volume introduction.

Studies of the subject matter of traditional Christian art (iconography) provide basic information for reading about content and symbolic function in narrative visual art. There are many encyclopedias of iconography, but the most recent and the best for Christian subject matter is found in the volumes by Gertrud Schiller, *Iconography of Christian Art* (New York Graphic Society, 1972 and following). A more general introductory study is available in one paperback volume, James Hall's *Dictionary of Subjects and Symbols in Art* (Harper and Row, 1979 [1974]). This book serves as a reliable handbook for viewing paintings from varied periods and styles.

If one is interested in the seventeenth and eighteenth centuries and in Christian attitudes reflected in American art and architecture, two good studies are Marian C. Donnelly's *The New England Meeting Houses of the Seventeenth Century* (Wesleyan University Press, 1968) and the first volume of Jules Prown's *American Painting* (Rizzoli, 1980). Especially helpful in this regard is the catalogue of an exhibition of American religious art from 1700 to 1900 by Jane Dillenberger and Joshua Taylor entitled *The Hand and the Spirit* (University Art Museum, Berkeley, 1972).

The story becomes complicated in the modern period because traditional religious definitions and subject matter in the arts have broken down. It is fascinating to observe, however, that a religious dimension remains constant even in the midst of change. Simply put, the problem is how to discover the authentic religious consciousness in the arts of the late-nineteenth and twentieth centuries. One can begin with the visionary art of William Blake in Anthony Blunt's *The Art of William Blake* (Columbia University Press, 1959).

Some nineteenth-century art movements addressed specifically religious questions. For instance, A. W. N. Pugin's *The True Principles of Pointed or Christian Architecture* (St. Martin's Press, 1973 [1841]) and Vincent van Gogh's *Complete Letters* (three volumes, New York Graphic Society, 1958). Curious phases claiming religious motivation are seen in Edward Lucie-Smith's *Symbolist Art* (Oxford University Press, 1972), Robin Ironside's *Pre-Raphaelite Painting* (Phaidon, · 1948), and Charles Chassé's *Les nabis et leur temps* (La Bibliotheque des arts, 1960).

For a glimpse at twentieth-century religious attitudes in modern art, see the anthology by Herschel B. Chipp, *Theories of Modern Art* (University of California Press, 1968), keeping in mind questions about the nature of the "religious" in these sources. Personal points of view are recorded in works like Wassily Kandinsky's *Concerning the Spiritual in Art* (Wittenborn, Shultz, 1947), Hans Jaffe's *De Stijl* (London, no date), and Pierre Courthion's *Georges Rouault* (Abrams, 1962). Jane Dillenberger has made some of the modern material available to religious studies in two different volumes and numerous articles; see her *Secular Art with Sacred Themes* (Abingdon, 1969), and the catalogue for the exhibition she and John Dillenberger organized, entitled *Perceptions of the Spirit in Twentieth-Century American Art* (Indianapolis Museum of Art, 1977).

The story reaches a peak in the works of Barnett Newman and Mark Rothko: by the 1970s they had produced an art that sought great religious and moral depth. See Lawrence Alloway's *Barnett Newman: The Stations of the Cross* (The Solomon R. Guggenheim

Museum of Art, 1966) and Diane Waldman's commentary in *Mark Rothko* (The Solomon R. Guggenheim Museum of Art, 1978).

All of the texts cited here concern the visual language of the religious experience—a language that is too often neglected in modern religious studies and practice. Reclaiming this major facet of the Christian tradition, rediscovering the authentic language of the arts for the life of the church, and incorporating this material into religious studies can broaden and enrich our understanding of Christianity.

Special Topic Bibliographies

These special topic bibliographies have been prepared as introductions to the various approaches to the inter-disciplinary study of religion and the visual arts. None of these listings is comprehensive or complete. The materials selected for inclusion have been chosen for their availability and intelligibility for students beginning this type of inquiry. The section on Christian Art complements John Cook's bibliographic essay. The editor wishes to thank Catharine J. Allen, David and Linda Altshuler, William Cenkner, Jane Dillenberger, John W. Dixon, Lois Ibsen al Faruqi, and Richard B. Pilgrim for their assistance in the development of these special topic bibliographies.

Sourcebooks in Religion and Art

Bernen, Robert and Satia. *Myth and Religion in European Painting, 1270–1700: The Stories as the Artists Knew Them.* New York: Constable, 1973.

Cirlot, J. E. *A Dictionary of Symbols.* New York: Philosophical Library, 1972.

Cooper, J. C. *An Illustrated Encyclopedia of Traditional Symbols.* London, 1978.

Encyclopedia of World Art. (15 volumes) New Jersey: McGraw-Hill Book Co., 1959–1968.

Ferguson, George. *Signs and Symbols in Christian Art.* New York: Oxford University Press, 1954.

Moore, Albert C. *Iconography of World Religions: An Introduction.* Philadelphia: Fortress Press, 1977.

New Catholic Encyclopedia. (15 volumes) New Jersey: McGraw-Hill Book Company, 1967.

Theories of Religion and Art

Bowlam, David and James L. Henderson. *Art and Belief.* New York: Schocken Books, 1970.

Brandon, S. G. F. *Man and God in Art and Ritual; A Study of Iconography, Architecture and Ritual Action as Primary Evidence of Religious Belief and Practice.* New York: Charles Scribner's and Sons, 1975.

Burckhardt, Titus, *Sacred Art in East and West.* London: Perennial, 1967.

Hunter, Howard, Editor. *Humanities, Religion and the Arts Tomorrow.* New York: Holt, Rhinehart and Winston, 1972.

Laeuchli, Samuel. *Religion and Art in Conflict.* Philadelphia. Fortress Press, 1980.

Maritain, Jacques. *Creative Intuition in Art and Poetry.* Princeton: Princeton University Press, Bollingen Series #35, 1978.

Martland, Thomas R. *Religion as Art, An Interpretation.* New York: SUNY Press, 1981.
van der Leeuw, Gerardus. *Sacred and Profane Beauty: The Holy in Art.* New York: Holt, Rhinehart and Winston, 1953 (1932).
Weiss, Paul. *Religion and Art.* Milwaukee: Marquette University Press, 1963.

Primitive Religious Art
Anderson, Richard L. *Art in Primitive Societies.* Englewood Cliffs, N.J.: Prentice-Hall, Inc., 1979.
Armstrong, Robert Plant. *The Powers of Presence: Consciousness, Myth and Affecting Presence.* Philadelphia: University of Pennsylvania Press, 1981.
Banton, Michael, Editor. *Anthropological Approaches to the Study of Religion.* London: Tavistock Publications, 1966.
Bateson, Gregory. *Steps to an Ecology of Mind.* N.Y.: Ballantine Books, 1972.
Boas, Franz. *Primitive Art.* N.Y.: Dover Publishing Co., 1972 (1955).
Donnan, Christopher. *Moche Art and Iconography.* Los Angeles: U.C.L.A. Latin American Center Publications, 1976.
Griaule, Marcel. *Conversations with Ogotemmeli: An Introduction to Dogon Religious Ideas.* London: Oxford University Press, 1965.
Jopling, Carol F., Editor. *Art and Aesthetics in Primitive Societies.* N.Y.: E. P. Dutton, 1971.
Levy, Gertrude R. *Gate of the Horn: A Study of the Religious Conceptions of the Stone Age.* New York: Humanities Press, 1968.
Munn, Nancy. *Walbiri Iconography: Graphic Representation and Cultural Symbolism in a Central Australian Society.* Ithaca: Cornell University Press, 1973.
Otten, Charlotte, Editor. *Anthropology and Art: Readings in Cross-Cultural Aesthetics.* New York: Natural History Press/Doubleday, 1971.
Reichard, Gladys. *Navaho Religion: A Study of Symbolism.* Princeton: Princeton University Press, Bollingen Series #18, 1963.
Scully, Vincent. *The Earth, the Temple and the Gods.* New Haven: Yale University Press, 1982.
Thompson, Robert F. *African Art in Motion.* Berkeley: University of California Press, 1974.

Hindu Art
Archer, W. G. *The Loves of Krishna in Indian Painting and Poetry.* New York: Grove Press, nd.
Arguëlles, José and Miriam. *Mandala.* Boulder: Shambala Press, 1972.
Basham, A. L. *The Wonder That Was India.* New York: Grove Press, 1959 (1954).
Binyon, Laurence. *The Spirit of Man in Asian Art.* New York: Dover Publishing, 1965 (1936).
Coomaraswamy, Ananda K. *History of Indian and Indonesian Art.* New York: E. Weyhe, 1927.
———. *The Dance of Śiva.* New York: Noonday Press, 1957.
———. *The Transformation of Nature in Art.* New York: Dover Publishing, 1956.
———. *The Christian and Oriental Philosophy of Art.* New York: Dover Publishing, 1956.
Eyck, Diana L. *Darśan: Seeing the Divine Image in India.* Chambersburg, Pa.: ANIMA Books, 1981.
Frederic, Louis. *The Art of India: Temples and Sculptures.* New York: Harry N. Abrams, Inc., nd.
Kramrisch, Stella. *The Hindu Temple.* Calcutta: University of Calcutta, 1946.
———. *The Art of India: Traditions of Indian Sculpture, Painting and Architecture.* New York: Phaidon Publishers, 1965.
———. *Manifestations of Śiva.* Exhibition Catalogue. Philadelphia: Philadelphia Museum of Art, 1981.

Larson, Gerald J., Pratapaditya Pal and Rebecca P. Gowen. *In Her Image: The Great Goddess in Indian Asia and the Madonna in Christian Culture.* Exhibition Catalogue. Santa Barbara: U.C.S.B. Art Museum, 1980.
Murray, Chris and Kim. *Illuminations of the Bhagavad-Gita.* New York: Harper and Row, Inc., 1980.
Northrop, F. S. C. *The Meeting of East and West.* New York: Macmillan Co., 1946.
Rawson, Phillip. *The Art of Southeast Asia.* London: Thames and Hudson, 1967.
Rowland, Benjamin, Jr. *The Art and Architecture of India.* Baltimore: Penguin Books, 1953.
Tucci, Guiseppi. *The Theory and Practice of the Mandala.* New York: Samuel Weiser, Inc., 1969.
Zimmer, Heinrich, *Myths and Symbols in Indian Art and Civilization.* Princeton: Princeton University Press, 1974 (1946).

Buddhist Art

Awakawa, Yasuichi. *Zen Painting.* New York: Kodansha International, 1970.
Boger, H. Patterson. *The Traditional Arts of Japan.* London: Allen and Unwin Co., 1964.
Covell, Jon and Sobin Yamada. *Zen at Daitokuji.* New York: Kodansha International, 1974.
Dürkheim, Karlfried. *The Japanese Cult of Tranquility.* New York: Samuel Weiser, 1974.
Fontein, Jan and Money Hickman. *Zen Painting and Calligraphy.* Boston: Museum of Fine Arts, 1970.
Herrigel, Eugene. *Zen in the Art of Archery.* New York: Random House, 1971.
Hisamatsu, Shin'ichi. *Zen and the Fine Arts.* New York: Kodansha International, 1971.
────── and Paul Tillich. "Dialogues, East and West," *Eastern Buddhist.* Part I: IV/2 (1971): 89–107; Part II: V/2 (1972): 107–128; Part III: VI/2 (1973): 87–114.
Holbron, Mark. *The Ocean in the Sand.* Boulder: Shambala Publications, 1978.
Kageyama, Haruki. *The Arts of Shinto.* New York/Tokyo: Weatherhill/Shibundo, 1973.
Mizuno, Seiichi. *Asuka Buddhist Art: Hōryu-ji.* New York/Tokyo: Weatherhill/Heibonsha, 1974.
Northrop, F. S. C. *The Meeting of East and West.* New York: Macmillan Co., 1946.
Okazaki, Jōji. *Pure Land Buddhist Painting.* Tokyo/New York: Kodansha International, 1977.
Pilgrim, Richard B. "The Artistic Way and the Religio-Aesthetic Tradition in Japan," *Philosophy East and West.* 27/3 (1977): 285–305.
──────. *Buddhism and the Arts of Japan.* Chambersburg, Pa.: Anima Books, 1981.
Rambach, Pierce. *The Secret Message of Tantric Buddhism.* New York: Skira/Rizzoli, 1979.
Rosenfield, John M. and Shūjirō Shimada. *Traditions of Japanese Arts.* Cambridge: Harvard University Press, 1970.
Sawa, Takaaki. *Art in Japanese Esoteric Buddhism.* New York/Tokyo: Weatherhill/Heibonsha, 1972.
Seckel, Dietrich. *The Art of Buddhism.* New York: Crown Publishers, Inc., 1964.
Suzuki, Daisetz T. *Zen and Japanese Culture.* Princeton: Princeton University Press, 1959.
Ueda, Makoto. *Literary and Art Theories of Japan.* Cleveland: Press of Western Reserve University, 1967.
Warner, Langdon. *The Enduring Arts of Japan.* New York: Grove Press, 1952.
Yoshikawa, Itsuji. *Major Themes in Japanese Art.* New York/Tokyo: Weatherhill/Heibonsha, 1976.

Jewish Art

Barnett, R. D. *Catalogue of the Permanent and Loan Collections of the Jewish Museum.* London: Harvey Miller, 1974.

Bialer, Yehuda L. and Estelle Fink. *Jewish Life in Art and Tradition from the Collection of the Sir Isaac and Lady Edith Wolfson Museum.* Jerusalem: Heichal Shlomo, 1980.

Davidovitch, David. *The Ketubah: Jewish Marriage Contracts.* Tel Aviv: E. Lewin-Epstein, Ltd., 1979.

Eis, Ruth. *Hanukkah Lamps of the Judah Magnes Museum.* Berkeley: Judah Magnes Museum, 1977.

Epstein, Shifra *et al. The Maurice Spertus Museum of Judaica: An Illustrated Catalog of Selected Objects.* Chicago: Spertus College of Judaica Press, 1974.

Goodenough, Erwin. *Jewish Symbols of the Greco-Roman World.* (13 volumes) N.Y.: Pantheon Books, 1953–1968.

Gutmann, Joseph. *Beauty in Holiness: Studies in Jewish Customs and Ceremonial Art.* New York: KTAV, 1970.

———. *Hebrew Manuscript Painting.* New York: George Brazilier, 1978.

———. *Jewish Ceremonial Art.* New York: Thomas Yoseloff, 1964.

———. *No Graven Images: Studies in Art and the Hebrew Bible.* New York: KTAV, 1971.

———. *The Synagogue: Studies in Origins, Archeology and Architecture.* New York: KTAV, 1975.

Kanof, Abraham. *Ceremonial Art in the Judaic Tradition.* Raleigh, N.C.: North Carolina Museum of Art, 1975.

———. *Jewish Ceremonial Art and Religious Observance.* New York: Harry N. Abrams, 1970.

Kayser, Stephen, Editor. *Jewish Ceremonial Art.* Philadelphia: Jewish Publication Society of America, 1955.

Kedourie, Elie, Editor. *The Jewish World.* New York: Harry N. Abrams, 1979.

Kirshenblatt-Gimblett, Barbara. *Fabric of Jewish Life.* New York: The Jewish Museum, 1977.

Landsberger, Franz. *The History of Jewish Art.* Cincinnati: Union of American Hebrew Congregations, 1946.

Mann, Vivian, *et al. Danzig 1939: Treasures of a Destroyed Community.* Detroit: Wayne State University Press, 1980.

Mayer, Leo A. *Bibliography of Jewish Art.* Jerusalem: Magnes Press, 1967.

Namenyi, Ernest. *The Essence of Jewish Art.* New York: Thomas Yoseloff, 1960.

Narkiss, Bezalel. *Hebrew Illuminated Manuscripts.* Jerusalem: Keter Publishing House, 1969.

———, Editor. *Journal of Jewish Art.* (Vols. 1–5, 1974–1978, published in Chicago by Spertus College; vols. 6ff, 1979, published in Jerusalem by the Center for Jewish Art, Hebrew University).

Pappenheim, Shlomo. *The Jewish Wedding.* New York: Yeshiva University Museum, 1977.

———. *Purim: The Face and the Mask.* New York: Yeshiva University Museum, 1979.

Roth, Cecil, Editor. *Jewish Art.* Greenwich: New York Graphic Society, 1961

Wigoder, Geoffrey, Editor. *Jewish Art and Civilization.* New York: Walker and Co., 1972.

Wischnitzer, Rachel. *The Architecture of the European Synagogue.* Philadelphia: Jewish Publication Society of America, 1964.

Yerushalmi, Yosef Hayim. *Haggadah and History: A Panorama in Facsimile of Five Centuries of the Printed Haggadah.* Philadelphia: Jewish Publication Society of America, 1975.

Christian Art

Davies, Horton and Hugh. *Sacred Art in the Secular Century*. Collegeville: The Liturgical Press, 1980.

Dillenberger, Jane. "Folk Art and the Bible," *Theology Today*. Vol. 36:4 (January 1980): 564–568.

——— with J. C. Taylor, R. Murray and R. Soria. *Perceptions and Evocations: The Art of Elihu Vedder*. Washington, D.C.: The Smithsonian Institution Press, 1979.

———. "Mormonism and American Religious Art," in *Reflections on Mormonism: Judaeo-Christian Parallels*. Edited by T. G. Madsen. Provo: Brigham Young Press, 1978.

———. "Seeing Is Believing," *Journal of Current Social Issues*. Volume 15.3, (Fall 1978): 68–73.

———. "Visual Arts and the Seminary," in *ARC Directions, Occasional Papers of the Fellows of the Society for Art, Religion and Contemporary Culture*. New York, 1974.

——— with John Dillenberger. "Picasso's Crucifixion," in *Humanities, Religion and the Arts Tomorrow*. Edited by Howard Hunter. New York: Holt, Rhinehart and Winston, 1971.

———. "The Abstraction of Agony. Barnett Newman's *Stations of the Cross*," *Religion in Life*. Vol. 38 (Summer 1969): 183–197.

———. *Style and Content in Christian Art*. Nashville: Abingdon Press, 1965.

Dillenberger, John. *Benjamin West: The Context of His Life's Work*. San Antonio: Trinity University Press, 1977.

———. "Perception in Art and Religion," *Arts and Society*. (Spring/Summer 1976).

Dixon, John W. *Art and the Theological Imagination*. New York: The Seabury Press, 1980.

———. *Nature and Grace in Art*. Chapel Hill: University of North Carolina Press, 1964.

———, "Is tragedy essential to knowing? A critique of Dr. Tillich's aesthetic," *The Journal of Religion*. Vol. 43, (October 1963): 271–284.

Eversole, Finley, Editor. *Christian Faith and the Contemporary Arts*. Nashville: Abingdon Press, 1962.

Harned, David B. *Theology and the Arts*. Philadelphia: Westminster Press, 1966.

Hazelton, Roger. *A Theological Approach To Art*. Nashville: Abingdon Press, 1967.

———. *Ascending Flame, Descending Dove*. Philadelphia: Westminster Press, 1976.

Heyer, George S. *Signs of Our Times: Theological Essays on Art in the Twentieth-Century*. Grand Rapids: William B. Eerdmanns, 1980.

Kung, Hans. *Art and the Question of Meaning*. New York: The Crossroad Publishing Company, 1981.

Lowrie, Walter. *Art in the Early Church*. New York: Norton Classics, 1969 (1947).

Martin, David F. *Art and the Religious Experience: The "Language" of the Sacred*. Lewisburg: Bucknell University Press, 1972.

Morey, Charles R. *Christian Art*. New York: Norton Classics, 1958.

Nichols, Aidan. *The Art of God Incarnate, Theology and Symbol from Genesis to the Twentieth-Century*. New York: Paulist Press, 1980.

Regamey, Pie-Raymond. *Religious Art in the Twentieth-Century*. New York: Herder and Herder, 1963 (1952).

Ross-Bryant, Lynn. *Imagination and the Life of the Spirit*. Chico: Polebridge Books, 1981.

Rubin, William S. *Modern Sacred Art and the Church of Assy*. New York: Columbia University Press, 1961.

Schwarz, Rudolf. *The Church Incarnate: The Sacred Function of Church Architecture*. Chicago: Henry Regnery, 1958.

Steinberg, Leo. *Michelangelo's Last Paintings; The Conversion of St. Paul and the Crucifixion of St. Peter in the Capella Paolina, Vatican Palace*. London: Phaidon, 1975.

Tillich, Paul, "Existentialist Aspects of Modern Art," in *Christianity and the Existentialists*. Edited by Carl Michalson. New York: Charles Scribner's and Sons, 1956; pp. 128–147.

———. "Protestantism and Artistic Style," *Theology of Culture*. New York: Oxford University Press, 1972 (1959), pp. 68–75.

Wolterstorff, Nicholas. *Art in Action: Towards A Christian Aesthetic*. Grand Rapids: William B. Eerdmanns, 1980.

Islamic Art

Arnold, T. W. *Painting in Islam*. New York: Dover Publications, Inc., 1965 (1928).

Aslanpa, Oktay. *Turkish Art and Architecture*. New York: Praeger, 1971.

Burckhardt, Titus. *Art of Islam: Language and Meaning*. London: World of Islam Publications, 1976.

———. *Sacred Art in East and West: Its Principles and Methods*. London: Perennial Books, 1967.

Creswell, K. A. C. *Early Muslim Architecture*. Oxford: Clarendon Press, 1969.

Denny, Walter B. *Oriental Rugs*. Washington: Cooper-Hewitt Publishers, The Smithsonian Institution, 1979.

Dundan, Alistair. *The Noble Sanctuary*. London: Longman Group Ltd., 1972.

Dy Ry, Carel. *Art of Islam*. New York: Harry N. Abrams, Inc. 1970.

Ettinghausen, Richard. *Arab Painting*. New York: Rizzoli, 1977 (1962).

Grabar, Oleg. *The Formation of Islamic Art*. New Haven and London: Yale University Press, 1973.

Gray, Basil. *Persian Painting*. New York: Rizzoli, 1977 (1961).

Grube, Ernst. *The World of Islam*. New York: McGraw-Hill Book Co., 1966.

Hill, Derek and Oleg Grabar. *Islamic Architecture and Its Decoration, A.D. 800–1500.* Chicago: The University of Chicago Press, 1964.

Hoag, John D. *Western Islamic Architecture*. New York: George Braziller, 1963.

Hrbas, Milos and Edgar Knoblach. *The Art of Central Asia*. London: Paul Hamlyn, 1965.

Khatibi, Abdelkebir and Mohammed Sijelmassi. *The Splendour of Islamic Calligraphy*. London: Thames and Hudson, 1976.

Kühnel, Ernst. *Islamic Arts and Architecture*. London: G. Bell and Sons, Ltd., 1966.

Kuran, Aptullah. *The Mosque in Early Ottoman Architecture*. Chicago: The University of Chicago Press, 1968.

Lewis, Bernard, Editor. *The World of Islam*. London: Thames and Hudson, 1976.

Lings, Martin. *The Quranic Art of Calligraphy and Illumination*. London: World of Islam Publications, 1976.

Pope, Arthur Upham. *Persian Architecture: The Triumph of Form and Color*. New York: George Braziller, 1965.

Rice, David Talbott. *Islamic Art*. New York: Praeger, 1965.

El-Said, Issam and Ayse Parman. *Geometric Concepts in Islamic Art*. London: World of Islam Publications, 1976.

Scerrato, Umberto. *Monuments of Civilization: Islam*. New York: Grosset and Dunlop, 1976.

Sebag, Paul. *The Great Mosque of Kairouan*. London and New York: Collier-Macmillan, The Macmillan Co., 1965.

Seherr-Thoss, Sonia P. *Design and Color in Islamic Architecture*. Washington: Smithsonian Institution Press, 1968.

Wilber, Donald N. *The Architecture of Islamic Iran: The II Khänid Period*. Princeton: Princeton University Press, 1955.

Welch, Stuart Carey. *A King's Book of Kings*. New York: The Metropolitan Museum of Art, 1972.

Contributors

DOUG ADAMS is Associate Professor of Christianity and the Arts at the Pacific School of Religion and Chairperson of the Doctoral Faculty in Theology and the Arts at the Graduate Theological Union. A former Post-Doctoral Fellow in Art History at the National Museum of American Art, Adams is the author of many articles on the relationship between religion and the visual arts.

DAVID ALTSHULER is Charles E. Smith Professor of Judaic Studies and Chairman of the Committee on Judaic Studies at The George Washington University.

LINDA ALTSHULER is Director of the B'nai B'rith Klutznick Museum of Jewish Art, Washington, D.C. Her publications include articles on Jewish art and dance in the *National Jewish Monthly*.

DIANE APOSTOLOS-CAPPADONA is a member of the faculties of The George Washington University; Georgetown University S.S.C.E.; and Mount Vernon College. The author of several articles synthesizing artistic and spiritual modes of being, she is presently engaged in a study of the spiritual dimensions of space and sculpture in the art of Isamu Noguchi.

JOHN W. COOK is Associate Professor of Religion and the Arts, and Director of the Religion and Arts Program at Yale University. His graduate studies were at the University of Bonn, Germany; and Yale University.

ANANDA K. COOMARASWAMY was Curator of Indian Art, Boston Museum of Fine Arts. In his many important texts, Coomaraswamy combined his work as art historian, philosopher, orientalist and linguist.

CECILIA DAVIS CUNNINGHAM is a potter and art historian. She has taught in the United States and Italy, and reviews art books for *Best Sellers*.

STEPHEN DE STAEBLER is Professor of Art at San Francisco State University. His sculptures have been commissioned for the Sanctuary of the Holy Spirit Chapel, Newman Hall, Berkeley; the Bay Area Rapid Transit District, Embarcadero and Concord Stations; Pacific Mutual Plaza, Newport Beach; the University of California Art Museum, Berkeley; and many private collections. DeStaebler's artwork has been selected for major international exhibitions including the "Biennale de Paris," Musée d'Art Moderne; "International Exhibition of Ceramic Art," Japan; "Century of Ceramics in the United States," Everson Museum, New York; "One Hundred Years of California Sculpture," The Oakland Museum; "20 American Artists," San Francisco Museum of Modern Art; and most recently, "Art and/or Craft," Art Museum, Kanazawa, Japan.

JANE DILLENBERGER is a member of the faculty of Hartford Seminary and of Trinity College, Hartford. She is the author of several books on religion and art, was curator of the exhibitions, "The Hand and the Spirit: Religious Art in America, 1700–1900" and "Perceptions of the Spirit in Twentieth-Century American Art," and is the co-author of the catalogues for these exhibitions.

JOHN DILLENBERGER, theologian and cultural historian, is President of Hartford Seminary. He is co-author of *Perceptions of the Spirit in Twentieth-Century American Art*, and his most recent book is *Benjamin West: The Context of His Life's Work* (Trinity University Press, 1977).

JOHN W. DIXON, JR., is Professor of Religion and Art at the University of North Carolina at Chapel Hill. He received his PhD from the Committee on Social Thought of the University of Chicago in 1953. He is the author of *Nature and Grace in Art; Art and the*

Theological Imagination; The Physiology of Faith; and numerous articles on religion and art.

MIRCEA ELIADE is Sewell L. Avery Distinguished Service Professor at the Divinity School, The University of Chicago. Among his many important books are *The Sacred and The Profane; Yoga, Immortality and Freedom;* and *Cosmos and History.*

LOIS IBSEN AL FARUQI teaches world religions and the arts at Temple University. She has published on religion and art; Islamic art; music in Islamic culture; dance of the Muslim peoples; and women and the family in Islamic Society.

LANGDON B. GILKEY is Shailer Matthews Professor of Theology at The Divinity School, The University of Chicago. His most recent book is *Society and the Sacred* (Crossroad Publishing, 1981).

WASSILY KANDINSKY was a non-objective painter of the early twentieth-century. His text, *Concerning the Spiritual in Art,* is one of the most important documents in the development of modern art.

KAREN LAUB-NOVAK is a painter, printmaker, sculptor and commercial illustrator. Her works have been exhibited in the United States and Europe. She has taught at several colleges and is a popular guest lecturer in art and mysticism at colleges and universities.

T. R. MARTLAND is Associate Professor of Philosophy, SUNY/Albany. He is a member of the Editorial Board of the *Journal of Comparative Literature & Aesthetics;* Guest Editor of the *Annals of Scholarship;* and a former Chair of the Executive Committee of the International Association for Philosophy and Literature (1980–1981). His articles have appeared in *Religious Studies; Journal of the American Academy of Religion; Philosophy and Phenomenological Research; The Review of Metaphysics; British Journal of Aesthetics; The Journal of Aesthetics and Art Criticism; Journal of Philosophy;* and *Anglican Theological Review* among others. His most recent book is *Religion As Art, An Interpretation,* (SUNY Press, 1981).

BARBARA NOVAK is Professor of Art History, Barnard College and Columbia University. Her most recent book is *Nature and Culture:*

American Landscape and Painting, 1825–1875 (Oxford University Press, 1980).

THOMAS FRANKLIN O'MEARA, O.P., is Professor of Theology, University of Notre Dame. A past President of the Catholic Theological Society of America, his most recent book is *Romantic Idealism and Roman Catholicism: Schelling and the Theologians* (University of Notre Dame Press, 1982).

RICHARD B. PILGRIM is Associate Professor of Religion, and Director of the Graduate Program, Department of Religion, Syracuse University. His most recent book is *Buddhism and the Arts of Japan* (Anima Books, 1981).

CHARLES SCRIBNER III is a specialist in the art of the Counter Reformation, and has published articles on Caravaggio, Rubens, and Bernini. He is the author of *The Triumph of the Eucharist: Tapestries Designed by Rubens* (UMI Research Press, 1982), and is currently vice-president and director at Charles Scribner's Sons publishing firm in New York City.

LEO STEINBERG, Benjamin Franklin Professor of the History of Art, University of Pennsylvania, has published and lectured widely in the fields of Renaissance, Baroque, and modern art. His books include *Other Criteria: Confrontations with 20th-Century Art, Michelangelo's Last Paintings,* and *Borromini's San Carlo alle Quattro Fontane.* In the spring of 1982, he delivered the Andrew W. Mellon Lectures in the Fine Arts at the National Gallery of Art, Washington, D.C., under the title "The Burden of Michelangelo's Painting," to be published by Princeton University Press.

JOSHUA C. TAYLOR was Director of the National Museum of American Art (Smithsonian Institution) and President of the College Art Association. His major books include *Learning to Look* (University of Chicago Press, 1957); and *The Fine Arts in America* (University of Chicago Press, 1976).

PAUL TILLICH was John Nuveen Professor of Theology at The Divinity School, The University of Chicago. His books include *The Courage To Be; Theology of Culture;* and *The Protestant Era.*

DAVID TRACY is Professor of Theology, The Divinity School, The University of Chicago. His most recent book is *The Analogical Imagination* (Crossroad Publishing, 1981).

ROGER WEDELL is Staff Executive at Thanks-Giving Square, Dallas, Texas. He lectures and presents workshops in the fields of worship, religion and fine arts. He is a member of the American Academy of Religion, the Sacred Dance Guild International, the College Art Association and the Mimesis Institute. He serves on the Editorial Board of *Modern Liturgy* magazine.

NICHOLAS WOLTERSTORFF is Professor of Philosophy, Calvin College. His most recent books are *Art in Action, Towards A Christian Aesthetic* (Eerdmanns, 1980), and *Worlds and Works of Art* (Oxford University Press, 1981).

MELINDA WORTZ is Director, Fine Arts Gallery, University of California, Irvine. A regular contributor to *Arts Magazine, Artnews* and *Artforum*, she has prepared many exhibition catalogues including the introductions for the James Turrell Exhibition, Whitney Museum of American Art; and the Larry Bell Exhibition, Hudson River Museum.